MW00962792

The authors and publisher have endeavored to ensure all facts are correct.
Please note any corrections and send to the address below.

Published by Spice of Life Books Inc.

National Library of Canada Cataloguing in Publication Data

Pavicic, Liliana, 1964-
        More than just dinner and a movie

Includes bibliographical references and index.
ISBN 0-9688597-0-4

Cookery. 2. Motion pictures-Miscellanea. I. Pirker-Mosher, Gordana, 1967-II. Title.

TX715.P38 2001   641.5   C2001-901463-5

Printed in Canada by Dollco Printing

Cover and interior book design by Corinne Nyffenegger
Food Photography by Roy Timm
International Standard Book Number: 0-9688597-0-4

All inquires should be addressed to:
Spice of Life Books Inc.
P.O.Box 84012
Burlington, Ont
L7L 6S2
e-mail: authors@morethanjustdinnerandamovie.com
www.morethanjustdinnerandamovie.com

Dedications

To my two daughters Aleksandra and Angie, who have surprised me many times with their cooking skills and delicious creations. I hope you both follow your dreams and never give up... they do come true! To my husband and my family, for their continued support in all my interesting and challenging endeavors. And to all my friends and associates, a special thanks for purchasing our first book and coming out to our book signing events to support us. But mostly to my friend Liliana (Lil) who shares my joys, sorrows and the same crazy ideas... this is a fun journey — I am glad it's with you!

Gordana

A big thank you to my husband Vlado, who came up with the basic idea for this book. To my two sons, Luka and Andrei, who are already showing some promise in the kitchen (with two parents who enjoy cooking it must come naturally) — I dedicate this book with love, and the hope that they will be able to dream big and work hard to make their dreams come true! Thank you to other family members and especially my sisters, Gina and Sandra, for their support. Lastly, thank you to Gordana for always being there!

With good friends and family anything is possible.

Liliana

How This Book Came About!

Fate played a role! It was the mid-eighties and we had both entered a Miss Canadian-Yugoslav beauty contest with the hopes of winning the contest and enjoying the prize, which was a trip to the country of our roots. Being that the two of us were outgoing and friendly, and not the least bit competitive; we ended up connecting at the contest and formed a strong friendship very quickly. The next summer, we ended up travelling together to the former Yugoslavia, and travelled throughout many of the regions and spent an idyllic two weeks on the Adriatic coast enjoying ourselves in the spectacular city of Dubrovnik, the pearl of the Adriatic.

Even as teenagers we dreamt of our future and purchased items on our trip to tuck away for the time when we would have our own homes: tablecloths, dinnerware, crystal, etc. We especially treasured heirloom table linens given to us by our grandmothers. Our interest in food was evident as we wined and dined our way across the country, collecting recipes along the way!

We always knew that our shared passion for food and entertaining along with other combined interests would keep our friendship intact for many years. We had mulled over the idea of writing a cookbook some years ago, however, with our new found careers, motherhood and the many responsibilities that come along with adulthood, our dream of one day being published took a few years longer than expected. We were pleased when our first cook book was published in September of 2000. "The Best of Croatian Cooking" was released by Hippocrene Books Inc, of New York. Hippocrene is the world's biggest publisher of international cookbooks. The success of our first cookbook motivated us to continue writing and set some new creative goals for ourselves.

In planning this project we kept in mind that the fast-paced lifestyle of North Americans has not slowed down. People cherish their weekends and try to plan events with significant others, family members and friends in mind. Watching movies is usually on the weekend agenda (ever notice how busy your local video store is Friday evenings?) Most people also attempt to prepare more elaborate meals on the weekend, often trying out new foods and recipes. Knowing this, and taking into account the rise in popularity of thematic dinner parties, we planned a cookbook that ties all of these ideas together. More Than Just Dinner and a Movie celebrates award winning films of the past 70 years, providing a summary of each film, information about the actors and awards, as well as some fun trivia! Menus with accompanying recipes (over 200 recipes) that are linked to the film, beverage recommendations and music suggestions, as well as ideas for setting the stage or mood, round out the plan for a fantastic event. After planning and enjoying a full thematic film evening you will never want to watch a film any other way!

Good film, just like good literature enriches our lives. It is timeless and allows to become armchair travellers—to experience new cultures or to go back in time. Sometimes films mirror our lives, or allow us to dream of what is possible or even help us find a solution to our dilemmas. Cinematherapy is as powerful as bibliotherapy (seeking validation and guidance from books)—there are films that examine every facet of human life and all of its joys and sorrows. Excellent films make us realize that we are all a part of something much larger than ourselves, and that everyone and everything is connected, we are all explorers on this journey called life.

We sincerely hope you enjoy the book and create some special evenings and cherished memories! Lights, camera action. . . it's now up to you!

Best wishes,

Gordana and Liliana

How To Use This Book

This book really is for anyone that enjoys movies. It is especially appealing to those who are searching for something different to do with their partner or with someone whom they are dating and ready to become more serious with. After all, what could be more intimate than shopping and cooking together and then snuggling up to watch a great movie! Here are a few simple steps to maximize use of this book.

1. Peruse the film summaries to choose a movie and set a date for your event.

2. Have a look at the recipes and make a required ingredient list.

3. Choose music for the event. Remember, you don't always have to actually buy a CD, borrow from your public library instead.

4. Read through setting the stage section and make a list of what you need to do or obtain prior to the event. We have provided a number of ideas for each movie, they are a base to build on—augment them with your own creative touches!

5. Shop together with your special person. Discover new places to shop in your own city by visiting ethnic neighbourhoods and supermarkets to buy items for the menu and thematic setting.

6. Make it an event! Start preparation early in the day. Decide when you are going to eat (before, during or after the movie) and get the food preparation under way. Decorate using the ideas garnered from the book as well as your own. Cook the meal, pop in the movie and sit back and enjoy a rewarding and entertaining evening!

TABLE OF CONTENTS

The starting page for each section is shown. All Movies are in alphabetical order.

1930's

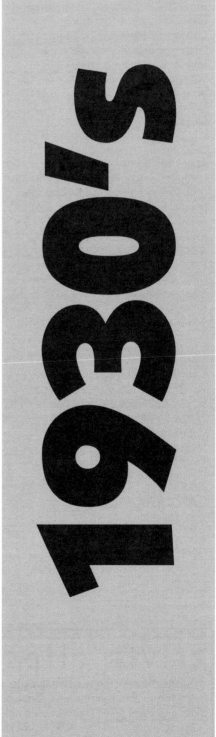

1933- Hitler becomes chancellor of Germany.

1935- Invention of radar.

1935- When Bugs Bunny first appeared he was called Happy Rabbit.

1938- Time magazine's "Man of the Year" was Adolf Hitler.

1935- The Mildred sisters and Patty Hill originally wrote the song "Happy Birthday to You" as "Good Morning to You." The words were changed and it was published, the rest is history.

1937- Spam was the first meat product that did not need refrigeration. The military liked its convenience and portability, and used it during World War II.

1939- There was a major modification of the internal combustion engine that gave birth to the jet engine. The engine had its first test in 1937. The first jet flight took place on Aug. 27, 1939.

1938- The first U.S. Minimum Wage Law was instituted. The minimum wage at the time was 25 cents per hour.

1930- Twinkies were born when Continental Baking company manager, James Dewar, of Illinois decided Depression-idled baking pans might be used to create a cheap snack. He took the name from an ad for Twinkle Toe Shoes, and charged a nickel for a pack of two. The original filling was banana cream.

1939-45- World War II On Sept. 1, 1939, Germany invaded Poland. On September 3, 1939 England and France demanded that Germany withdraw its troops. When Germany refused, England and France declared war on Germany. The start of the war climaxed a series of warlike acts between 1931 and 1939 by Germany, Italy, and Japan. The acts of these aggressor nations included taking territories that did not belong to them.

1929-40- The drought that created the 1930's Great Plains Dust Bowl compounded the damage caused by the economic downturn. The theme song of the period became "Brother, Can You Spare a Dime?"

alexander nevsky (1938)

This epic, directed and co-written by Sergei Eisenstein is based on an actual battle that took place at a lake near Novgorod in Northwest Russia. Current events of the late 1930's influenced the film: though it is set in the 13th century, through symbolism it aimed to boost Russian patriotism, using the wicked Teutonic knights and the like-minded Tartars to represent the looming threat of Hitler and his hordes. The message in the film suggests that since historically Russians had been victorious against Teutonic invaders...If need be they could stand united and defeat them again. The film was very effective as anti-Hitler propaganda not only in the Soviet Union but also around the world. The hero of the film is charismatic "knyaz" or Prince Alexander Nevsky (portrayed by Nikolai Cherkasov) who along with his followers is attempting to save the population from the barbaric knights whose evil knows no bounds... they even commit infanticide. The spectacular battle scenes viewed from today's standpoint may inspire some to giggle at the exaggerated reactions of some of the extras in the film, nevertheless the visuals are amazing and the film is a must-see!

FEATURED ACTORS
Nikolai Cherkasov
 (Prince Alexander
 Yaroslavich Nevsky)
Nikolai Okhlopkov (Vassily Buslaj)
Andrei Abrikosov (Gavrilo Oleksich)
Dmitri N. Orlov
 (Ignat, Master Armourer)
Vasili Novikov
 (Pavsha, Governor of Pskov)

DIRECTOR - Sergei Eisenstein

AWARDS WON
5 Best Films   1939 National
                  Board of Review of
                  Motion Pictures

menu

breaded chicken patties • russian onion salad • eastern empire rice • crusty bread • fresh berry kissel mousse

breaded chicken patties

serves 6

5	slices white bread	1/2 tsp	white pepper
1/4 cup	milk	2 cups	dried bread crumbs
2 lbs	lean ground chicken	1/4 cup	cooking oil
1/4 lb	unsalted butter, softened	1/4 cup	flat leaf parsley, chopped
3/4 tsp	salt	3/4 cup	sour cream or yogurt

- Put bread slices in a bowl and pour in the milk. Soak the bread for 15 minutes. Squeeze the bread dry being careful not to tear it up. Combine ground chicken with the bread slices.
- Gradually beat in the butter that you have softened, along with the salt and pepper, until the mixture is smooth. Make 6 patties from this mixture.
- Roll patties in the bread crumbs, coating them completely.

- Heat oil in a deep frying pan over medium- high heat. Fry the patties for approximately 5 to 6 minutes per side or until done to suit your taste.
- Stir chopped parsley into sour cream or yogurt and garnish each patty with a dollop of plain yogurt or sour cream on each patty. Serve with crusty bread.

 Rather than frying the patties you may broil them. Use low fat sour cream or yogurt.

russian onion salad

serves 4

2	large Bermuda onions, sliced	1/2 tsp	fresh rosemary, chopped
1 tbsp	fresh lemon juice	1/4 tsp	salt
2	large oranges, peeled, seeded and chopped	1/4 tsp	freshly ground pepper
2 tbsp	fresh orange juice	1	hard-boiled egg, chopped
1/2	medium cucumber, peeled and sliced	(optional)	lettuce leaves
4 tbsp	olive oil		

- Mix all ingredients in a large bowl. Cover and chill.
- Place on a bed of lettuce leaves.

trivia clips

Stalin had supported the film upon its release in 1938 as a tool to warn the Russian people to be careful of German aggression, then the film was deemed too anti-German at the time of the Russo-German non-aggression pact which took place later the same year. The film once again gained favour with the Soviet government after the German invasion of Russia in 1941 at which point the government used the film to foster Russian patriotism as well as anti-German sentiment.

alexander
nevsky (1938)

eastern empire rice

serves 6 to 8

This dish has definite Middle Eastern influences as is evident by the use of dried fruits and almonds. The smell will take you on a journey to a bazaar with abundant stalls of dried fruits, nuts, spices and silks!

2 cups	Basmati rice	1 tsp	salt
1/2 cup	dried apples, diced	1 cup	fresh Crimini or button mushrooms, sliced
1/2 cup	dried apricots, diced		
1/2 cup	dried dates, chopped	1 tsp	cinnamon
1/2 cup	raisins	1/2 tsp	allspice
1/2 cup	prunes, pitted and chopped	1/2 cup	slivered almonds, toasted

- In a large pot, bring enough water to a boil to cook the rice (see package directions for quantity of water required). Add rice, stir, and reduce heat.
- Add the dried fruits and salt, cook for 15 minutes on medium heat.
- Add remaining ingredients except for the almonds, stir, cover and continue to cook until all the water has been absorbed.
- Garnish with the toasted slivered almonds, and serve.

Buy the dried fruits and nuts at a bulk food store so that you can buy the small amounts required.

To toast nuts, place in a skillet over medium heat and stir frequently to avoid burning. Remove from heat and put into a separate container when done to avoid further toasting!

fresh berry kissel

1-1/2 lbs	fresh berries (strawberries, raspberries, cranberries, etc.)		corn starch
		1/2 to 3/4 cup	light cream
6 cups	cold water		berries for garnish (optional)
1/4 cup	sugar, or to taste		

- Wash and hull berries if necessary. Place them in a bowl and mash them using a fork. Strain and reserve the juice. Measure the juice and add enough water to make 6 cups of liquid altogether.
- Place the berries into a saucepan and add 5 cups of the liquid, reserving one cup for later use. Simmer over medium heat until the berries are soft. Then strain, measure amount of liquid left and reheat the liquid.
- Add the sugar, be careful not to add too much as the kissel should be tart.
- Now add 2 teaspoons of cornstarch (per cup of liquid that is reheating), into the reserved cup of liquid. Stir well to dissolve all of the cornstarch and now add it to the hot fruit syrup.
- Let the liquid boil for 1 to 2 minutes until it becomes clear.
- Pour into serving dishes.
- Serve chilled with a drizzle of light cream on top. Garnish with fresh berries if desired.

 In place of light cream drizzle with evaporated skim milk.

A kissel is a fruit juice based pudding usually thickened with corn or potato starch. The fruit used can be fresh, frozen or canned. There are 3 types of kissel: the solid mold, the creamy pudding or the kissel beverage.

BEVERAGES

What else but vodka! We suggest you try iced vodka, either plain or in a variety of other flavours.

Stolichnaya (Russia), Cristall (Russia) and Finlandia (Finland) make a number of flavoured vodkas such as cranberry.

MUSIC

Red Army Chorus
(Le Chant du Monde)

or

Russian Folk Songs Vols. 1 & 2
(A World of Music).

SETTING THE STAGE

Decorate in the traditional Russian colours of red, white and blue or buy and old Soviet flag with a hammer and sickle and use it as a tablecloth. If you have a set of Russian nesting or Matrushka dolls, use them to decorate your table.

Serve your vodka well chilled in a decorative ice bucket or better yet create your own unique ice bucket... Take a large juice or milk carton and cut off the top portion. Place a bottle of vodka (and it doesn't have to be a full bottle) in the carton and pour in about 1/2 cup of water. Now add some slices of citrus fruit, strawberries, cranberries, etc. Add greenery such as small boughs of pine or fir. Freeze in the upright position. When the layer is frozen, layer again with water and the decorative garnishes until only the neck of the bottle is visible. Prior to serving, run the carton under warm water and remove the carton to reveal a stunning "ice bucket" around the vodka bottle. Rest bottle on a silver tray or attractive plate surrounded by more greenery or even fresh flowers. This alone would create an exquisite centrepiece.

all quiet on the
western front (1930)

Based on the novel by Erich Maria Remarque, this film shows the horror of trench warfare. A line at the beginning of the film sums it up, "this story will try to simply tell of a generation of men who, even though they may have escaped its shells were destroyed by the war..." This is a classic anti-war film, which may seem strange considering the basic story line as is told from the viewpoint of German soldiers. It begins with a group of friends whose patriotism has been aroused by the events around them. They decide to enlist and are quickly sent to the Western front. A "front" is where the war is fought first hand, in other words, in the thick of the action. The Western Front extended from Belgium all the way through Germany and Switzerland, basically east of the river Marne. Soon after arriving, the young men go through sobering battle experiences and view firsthand the inevitable deaths that go hand in hand with warfare. Their patriotic illusions of what war is about are quickly shattered by the dismal reality of the senselessness of war. One of the characters, Paul Baumer, is changed forever by the war, and the film deals with his inner struggle and turmoil. The final scene is quite touching and reminds us that beauty can be found everywhere... even in the trenches.

FEATURED ACTORS

Lew Ayres (Paul Baumer)
Ben Alexander (Kemmerick)
Louis Wolheim (Katczinsky)
John Ray (Himmelstoss)
George "Slim" Summerville (Tjaden)
Raymond Griffith (Gerard Duval)
William Blackwell (Albert)
Marion Clayton (Miss Baumer)
Russell Gleason Rhodes (Muller)

DIRECTOR - Lewis Milestone

AWARDS WON

Best Picture	1930 Academy Awards
Best Director	1930 Academy Awards
10 Best Films	1930 Film Daily Award
10 Best Films	1930 National Board of Review Award
10 Best Films	1930 New York Times
Award	1930 Photoplay
U.S. National Film Registry	1990 Library of Congress
100 Greatest American Movies	1998 American Film Institute

menu

moules à la belgique • belgian-style french fries • flavoured mayonnaise • apple strudel • a selection of belgian, german or swiss chocolates

Many European cuisines feature a spectacular assortment of grilled meat dishes, cabbage and roasted potatoes. If nothing in our menu tantalizes your taste buds, you could purchase cabbage rolls, knackwurst sausages, Viennese wieners; even red cabbage at local European delicatessens. Serve a selection of meats on a wooden or silver platter surrounded by potatoes or cabbage.

moules à la belgique
serves 4

2 lbs	mussels, washed and debearded
1	onion, finely chopped
2	cloves garlic, chopped
2 tsp	fresh thyme, chopped
1 bottle	Belgian beer (see beverages below)
1/2 tsp	hot pepper flakes
1/2 cup	flat leaf parsley, chopped
2 tbsp	lemon juice
1/4 cup	butter
	salt and freshly ground pepper to taste

- In a large, deep pot, combine onions, garlic, thyme, lager, hot pepper flakes and parsley. Bring to a boil over high heat.
- Add mussels, cover and steam for three minutes, shaking the pan frequently. Uncover and remove mussels as they open and transfer to a large bowl. Discard any unopened mussels.
- Next, add lemon juice, butter, salt and pepper to sauce left in deep pot. Bring to a boil.
- Pour over mussels in bowl, straining the liquid if desired.

belgian-style french fries
serves 4 to 6

In Belgium and many other European countries, fries are served with mayonnaise. For those who haven't tried this combination, you will be pleasantly surprised!

There is a trick to these crispy fries; the potatoes are fried twice. The first time cooks them through and makes them tender. The second time, which can be done hours later just before serving, turns them golden brown and deliciously crisp. If you have an electric deep fryer, it'll come in handy for this recipe. If not, don't despair as you can use a 4-quart fryer with a basket insert. Alternatively, use a heavy pot that is at least 5 inches deep, a long-handled fried-food skimmer or very large, long-handled slotted spoon, and a deep-fat thermometer.

Use starchy potatoes such as Yukon Gold or russet. The size of the fries is up to you. Some people like them very thin and crunchy. Others prefer them quite large so that they can be crispy on the outside and soft in the center. Keep in mind though that thinly cut potato sticks need a shorter frying time, and the thicker ones take a little longer. Remember that when frying anything in deep fat, always keep a lid close by.

trivia clips

The Western Front ran about 300 miles across the face of Western Europe.
Lew Ayres, the lead actor, became a conscientious objector during WW II. He served as a medic and a chaplain's assistant.
After his well-respected novel was published, the author, Erich Maria Remarque, had his German citizenship revoked by the Nazi party.

belgian-style french fries continued

In case of fire, turn off the heat and cover the pan.

3 - 4 cups	vegetable oil for frying
2 lbs	Yukon Gold or russet baking potatoes, potatoes, peeled, rinsed and dried
	salt to taste

- Pour enough oil into a deep fryer to reach at least halfway up the sides of the pan, but not more than three-quarters of the way up. Heat the oil to 325°F.

- Cut the potatoes into sticks 1/2 inch wide and 2-1/2 to 3 inches long. Dry all the pieces thoroughly in a clean dish towel. This will keep the oil from splattering. Divide the potato sticks into batches of no more than 1 cup each. Do not fry more than one batch at a time.

- When the oil has reached the desired temperature, fry the potatoes for 4 to 5 minutes per batch. They should be lightly coloured but not browned. If your fryer has a basket, simply lift it out then remove the fried potatoes. Otherwise, use a long-handled skimmer to lift out the potatoes. Be sure to bring the temperature of the oil back to 325°F in between batches. At this point the fries can rest for several hours at room temperature until you are almost ready to serve them.

- Heat the oil to 325°F. Fry the potatoes in 1-cup batches until they are nicely browned and crisp, 1 to 2 minutes. Drain on fresh paper towels or brown paper bags and place in a warmed serving bowl lined with more paper towels. Sprinkle with salt and serve. Never cover the potatoes to keep them hot as they will immediately turn soft and limp. If you are inclined to perfectionism, leave some potatoes to fry halfway through the meal so you can serve them crisp and piping hot.

Here are a couple of recipes for flavourful mayonnaise to enjoy with your Belgian fries! Yield: 1/2 cup for all mayonnaise recipes

 Low fat mayonnaise is okay to use.

garlic and parsley mayonnaise

6 tbsp	good quality mayonnaise	1/2 tbsp	parsley, chopped
2	large garlic cloves, pressed	1tsp	extra-virgin olive oil
1 tsp	fresh lemon juice		salt to taste
			pinch of pepper

- Whisk mayonnaise, garlic, lemon juice, parsley and 1 teaspoon olive oil in small bowl to blend.

- Season with salt and pepper.

curry mayonnaise

1/2 cup	good quality mayonnaise	1/8 tsp	cayenne
1 tsp	curry powder		paprika
1 tbsp	fresh lime juice		for garnish

- In a bowl, stir together the mayonnaise, curry powder, lime juice, and cayenne.

- Chill the mayonnaise, covered, for 1 hour and garnish with paprika.

all quiet on the
western front (1930)

SETTING THE STAGE

From the very earliest movies to today's box office hits, movies have affected our hearts and souls. Throughout history, wars have been portrayed in different ways. Sometimes sending a soldier off to war was a proud moment and much-celebrated patriotic event. Other times, cold realism magnified humankind's trials and tribulations during times of war. We thought that the "Great Wars" of the twentieth century were behind us, but one only has to reflect on the events of the 1090's in Europe and elsewhere to realize that we still have not learned our lesson.

We hope this film will inspire you to learn a little about your family's "war history". Were any of your relatives involved in armed conflict or victims of war? Together, may want to gather your old photos and work on a family tree, or memory book. Such collections of old photos and stories are priceless. Rummage through the photo drawers or albums of grandparents, aunts, uncles and any other relatives. Ask for an extra copy or make a copy of photographs that you don't have. Include old letters, newspaper clippings, etc. in your memory book. Write down oral stories or better yet, videotape relatives sharing their war stories. These vignettes of family history are important to preserve for future generations and to share with friends, family and loved ones. Maybe we can still learn something from them, and if nothing else, honour their memory.

apple strudel

Yield: 12 to 15 slices

8	large cooking apples, peeled, cored and diced
2 tsp	cinnamon
1 tbsp	grated lemon rind
3/4 cup	sugar
3/4 cup	raisins
12 to 14	phyllo dough sheets
1/2 cup	melted butter or cooking spray
3/4 cup	ground or finely chopped nuts
	powdered sugar for garnish

• Preheat oven to 350°F. Combine all of the ingredients except for the nuts, phyllo and powdered sugar. Mix well. Place filling about 2 inches from edge of stacked phyllo dough sheets (6 to 7 sheets stacked together by brushing each sheet with butter or spraying with cooking spray), sprinkle nuts on top of the filling prior to rolling the dough, jellyroll fashion.

• Place on greased baking sheet. Bake for about 45 minutes or until golden. Let cool slightly before slicing and serving. Garnish with powdered sugar.

trivia clips
The trench warfare of World War 1 lasted three years and took several million lives.
The First World War was the first conflict in which airplanes were used to attack enemy positions.

bride of frankenstein (1935)

menu experimental pizza bread or monster mash pita wraps • brainless salad • lady fingers raspberry trifle

experimental pizza bread serves 4

The deep hollow created by emptying the bread is filled with lots of tasty goodies.

1	large loaf French bread	1/2 lb	mozzarella cheese, coarsely grated
3/4 lb	Italian or Mexican sausage (hot or mild), casings removed	3	small cans (about 12 ounces in all) eggplant appetizer (caponata)
1	10-ounce package frozen chopped spinach, thawed, squeezed very dry	3/4 cup	purchased marinara sauce or pizza sauce
1/2 cup plus 2 tbsp	homemade or purchased pesto sauce		

• Position rack in center of oven and preheat oven to 375°F. Horizontally, cut off top 1/3 of bread and reserve for another use. Scoop or cut out interior of bread, leaving 1/2-inch shell. Place shell on large baking sheet.

• Fry sausage in a heavy medium sized skillet over medium-high heat until cooked through, breaking up with fork, about 10 minutes. Drain all fat from skillet.

• Combine spinach and 1/2 cup pesto in small bowl. Sprinkle half of cheese over bottom of bread shell. Spread spinach mixture over cheese. Arrange sausage evenly over spinach layer. Spread eggplant appetizer over sausage layer.

• Bake pizza until filling is heated through, about 20 minutes. Combine marinara sauce with remaining cheese and spread over top of pizza. Dot with remaining 2 tablespoons pesto. Bake until cheese melts and topping bubbles, about 12 minutes. Cut into slices and serve.

Hollywood's most successful bogeyman, Boris Karloff, stars as the monster in this classic horror flick. The film opens with a spectacular thunderstorm as the backdrop to a conversation between Lord Byron, Percy Shelley and his spouse, Mary. Mary Shelley is a writer who has already penned a gruesome tale with the title "Frankenstein". She proceeds to relate the tale's sequel to the two men, who sit hanging on to her every word...The monster is on a rampage after surviving a fire in the old mill. After a short period of incarceration, he is taken in by a blind hermit who teaches him to speak. In the meantime, the languishing creator of the monster, Henry Frankenstein, learns that his former mentor, Doctor Praetorius, plans to carry out another experiment. This time he sets out to create a female, a bride for the monster! Will the two creatures "connect"? Watch and find out! Though the film is a product of Hollywood, there is an unmistakable thread of British humour that runs through it which makes it quite enjoyable.

Macabre fantasy still captures today's audiences and those who enjoy the adrenaline rush from watching movies in this genre must see this film!

FEATURED ACTORS
Boris Karloff (The Monster)
Colin Clive (Dr. Henry Frankenstein)
Valerie Hobson
    (Elizabeth Frankenstein)
Ernest Thesiger (Dr. Praetorius)
DIRECTOR - James Whale

trivia clips

Not long before filming began, Colin Clive broke his leg in a horse riding accident. Consequently, most of Dr. Frankenstein's scenes were shot with him in a sitting position.

When filming the scene where the monster emerges from the burnt windmill, Boris Karloff slipped and fell into the water-filled well and broke his leg.

The metal struts used to stiffen his legs (for the famous "monster lurch") helped keep the bones in place until they could be properly set. Hmmm... 2 broken legs connected to the film. Is it coincidence or something else at work? You be the judge.

Oops, a film blooper! When the castle self-destructs, the Doctor can be seen against the far wall. Yet he is next seen outside, in the arms of his beloved, watching the explosions.

bride of frankenstein (1935)

BEVERAGES

A variety of shooters (including non-alcoholic) can be served and are fun to make! Use a straw or a clean medicine dropper, draw up a small amount of grenadine syrup and add to the clear shooters or clear non-alcoholic drinks. The syrup will float and slowly trickle down to the bottom of the shooter glass, it will look like veins! Alternatively, make your favourite punch, and rather than using regular ice cubes to keep the punch cold, try this; take a latex or non-latex glove (available at drugstores) and wash well. Fill with water mixed with green food colouring, and freeze. When frozen, peel off the glove and you now have a "monster's hand" to cool your punch in a ghoulish fashion.

RIGOR MORTIS SHOOTER:

1/3 ounce coffee liquor, 1/3 ounce Bailey's Irish Cream, 1/3 ounce bourbon. Layer into a shooter glass.

GUTS:

3/4 ounce sloe gin, 1/4 ounce Bailey's Irish Cream (pour Bailey's into sloe gin)

BLOODY MARY

(see main beverages page)

MUSIC

"The Monster Mash" (Polygram) by Bobby Pickett and the Crypt-Kickers is a well-known song that is perfect for the occasion, as is Edgar Winter's "Frankenstein" found on his "They Only Come Out at Night" CD (Epic). A great theme party compilation with songs by a number of artists, including Pickett, is "Elvira Presents Haunted House Hits" (Rhino). This collection includes songs such as "The Purple People Eater", "Ghostbusters" and more.

monster mash pita wraps

There is enough garlic in here to ward off any vampires or scary goblins that come your way! Everyone will have garlic breath so they will be protected.

12	large garlic cloves (unpeeled)	room temperature
5 tbsp	olive oil	
1/2	cucumber, peeled and seeded, very thinly sliced	
1/2	small red onion, very thinly sliced	
2 tbsp	red wine vinegar	
1 tbsp	sesame seeds, toasted	
1 tsp	dried oregano	
4 ounces	cream cheese,	

3 tbsp	black olives, chopped
3 tbsp	green olives, chopped
4	6-inch pita bread rounds, cut horizontally in half
8 tbsp	grated Monterey Jack cheese
8 tbsp	grated cheddar cheese
	butter, room temperature
1	red bell pepper, cut into strips

- Preheat oven to 350˚F. Place garlic in small baking dish. Top with 2 tablespoons oil. Bake until tender, about 25 minutes. Cool.

- Combine cucumber, onion, vinegar, sesame seeds, oregano and 3 tablespoons oil in medium bowl. Let stand 30 minutes.

- Peel and chop garlic. Place in small bowl. Mix in cream cheese and chopped black and green olives.

- Drain cucumber salad. Spread 1/4 of cream cheese mixture on cut side of each of 4 pita halves.

- Spoon 1/2 cup cucumber salad over each. Sprinkle both cheeses on top of salad. Cover with remaining 4 pita halves.

- Heat medium skillet over medium heat. Butter both sides of each pita. Working in batches, cook pitas in skillet until cheese melts, about 3 minutes per side. Garnish with peppers. Cut into smaller wedges.

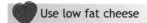 Use low fat cheese

brainless salad

Serves 4 to 6

1 lb	elbow macaroni
1 cup	frozen peas
1/2 cup	mayonnaise
3 tbsp	fresh lemon juice
2 tbsp	milk plus additional if necessary

1/2 lb	piece cooked ham, diced
2	celery ribs, sliced
3/4 cup	packed fresh parsley leaves, chopped
1/2 cup	dried currants
	salt and pepper to taste

- Fill a 6-quart pot three-fourths full with salted water and bring to a boil. Cook macaroni in boiling water 5 minutes, or until just tender (using package instructions as a guide). Add peas and cook for last 2 minutes. In a colander, drain macaroni and peas and rinse under cold water. Drain well.

- In a large bowl, whisk together mayonnaise, lemon juice and 2 tablespoons milk. Add macaroni, peas, ham, celery, parsley, currants, and salt and pepper to taste. Toss to combine well. Salad may be made 2 days ahead and chilled, covered. If salad looks dry, toss with additional milk before serving. Serve salad at room temperature or chilled.

bride of
frankenstein (1935)

lady fingers
raspberry trifle serves 10 to 12

You can never get enough of raspberries. Guests will swoon over this dessert!

2	packages vanilla pudding mix		2	packages lady fingers biscuits
3/4 cup	raspberry preserves		3/4 cup	cream sherry or orange flavoured liqueur
3	10-ounce packages frozen raspberries in syrup, thawed and drained (reserve 1/4 cup syrup)		1-1/4 cups	chilled whipping cream or dessert topping

- Prepare pudding mix according to package instructions. Place in freezer until cold, stirring often, about 15 minutes.

- Mix preserves and 1/4 cup reserved raspberry syrup in small bowl. Line bottom of glass bowl that is 8 inches in diameter, and 4 to 5 inches deep (about15-cup capacity) with layer of lady fingers, trimming to fit. Brush 1/4 cup sherry over lady fingers. Next, spread 1/4 cup preserve mixture over top of the lady finger layer.

- Reserve 12 raspberries and set aside. Sprinkle 1/3 cup raspberries over preserves, then pour 1 cup pudding over top. Repeat layering 2 more times. Cover; chill 2 hours. (Can be made 1 day ahead. Keep chilled.)

- Beat cream in large bowl until stiff peaks form. Spoon cream onto trifle. Garnish with the reserved fresh raspberries.

 Use low fat whipped topping or skim milk if you prepare dessert topping.

SETTING THE STAGE

This would be the ultimate Halloween party! And for those without a "crypt," basement parties will do just fine. Fill a few bowls around your house with dry ice and make sure to dim the lights. Use candles to light your dungeon. Ask your guests to dress in costume, perhaps as Mr. and Mrs. Frankenstein. Get a small collection of test tubes and beakers to use for drinks (shooters). Use a variety of coloured of liqueurs for a ghastly display. Play some fun games, set up an experiment requiring your guests to guess what they are tasting. Blindfold your guests and let them sample some of your creations: a bowl full of cold spaghetti (guts), Jell-O-with olives inside (brains) and a bowl of ketchup (blood). Use rustic style plates such as those for camping, stainless steel platters, black iron kettles, and cauldrons.

city lights (1931)

This 1931 silent film is considered by many reviewers to be Charles Chaplin's finest. He co-wrote, produced, directed, scored and edited the film. Even though spoken words had been introduced into films 3 years earlier, Chaplin decided to use only music and sound effects. The film has been called a comedy in pantomime and it plays on the universal themes of the blindness of love and the healing that refreshes the soul when one becomes selfless. In this film, the Little Tramp once again takes centre stage as he falls in love with a blind flower girl. Through a series of coincidences, the flower girl somehow forms the impression that the Tramp is a millionaire! In an interesting twist to the story line, the Tramp actually saves a suicidal millionaire who is having a love affair with the bottle. When inebriated he treats the Tramp like a pal, however, when sober he doesn't even recognize him. The altruistic tramp attempts to raise money so that his love, the blind flower girl, can have an eye-saving operation to bring back her sight. The boxing scene between the scrawny tramp and Hank Mann, who plays the boxer, is one of the highlights of the movie as is the touching scene in which the girl receives the gift of sight and finally sees her materially destitute, but spiritually rich benefactor.

FEATURED ACTORS
Charles Chaplin (The Tramp)
Virginia Cherrill (The Blind Girl)
Harry Myers (The Millionaire)
Allan Garcia
   (The Millionaire's Butler)
Hank Mann (The Boxer)
Florence Lee
   (Blind Girl's Grandmother)
Albert Austin (street cleaner)
Jean Harlow (guest)
James Donnelly (foreman)
Henry Bergman (mayor/janitor)
John Rand (tramp)
Stanhope Wheatcroft (man in cafè)
Eddie Baker
   and Henry Bergman (janitor)
Robert Parrish and John Rand (tramp)

DIRECTOR - Charles Chaplin
(as well as Editor / Composer (Music Score) / Producer / Screenwriter)

menu
straciatella soup • sausages with maple baked beans • choucroute • country style bread (store bought) • cheese and fruit platter

straciatella soup
serves 4

"Straciatella" means little rags or strings, which is what the eggs resemble when they are cooked.
A good stock is absolutely essential for this soup as are the eggs and the cheese. The spinach may be replaced with other greens, such as Swiss chard or kale, use what you can find. Cooked peas work well as a substitute for the greens.

2	eggs	4 cups	chicken stock or beef stock or vegetable stock
4-1/2 tsp	finely grated good quality Parmesan cheese	1 lb	spinach or Swiss chard, stemmed and leaves cut across into narrow strips, (or peas)
pinch	coarse sea salt, plus 1-1/2 teaspoons iodized salt		freshly ground black pepper, to taste
pinch	freshly grated nutmeg		
1 tbsp	all-purpose flour		

- In a small bowl, stir together the eggs, cheese, pinch of salt, the nutmeg, and flour (try not to get the eggs too frothy).

- In a medium saucepan, bring the stock to a boil. Place a colander with widely spaced holes over the boiling stock. Pour the egg mixture through the colander. Remove the colander and stir the soup once or twice (alternatively, slowly pour in the egg mixture and stir soup with a whisk). If using the greens, lower the heat and stir them in just to heat through. If using cooked green peas, add them at this point. Remove from heat and season with remaining salt and pepper to taste. Serve immediately.

 Use low fat broth, or if making your own, cool broth and skim the fat off the surface.

SAUSAGES
We suggest using a European style sausage such as smoked bratwurst. Shop at a Euro style butcher's or an upscale supermarket for the best quality. There are many types of sausages available — you may wish to ask for small samples to taste as they are often precooked. Prepare sausages according to package or butcher's directions.

 Buy a lean low fat sausage.

trivia clips
It took 342 takes before Chaplin was satisfied that he had adequately conveyed the idea that the blind girl had thought the tramp was wealthy after he bought flowers from her.

city lights (1931)

maple baked beans

serves 4 to 6

This dish has definite Middle Eastern influences as is evident by the use of dried fruits and almonds. The smell will take you on a journey to a bazaar with abundant stalls of dried fruits, nuts, spices and silks!

2 cups	dried navy beans, picked over and rinsed		1/2 lb	bacon, chopped
1	onion, chopped		8	cups water
1	large garlic clove, finely chopped		1/2 cup	maple syrup
			1 tsp	dry mustard
			1 tsp	paprika

- In a 7-1/2 quart ovenproof heavy kettle measuring about 12 inches across, combine beans, onion, garlic, bacon, and water and simmer, partially covered, 1 hour. Reserve 1/2 cup cooking liquid.
- Preheat oven to 300°F. In a bowl stir together reserved cooking liquid, maple syrup, mustard, and paprika

until well combined and stir into bean mixture, with enough additional water to just cover beans. Cover and bake beans for about 5 hours, adding just enough water at hourly intervals to keep mixture just covered.

 Use turkey bacon or reduce the quantity of bacon called for in recipe.

choucroute

We suggest buying a can of choucroute (sauerkraut cooked in white wine) at a local European delicatessen or at better supermarkets. Heat according to directions on label. If this doesn't tickle your taste buds, substitute your favourite green salad!

fruit and cheese platter

Serve at least 2 types of cheese, we suggest including Brie or Camembert and at least 3 to 4 types of fruit. Be certain to include some tropical fruit such as pineapple, papaya or mango! Peel the fruit if required and slice. Arrange decoratively on a platter.

trivia clips

Leading lady Virginia Cherill was fired near the end of filming for being tardy for a shoot. Georgia Hale, Chaplin's leading lady in "Gold Rush" was then hired and shot some of the end scenes, but Virginia was soon re-hired after Chaplin realized that the cost of re-shooting all of the scenes would be prohibitive. Even so, savvy Virginia managed to negotiate a 100% pay raise!

AWARDS WON

10 Best Films	1931 National Board of Review of Motion Pictures
U.S. National Film Registry	1991 Library of Congress
100 Greatest American Movies	1998 American Film Institute

BEVERAGES

Try a good European pilsner, lager or ale: try Bitburger Premium Pilsner (Germany), Tuborg Gold Label (a great lager from Denmark) or you may wish to try a Trappist Ale brewed by Trappist monks in Belgium- Rochefort 8 or La Trappe Dubbel. Historically the church has had a hand in brewing for hundreds and hundreds of years!

Coffee

MUSIC

The world was at war in the 1930's and economic depression swept the country. Jazz music became a popular mode of expression and it was heard in ballrooms and clubs across the nation.

Billie Holiday's Greatest Hits CD is an irresistible collection of her hits from the 30's and early 40's. The 30's was also an era when swing music and the big bands became popular. The music of Glen Miller, Benny Goodman, and Duke Ellington is a good introduction to the big band sound.

Good old American Blues would also be perfect. Not only was the music becoming more popular during this era, but also its soulfulness reflects the tough decade that was the 1930's. Anything by Bessie Smith or W.C. Handy (also known as the father of the blues because he brought the world's attention to blues music) would be suitable.

SETTING THE MOOD

Use a colourful scarf as a tabletopper. Put some daisies in an old teapot, a small metal pail or a small glass bottle such as those used for bottled water. Put a candle in an old wine bottle, and napkins and condiments in a basket. Use mismatched dinnerware as long as it doesn't clash. Improvisation and shabby chic are the key elements!

gone with the wind (1939)

Released in 1939, this film made box office history as one of the highest grossing films of its time. A lavish romance set against the backdrop of the Civil War; the multi-Academy Award-winning "Gone With the Wind" features a legendary cast. Historically romantic in its treatment of many aspects of the era, it nevertheless gives a fascinating view of the American South of long ago. Scarlett's tumultuous relationship with Rhett Butler was deemed to be one of the greatest epic love stories ever translated into film. The film tells the tale of a selfish woman who doesn't want to admit her true feelings for the man she loves, and in the end loses him. Her life's story occurs during one of the most turbulent periods in America's history. The film follows Scarlett from her young, seemingly innocent days on a feudalistic plantation to the war torn streets of Atlanta; from her first love whom she has always desired to three husbands. From the utmost luxury to absolute starvation and poverty; from her innocence to her understanding of the trials and tribulations of life. This is a movie you'll want to see more than once!

FEATURED ACTORS
Clark Gable (Rhett Butler)
Vivien Leigh (Scarlett O'Hara)
Leslie Howard (Ashley Wilkes)
Olivia de Havilland
   (Melanie Hamilton)
Hattie McDaniel (Mammy)

DIRECTOR - Victor Fleming

menu southern-style corn fritters with salsa • oven barbecued chicken or georgia peach spareribs • roasted garlic mashed potatoes • biscuits • pecan pie

southern-style corn fritters with salsa serves 4

This is a unique way to use fresh corn!

For salsa:

4	plum tomatoes, coarsely chopped
2/3 cup	white onion, chopped
4 tbsp	fresh cilantro, chopped
2 tbsp	pickled jalapeño chilies, chopped
2 tbsp	fresh lime juice
	salt to taste

- Accompaniment: sour cream (low fat sour cream is okay to use)
- Salsa: Stir together all salsa ingredients and season with salt.
- Make fritters: Cut corn kernels from ears with a sharp knife and scrape cobs to extract juice; discard cobs. Whisk together egg and milk until smooth and stir in cornmeal, flour, and salt. Stir in corn and its juice.

For fritters:

4	ears corn, shucked
2	large eggs
1 cup	milk
2/3 cup	coarse yellow cornmeal
5 tbsp	all-purpose flour
1/4	tsp salt
3 to 6 tbsp	vegetable oil

- Heat 1 tablespoon oil in a 12-inch non-stick skillet over moderate heat until hot, but not smoking. Drop in 2 tablespoons batter for each fritter. Fry until lightly browned, about 2 minutes per side, and drain on paper towels. Continue making the rest of the fritters, adding oil as necessary.
- Serve fritters with salsa.

oven barbecued chicken serves 2 to 4

1-3 lb	fryer chicken (cut up)
	seasoned flour (with salt and pepper)
1/4 cup	cooking oil
1 cup	ketchup
1/4 cup	vinegar
1/3 cup	water

2 tbsp	lemon juice
1 tbsp	Worcestershire sauce
2 tbsp	melted butter or margarine
4 tbsp	brown sugar
1	medium onion, diced

- Preheat oven to 325(F. Coat chicken pieces with seasoned flour. In a large skillet heat the oil, add the chicken pieces and brown evenly. Then place the chicken in a baking dish. In a saucepan, combine the rest of the ingredients and bring to a boil. Pour this over the chicken and cover baking dish with foil. Bake at 325 for one hour and 30 minutes, removing foil for the last 15 minutes of baking time.

Use a non-stick skillet and reduce the oil required for browning. Use light butter or margarine.

 Did you know that... Fried chicken is the most popular meal ordered in sit-down restaurants in the U.S. Van Camp's Pork and Beans were a staple food for Union Soldiers during the Civil War.

gone with the wind (1939)

georgia peach spareribs

serves 4

3 lbs	spareribs, quartered		2 tbsp	flour
1 tsp	salt		2 tbsp	prepared mustard
1	large can peach halves (in heavy syrup)		1/4 tsp	ground cloves
1 cup	ketchup		1 tsp	salt
2 tbsp	Worcestershire sauce		3/4 tsp	black pepper
1/4 cup	minced onion			

- Preheat oven to 375°F. Arrange the ribs in a shallow roasting pan, meaty side up; sprinkle with 1 teaspoon salt. Drain the peaches, saving the syrup. In a saucepan, blend the syrup with the ketchup, Worcestershire sauce, onion, flour, mustard, cloves, salt, and pepper; heat to boiling, then pour over the ribs. Bake at for one hour and 30 minutes or until tender. Baste often, turn once at approximately 1 hour. Place the peaches, cut side down around the ribs. Bake 10 more minutes, basting with sauce.

roasted garlic mashed potatoes

Roasted garlic is added to the decade's ultimate comfort food: smooth and creamy mashed potatoes.

1	large head garlic		2/3 cup	half and half cream
1 tsp	olive oil		5 tbsp	butter, cut into 5 pieces
2-1/2 lb	russet potatoes, peeled, cut into 1/2-inch pieces			salt and pepper to taste

- Preheat oven to 400°F. Place garlic on large square of foil. Drizzle with oil. Wrap foil around garlic to enclose and bake garlic until soft, about 40 minutes. Once garlic has cooled, separate cloves and press them between fingertips to release from skins.
- Cook potatoes in large pot of boiling, salted water until tender, about 20 minutes. Drain and return potatoes to same pot. Add garlic and mash together.
- Bring half and half to simmer in small saucepan. Add half and half and butter pieces to potatoes; mash and stir to blend. Season with salt and pepper.

 Use light butter and evaporated skim milk instead of half and half cream.

? Did you know that... Hattie McDaniel was the first African American to win an Oscar!!

trivia clips

In 1939, the Hollywood Production Code dictated what could and could not be shown or said on screen. David O. Selznick had to pay a fine of $5,000 to keep the most memorable last line in the film, "Frankly my dear I don't give a damn". Other suggested alternatives were "Frankly my dear, I just don't care," "it makes my gorge rise," "my indifference is boundless," "I don't give a hoot," and "nothing could interest me less."

AWARDS WON

Best Actress (Vivien Leigh)	1939 Academy Award
Best Art Direction (Lyle Wheeler)	1939 Academy Award
Best Cinematography (Ernest Haller)	1939 Academy Award
Best Cinematography (Ray Rennahan)	1939 Academy Award
Best Director (Victor Fleming)	1939 Academy Award
Best Editing (James Newcom)	1939 Academy Award
Best Editing (Hal Kern)	1939 Academy Award
Best Picture	1939 Academy Award
Best Supporting Actress (Hattie McDaniel)	1939 Academy Award
Best Writing Screenplay (Sidney Howard)	1939 Academy Award
Honourary and Other Awards (W.C. Menzies)	1939 Academy Award
10 Best Films	1939 Film Daily Award
10 Best Films	1939 National Board of Review of Motion Pictures Award
Best Actress (Vivien Leigh)	1939 New York Film Critics Circle Award
Best Direction (Victor Fleming)	1939 New York Film Critics Circle Award
Best Film (Victor Fleming)	1939 New York Film Critics Circle Award
Best Film (David O.Selznick)	1939 New York Film Critics Circle Award
Best Picture	1939 New York Film Critics Circle Award
10 Best Films	1939 New York Times Award
Award	1939 Photoplay Award
10 Best Films	1940 National Board of Review of Motion Pictures Award
U.S. National Film Registry	1989 Library of Congress Award
100 Greatest American Movies	1998 American Film Institute Award

continued

SETTING THE STAGE

When we think about Southern cooking, most of us have images of lots of food, picnics and good old-fashioned Southern hospitality. Turn this event to an outdoor picnic—indoors. Light a few citronella candles and set the table with a red and white checked tablecloth. You could turn this into an elegant buffet for 4 or more, or an intimate dinner for two. Decorate a picnic basket (or any basket for that matter) and use this as your centrepiece. Wrap the utensils in a variety of different coloured napkins and place in the basket. Gather all your favourite plates (they don't have to match!) and let everyone help themselves to the food. To make your guests feel as if they are they are going on a picnic, tell them to bring a small dessert or salad to include in your buffet. Don't worry if this seems like too much food, the movie is over three hours long-set intermission and enjoy the treats!

BEVERAGES

Your favourite American ice cold beer or you may wish to try Kingfisher Lager (Indian style beer brewed in England)

Mint Julep (see main beverages page)

Coffee with dessert is a must! See the main beverages page for a variety of coffees.

MUSIC

Listen to some great American blues artists like Robert Johnson. His "King of the Delta Blues Singers" (Columbia) and "All Time Blues Classics" (Music Memoria) are a great introduction to this music genre. Alternatively, a compilation CD like Cinema Serenade 2: The Golden Age (Sony), featuring movie music performed by the renowned team of violinist Itzhak Perlman would be suitable.

biscuits

serves 4 to 6

This quick recipe can easily be doubled.

2 cups	all-purpose flour
1 tbsp	baking powder
1 tsp	salt

| 3/4 stick | (6 tbsp) cold unsalted butter |
| 3/4 cup | heavy cream |

- Preheat oven to 425˚F and lightly grease a baking sheet.
- Into a large bowl sift together flour, baking powder, and salt. Cut 5 tablespoons butter into the flour mixture with your fingertips or with a pastry blender until mixture resembles coarse meal. Add cream, stirring with a fork until just combined. Transfer mixture to a lightly floured surface and gently knead about 3 times until it forms a dough. Pat dough into a circle shape (about 1/2 inch thick).
- Using a 2-1/2 inch round cutter cut out biscuits and arrange about 1 inch apart on baking sheet. Gather and pat out scraps and cut out more biscuits.
- Melt remaining tablespoon butter and lightly brush onto biscuits. Bake biscuits in middle of oven until pale golden and cooked through, about 20 minutes.

 In place of heavy cream use evaporated 2% or evaporated skim milk.

 Purchase store bought biscuits and warm up prior to serving, or buy the ready-to-bake biscuit dough that comes in a tube.

pecan pie

Yield: 10 slices

1/2 cup	butter, at room temperature
1/2 cup	sugar
3/4 cup	white corn syrup
3 tbsp	honey

3	eggs, lightly beaten
1-1/2 tsp	vanilla
2 cups	pecans, coarsely chopped
	Unbaked 9-inch pie shell

- Preheat oven to 350˚F. Cream the butter well, then slowly add the sugar and continue to mix until fluffy. Slowly stir in the syrup, honey, eggs, vanilla, and half of the nuts. Pour mixture into the pie shell, then top with the rest of the nuts. Bake at for 1 hour. Cool before slicing. For an extra special treat serve with vanilla ice cream on the side.

 Rather than a calorie dense pie, prepare a low fat vanilla or butterscotch pudding. Garnish with chopped pecans and a small dollop of whipped cream.

 Buy a ready-made pecan pie at the supermarket or your neighbourhood bakery! While enjoying your meal warm the store bought pie in the oven and fill the air with the sweet scent of pecans-serve warm. Your guests will think you just made it!

Margaret Mitchell wrote her novel between 1926 and 1929. In the early drafts, the main character was named "Pansy O'Hara". Do you think Scarlett's character would have been as popular if she was named Pansy?

Name another popular movie directed by Victor Fleming in 1939? Hint-ruby slippers and Kansas.

During the American Civil war, 200,000 Black Americans served in the Union Army; 38,000 of them gave their lives; and 22 won the Medal of Honour.

In 1865, several veterans of the Confederate Army formed a private social club in Pulaski, Tennessee, called the Ku Klux Klan.

it happened one night (1934)

Veteran heartthrob Clark Gable stars in this romantic comedy which snatched 5 major Academy awards in 1934. Frank Capra directed "It Happened One Night" in which Claudette Colbert plays Ellie Andrews. A spoiled heiress, who ends up marrying the man of her dreams despite her family's disapproval. Ellie's father conjures up plans to keep her from her husband, King Westley, known as the society aviator. He thinks Westley is a playboy and he proceeds to have the nuptials annulled and whisks his daughter on board the family yacht where he holds her, a virtual prisoner. Determined to get back to her husband, Ellie jumps ship near Miami to search for him in New York. She ends up at the nearest bus depot. On the bus, she meets street-smart reporter Peter Warne. They end up travelling together. Warne finds out her true identity along the way and hopes to get a great story. As they near new York City, with their many misadventures coming to an end; they reluctantly find that they are in love and afraid to admit it to each other. After she mistakenly thinks that Warne has run out on her Ellie returns to King Westley, but for how long?

menu spicy meatloaf • "smashed" potatoes with caramelized onions • your favourite tossed green salad • lemon meringue pie • vanilla milkshakes

spicy meatloaf
serves 4 to 6

2 tsp	olive oil
1	onion, chopped
2	cloves garlic, finely chopped
2 lb	extra-lean ground beef
3	egg whites, or 1 whole egg
1 tbsp	Dijon mustard
1 tbsp	Worcestershire sauce
1/2 tsp	hot pepper sauce
1 tsp	salt
1/2 tsp	pepper
1-1/2 cups	fresh breadcrumbs
3/4 cup	salsa (mild or medium)
2 tbsp	fresh cilantro, chopped

Topping

1/4 cup	tomato sauce, salsa or ketchup

• Preheat oven to 350°F. Heat oil in large skillet. Add the onion, garlic and cook gently until tender. Set aside to cool. In a large bowl combine ground beef, egg whites, mustard, Worcestershire sauce, hot pepper sauce, salt, pepper, breadcrumbs, salsa and cilantro. Add cooled onion mixture and knead ingredients together lightly until blended.

• Line large loaf pan with parchment paper or foil and place mixture in pan. Cover with foil and bake covered with foil in oven for 45 minutes. Uncover meatloaf, brush with topping and bake uncovered for another 20 minutes. Cool for 10 minutes before serving.

"smashed" potatoes with caramelized onions
serves 4 to 6

3 tbsp	butter
3/4 lb	onions, thinly sliced
1 tsp	sugar
1-1/2 lb	Yukon Gold potatoes, peeled and diced
1 tsp	salt plus more for salting water
scant 1/2 cup	milk
1/2 tsp	ground black pepper

• In a large skillet, melt 2 tablespoons butter over medium-low heat. Add the onions and sugar; cook, stirring occasionally, until onions turn dark golden brown - about 30 minutes.

• Place potatoes in a 4-quart saucepan. Cover with salted water. Cook potatoes over medium-high heat until soft-about 25 minutes. Drain potatoes and return to saucepan. Using a potato masher or an electric hand mixer on low speed, mix together potatoes, remaining tablespoon butter, milk, salt, and pepper until well combined. Fold in caramelized onions and serve.

 Use evaporated skim milk to lower fat yet maintain creamy taste. Use light butter or non-hydrogenated margarine.

FEATURED ACTORS

Clark Gable (Peter Warne)
Claudette Colbert (Ellie Andrews)
Walter Connolly (Alexander Andrews)
Roscoe Karns (Oscar Shapely)
Jameson Thomas (King Westley)

DIRECTOR - Frank Capra

trivia clips

Frank Capra's nickname was "Capra-corn"

"I made mistakes in drama. I thought drama was when actors cried. But drama is when the audience cries." Frank Capra in Cinéma, Cinémas, No. 12, Antenne 2 (French television), February 1983

lemon meringue pie

Yield: 1 pie

Here is a classic lemon meringue pie recipe that is a guaranteed hit. In the past, many diners lined up a variety of pies and cakes on the counter under glass domes to entice customers to order the desserts. Things have not changed since then. Coffee shops may serve a variety of fancy coffees as well as other beverages, but desserts are still a big draw. Biscotti with your cappuccino?

Pie Pastry

1-1/4	cups all-purpose flour	2 tbsp	cold vegetable shortening
6 tbsp	cold unsalted butter, cut into bits	1/4 tsp	salt
		2 to 4 tbsp	ice water

- In a bowl, with a pastry blender, or in a food processor blend or pulse together flour, butter, shortening, and salt until mixture becomes mealy. Add 2 tablespoons ice water and toss or pulse until water is absorbed. If necessary, add enough of remaining

ice water to form a dough and then form dough into a disk. Lightly dust dough with flour and chill, wrap in wax paper, then chill for an hour.

- Makes enough dough for a 9-inch to 10-inch single-crust pie.

Lemon Meringue Pie Filling

1	pie crust (see previous recipe)	1 tbsp	grated lemon peel
1-1/4 cups	plus 1/3 cup sugar	pinch	of salt
1 1/2 cups	water	1/2 cup	fresh lemon juice
6 tbsp	cornstarch	2 tbsp	unsalted butter, room temperature
5	large eggs, separated	1/2	tsp cream of tartar

- Position rack in center of oven and preheat oven to 350°F. Take pie crust out of refrigerator. Place on a floured pastry board, and roll out with a rolling pin to about 10 to 11 inches in diameter. If crust cracks, wet fingers and push edges together. Sprinkle flour over crust. Place crust floured side down in 9-inch-diameter glass pie dish. Fold edges over; crimp decoratively. Pierce crust all over with fork. Bake until crust is pale golden, about 12 minutes. Cool crust completely on rack.

- Whisk 1-1/4 cups sugar, water, 5 tablespoons cornstarch; egg yolks, lemon peel and salt in heavy medium saucepan to blend. Whisk over medium heat until mixture comes to a boil. Whisk until mixture thickens, about 2 minutes.

- Remove from heat. Add lemon juice and butter; whisk until smooth. Cool completely, about 1 hour, stirring occasionally.

- Preheat oven to 350°F. Mix 1/3 cup sugar and 1 tablespoon cornstarch in small bowl. Beat egg whites in large bowl until foamy; add cream of tartar and beat until soft peaks form. Add sugar mixture 1 tablespoon at a time, beating until stiff peaks form after each addition.

- Spread cooled lemon filling in crust. Spoon dollops of meringue around edge of pie on top of filling. Spoon remaining meringue onto center of pie. Spread meringue to cover filling, mounding in center and sealing completely to the crust edge. Using rubber spatula or spoon, swirl meringue decoratively, forming peaks. Bake pie until meringue peaks are light brown, about 12 minutes.

- Transfer to rack and cool completely. Refrigerate pie until cold, about 1-1/2 hours. (Can be prepared 3 hours ahead. Keep refrigerated.)

AWARDS

Best Actor (Clark Gable)	1934 Academy Award
Best Actress (Claudette Colbert)	1934 Academy Award
Best Adapted Screenplay (Robert Riskin)	1934 Academy Award
Best Director (Frank Capra)	1934 Academy Award
Best Picture	1934 Academy Award
10 Best Films	1934 Film Daily Award
10 Best Films	1934 National Review of Motion Pictures
10 Best Films	1934 New York Times Award
Best Picture	1934 Venice Film Festival
U.S. National Film Registry	1993 Library of Congress
100 Greatest American Movies	1998 American Film Institute

it happened
one night ₍₁₉₃₄₎

vanilla milkshake

serves 1

1/2 cup	milk	1 pint	vanilla ice cream
1/2 cup	heavy cream	1 tsp	vanilla extract

- Put all ingredients in a blender and frappè until frothy. Serve in a tall glass.

 Use evaporated skim or 2% milk in place of cream. Use low fat ice cream or frozen yogurt.

BEVERAGES

Milkshakes

Soft drinks

Your favourite American beer

MUSIC

Willy Nelson's "On the Road Again" and John Denver's "Greatest Hits" would suit this theme.

SETTING THE STAGE

Since this is an "on the road" romance, we thought that diner "cuisine" would be most suitable! Think about the car trips you may have taken as a child with your family. Wasn't one of the best parts stopping at various diners and greasy spoons as you travelled all over the country. Portions at diners are usually generous, and though it may not be haute cuisine it is certainly tasty! Make up some bus boarding passes, and as your guests arrive, give them each a ticket. At the end of the night draw for a door prize. Make up a small gift bag of travel supplies like toothpaste, personal soaps, mints, etc.

Set the table with paper place mats purchased at a party supply store. Write out a menu of the dinner specials. Set up a display of trip memorabilia you have, and don't forget the photo album!

Maybe you could even lay out some plans for your own road trip, or perhaps reminisce about those trips you took as a child with your family!

trivia clips

Name an American movie classic directed by Frank Capra that is traditionally viewed at Christmas time. Despite its popularity now, the movie was a box office flop. Capra never earned any money from this box office flop (Hint: An angel showed the character how wonderful the character's life was).

"Kiss my grits" was a saying made popular by a waitress on a long running 1970's sitcom. Can you name the show and the diner? Hint: Linda Lavin played the lead as a divorced single mother raising her son).

mutiny on the bounty (1935)

"Mutiny on the Bounty," a novel written by Charles Nordhoff and James Norton Hall, was published in 1932. It is one of the most stirring sea adventures ever told(the historic voyage of the H.M.S. Bounty that culminated in Fletcher Christian's mutiny against Captain Bligh. The yarn about the ship and the mutiny that took place on it in 1789 sparked the interest of MGM Studios. They invested two million dollars (an enormous sum for film production in 1935) in production costs alone! Filming took place on location in Tahiti. MGM's investment paid off handsomely, as the film won the Oscar for Best Picture in 1935 along with numerous other nominations. Though historians argue over some of the facts regarding the story, the plot line of the movie follows the main events as they were recorded. Namely, the story deals with a ship sailing from Britain to Tahiti to obtain a cargo of breadfruit. The notorious Captain Bligh (Charles Laughton) is in command of the HMS Bounty and the first mate is Fletcher Christian (Clark Gable), who has no affinity for his captain from the onset of the journey. Bligh's actions towards his crew don't win him any friends, especially on the voyage back to England. He enforces discipline by flogging, puts the crew on meagre rations and plays a role in the death of the ship's doctor. All of these events lead many of the crew to despise Bligh, so when Christian leads a mutiny, many of the crew support him. Bligh and those few officers loyal to him are set adrift in an open boat. Christian, now in command of the HMS Bounty, returns the ship and remaining crew to the paradise they enjoyed in Tahiti. What none of them could foresee was the return of the formidable Captain Bligh...

menu

nut encrusted red snapper with south seas salsa • coconut rice • green salad with vinaigrette dressing • vanilla ice cream with tropical fruit sauce

nut encrusted red snapper with south seas salsa
serves 4 to 6

2	large red bell peppers, cut into 1/4-inch pieces
1	mango, peeled and pitted, cut into 1/4-inch pieces
1	papaya, peeled and seeded, cut into 1/4-inch pieces
1 cup	fresh pineapple, peeled, cut into 1/4-inch pieces
1 cup	fresh cilantro, finely chopped
1/2	small red onion, finely diced
2 tbsp	fresh lime juice
1 tbsp	extra virgin olive oil
1 tbsp	white wine vinegar
1 tsp	garlic, finely chopped
1/4 tsp	cayenne pepper or paprika
	salt and pepper to taste
1/2 cup	all-purpose flour
2	large eggs
	salt and pepper to taste
3 cups	ground nuts (cashews, macadamia, hazelnuts, etc., mixture okay)
4 tbsp	olive oil
6	6-ounce red snapper fillets (grouper may be substituted)

- To make the salsa: Combine first 11 ingredients in large bowl and stir to blend. Season salsa to taste with salt and pepper.

- For the fish: Preheat oven to 350˚F. Place flour in shallow bowl. Whisk eggs in small bowl to blend. Sprinkle fish with salt and pepper and then coat fish with flour. Dip fish into eggs, then nuts, coating completely. Heat 2 tablespoons oil in each of 2 heavy large skillets over medium heat. Place 3 fillets in each skillet; cook until golden brown, about 2 minutes per side. Transfer fillets on to large baking sheet.

- Bake fish until just opaque in center, about 7 minutes. Divide salsa among 6 plates. Top with fish and serve.

 Use egg substitute in place of eggs.

 The salsa can be prepared 1 day ahead. Cover and refrigerate. Bring to room temperature before serving.

trivia clips

Charles Laughton, who played Captain Bligh, had a fear of the ocean and spent much time off camera being seasick!
As moustaches were not permitted in the British Navy during the time the HMS Bounty sailed, Clark Gable had to shave off his trademark moustache for the role.

mutiny on the bounty (1935)

coconut rice

serves 4 to 6 as a side dish

The texture of this rice is moist and sticky, so do not expect fluffy individual grains.

1-1/2 cups	canned, unsweetened coconut milk
1-1/2 cups	water
1/2 tsp	salt

1-1/2 cups	long-grain white rice
	sweetened flaked coconut, toasted (for garnish)

- In a small saucepan combine coconut milk, water and salt. Stir well and bring to a boil. Stir in rice. Reduce heat to moderately low and simmer rice, covered, until most of liquid is absorbed, about 15 minutes. Remove pan from heat and let rice stand, covered, 5 minutes.
- Serve rice sprinkled with toasted, flaked coconut.

♥ Use low fat coconut milk.

green salad with vinaigrette dressing

As the flavours of the fish are quite complex it is best to stick to a simple salad which will not detract from the fish. Use your favourite salad greens, add a simple vinaigrette dressing, and season with salt and pepper. Here is a good basic vinaigrette dressing with a few variations included.

2 tbsp	vinegar
1/2 tsp	salt

1/4 tsp	freshly ground pepper
1/2 cup	olive or vegetable oil

- In a small bowl, mix the vinegar and salt and let stand a few minutes. Add the pepper and slowly whisk in the oil. Taste for acidity and saltiness. Before using, stir to blend, or store in a jar with a tight lid for future use. Shake well before using.
- Mustardy Vinaigrette Dressing: Add 1 to 1-1/2 teaspoons Dijon mustard.

Blend well. Include minced onion and garlic, if desired.

- Onion or Garlic Vinaigrette Dressing: Add 1 to 2 tablespoons minced onion, scallions, or shallots or 1/2- 1 teaspoon minced garlic.
- Vinaigrette Dressing with Fresh Herbs: Add 2 teaspoons fresh chopped herbs, such as basil, chervil or tarragon.

FEATURED ACTORS
Clark Gable
(1st Mate Fletcher Christian)
Charles Laughton
(Capt. William Bligh)
Franchot Tone (Roger Byam)
Dudley Digges (Bachus)
Donald Crisp (Burkitt)
Movita Wallis Clark (Morrison)
Herbert Mundin (Smith)
Maria "Movita" Castaneda (Tehani)
Francis Lister (Capt. Nelson)
Mamo Clark (Maimiti)

DIRECTOR - Frank Lloyd

AWARDS WON

Best Picture	1935 Academy Award
Best Films	1935 Film Daily Award
10 Best Films	National Board of Review of Motion Pictures Award
Best Actor (Charles Laughton)	1935 New York Film Critics Circle Award
Best Picture	1935 New York Film Critics Circle Award
100 Greatest American Movies	1998 American Film Institute Award

BEVERAGES

Pre-dinner cocktails could include (see main beverages page) a Mango Daiquiri or Tropical Dream.

A Chardonnay would complement the fish. Here are some to try: Calvet Chardonnay Vin De Pays D'Oc (France), Banrock Station Unwooded Chardonnay (Australia) and Henry of Pelham Reserve Chardonnay VQA (Canada)

MUSIC

Find authentic Tahitian music... try your public library or the world music section of a large music store. There is a compilation entitled "Music of Tahiti" that is quite good, as is anything by Vanfau Records. A wonderful alternate Polynesian choice would be the late Hawaiian singer, Israel Kamakawiwo'ole. One of his popular albums is "Facing Future" and it features some songs familiar to us all, such as "Country Roads" and "Somewhere Over the Rainbow". If all else fails you can't go wrong with some good old reggae sounds, especially music by Bob Marley!

SETTING THE MOOD

Decorate your drink glasses with umbrellas, use colourful straws. Set your table with tropical pink and citrus colours. Buy some orchids or other tropical flowers—even a few will make an impact, and use them as a centrepiece. Go to a party store and buy Polynesian leis and wear with your favourite summer beachwear. After all, you're sailing to Tahiti!

vanilla ice cream with tropical fruit sauce

serves 4 to 6

1/4 cup	sweet butter
1/2 cup	packed dark brown sugar
1/4 cup	guava, mango or papaya nectar
1 tbsp	dark rum
1 tbsp	crystallized ginger, minced
1/8 tsp	ground nutmeg
1/8 tsp	ground allspice
1/2 cup	fresh pineapple, peeled and diced
1	kiwi, diced
1	banana, peeled and sliced
1 cup	mango, papaya or guava, peeled and diced (may be a combination of fruits)
	vanilla ice cream
	toasted sweetened coconut (optional)

- Melt butter in large, heavy skillet over medium heat. Add brown sugar, nectar and rum; stir until sugar dissolves. Increase heat and boil until syrupy, about 4 minutes. Mix in ginger, nutmeg and allspice. Add pineapple, kiwi, banana and mango (or papaya or guava) and sauté just until heated through, about 1 minute. Let cool 2 minutes.

- Scoop ice cream into bowls. Spoon warm sauce over ice cream. Sprinkle with coconut and serve immediately.

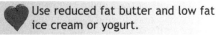 Use reduced fat butter and low fat ice cream or yogurt.

ninotchka (1939)

menu   wild mushroom soup • green salad with french farmhouse herb dressing • roast lamb with pistou • mediterranean style tomato rice with olives • pear clafoutis

wild mushroom soup

serves 4 to 6

Adding potatoes to the purèe gives this soup its thick, creamy texture.

2 cups	warm water
3/4 ounce	dried porcini mushrooms
2 tbsp	butter or olive oil
1 cup	onion, chopped
1 cup	carrots, peeled and chopped
1/2 cup	chopped leek (white and pale green parts only)
22 ounces	fresh mushrooms (such as crimini, shiitake or portobello), sliced
1/2 cup	dry white wine

4 cups	(or more) chicken or vegetable stock
1 cup	Yukon Gold potato, peeled and diced
1 tbsp	fresh thyme, chopped or 1 teaspoon dried
1	bay leaf
1/4 cup	whipping cream
1/4 cup	milk
	salt and pepper to taste
	Chopped fresh parsley or chives

- Combine 2 cups warm water and dried porcini mushrooms in small bowl. Let mushrooms soak until soft, about 30 minutes. Using slotted spoon, remove mushrooms from liquid. Squeeze excess liquid from mushrooms back into bowl. Strain 1 cup soaking liquid into another small bowl, leaving any sediment behind.

- Melt 1 tablespoon butter or oil in a large, heavy pot over medium heat. Add onion, carrots and leek. Sautè until vegetables are tender and pale golden, about 10 minutes. Add remaining 1 tablespoon butter or oil and fresh mushrooms; sautè until mushrooms are tender and brown, about 10 minutes. Stir in porcini and wine. Cook until liquid evaporates, about 5 minutes. Add 4 cups stock, potato, thyme, bay leaf and 1 cup reserved porcini soaking liquid. Bring to boil. Reduce heat and simmer until potato is very soft, stirring occasionally, about 30 minutes.

- Discard bay leaf. Cool slightly. Working in batches, purèe soup in blender. Return soup to pot. Mix in cream and milk. Bring to simmer. Season with salt and pepper. (Can be prepared 1 day ahead. Cover and refrigerate. Re-warm before serving, thinning with more stock, if desired.) Ladle soup into bowls. Sprinkle with chopped parsley.

 Use evaporated 2% or skim milk in place of cream.

 The soup can be made the day before, just reheat gently and remove from heat before it boils.

The alluring Greta Garbo plays the fascinating Ninotchka. This comedy starts in Russia with three Russian delegates being dispatched to Paris to sell some valuable Imperial jewelry. The former owner of the jewelry, Grand Duchess Swana (Ina Claire) is understandably upset when she learns of the whereabouts of her precious gems. She dispatches her boyfriend Count Leon Dalga, played by the dashing Melvyn Douglas, to retrieve her cache of jewels. He has a plan for the trio of delegates and he begins to wine and dine them... Moscow smells danger in the air and sends in comrade Ninotchka who declares that "love is just a chemical reaction" as a response to the Count's charming ways. Leon does finally win Ninotchka over, and in a twist to the plot truly falls in love with her! This tale of espionage and love also features well-known horror film actor Bela Lugosi in one of his last supporting roles in a high-budget film.

FEATURED ACTORS
Greta Garbo (Ninotchka)
Melvyn Douglas (Count Leon Dalga)
Bela Lugosi (Commissar Razinin)
Sig Rumann (Michael Iranoff)
Felix Bressart (Buljanoff)
Ina Claire (Grand Duchess Swana)
Alexander Granach (Kopalski)

DIRECTOR - Ernst Lubitsch

AWARDS WON

10 Best Films	1939 Film Daily Award
10 Best Films	1939 National Board of Review of Motion Pictures Award
10 Best Films	1939 New York Times Award
U.S. National Film Registry	1990 Library of Congress Award

trivia clips
MGM decided to cast Greta Garbo in order to better market the film in Europe and boost foreign revenues.

BEVERAGES

Kittling Ridge Cabernet Sauvignon (Canada), Hardy's Australian Shiraz (Australia)

French Roast Coffee (buy a small amount and grind just before serving)

MUSIC

Edith Piaf, also called the sparrow of Paris (Piaf means sparrow in French) was one of the most popular singers ever in France. Her wistful, bittersweet tunes will evoke a nostalgic feeling for times gone by...Try "The Best of Edith Piaf" (Delta) or "Cocktail Hour" (Colombia River).

SETTING THE MOOD

Some of the scenes take place in fancy Parisian restaurants. Bring out your best plates and cutlery. Use linen napkins or very fancy paper ones that are colourful and unusually shaped. Set out finger bowls with lemon slices. Buy some elegant, long-stemmed flowers and place them in a crystal vase or place one flower by each table setting for a simple, yet graceful impact. Dim the lights and set out various candles-put a sultry chanteuse such as Edith Piaf on the stereo and enjoy a long drawn out French style meal!

green salad with french farmhouse herb dressing serves 4 to 6

1 head	green salad (Romaine or Boston), washed, dried and torn into pieces suitable for spearing with a fork	1/3 to 1/2 cup	olive oil, or to taste
		1-1/2 tsp	minced fresh Italian or flat leaf parsley leaves
Add whatever you wish of the following: chopped pepper, radishes, celery, or grated carrot.		1-1/2 tsp	minced fresh chives
		1-1/2 tsp	minced fresh tarragon or 1/2 teaspoon dried
2 tbsp	red or white wine vinegar	1-1/2 tsp	minced fresh chervil or 1/2 teaspoon dried
1/2 tsp	honey Dijon-style mustard	1-1/2 tsp	minced fresh thyme or 1/2 teaspoon dried

- In a bowl combine the vinegar, the mustard, and salt and pepper to taste, add the oil in a stream, whisking the dressing until it is emulsified.

- Stir in parsley, chives, tarragon, chervil and thyme.

roast lamb with pistou serves 4 to 6

Pistou is the french term for pesto sauce. The difference is that the pistou is made without the addition of nuts.

Pistou		Lamb	
6 to 8	large garlic cloves	1	5 to 6 lb leg of lamb, boned, rolled, tied
2	1/2 ounce packages fresh basil leaves, trimmed, coarsely chopped	3	garlic cloves, slivered
		4 tbsp	chopped fresh basil
1/2 cup	olive oil		olive oil
3/4 cup	grated Parmesan cheese		salt and pepper
	salt and pepper	4	large tomatoes
			fresh basil leaves

For pistou:

- In a food processor chop garlic finely. Add basil and oil, process until finely chopped and mixed into a purèe. Mix in cheese. Season with salt and pepper. Transfer to small bowl.

For lamb:

- Preheat oven to 450˚F. Form slit in lamb with tip of sharp knife. Insert garlic sliver and some of the chopped basil into slit. Repeat all over lamb. Place lamb on rack in roasting pan. Brush generously with oil. Sprinkle with salt and generous amount of pepper. Roast 20 minutes. Reduce oven temperature to 375˚F. Continue roasting until thermometer inserted into thickest part of lamb registers 130˚F, basting occasionally with drippings, about 1 hour longer. Cool 1 hour. Slice tomatoes; place around edge of platter. Slide basil leaves between tomato slices. Slice lamb; arrange on platter. Drizzle pistou over lamb and tomatoes.

 Use prepared pesto sauce instead of making your own pistou.

mediterranean style
tomato rice with olives serves 4 to 6

4 tbsp	extra-virgin olive oil	1-1/2 cups	long-grain rice
1/2 cup	scallions, thinly sliced	1/4 cup	parsley, chopped
1 cup	onions or leeks, finely chopped		freshly ground black pepper
pinch	of salt		oily black olives for garnish
1/2 cup	tomato paste		

- Heat 3 tablespoons of the olive oil in a 10-inch straight-sided skillet. Add the scallions, onions, a pinch of salt, and 1/4 cup water and cook, covered, over medium-low heat for 10 minutes. When the water evaporates, slowly let the onions turn golden, stirring occasionally. Add 3 cups water and the tomato paste. Stir to mix, and add the rice. Cover and cook for 10 minutes. Add freshly ground pepper.

- Garnish with chopped parsley and olives.

clafoutis
serves 4 to 6

4	large eggs	1 tsp	vanilla extract
1/2 cup	sugar	1 tsp	grated lemon peel
pinch	of salt	3	large pears, peeled, cored and sliced
1/3 cup	all-purpose flour		powdered sugar
1 cup	milk		
1/4 cup	unsalted butter, melted		

- Preheat oven to 325°F. Generously butter a 9-inch-diameter deep-dish glass pie plate. Beat eggs, 1/2 cup sugar and salt in medium bowl to blend. Whisk in flour. Add milk, butter, vanilla and lemon peel and whisk until smooth. Arrange pears in bottom of prepared plate. Pour custard over pears.

- Bake until clafoutis is set in center and golden on top, about 55 minutes. Sprinkle powdered sugar over top and serve.

top hat (1935)

This couple met by luck and ended up as America's sweethearts, tapping their toes in sync for years to come. Fred Astaire and Ginger Rogers were well-received by the movie-going public in their first appearance in the flick "Flying Down to Rio" released in 1935. Their screen magic was electrifying and "Top Hat" was created specifically to show off their talents. Audiences enjoyed watching Fred Astaire and Ginger Rogers float across the dance floor dancing cheek to cheek and bringing a little bit of Broadway to the silver screen. The legendary Irving Berlin wrote all the brilliant songs for "Top Hat" which was filmed entirely in London, England even though a part of the story takes place in Venice. The story line features the character Dale Tremont (Rogers), a fashion model preparing for her upcoming movie debut. The young starlet's beauty sleep is disturbed by a tap dancing stage star Jerry Travers (Astaire), who continually practices on the floor directly above hers. The two meet, flirt, dance and fall in love- with a few complications along the way.

FEATURED ACTORS
Fred Astaire (Jerry Travers)
Ginger Rogers (Dale Tremont)
Edward Horton (Horace Hardwick)
Helen Broderick (Madge Hardwick)
and Erik Rhodes (Alberto Beddini)

DIRECTOR – Mark Sandrich

AWARDS WON

10 Best Films	1935 Film Daily Award
U.S. National Film Registry	1990 Library of Congress

menu
antipasto platter • spaghettini salad • garlic bread • angel food cake with strawberries and devonshire cream

antipasto platter
serves 6 to 8

Don't worry about the large amount of food in this dish-the leftovers are tasty and will last for a few days. If you wish though, you may cut the recipe in half.

For the marinade:

2	large garlic cloves, minced
2 tbsp	balsamic vinegar
2 tbsp	red or white wine vinegar
1/2 tbsp	fresh rosemary, chopped (or 1/2 teaspoon dried rosemary, crumbled)
1/2 tbsp	fresh basil, chopped (or 1 teaspoon dried basil, crumbled)
1/2 tbsp	fresh oregano, chopped (or 1 teaspoon dried oregano, crumbled)
1/4 tsp	dried hot red pepper flakes, or to taste
1/2 cup	extra virgin olive oil

3	large carrots, cut diagonally into 1/4-inch-thick slices
2	small fennel bulbs (about 1-1/2 pounds), cut crosswise into 1/4-inch slices (about 3 cups)
2	red bell peppers, roasted and cut into strips
2	yellow or orange bell peppers, roasted and cut into strips
1	12-ounce jar hot pickled peppers (pepperoncini), drained well
3/4 lb	black or green brine-cured olives or a combination
1/4 lb	sun-dried tomatoes packed in oil, drained and cut into strips
3/4 lb	marinated or plain bocconcini
1/2 lb	soppressata salami
12	small button mushrooms, cleaned
2	small jars marinated artichoke hearts, rinsed and drained well
1/3 cup	fresh Italian parsley leaves, minced plus, if desired, parsley sprigs for garnish

Make the marinade:

• In a small bowl whisk together garlic, vinegars, rosemary, basil, oregano, red pepper flakes, and salt and pepper to taste. Add the oil in a stream, whisking, until the marinade is emulsified.

• In a large saucepan of boiling water blanch the carrots and the fennel for 3 to 4 minutes, or until they are crisp-tender. Drain them, and plunge them into a bowl of ice and cold water. Let the vegetables cool then drain them well. In a large bowl toss together the carrots, the fennel, the roasted peppers, pepperoncini, olives, sun-dried tomatoes, bocconcini, soppressata, mushrooms, artichoke hearts, minced parsley and marinade until the antipasto is well combined. Chill the antipasto, covered, for at least 4 hours or overnight. Transfer the antipasto to a platter, garnish it with the parsley sprigs, and serve it at room temperature.

 Make the antipasto the day before or buy prepared antipasto at better supermarkets or gourmet food stores.

continued

spaghettini salad

serves 4 to 6

This refreshing salad-style pasta can be served warm or at room temperature. Perfect if you have to leave the table to dance in between courses.

1 lb	spaghettini	2 tsp	hot pepper flakes,
5	tomatoes, seeded and diced	1 tbsp	capers, chopped
1	bunch arugula or watercress, coarsely chopped	1/4 tsp	freshly ground pepper salt to taste
1/2 cup	flat leaf parsley, chopped	1/4 cup	extra virgin olive oil
1	head radicchio or leaf lettuce, coarsely chopped	3 to 4 tbsp	balsamic vinegar
3	cloves garlic, minced	1/4 cup	black olives, pitted and chopped
			freshly grated Parmesan cheese

- Bring large pot of water to boil. Add spaghettini and cook until tender, but firm. Meanwhile, in a large shallow dish, combine tomatoes, arugula, parsley and radicchio. Stir in garlic, hot pepper flakes, capers, pepper and salt. Stir in oil, vinegar and olives.

- Drain pasta well and combine immediately with sauce. Taste and adjust seasoning if necessary. Sprinkle with Parmesan cheese. Serve with the garlic bread and extra Parmesan for sprinkling on top.

garlic bread

serves 4 to 6

1/2 cup	butter, melted	4 tbsp	grated Parmesan cheese
4	garlic cloves, minced		paprika
1	large loaf French bread baguette, halved lengthwise		pepper

- Preheat broiler. Combine butter and garlic. Place bread on baking tray. Brush bread halves with butter mixture. Sprinkle each bread half with

2 tablespoons Parmesan cheese. Season with paprika and pepper. Broil until golden. Cut into 1-inch slices and serve.

top hat (1935)

BEVERAGES

Before dinner, have champagne of course, with fresh strawberries in each glass! Or you may want to serve a Kir Royale, which is made by topping champagne with Crème de Cassis, a liqueur made from blackberries.

During dinner any of these wines would be a hit: Yvon Mau Semillon Sauvignon (France), Fetzer Fumè Blanc (California). They are all wonderful if you prefer white. If you drink red wine try: Peller Estates Oakridge Merlot (Canada), or Ruffino Chianti (Italy).

Coffee Italian style
(espresso or cappuccino)

MUSIC

"Irving Berlin, A Hundred Years" (Columbia) is a phenomenal collection featuring vocals by Benny Goodman, Eddie Cantor, Dinah Shore, Fred Astaire, Tony Bennett and Johnny Mathis among others. "Irving Berlin, 100 years of Genius" (CBS U.K.) is also a good compilation of songs by this American legend. The vocals on this collection are performed by various artists such as Andy Williams, Doris Day, and Barbra Streisand.

SETTING THE STAGE

This could be a very romantic dinner for two. First set the table with a crisp white tablecloth, and add fancy plates with chargers (a large, usually ornate metal or glass decorative base for dinner plates). Place white floating candles in a crystal bowl and sprinkle a few silver sparkles on the table. You mat want to move your table to the far side of the room to create a small dance floor for an intimate twirl. Purchase or borrow a few long wall mirrors and place around your dance area. Or if planning a group dinner, call your local dance studio and book hour of dance time with an instructor. Then go home to eat, and watch the film to see how you measure up to Fred and Ginger!

trivia clips

Before Fred Astaire became a national icon on the Broadway scene, he was rejected by a few agents who classified him as, "not very good looking and dances a little," "don't think he should be in this business" and "won't last".
"People think I was born in top hat and tails." Fred Astaire (1899-1987) Evening Standard, 21 May 1976

angel food cake with strawberries and devonshire cream

serves 6 to 8

Some say Fred and Ginger danced like "angels". If you can't join them then try this dessert-it is heavenly! Since the rest of the menu is Italian we thought the dessert could use some English influence, hence the Devonshire cream.

angel food cake with strawberries

1-1/2 cups	powdered sugar		2 tsp	vanilla extract
1 cup	cake flour		1 cup	granulated sugar
2 cups	large egg whites (about 15), at room temperature			
2 tsp	cream of tartar		1 pint	fresh strawberries, hulled and sliced
3/4 tsp	salt			

- Preheat oven to 375˚ F. In small bowl, stir powdered sugar and cake flour; set aside. In a separate large bowl, add egg whites, cream of tartar, salt and vanilla extract. Beating at high speed, sprinkle in granulated sugar, 2 tablespoons at a time; beat just until sugar dissolves and whites form stiff peaks.

- With a rubber spatula, fold in flour mixture, about 1/4 cup at a time, just until flour is blended. Pour mixture into a 10-inch tube pan sprayed with cooking spray. Using spatula, cut through the batter to ensure there are no air bubbles. Bake for 35 minutes or until top of cake springs back when lightly touched by a finger. Remove from oven and invert cake on a drying rack; cool completely and remove to serving plate.

- If desired cut cake in half horizontally and place strawberries between the layers. Otherwise, serve strawberries along side cake slices.

mock devonshire cream

Yield: 3 cups

1/2 cup	cold water		1 cup	chilled whipping cream
1 tsp	unflavoured gelatin		1/4 cup	sugar
1 cup	chilled sour cream		2 tsp	vanilla extract

- Place water in small saucepan. Sprinkle gelatin over water. Let stand until gelatin softens, about 10 minutes. Stir mixture over low heat until gelatin dissolves. Let stand just until cool but not set, about 10 minutes.

- Place sour cream in medium bowl. Stir in gelatin mixture. Beat whipping cream, sugar and vanilla in medium bowl until soft peaks form; fold into sour cream mixture in 2 additions. Cover; chill at least 1 hour. (Can be made 1 day ahead. Keep chilled.)

trivia clips

This famous redhead appeared in a small role as a flower clerk in "Top Hat". In the 1950's she married a Cuban bongo-playing bandleader and they later had their own television comedy. Can you guess her name?

Irving Berlin wrote the American classic "God Bless America" and did not receive any royalties as he donated all the royalties to Boy Scouts of America.

wuthering heights (1939)

broiled cornish hens with lemon and herbs on a bed of rice

serves 4

3 cups	cooked rice (white or a mixture of white and wild rice)	1/4 tsp	dried rosemary leaves, crushed
1 tbsp	butter	1/4 tsp	black pepper
2	1-1/2-lb fresh or frozen (thawed) Rock Cornish hens	2 tbsp	lemon juice
	salt	3 tbsp	parsley, chopped
1/2 tsp	dried thyme leaves		lemon slices for garnish

- Preheat broiler to 350°F. In saucepan, prepare rice as package directs using 1 tablespoon butter; keep warm.

- Cut each Cornish hen in half. In a small roasting pan (about 14" by 10"), arrange hens, skin-side down; sprinkle with 1/4 teaspoon salt. With roasting pan 5 to 7 inches from source of heat, broil hens about 15 minutes.

- In a cup, mix dried thyme, dried rosemary, pepper, and 1/2 teaspoon salt. Turn hens; sprinkle with herb mixture. Broil hens about 15 minutes longer, basting once or twice with pan drippings, until golden brown and juices run clear when thickest part of hens is pierced with a knife.

- Remove hens to warm large platter; skim fat from drippings in roasting pan. Add lemon juice to roasting pan, stirring to loosen brown bits; spoon over hens on platter. Stir parsley into rice; serve with hens. Garnish with lemon slices.

baby potatoes with rosemary

serves 4

2-1/2 lb	assorted small potatoes (red, white, purple, golden), each cut in half or into quarters if large	2 tsp	paprika
		1-1/2 tsp	salt
1/4 cup	olive oil	1/2 tsp	coarsely ground black pepper
2 tbsp	fresh rosemary, chopped		rosemary sprigs for garnish

- Preheat oven to 425° F. Place potatoes in large roasting pan (17" by 11-1/2"); toss with olive oil, chopped rosemary, paprika, salt, and pepper. Roast potatoes 30 to 40 minutes, turning occasionally with metal spatula, until golden and fork-tender. Garnish with rosemary sprigs.

♥ Reduce the amount of olive oil called for to 2 tablespoons. Liberally spray roasting pan you with cooking spray.

trivia clips

Laurence Olivier, was very upset that the love of his life, Vivien Leigh did not get the role of Catherine.

The final shot of Catherine and Heathcliff walking hand in hand into the after world was filmed using the actors' stand-ins.

During the 1930's romanticism was sweeping Hollywood and this film based on Emily Brontë's novel, came out of that movement. Those who have read the novel will find that the movie doesn't follow the novel through to the end, however, they probably won't be disappointed by the film. The focus of the film is the intense relationship between Catherine Earnshaw (who was born into wealth), and her dark, brooding gypsy foster brother. Catherine chooses the path taken by most woman of her social standing, that is, marrying for convenience and wealth. What she doesn't plan on is her ability to control her passionate feelings for Heathcliff. In the interim, Heathcliff acquires some money and sets out on a vengeful course: he marries the sister of Edgar Linton, Catherine's husband. Neither of the two couples is happy or satisfied. Fate and unfulfilled desires lead to Catherine's early demise, but not before she and Heathcliff have pledged eternal love. Is their love really eternal? Watch the film and find out...

FEATURED ACTORS

Merle Oberon (Catherine Eamshaw)
Laurence Olivier (Heathcliff)
David Niven (Edgar Linton)
Flora Robson (Ellen Dean)
Geraldine Fitzgerald
  (Isabella Linton)
Donald Crisp (Dr. Kenneth)
Hugh Williams (Hindley Earnshaw)
Harold Entwistle (Beadle)
Rex Downing (younger Heathcliff)
Cecil Humphreys (Judge Linton)
Cecil Kellaway (Mr. Earnshaw)

DIRECTOR - William Wyler

AWARDS WON

10 Best Films	1939 Film Daily Award
10 Best Films	1939 National Board of Review of Motion Pictures Award
10 Best Films (William Wyler)	1939 New York Film Critics Circle Award
Best Picture	1939 New York Film Critics Circle Award
10 Best Films	1939 New York Times Award
100 Greatest American Movies	1998 American Film Institute Award

wuthering
heights (1939)

BEVERAGES

Mead, a wine made from honey, would be an authentic drink, most lords of the manor made it in-house. Luckily, commercial mead is now available. You'll pay a little bit more than you would for an average bottle of wine, but it will add to the atmosphere of the evening. Try Moniack Mead from Scotland.

A nice, light wine to try would be Beaujolais Nouveau Georges Duboeuf Beaujolais or Pisse-Dru, both from France are good ones to try if it happens to be November or December. This is the time of year that these light and delicate wines are available. They are released a few weeks after the harvest, usually the third Thursday of November. Beaujolais is meant to be consumed before Christmas. Italy also has its own version of Beaujolais Nouveau, called vino novello.

At any other time of year you may wish to serve a Chardonnay such as: Gallo of Sonoma (California), Banrock Station Unwooded Chardonnay (Australia) or Fortant De France Chardonnay (France).

MUSIC

Kate Bush's song "Wuthering Heights" is on both her "Whole Story" CD (EMI) or "Burning Desire" (Castle). For a new age blend of Celtic music you might try anything by Enya, or to evoke a melodramatic mood listen to Gregorian chants. Canadian sensation, Loreena McKennitt also has a wonderful array of songs that incorporate Celtic, folk and ethnic sounds. Unlike any other style her musical fusion, with its haunting melodies, will make you feel as if you are in an old castle. A suitable alternative would be a compilation CD like "Cinema Serenade 2: The Golden Age" (Sony), featuring movie music performed by the renowned team of violinist Itzhak Perlman would be suitable.

SETTING THE MOOD

Use brocade or tapestry type prints for setting the table. Tall candles are compulsory, the more the better; especially in silver or brass candelabra. Bring out your silverware and silver goblets if you have them, otherwise use crystal. A large fruit bowl full of various fruits and nuts in the shell, surrounded by some greenery makes a nice centrepiece.

green salad with naked vinaigrette Yield: 1 cup

Use your favourite salad greens or perhaps a mesclun mix-the key is to make the salad as simple as possible since the rest of the meal is seasoned with herbs.

2/3 cup	olive or canola oil	2 tsp	salt
1/4 cup	red or white wine vinegar	1/8 tsp	pepper

- In a small bowl, whisk all ingredients to combine. Pour over salad and toss.

easy mocha-chocolate mousse serves 4

12 ounces	good quality bittersweet chocolate, chopped	6	eggs, separated
3/4 cup	espresso or double strength brewed coffee	2 to 3 tbsp	brandy, rum or coffee liquor

- Put the chocolate into a blender or food processor and pour in the hot coffee. Blend until the chocolate has melted and the mixture is smooth. Blend in the egg yolks one at a time and then blend in the liquor. Transfer into a bowl and set aside.

- Next, beat the egg whites in a separate bowl at high speed until soft peaks form. Fold the whites into the chocolate mixture blending until no white shows. Pour the mousse into individual dessert cups. If you don't have dessert cups, just use wineglasses!

 Use an instant chocolate mousse, it's usually lower in calories and fat than the rich home-made version. European delicatessens or gourmet food stores usually carry such products.

---

trivia clips

"If you can reveal to an audience what lies within them, you can be as important as a philosopher, a psychiatrist, a doctor, a minister or whatever. You have to feel and love not only your own role-or some element in it-but also feel and love the audience. Sounds sentimental I'm afraid, but there you have it."
Laurence Olivier (1907-1989), Daily Mail, 28 March 1979

Fabulous 40's

1940- Hattie McDaniel becomes the first Black-American actress to win an Oscar. She won the Best Supporting Actress award for her role as Mammy in "Gone with the Wind".

1941- Germany invades the U.S.S.R The German invasion began on June 22, 1941, with massive assaults along the Soviet borders from the Gulf of Finland in the north, to the Black Sea in the south. There were 150 German divisions supported by 2,500 aircraft. Winter set in, the same harsh Russian winter that drove Napoleon's troops out of Russia in 1812. The Germans had not been provided winter clothing or boots. Many froze to death in the snow and devastating cold. Meanwhile, the Soviet military recouped, attacked sporadically, and waited for spring. The Germans would counterattack, but their momentum was gone. From winter 1941-42 the Soviets took the offensive against the Germans and pushed them westward to Berlin by 1945.The two most dramatic events of this theatre of war were the siege of Leningrad, when the brave city was battered and starved for about 900 days without ever giving up, and the Battle of Stalingrad, one of the great land battles in world history, which the Soviets finally won.

1945- Tito comes to power in Yugoslavia.

1945- The United Nations as we know it is formed. The new assembly opened in San Francisco, California, on April 25, 1945, and drafted the United Nations Charter.

1945- WW II ends.

1945- A computer at Harvard malfunctioned and Grace Hopper, who was working on the computer, investigated, found a moth in one of the circuits and removed it. Ever since, when something goes wrong with a computer, it is said to have a bug in it.

1947- American airman Major Chuck Yeager is the first person to break the sound barrier by flying faster than the speed of sound on Oct. 14, 1947. Breaking the sound barrier means flying an airplane faster than the speed of sound, 740 miles (1,190 kilometers) per hour. Since Yeager's flight, many military aircraft designed to fly at supersonic speeds have been built. The fastest have achieved about 2.5 times the speed of sound.

1947- Dead Sea Scrolls unearthed. This miscellaneous assortment of leather and papyrus manuscripts was so named because it was found in caves near the Dead Sea. Over 400 manuscripts were found. Some of the oldest documents are parts of the Hebrew Bible. The writings date from 100 BC to AD 68, and were written in ancient Hebrew, Aramaic, and Greek.

1948- Holography, a technique by which the image of a three dimensional object is recorded on film so that when the film is illuminated under the proper conditions, a three dimensional image of the object is created, was invented by Dennis Gabor, a Hungarian-born physicist. He was awarded the Nobel prize for physics in 1971. The development of the laser in the 1960s greatly improved the means of obtaining holograms.

1948- Invention of the transistor. In the 20th century no more useful invention has been made than the transistor. It is a solid-state device that regulates, amplifies, or generates electrical signals. The transistor replaced the cumbersome and shorter-lasting vacuum tube and made possible the electronics revolution of the late 20th century. The transistor was invented in 1948 by three physicists at Bell Laboratories: John Bardeen, Walter H. Brattain, and William B. Shockley.

1949- Eugenia Anderson is the first American woman to be appointed ambassador to a foreign country. (Ambassador to Denmark)

1949- Gwendolyn Brooks is the first Black woman to win a Pulitzer Prize.

Fabulous 40's

black narcissus (1947)

This British sensual melodrama is unusual in its subject matter, the battle between religion and eroticism. Not so unique, you say? Well, it is when nuns are at the centre of the tension! The movie is set in India, in the Himalayas, at an Anglican hospital and school complex. The structure was previously used to house a general's harem. This thought alone is troubling for the nuns, never mind the suggestive paintings that still adorn the walls of the building. Things become even more complicated for the nuns when the General's son, a handsome young man who wears the scent of black narcissus enters the picture. As if this weren't enough, an Englishman, Mr. Dean who exerts a powerful sexual presence, also arrives to throw the sisters into emotional turmoil. They begin to question their faith and choice of vocation. Ultimately, the destabilization leads to tragedy and the sisters fail to found a convent.

FEATURED ACTORS
Deborah Kerr (Sister Clodagh)
Sabu (young Prince)
David Farrar (Mr. Dean)
Kathleen Byron (Sister Ruth)
Flora Robson (Sister Philippa)

DIRECTOR ~ Michael Powell

AWARDS WON

Best Art Direction	1947 Academy Award
Best Cinematography	1947 Academy Award
Best Actress (Deborah Kerr)	1947 New York Film Critics Circle Award

menu
samosas (store bought) • tandoori chicken on a stick with yogurt dip • passage to india rice • naan • kulfi

Most supermarkets now carry a variety of samosas in mild and hot versions. As a condiment for the samosas you may wish to pick up an array of commercially prepared hot sauces, chutneys or even a lime pickle.

Grill or broil the chicken when the rice is set to cook, that way they will both be done at about the same time.

tandoori chicken on a stick with yogurt dip
serves 6

2 lbs	chicken breast fillets, cut into 1-inch cubes
1/2 cup	commercial tandoori paste
3/4 cup	plain yogurt
pinch	ground saffron
3 tbsp	fresh cilantro, chopped

Yogurt Dip

1 cup	plain yogurt
2 tbsp	fresh cilantro, chopped
1 tbsp	fresh chives or green onions, chopped
1/2 tsp	lime rind, finely grated

• Soak bamboo skewers for at least 1/2 hour in water prior to using. Thread chicken cubes onto skewers and place skewers into a shallow dish. Combine remaining ingredients in a medium sized bowl. Brush chicken with tandoori mixture; cover, refrigerate at least 3 hours or overnight.

Grill chicken on the barbecue or under the broiler in your oven at 350°F, turning once, until the chicken is done.

Yogurt Dip: Combine all of the ingredients in a small bowl. Refrigerate until serving time.

trivia clips
Sister Clodagh's flashbacks were censored in the film's American release so they wouldn't offend the Catholic Legion of Decency.
The film is based on a novel by Rumer Godden.
The wild Himalayan setting in the film was actually Horsham, Sussex. They filmed in in a studio and a garden.

black narcissus (1947)

passage to india rice

serves 6 to 8

2 tbsp	cooking oil
1/4 cup	sultana raisins
1/4 cup	almonds
2	onions, chopped
2	garlic cloves, minced
1/2 inch	piece fresh ginger root, peeled and grated
2 tbsp	tomato paste
1 tsp	ground coriander
1 tsp	ground cumin
1 tbsp	garam masala
1/2 tsp	ground cloves
1-1/2 cups	cauliflower florets, blanched
3	medium potatoes, peeled, cubed and parboiled
1	small zucchini, sliced and blanched
1 cup	okra, sliced
1	small eggplant, cubed, salted and rinsed
3	tomatoes, blanched, peeled, seeded and sliced
2 cups	Basmati or long-grained rice
pinch	of turmeric
	salt
1-1/4 cups	vegetable stock
1/2 tsp	lime juice
	fresh cilantro for garnish
	lime wedges for garnish

- Heat the oil in a large skillet over medium high heat. Add the raisins and almonds; sautéing for 2 minutes. Remove with a slotted spoon and set aside. Add the onion, garlic and ginger to the skillet; fry for 2 minutes. Then slowly stir in the tomato paste and all the spices. Reduce the heat and cook gently for about 2 minutes stirring constantly. Add all the vegetables, stir and cook for 5 minutes. Add pepper to taste.

- Meanwhile, prepare rice according to package directions, adding turmeric, and salt to the water used for cooking the rice. When done, place rice on a large serving platter, reserving 1/3 of the rice.

- Pile the vegetables onto the rice, then top with remaining rice. Sprinkle the raisins and almonds over this top layer of rice. Garnish with fresh cilantro leaves. Serve immediately.

 Make the vegetable portion of the recipe the day before, reheat gently in a microwave.

BEVERAGES

A dry Reisling such as Leon Beyer Reisling (France) would be a solid choice as would be a Banrock

Station Unwooded Chardonnay (Australia), if you wish to serve white wine. Red wines are more difficult to match with the spices in Indian cuisine, but a safe bet would be Periquita (Portugal) or a Beaujolais such as Duboeuf Beaujolais Brouilly (France).

Beer is always a good match for Indian food, we recommend Kingfisher Premium Lager (England) or an authentic Indian beer like Kalyani Export Special.

MUSIC

For classical Indian music we suggest: Ravi Shankar "Ragas" (Fantasy) or anything by Anindo Chatterjee. Another solid, classical Indian music selection is "Call of the Valley" (EMI), by classical musicians Shivkumar Sharma, Brijbushan Kabra and Hariprasad Chaurasia.

For those who prefer something more modern, we suggest "The Rough Guide to Bhangra" (World Music Network). Bhangra is an updated folk music style that originated in West Punjab. The music is great for dancing and has nuances of other world music styles. The music has received mainstream play in Europe, especially in the U.K.

naan

Yield: 10 naan

2 tbsp	sugar
1/4 cup	warm water
4 tsp	active dry yeast
1 cup	plain yogurt
1 cup	buttermilk

2 tsp	salt
1 tsp	baking soda
4-3/4 cups	all-purpose flour (approx)
optional garnishes:	poppy or sesame seeds, and butter if using garnish

- In a large bowl, dissolve sugar in water; sprinkle with yeast. Let stand for 10 minutes in a warm, draft-free place until frothy (we suggest in your oven with the oven light turned on). Whisk in yogurt, buttermilk, salt and baking soda.

- Stir in 2 cups of the flour until combined, then stir in enough of the remaining flour to make a soft dough. Turn out onto a lightly floured surface; knead for 5 minutes, dusting with flour to prevent sticking. Place dough in a greased bowl (use cooking spray), turning to grease all over. Cover with plastic wrap and place in warm, draft-free place (see previous suggestion) until doubled in bulk, about 1 hour.

- Grease baking pans and set aside. Punch down dough and divide into 10 pieces. Roll out each piece with rolling pin into ovals. If using garnish, brush naan with butter, and sprinkle sesame or poppy seeds over top. Place on greased baking pans, allow to rise for 30 minutes.

- Meanwhile, preheat oven to 450°F. Place baking stone or an inverted baking sheet into oven. If using an inverted baking sheet, grease with cooking oil or cooking spray prior to heating. Using a long-handled spatula, transfer ovals to oven, onto inverted baking sheet or baking stone. Bake for about 3 minutes or until golden brown, lifting to check underneath for doneness. Flip and bake until other side is also golden. Transfer to rack and let cool slightly.

 Buy commercial naan at ethnic supermarkets, or in large city grocery stores. The naan may be made up to one month ahead Just wrap each naan individually when done, in plastic wrap and freeze in an airtight container. To reheat; wrap each naan in foil and heat at 350°F for 5 to 7 minutes prior to serving.

kulfi

serves 6

This is the Indian version of ice cream. We think you'll find it refreshing and delicious!

2 cups	milk
3/4 cup	sugar
1 tbsp	corn starch
1-1/2 cups	evaporated milk

2 tbsp	pistachio nuts, chopped
2 tbsp	almonds, chopped
2 tsps	rosewater or orangewater
	gourmet cookies (optional)

- Place milk and sugar in a medium pan. Stir over low heat until milk is almost boiling and sugar dissolved.

- Blend cornstarch with a bit of the evaporated milk and stir into the milk and sugar mixture. Stir over low heat 3 to 4 minutes or until mixture thickens. Remove from heat and allow to cool slightly. Stir in the remaining evaporated milk, pistachios, almonds, and rosewater.

- Pour mixture into an ice cream maker and chill/churn for about 30 minutes or until firm.

<u>Freezer method:</u> Pour prepared mixture into a metal pan or bowl and freeze until the edges are firm. Remove from freezer, transfer to mixing bowl and beat with a mixer at medium speed until light and creamy.

- Return mixture to metal container, freeze until firm. For an extra special presentation, serve in stemmed glasses with gourmet cookies (those shaped like small fans or round cigars) tucked behind the scoops of ice cream.

 Use evaporated skim milk in place of regular milk and evaporated 2% milk where evaporated milk is called for. With this method you retain creamy taste and reduce fat.

 Buy prepared kulfi or other Indian desserts at Indian grocers. A good last minute substitute would be mango sorbet.

SETTING THE MOOD

People have always been drawn to India and its culture because it seems so much more exotic when compared to our own "Western" culture. Capitalize on that to set the mood for the evening. If you are lucky enough to be close to a large cosmopolitan centre (as we are, close to Toronto), then find out where there are authentic shops catering to Indian clientele. Pick up some incense and vibrant fabrics to use to turn your home into a more exotic locale. Use tableware and fabrics in gold, silver, bronze and jewel tones to create a rich, mysterious atmosphere. Drape sheer organza fabrics over doorways, or use beaded curtains. Buy colourful children's bangles at an Indian store to use as napkin rings or use jewel tone organza ribbons to tie up napkins. Splurge and buy a few exotic flowers, such as orchids, and use them as a centrepiece, or float them in a crystal bowl along with some floating candles-the candles will disperse the scent of the flowers. Be adventurous in your style of dress, perhaps you could pickup a sari for yourself- be more daring with your make-up.

casablanca (1942)

The film takes place in the early days of World War II. The lead character, Victor Laszlo, is a leader in the Czech resistance movement who escapes from a German concentration camp to Casablanca, Morocco. His plan is to go to Lisbon and then to the United States. All his plans hinge upon the actions of one man, Rick, who is a deeply disillusioned man. More dangerously though, Rick is very much in love with Victor Laszlo's wife, Ilsa, who happens to be his long lost love who walked out of his life in Paris. Rick has every reason to want Laszlo out of the picture...

No collection of movies is complete without this consummate American classic that was first released in 1942. Its enduring qualities attest to excellent film making and superb acting, making it one of the most popular movies ever made. The themes of romantic love and redemption transcend history and add to the film's timeless appeal.

FEATURED ACTORS
Humphrey Bogart (Rick Blaine)
Ingrid Bergman (Ilsa)
Paul Henreid (Victor Laszlo)
Claude Rains
        (Captain Louis Renault)
Peter Lorre (Ugarte)
Sydney Greenstreet (Senor Farrari)
Conrad Veidt
        (Major Heinrich Strasser)
Dooley Wilson (Sam)

DIRECTOR ~ Michael Curtiz

AWARDS WON

Best Picture	1943 Academy Award
Best Director	1943 Academy Award
Best Screenplay	1943 Academy Award
Ten Best Films	1945 National Board of Review Award

menu

harira (moroccan chicken, chickpea, and lentil soup) • black olives with harissa • moroccan chicken • moroccan vegetable couscous • pita bread (store bought, to serve with main dish) • tomato and cucumber salad with yogurt mint dressing • sunshine date baklava

harira

serves 6 to 8

In Morocco, this soup is often made with lamb as well as chicken and is traditionally served after sundown during the month of Ramadan to break each day's fast.

1	whole chicken breast, halved
4 cups	chicken broth
4 cups	water
1	28 to 32 ounce can whole tomatoes, drained and coarsely puréed
1/4 tsp	crumbled saffron threads
2	medium onions, finely chopped
1	19-ounce can chickpeas, rinsed
1/2 cup	raw long-grain rice
1/2 cup	lentils
	salt and pepper to taste
3/4 cup	finely chopped fresh coriander
3/4 cup	finely chopped fresh parsley leaves

• In a heavy stockpot (at least 5 quarts) simmer chicken in broth and water 17 to 20 minutes, or until chicken is just cooked through. Using a slotted spoon, transfer chicken to a cutting board. To stockpot. add tomatoes, saffron, onions, chickpeas, rice, and lentils and simmer, covered, 30 minutes, or until lentils are tender.

• Shred chicken, discarding skin and bones, and stir into soup with salt and pepper to taste. Just before serving, stir in coriander and parsley.

 Soup may be prepared 4 days ahead (cool uncovered before chilling covered).

trivia clips

The script for Casablanca was adapted by Julius and Philip Epstein and Howard Koch from an unproduced play called "Everybody Comes to Rick's" by Murray Burnett and Joan Alison.

"Rick's Café Américain" was modelled after Hotel El Minzah in Tangiers.

continued

black olives with harissa serves 6 to 8

The spicy North African condiment called harissa is often mixed with olives or served with salads, couscous, or tagines meat or poultry stews.

1 lb	oil-cured black olives (preferably Moroccan)		2	garlic cloves
			1/2 tsp	coarse salt, or to taste
For harissa:			1	medium red bell pepper, roasted (procedure follows) and coarsely chopped
1 tsp	cumin seed			
1/2 tsp	coriander seeds		1 tbsp	olive oil
1/2 tsp	caraway seeds			
2	dried hot red chilies, stemmed but not seeded (about 2 inches in length)			

- In a colander rinse olives under cold water 1 minute. In a large bowl cover with cold water and soak 1 hour to remove excess salt. Drain well.

- Make harissa: In a mortar and pestle, an electric spice grinder, or a cleaned coffee grinder, finely grind seeds. If using a mortar and pestle, add chilies, garlic, and salt and pound to taste. If using a spice or coffee grinder, transfer seeds to a small food processor and add chilies, garlic, and salt. Grind mixture to a paste.

- Add roasted pepper and oil and pound or purée to a coarse paste.

- In a large bowl, stir together harissa and olives; chill and marinate, covered, at least 6 hours or overnight. Olives may be prepared 1 week ahead and kept chilled, covered.

- Serve olives at room temperature.

- To roast peppers: Using a long-handled fork, char peppers over an open flame or on a rack set over an electric burner, turning, until skins are blackened, 4 to 6 minutes. You may also roast peppers under a preheated broiler about 2 inches from heat, turning every 5 minutes, 15 to 20 minutes, or until skins are blistered and charred. Transfer peppers to a bowl and let stand, covered, until cool enough to handle. Keeping peppers whole, peel them, starting at blossom end. Cut off pepper tops and discard seeds and ribs.

 Buy ready-made harissa at Middle Eastern or Mediterranean food stores. Jars of roasted peppers may be purchased at better supermarkets.

trivia clips

In Germany, one of the most famous, often quoted movie lines is "I look in your eyes, little one." This is the way German translators and subtitle writers chose to translate the movie's line"Here's looking at you, kid." Sometimes you can't translate literally!
Conrad Veidt, who played Major Heinrich Strasser, was well known for his intense hatred of the Nazis.

moroccan chicken

serves 6 to 8

Spicy harissa is once again featured in this braised-chicken dish.

2 tbsp	caraway seeds	4	garlic cloves, peeled
2 tbsp	purchased harissa (homemade or store-bought)	1/2 tsp	saffron threads
2 tbsp	fresh lemon juice	2	3 pound whole chickens, cut in half, backbones removed
2 tbsp	ground cumin	1/4 cup	(1/2 stick) butter
1-1/2 tbsp	ground coriander	3 cups	minced onions
1 tbsp	paprika	4 cups	(approx) water
1 tbsp	olive oil	1/4 cup	chopped fresh cilantro
2 tsps	salt		salt to taste
1	1 inch piece peeled fresh ginger		

• Stir caraway seeds in small, heavy skillet over medium heat until fragrant, about 1 minute. Transfer to processor. Along with next 10 ingredients, purée until coarse paste forms. Rub paste all over chicken halves.

• Melt butter in large pot over medium heat. Add onions; sauté until onions begin to soften, about 5 minutes. Add chicken halves to pot. Add enough water to almost cover chicken. Bring to boil. Reduce heat; cover and simmer until chicken is tender, turning once, about 45 minutes.

• Transfer chicken, skin side up, to baking sheet. Add cilantro to liquid in pot. Boil until reduced to 3 cups, about 20 minutes. Season with salt. Meanwhile, preheat broiler. Broil chicken until golden brown, about 6 minutes. Transfer chicken to platter. Serve with braising liquid.

 Reduce butter called for in the recipe and use a non-stick skillet for sauteing

trivia clips

Dooley Wilson (Sam) was a professional drummer who, in Casablanca, faked playing the piano. As the music was recorded at the same time as the film, the piano music one heard was actually a recording of Elliot Carpenter performing behind a curtain.
The timely real-life invasion of Casablanca was used to promote this film, and undoubtedly contributed to its success.
Contrary to popular belief, Rick never says "Play it again, Sam." He says "You played it for her, you can play it for me. Play it!" Ilsa says "Play it, Sam. Play "As Time Goes By".

moroccan vegetable couscous   serves 6 to 8

3/4 cup	slivered almonds		1 cup	dry white wine
2 tbsp	olive oil		2/3 cup	golden raisins
1	red onion, chopped		1-1/2	cups canned vegetable broth
8 cups	mixed cut-up vegetables (such as carrots, zucchini, leeks, squash and cauliflower)			salt and pepper to taste
			2	5 to 7 ounce boxes couscous
1 cup	frozen peas		1/4 cup	cilantro, chopped (optional)
2-1/2 tsps	ground cumin			
2-1/2 tsps	ground coriander			

• Place almonds in medium sized, heavy skillet. Stir over medium heat until almonds are pale golden, about 4 minutes. Transfer almonds to bowl. Add oil to same skillet. Increase heat to medium-high. Add vegetables, cumin and coriander; sauté until vegetables just begin to soften, about 3 minutes. Add wine and raisins. Boil until wine is reduced by half, about 3 minutes. Add vegetable broth.

Partially cover skillet; simmer until vegetables are tender, about 6 minutes. Season with salt and pepper.

• Meanwhile, prepare couscous according to package directions.

• Mound couscous on platter. Spoon vegetable topping and juices over it. Sprinkle with almonds, and of so desired- garnish with chopped cilantro. Serve.

tomato and cucumber salad with yogurt mint dressing   serves 6 to 8

2	medium cucumbers, peeled and diced		1-1/2 tbsp	fresh mint, chopped finely
4	medium tomatoes, diced		1 cup	plain yogurt, preferably Balkan style
	salt and pepper to taste			

• Place all ingredients except mint, in a bowl. Stir to coat and garnish with fresh chopped mint prior to serving.

 Use low fat yogurt.

BEVERAGES

For those who prefer white wines, Rothschild Sauvignon Blanc (France) is an ideal complement to this menu. An alternate choice would be Ruffino Orvieto Classico (Italy). Fetzer Zinfandel (USA) would be suitable for red wine drinkers. Those who prefer beer may wish to try Duvel Belgian Beer.

Mint Iced Tea (see Lawrence of Arabia menu)

Coffee with dessert

MUSIC

A good choice of music for this event would be the "Rough Guide to North African Music" or anything by Maroc, especially the CD entitled "Confrerie Des Jilala", a compilation of devotional Islamic music with haunting tones and interesting rhythms. Other great choices are: Hassan Hakmoun, a Gnoua style musician (Gnoua is a mixture of religious Arabic music and African rhythms), has the following CD's, "The Fire Within" (Music of the World) or his "Gnawa Music of Marrakesh" (Axiom). Samira Bensaid is a female vocalist who performs in the classic tradition. For an example of the Andalousian style, listen to Usta Massano Taz's "Musique Classique Andalouse de Fes" (Ocora). Alternatively, a compilation CD like "Cinema Serenade 2: The Golden Age" (Sony), featuring movie music performed by the renowned team of violinist Itzhak Perlman would be a good mainstream musical choice.

SETTING THE STAGE

Visit an area of the city where Arabic and African stores can be found. Buy some colourful plates, tableware, cushions or even a kilim rug. If you have any kilim rugs or tapestries, hang them on a wall for ambience. Enclose your dining area in sheer curtains or drape them from a light fixture (be careful that the fabric does not touch the light bulb). Turn a room into a tent- like setting and have your meal while seated on the floor on brocade cushions. Use a rich looking scarf or piece of fabric as a tablecloth. Dim the lights and use candles. If you are having guests, hire a belly dancer to perform or to even teach you and your guests this ancient Arabic dance form.

sunshine date baklava

serves 8 to 10

This version of the Greek and Turkish dessert features dates instead of nuts. Date palms flourish in the hot climate of the Mediterranean and Middle East and their fruit are often served for dessert. The sunshine in the title refers to the orange flavours in the recipe.

For syrup:

1/3 cup	sugar
3 tbsp	water
1 tbsp	fresh lemon juice
1 tbsp	honey
1 tsp	orange flower water
1/4 tsp	almond extract

For filling:

3 cups	whole pitted dates
1 tbsp	sugar
1 tbsp	grated orange peel
1 tbsp	grated lemon peel
1/2 tsp	ground cinnamon
1/4 cup	fresh orange juice

For baklava:

1/2 cup	sugar
2 tsps	ground cinnamon
12 sheets	fresh phyllo pastry or frozen, thawed (each about 18 x 14 inches)
1/2 cup	(1 stick) unsalted butter, melted

Make syrup:

Stir first 3 ingredients in small saucepan over low heat until sugar dissolves.

- Increase heat; boil 1 minute. Remove from heat. Mix in honey, orange flower water and almond extract. Cool.

Make filling:

- Combine first 5 ingredients in processor. Using on/off turns, process until dates are minced. Add juice; process until coarse paste forms.

Make baklava:

- Preheat oven to 350˚F. Mix sugar and cinnamon. Stack phyllo on work surface.

- Using bottom of 8 x 8 x 2 inch pan as guide, cut out two 8-inch-square stacks, making 24 squares.

- Butter inside of same pan. Place 2 phyllo squares in pan. Brush with butter; sprinkle with 1-1/2 tsps cinnamon sugar. Repeat layering of phyllo squares (2 at a time), butter and sugar 4 more times (a total of 10 phyllo squares). Spread half of filling over phyllo. Top with 2 phyllo squares. Brush with butter and

sprinkle with cinnamon sugar. Repeat with 2 more squares, butter and sugar. Spread with remaining filling. Layer 10 squares (2 at a time) over filling, brushing with butter and sprinkling with sugar in between every 2 squares. Using knife, score top into 16 squares (do not cut through to filling).

- Bake baklava until deep golden, about 30 minutes. Cut through scored lines to bottom of pan. Spoon cool syrup over hot baklava. Cool. (Can be made 1 day ahead. Cover. Let stand at room temperature.)

 Use butter flavour cooking spray instead of butter between baklava layers.

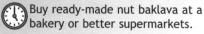 Buy ready-made nut baklava at a bakery or better supermarkets.

citizen
kane (1941)

Since Xanadu was located on the Florida coast, we thought we'd come up with a menu to showcase the best this state has to offer. Florida is synonymous with citrus fruit, so we feature some delectable dishes made with a splash of citrus!

chilled cucumber soup

serves 6

3 cups	buttermilk
3/4 cup	frozen orange juice concentrate, thawed
1	medium cucumber, halved lengthwise, seeded, and thinly sliced
2 tbsp	flat leaf parsley, chopped
1	small clove garlic, chopped finely
	pinch of pepper
1/4 tsp	salt
	parsley for garnish

• In a bowl, combine buttermilk, thawed juice concentrate, cucumber, parsley, garlic, pepper, and salt.

Cover and chill until serving time. Ladle into bowls and garnish with chopped parsley.

grilled shrimp salad with citrus dressing

serves 6

2-1/2 lbs	medium sized shrimp, shelled and deveined
1 lb	asparagus, washed and woody stems removed, chopped
2 tbsp	olive oil
2 cups	plain croutons
1	head Boston lettuce, washed and torn into small pieces
2	medium sized avocados, peeled and diced

Citrus Dressing:

2 tsps	grated orange rind
2/3 cup	fresh orange juice, not from concentrate
1 tsp	grated lemon rind
2 tbsp	lemon juice
1/2 cup	mayonnaise
3 tbsp	olive oil
2 tbsp	balsamic vinegar
2 tsps	sugar
1	clove garlic, chopped finely

• Dressing: Make dressing by blending all ingredients together until smooth. Set aside

• If using bamboo skewers, you should soak them in water for at least 1/2 hour prior to using. Shell and devein shrimp, leaving tails intact. Combine shrimp and 1/4 cup of the citrus dressing in large bowl, cover and refrigerate 1 hour.

• Add asparagus to pan of boiling water, boil 1 minute; drain. Set aside.

• Thread shrimp onto metal or bamboo skewers, all facing the same way. Brush with olive oil. Grill shrimp on an oiled rack set 5 to 6 inches over glowing coals until shells are pink and slightly charred and shrimp are just cooked through, 3 to 4 minutes on each side. (Alternatively, grill shrimp in a hot, well-seasoned ridged grill pan over moderate heat or if placed on skewers, on an oiled rack under the broiler in the oven using moderate heat).

• In a large salad bowl, mix together the croutons, asparagus, lettuce and avocado. Add the dressing and toss to coat. Divide salad amongst 6 plates. Place shrimp decoratively on top and serve immediately with breadsticks, if so desired.

♥ Use low fat mayonnaise.

This film is considered by many film critics to be the best American film ever made; it is compulsory viewing for students of Film Arts. Orson Welles's film debut introduced new conventions of storytelling and visual structure to the large screen by using flashbacks from the viewpoint of others to tell the story of the enigmatic Kane's life. Welles revealed much about his characters by the surroundings they occupied, for instance, the dying Kane's character is reflected in his vast, lonely, somewhat forlorn mansion. Surrounded all his life by wealth and power, still he would share the same fate as the common man. After all, money can't buy everything.

The movie opens showing wealthy and powerful Charles Kane lying on his deathbed in his palatial home named Xanadu. He dies whispering the word "rosebud". Soon after his death, a journalist who is working on an obituary piece about the late tycoon, is assigned the task of finding out the significance of Kane's last utterance. The reporter delves into Kane's private life, and much to his dismay does not discover the meaning of Kane's last spoken word. The viewers though, do find out the significance of the riddle of "rosebud" in the film's final moments.

FEATURED ACTORS
Orson Welles (Charles Foster Kane)
Joseph Cotton (Jedediah Leland)
Ray Collins (Boss Jim Gettys)
Paul Stewart (Raymond)
Dorothy Comingore (Susan Alexander)

DIRECTOR ~ Orson Welles

citizen
kane (1941)

AWARDS WON

Best Original Screenplay (Herman Mankiewicz)	1941 Academy Award
Best Original Screenplay (Orson Welles)	1941 Academy Award
10 Best Films	1941 Film Daily Award
10 Best Films	1941 National Board of Review of Motion Pictures
Best Film/ Best Picture	1941 New York Film Critics Circle Award
10 Best Films	1941 New York Times Award
U.S. National Film Registry	1989 Library of Congress Award
100 Greatest American Movies	1998 American Film Institute Award

BEVERAGES

Tropical lime coolers or margaritas (see main beverages page). If you prefer wine, try Yvon Mau Semillon Sauvignon (France) or your favourite Chardonnay. Beer lovers may wish to try Red Stripe (Jamaica), Cristal Lager (Cuba) or Tusker Premium Lager (Kenya).

MUSIC

"Cinema Serenade 2: The Golden Age" (Sony), features movie music performed by the team of renowned violinist Itzhak Perlman. "Nipper's Greatest Hits of the 1940's Vol. 1 & 2" (RCA); these two volumes will appeal to a wide range of listeners as various artists and styles are featured.

SETTING THE MOOD

Since most of us don't live in a home the size of Xanadu, and we can't replicate that- we'll just have to bring a bit of the sunshine state into our homes! Regardless of the season, use citrus colours for your table. Use a bowl of lemons or limes as a simple yet attractive centrepiece. Buy some pretty paper napkins that feature a tropical design. If you have been to Florida, display some of your favourite vacation pictures or put up a travel poster that you may have tucked away somewhere.

clementine trifle brûlée

serves 6

The caramel topping on this trifle makes for a spectacular presentation. Your guests will think you are quite the gourmet cook when they see this showcase dessert! The trifle is best made the day before serving, the caramel topping is added just prior to serving.

2	6 ounce packages vanilla pudding (not instant)	2 cups	clementine segments (drain if using canned)
2 tsps	ground ginger	1/2 cup	granulated sugar
1 cup	whipping cream		mint leaves for garnish (optional)
1/2 cup	orange flavoured liqueur		orange zest for garnish (optional)
2	boxes ladyfingers		

- Make pudding according to directions on package, adding the ground ginger with the milk. To make it extra creamy, we suggest using evaporated skim milk for some of the milk required to make the pudding. Set aside to cool.

- Use an electric mixer to beat whipping cream until stiff peaks form. Set aside.

- Put orange liqueur in bowl. Dip ladyfingers into liqueur and in a large transparent dessert bowl arrange a layer of ladyfingers on bottom, and along sides. The ladyfingers should not rise above the edge of the bowl. Add a layer of whipped cream on top of ladyfingers, then a layer of clementine segments, topping with another layer of the liqueur dipped ladyfingers. Next, add a layer of the vanilla pudding. Repeat the above steps for the subsequent layers, reserving some pudding for the very top layer. Cover and refrigerate trifle overnight.

- For the caramel topping: Place sugar and 1/4 cup of water in a heavy-bottomed pot over high heat on the stove until it turns golden brown. Watch very closely. Once the syrup has turned an amber colour, carefully spoon over trifle. If it becomes too hard to spoon, return to medium heat until it softens, and then resume spooning. Garnish with mint leaves and a few twirls of orange peel zest. Serve immediately, tapping the caramel topping to break through in order to spoon out portions of the trifle.

trivia clips

The film is loosely based on the life of powerful publishing magnate William Randolph Hearst who, after he getting wind of the project, offered RKO Pictures a large sum of money to burn the negatives. They refused and Hearst waged a campaign against the picture.

hamlet (1948)

menu danish cheese platter • danish meatballs • danish style open faced sandwiches (smørrebrød) • array of pickled vegetables (store-bought) • potato patties • rice pudding

In this film based on the classic Shakespearean play, a Danish prince seeks to avenge his father's death when he learns that his father was murdered by his uncle, who wanted to succeed him as King, and marry the Queen. The horrible secret burdening Hamlet eventually leads to violent behaviour on the part of the prince. Hamlet kills some of his family members as well as members of the family of courtier Polonius (Felix Aylmer), whose daughter Ophelia (Jean Simmons) is in love with Hamlet. This 1948 version is considered to be the best of all the dozen or so films produced based on the classic play. The complex, multi-faceted character of Hamlet is considered the ultimate role by most actors. The earliest film version was made in the silent picture era, and featured actor John Byron as Hamlet. Ethan Hawke played Hamlet in the most recent movie version, but it is the legendary actor Laurence Olivier who seems to be best remembered for his portrayal of the Danish prince. Olivier was director, producer, and star in this 1948 classic, which in turn became his masterpiece, winning four Academy Awards.

danish cheese platter

On a wooden or silver tray, place a variety of Danish cheeses such as Havarti, Danish Blue, Esrom and Tilsit. Flat breads, crackers or dark rye slices cut into triangles go great with this.

danish meatballs

Danish meatballs are the most common dish served in Denmark, the Danish name for them is Frikadeller.

1 lb	ground pork	1 tsp	salt
1 lb	ground lamb or beef	1 tsp	black pepper
3/4 cup	plain bread crumbs	1 cup	water
1	onion, finely chopped	6 tbsp	cooking oil

- Combine all the ingredient except cooking oil, in a bowl mix well. Use a spoon or your hands to form meatballs.
- Heat six tbsp cooking oil in a skillet over medium heat. Place the meatballs in the skillet, do not overcrowd. Turn them every few minutes or so, browning on all sides.

- Test them with a fork to make sure they are well done inside; they are not supposed to be pink in the centre. When done, place in casserole dish lined with a paper towel to absorb oil. Serve with the potato patties and salad.

FEATURED ACTORS
Laurence Olivier (Hamlet)
Eileen Herlie (Queen Gertrude)
Basil Sydney (King Claudius)
Felix Aylmer (Polonius
Terence Morgan II (Laertes)
Jean Simmons (Ophelia
Norman Wooland (Horatio)

DIRECTOR ~ Laurence Olivier

danish style open-faced sandwiches

As in many of the Scandinavian countries, the Danes also enjoy this style of sandwich which is a compulsory feature of a smorgasbord table. Here are some ideas for sandwiches. The key is to have an assortment of breads and toppings. Use your imagination and personal taste as guidelines.

- Cocktail shrimp on a french baguette with dilled cream cheese.
- Herring (in wine sauce), drained and chopped, on rye bread with red onions and green pepper.
- Scrambled eggs on mini-bagels (pumpernickel or rye) with strips of smoked salmon, and chopped capers.

- Sliced hard-boiled eggs with roasted red pepper strips and cheese on dark bread.
- Liver paté on dark bread.
- Sliced ham with mayonnaise, a slice of hard-boiled egg and pickled vegetable on rye bread.

trivia clips

Hamlet is most remembered for this one line in his soliloquy.
Hint: "To ___or not to___"
Denmark is said to be the oldest kingdom in the world. Queen Margrethe celebrated her Silver Jubilee in 1996 and is said to have the oldest lineage in Europe, dating from the early 900's A.D. and from the Viking King Gorm.

hamlet (1948)

continued

AWARDS WON

Best Actor (Laurence Olivier)	1948 Academy Award
Best Art Direction (Carmen Dillon)	1948 Academy Award
Best Art Direction (Roger Furse)	1948 Academy Award
Best Picture	1948 Academy Award
Best Film (Laurence Olivier)	1948 British Academy Award
Best Actor (Laurence Olivier)	1948 New York Film Critics Circle Award
Best Direction (Laurence Olivier)	1948 New York Film Critics Circle Award
Best Film (Laurence Olivier)	1948 New York Film Critics Circle Award
Best Actress (Jean Simmons)	1948 Venice Film Festival Award
Best Photography (Desmond Dickinson)	1948 Venice Film Festival Award
International Grand Prix	1948 Venice Film Festival Award
Best Actor (in drama)	1949 Golden Globe Award

array of pickled vegetables

Place pickled vegetables on a relish platter or in a separate dish and serve along side main course.

potato patties

serves 4 to 6

Potatoes are a staple on many Danish menus. These can be served as a meal on their own when accompanied with a salad. Often served warm as a snack.

3 or 4	medium potatoes
2 tsps	dry yeast
1/2 cup	warm milk for yeast
1/2 tsp	sugar

1-1/2 to 1-2/3 cups	flour
1/2 tsp	salt
1 cup	vegetable oil for frying

- Cook the potatoes in boiling salted water. Peel the potatoes and immediately mash them. Allow to cool.

- In a small bowl, mix the warm milk with the yeast and sugar. Let sit for 5 minutes.

- Mix mashed potatoes with flour, yeast mixture and salt. Start with 1-1/2 cups flour and add more flour to make the dough easier to knead. Knead well.

- Put the dough in a bowl and cover with tea towel. Let dough rise in a warm draft-free place until double in size, about 1 hour.

- Roll out the dough onto a floured board to 1/2 inch thickness (dust a little flour on the rolling pin as well). Cut into rectangles, squares or circles. Prick with a knife to keep big bubbles from forming.

- In a deep skillet, heat about 1 cup of oil at a medium high setting. Fry potato cakes in oil (adjust heat as needed, if it is too hot they will burn). Fry until golden, turning once. Remove and place on a plate lined with paper towel to absorb any extra oil. Serve as soon as possible.

trivia clips

In the year 2000 movie release of Hamlet (a modernized version), Ethan Hawke played an amateur filmmaker, whose father was CEO of "Denmark Corporate".

Many actors have played Hamlet. Can you name them all?

This actor also played Hamlet in 1969 but is best remembered as Hannibal. Who is he?

hamlet (1948)

rice pudding

serves 4 to 6

This dish is traditionally associated with Christmas, but is often eaten all through the winter. It is considered too heavy for a summer dish. The association with Christmas comes from the past when peasants at Christmas would put a bowl of rice pudding in the attic to appease the mythical "nisse". The diner who found the whole almond traditionally received an extra gift. This was an incentive for second helpings.

1 tbsp	butter
2 cups	milk
1 cup	rice
3/4 cup	almonds, chopped
1	whole almond
3 tbsp	sugar

1 tsp	vanilla extract
2 tbsp	Madeira wine or sherry (optional)
2 cups	whipping cream
	cherry preserves (optional)

- Smear the bottom of a pot with the butter, and then heat the milk to almost boiling. Add the rice gradually while stirring. Turn the heat down to low, cover pot with lid, and let the rice simmer for about 30 minutes. Let cool, then stir in almonds, sugar, vanilla and wine.

- Whip the cream and fold in gently. Cool and serve.

- For an extra special touch serve with cherry preserves on top.

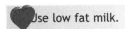 Use low fat milk.

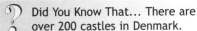 Did You Know That... There are over 200 castles in Denmark.

MUSIC

There is a soundtrack for the film. Entitled, not surprisingly, "Hamlet" (Virgin). You may also wish to listen to some Danish folk music. If so, try "Souvenirs from Denmark" (Discom).

BEVERAGES

Danes love their beer! Try Tuborg or Carlsberg, two of the best known brands.

SETTING THE MOOD

In Denmark, the Danes take time out of their busy day-to-day life to sit down and enjoy their meals. Simplicity is the key here, crisp damask tablecloths with linen napkins and fresh flowers. Select flowers that are in season or create a simple, but beautiful centrepiece by placing a decorative bowl of fresh lemons or oranges on the table. Slow down the pace and light the room with scented candles. Savour the moment.

trivia clips

This famous Australian bred actor also tried the role on for size in the early 90's, but he's probably better known as "Mad Max."

This Canadian actor moved at a fast "Speed" from the silver screen to the stage in his stab at the role.

This emergency room physician goes back to his native Croatia during the summer to play Hamlet during Dubrovnik's Summer Theatre Festival.

it's a wonderful life (1946)

Any compilation of movie classics from this decade wouldn't be complete without this somewhat bittersweet comedy drama. In the film, the main character named George Bailey played by America's favourite, James Stewart, is facing serious financial ruin and arrest. As he contemplates suicide in the small town of Bedford Falls on Christmas Eve, there appears an angel, Clarence Oddbody (Henry Travers) to help him. Clarence has not yet earned his wings, and the only way he can, is by helping George understand what life would have been like if he had never lived. Despite the selfless acts George performed throughout his life, he still considers himself a failure. Clarence takes George on a nightmare odyssey through a town George does not recognize. His friends do not recognize him, his wife who stuck by his side through thick and thin, is now the spinster librarian. Other revealing moments throughout this journey in time cause George to wake up and see things in a different light and realize how much of a positive impact he's had not only other people's lives, but also on the whole town. He concludes that ending his life is no longer the answer to his misery ... in fact, he realizes that despite all of his problems, he does have a wonderful life! This tearjerker is perfect to watch with family and friends, whether at Christmas or at any other time of the year.

menu

creamy pecan stuffed mushrooms • roast turkey breast with caramelized onion • canadian style brussels sprouts with chestnuts horseradish mashed potatoes • your favourite green salad (optional, recipe is up to you) • monte bianco

creamy pecan stuffed mushrooms serves 6

These are very good! Remember to save some room for all of the other items on the menu!

20	medium-sized mushrooms	2 tbsp	Italian style bread crumbs
1 pkg	(3 ounces) cream cheese, softened	2 tsps	chives, minced
2 tbsp	cooked, crumbled bacon	1 tbsp	white wine
1-1/2 tbsp	pecans, chopped	3 tbsp	melted butter

- Gently separate stems from mushroom caps. Preheat broiler to 375˚F.

- Mix until well combined: the cream cheese, bacon, pecans, breadcrumbs, chives and wine. Brush mushroom caps with the melted butter.

- Fill each cap with cream cheese mixture. Broil stuffed mushrooms for 3-5 minutes. Serve hot.

 Use reduced fat cream cheese and light butter or non-hydrogenated margarine.

Auld Lang Syne: This song is now generally sung at the end of a merry evening and at New Year's Eve the world over. It speedily took the place of Scotland's older parting song "Good Night and Joy Be with You All." It has become the traditional song among English-speaking peoples for bidding farewell to the old year and welcoming in the new.

trivia clips

The movie was neither a box-office success nor a critical favourite. It earned some recognition with 5 Oscar nominations, including Best Picture. For the next 28 years, the movie remained a cult favourite among movie buffs and Capra fans. It gained the stature of a classic after 1973 when it was shown annually on television during the Christmas season.

it's a
wonderful life (1946)

roast turkey breast with
caramelized onion <small>serves 6 to 8</small>

1 tbsp	olive oil	1/4 tsp	coarsely ground black pepper
2 cups	red or Bermuda onions, peeled and thinly sliced	1	bone-in turkey breast (about 7 pounds)
4	garlic cloves, peeled and thinly sliced	1/2 cup	dry red wine
2 tbsp	brown sugar	1 cup	chicken broth
1 tbsp	balsamic vinegar	1 tbsp	cornstarch
1/2 tsp	salt		

- In non-stick 10-inch skillet, heat olive oil over medium heat. Add onions and cook 8 to 10 minutes, stirring occasionally until onions are tender and golden. Add garlic and cook 1 minute longer. Stir in brown sugar, vinegar, salt, pepper, and 1 tbsp water; cook 1 minute. Transfer to bowl and cool to room temperature.

- Preheat oven to 325°F. With fingertips, gently separate skin from meat on turkey breast. Spread cooled onion mixture under skin. Place turkey breast, skin side up, on rack in medium roasting pan (about 14" by 10"). Cover turkey breast with a loose tent of foil (this prevents it from browning too quickly). Roast turkey 2-1/2 to 3 hours or until temperature on meat thermometer reaches 170°F. Start checking for doneness during last 30 minutes of roasting. To brown turkey breast, remove foil during last hour of roasting time and baste occasionally with pan drippings.

- Transfer turkey to carving board. Let stand 15 minutes to set juices for easier slicing.

- Meanwhile, prepare sauce: Remove rack from roasting pan. Skim and discard fat from drippings in pan. In large saucepan, heat red wine to boiling over high heat; boil for 2 minutes. Stir in chicken broth, 1/2 cup water, and pan drippings; heat to boiling. In cup, dissolve cornstarch in 1 tbsp water; whisk into boiling sauce, and boil 1 minute. Pour sauce through coarse sieve into bowl. Serve sauce with turkey breast.

- To carve the turkey breast: Hold it firmly on cutting surface with a carving fork. Using a sharp knife, make 1 long cut away from the wishbone to just above the wing joint to release meat from one side of the breastbone. On cutting surface, slice meat diagonally across the breast into 1/4-inch-thick slices. Repeat on other side. For the best presentation, carve turkey in the kitchen and arrange slices in shape of turkey breast on a platter.

FEATURED ACTORS
James Stewart (George Bailey)
Donna Reed (Mary Hatch Bailey)
Lionel Barrymore (Mr. Potter)
Thomas Mitchell (Uncle Billy)
Henry Travers (Clarence)

DIRECTOR ~ Frank Capra

AWARDS WON

10 Best Films	1946 National Board of Review of Motion Pictures
Best Director (Frank Capra)	1947 Golden Globe Award
U.S. National Film Registry	1990 Library of Congress Award

trivia clips

Christmas shopping over the Internet is increasing every year. Most who buy on-line do so to avoid lineups and crowds.
If you watch Frank Capra's films, you'll see that the raven named Jimmy appears in all of them.

it's a
wonderful life (1946)

BEVERAGES

Homemade Hot Chocolate (see main beverages section)

Eggnog (store-bought or homemade, see main beverages section)

Rosemount Estate Chardonnay (Australia), Chateau Lafayette Chardonnay (USA), or a Beaujolais such as Mommessin Beaujolais Villages Vieilles Vignes (France).

Liqueurs, dessert wines or ice wines with dessert. Sperone Marsala Cremovo Fine (Italy) or Samos Muscat Doux (Greece) are fine red and white dessert wines. Inniskillin ice wines are divine as are those by Reif and Southbrook (all from Ontario).

Specialty coffees
(see main beverages section)

MUSIC

Get in the spirit of the season with the following music choices:

"1940's Christmas" (Delta), featuring artists Bing Crosby, Judy Garland, Perry Como and Benny Goodman. "It's a Wonderful Life Christmas Album," (Cema Special Markets) or "It's a Wonderful Life Christmas Carols" (Telarc) by the Royal Philharmonic Orchestra. The latter also features some songs from another popular Christmas classic "Miracle on 34 th Street".

canadian style brussels sprouts with chestnuts   serves 6 to 8

This will please even those who say they don't like Brussels sprouts!

1 lb	Brussels sprouts	2 tbsp	butter
3/4 cup	chestnuts (fresh roasted or canned)	1 tsp	salt
1/3 cup	maple syrup	1/4 tsp	ground black pepper

- Preheat oven to 375°F. Bring 2 quarts of water and 1 tsp of salt to a boil in a large stockpot.

- If fresh chestnuts are used, cut an "X" into the shell with a paring knife, peel away as much of the shell as possible. Then toast chestnuts on a cookie sheet in the oven until the meat pulls from the shell, and the shell and skin can be easily removed.
If canned chestnuts are used, drain and dry them.

- Trim the outside leaves from the Brussels sprouts and cut 1/4 inch deep cross in the bottoms of each.

Drop them in the boiling salted water and cook until they are fork tender. Drain the sprouts and drop into ice water to shock and cool.

- Next, cut each Brussels sprout in half. Set aside momentarily.

- Add the maple syrup to a 10 inch sauté pan and warm. Add the Brussels sprouts and bring to a boil. Quickly add the chestnuts and stir in the whole butter. The syrup and butter will thicken and glaze the sprouts. Season with salt and pepper and serve.

horseradish mashed potatoes   serves 6 to 8

This is a tasty version of a classic holiday side dish!

6 to 8	medium Yukon Gold potatoes (about 2 pounds), peeled, each cut into 8 pieces	3 tbsp	freshly grated or prepared horseradish
			salt and pepper to taste
9 tbsp	(or more) warm milk	1 tbsp	fresh thyme, chopped
4-1/2 tbsp	cold butter, cubed		

- Cook potatoes in large pot of boiling salted water until very tender, about 20 minutes. Drain.

- Return potatoes to same pot. Add milk, butter and horseradish. Using an electric mixer, beat potatoes until creamy. Season to taste with salt and

pepper. You can prepare this side dish up to 2 hours ahead. Cover and let stand at room temperature. Re-warm over low heat, stirring constantly and thinning with more milk if necessary. Sprinkle with thyme before serving.

it's a
wonderful life (1946)

monte bianco

serves 6 to 8

This dessert is traditionally served during the holiday season, usually on New Year's Eve, in areas of Italy and France. The finished dessert resembles the mountain range in the Alps that is shared by these two countries. If you have never tried chestnuts as dessert, you'll be pleasantly surprised by this concoction!

6	squares (6 ounces) semi-sweet chocolate, coarsely chopped	1/4 cup	rum or brandy
		1 cup	whipping cream
2 cans	(15 to 19 ounces in total) sweetened chestnut purée	1 tbsp	powdered sugar
		1 tsp	vanilla

- In a bowl, over a saucepan of hot water, melt chocolate, stirring occasionally. Let cool.

- In another large bowl, combine chestnut purée, rum or brandy and chocolate. Cover and refrigerate for at least 2 hours to allow the flavours to blend (may be refrigerated for up to a day).

- Place mixture in a potato ricer, food mill, colander with large holes, or coarse mesh sieve over serving platter, press chestnut mixture

through the holes so that strands fall loosely into a mound. Gently rearrange strands to make more of a mountain shape, if so desired (or mold into a mountain shape with your hands). Set aside.

- In a bowl, whip cream with powdered sugar and vanilla until soft peaks form. Spoon the whipped cream over the top third of the chestnut mound to create "snowcaps". Serve immediately.

SETTING THE STAGE

The Christmas season is something most of us look forward to with much joy and anticipation. Since the story in the film takes place on Christmas Eve, some holiday cheer is required. Whether you already have your house decorated with holly and mistletoe or whether Christmas is months away, bring some seasonal touches to your table setting. Use hurricane lamps; fill an elegant crystal or glass bowl with Christmas ornaments or pine cones. Scented vanilla, cinnamon or evergreen candles heighten the mood. Use a white tablecloth with red or green napkins. Light a candelabra in which you have placed silver or gold tapers (candles). For those of you saving your special plates and silver which you tucked somewhere in the curio cabinet... now is the time to enjoy using them with family and friends, or just the two of you. Make your own crackers, use empty paper towel rolls. Fill with delectable chocolates and small trinkets, perhaps some lottery tickets and wrap "crackers" in gold or silver foil. Have one for each place setting. After all, it is a wonderful life and there is no time like the present. It is called the present because it truly is a gift. Celebrate it!!

laura (1944)

This film is based on a suspense novel written by Vera Caspary. Those who enjoyed films such as Dead Again (1991) and Vertigo (1958) will enjoy this intriguing thriller. Right at the beginning the viewer finds out that the title character, Laura, has allegedly been murdered... There are three main suspects: columnist Waldo Lydecker; good-for-nothing socialite Shelby Carpenter and Carpenter's wealthy, benevolent "friend" Anne Treadwell. The rugged New York City detective leading the investigation, becomes captivated by the enigma named Laura and spends a lot of time focussing on a painted portrait of her. One day while sitting in her apartment and mulling over the case, he is shocked when Laura comes through the door. We won't tell you anymore. You will have to watch the film to find out exactly what happens...

FEATURED ACTORS
Gene Tierney (Laura Hunt)
Dana Andrews (Mark McPherson)
Clifton Webb (Waldo Lydecker)
Vincent Price (Shelby Carpenter)
Judith Anderson (Anne Treadwell).

DIRECTOR ~ Otto Preminger

AWARDS WON

Best Cinematography (Joseph La Shelle)	1944 Academy Award
10 Best Films	1944 Film Daily Award
Best Direction (Otto Preminger)	1944 New York Film Critics Circle Award
U.S. National Film Registry	1999 Library of Congress Award

menu
simple pantry stroganoff on a bed of egg noodles • green salad with vinaigrette • marshmallow roll

Pantry supplies were at times very limited during the frugal forties, due to the war. Cooks had to be ingenious and create appetizing meals with few ingredients. We have tried to mirror that resourcefulness in our menu.

simple pantry stroganoff on a bed of egg noodles serves 4

2 tbsp	cooking oil
1	onion, finely chopped
1-1/2 lbs	lean ground beef or chicken
2 cups	button mushrooms, sliced
	salt and freshly ground pepper to taste
1	10-ounce can cream-of-mushroom soup

1 tsp	Worcestershire sauce
1/3 cup	tomato sauce
1/2 tsp	paprika
1/4 cup	sour cream
2 tbsp	flat leaf parsley, chopped
1	16-ounce package broad egg noodles
	hot sauce (optional)

• Heat cooking oil over medium high heat in a deep frying pan or large, heavy saucepan. When hot, add the onion and fry until translucent. Next, add the ground meat, and when the meat is no longer pink, add the mushrooms. Season with salt and pepper to taste. When the mushrooms are soft, stir in the cream-of-mushroom soup, Worcestershire sauce, tomato sauce and paprika. Reduce heat, and simmer till heated throughout, stirring frequently for 5 to 7 minutes. Remove from heat and stir in sour cream. Set aside until noodles are done.

• Prepare noodles according to package directions. Drain when done and transfer to serving dish.

• Serve stroganoff over noodles, garnish each serving with parsley. If you wish to kick up in terms the flavour-add a few drops of hot sauce to the stroganoff.

 Use low fat cream-of-mushroom soup and low fat sour cream.

trivia clips
Rouben Mamoulian was the director at the outset of the on screen adaptation of Caspary's novel, but behind-the-scenes events led to the film being credited to Preminger.

laura (1944)

green salad with vinaigrette

see index

marshmallow roll

serves 4 to 6

1	8 ounce package small, coloured marshmallows, quartered
1/4 cup	chopped nuts
1 cup	graham cracker crumbs
1/4 cup	Maraschino cherries, well drained, chopped
2/3 cup	sweetened condensed milk
1	small package flaked coconut

• In a mixing bowl, stir together the marshmallows, nuts, graham crackers and Maraschino cherries. Stir in the condensed milk and mix until well combined. Divide mixture in two. Wet hands and roll each half into a log shape.

• Sprinkle coconut on a pastry board or section of wax paper. Roll log in coconut until covered.
Wrap in plastic wrap and refrigerate for at least 2 hours. Slice just prior to serving. Wrap unused portions and refrigerate promptly.

BEVERAGES

Beer: Try Castle Lager (South Africa) or Beck's (Germany)

Coffee

MUSIC

Who else but "old blue eyes" Frank Sinatra crooning about love? Sinatra had his first number one hit in 1940 and continued to please audiences well into the 90's. We suggest "Frankly Sentimental" (Columbia) or a compilation of some of his best songs on "Portrait of Sinatra: Columbia Classics" (Sony). Alternatively, a compilation CD like "Cinema Serenade 2: The Golden Age" (Sony), featuring movie music performed by the renowned team of violinist Itzhak Perlman would be suitable.

SETTING THE MOOD

Turn this into a murder mystery night for your guests! Create an intermission part way through the film and have each person write down on a piece of paper who they think committed the murder and why. At the end of the film, review the answers and present the winner with a prize (perhaps the latest best-selling mystery novel). If you have made it an intimate dinner and movie for two... perhaps the loser can grant the winner a preordained wish of the winner, such as a half-hour massage... you get the idea!

trivia clips

"I've made a lot of schlock. But my wife [the late Coral Browne] waited five years for the right script-which won her the British Academy Award. Then she waited three years for the next right part. Somebody's got to pay the rent."
Vincent Price (1911-1993) Film Yearbook, 1989

the maltese falcon (1941)

This film, based on the classic detective novel of the same name by Dashiell Hammett, propelled Humphrey Bogart to genuine stardom. Bogart stars as Sam Spade, a San Francisco detective with his own code of ethics, which isn't to say that he can't be as unethical as some of the people he deals with in his line of work. Sam and his partner Miles Archer are offered a large retainer from a woman named Miss Wonderly, who seeks protection from a man named Floyd Thursby. Even though they don't believe their client has been completely honest with them, they need the work and the money. They accept the case not knowing the tragedy that will ensue. They have no idea their client is using a false name or that she is a trickster with an international reputation. She also doesn't reveal that she is in search of a mysterious jewel-encrusted statuette of a falcon.

FEATURED ACTORS
Humphrey Bogart (Samuel Spade)
Mary Astor (Brigid O' Shaughnessy)
Peter Lorre (Joel Cairo)
Sydney Greenstreet (Kasper Gutman)
Ward Bond (Detective Tom Polhaus)
Barton MacLane
   (Detective Lt. Dundy)

DIRECTOR ~ John Huston

AWARDS WON
10 Best Films	1941 National Review of Motion Pictures Award
U.S. National Film Registry	1989 Library of Congress Award
100 Greatest Movies	1998 American Film Institute Award

menu
cioppino • crusty bread (store bought) • cheese platter (optional) • coffee lovers cake

cioppino
serves 4 to 6

Cioppino is made with a variety of fresh fish and is quite similar to bouillabaisse, a famous seafood soup with a tomato base from the Provençal region of France. Tourists who travel to San Francisco usually make sure they have this dish at least once during their stay. The city's Italian immigrants are credited with developing this savoury fish stew.

Use the recipe as a guide and make substitutions according to the availability of fresh seafood ingredients in your area. Some versions of cioppino add crab. If you wish to do so, reduce the amount of fish by one pound and substitute one pound of crab instead.

4	garlic cloves, minced	1 tbsp	tomato paste
1/4 cup	olive oil	12	small hard-shelled clams or mussels, scrubbed well
1	medium onion, chopped fine	1 lb	medium shrimp, shelled, leaving tails intact
1	stalk celery, chopped		
1/2 tsp	dried hot red pepper flakes	1 lb	sea scallops, halved or quartered if very large
1	green bell pepper, chopped	2 lbs	white fish fillet (scrod, halibut, red snapper, sea bass), cut into 1-inch pieces
1 tbsp	red-wine vinegar		
1-1/2 cups	dry red or white wine		
1 tsp	dried oregano, crumbled		
1/2 tsp	dried thyme, crumbled	2 tbsp	minced fresh parsley leaves
1	bay leaf		hot sauce to taste
1	28-ounce can whole tomatoes including juice, puréed coarse		

- In a large, heavy stockpot, cook garlic in oil over medium heat, stirring, until pale golden.

- Add onion and cook, stirring, until softened. Add celery, pepper flakes and bell pepper and cook, stirring, until softened. Add vinegar and boil until evaporated. Add wine, oregano, thyme and bay leaf and simmer about 5 minutes. Stir in tomato purée and tomato paste and bring to a boil.

- Add clams or mussels (and crab; if using) and simmer, covered, 15 to 20 minutes, checking often and with tongs transferring clams or mussels as they open to a bowl (discarding unopened ones).

- If using crabs, transfer with tongs to a cutting board and remove top shells, adding any crab liquid to soup. Halve or quarter crabs (depending on size) and reserve, with any additional liquid, in a bowl. Add shrimp, scallops, and fish to soup and simmer, covered, 5 minutes, or until seafood is just cooked through. Stir in crabs gently, their liquid, and clams. Serve in large, deep bowls and garnish with parsley prior to serving. To spice up individual portions of the dish-add a splash of hot sauce!

- Cioppino is a substantial dish. Serve with your favourite fresh, crusty bread to fully appreciate the broth. Make sure you place a plate or bowl on the table for the discarded shells.

cheese platter

If you wish, you may serve some of your favourite cheeses on a platter alongside the cioppino. We suggest a wedge of Parmesan, Swiss and Gouda cheeses.

 Use reduced fat cheese.

coffee lovers cake

serves 8 to 10

Crumb Topping

1 tsp	instant coffee
1/2 cup	brown sugar
2/3 cup	all-purpose flour
1-1/2 tsps	cinnamon
1/4 tsp	allspice
6 tbsp	cold butter or margarine, diced
1-1/4 cups	walnuts, chopped
1/2 cup	good quality white chocolate, chopped
1/2 cup	good quality dark chocolate, chopped

Cake

1/2 cup	butter or margarine, softened
1 cup	sugar
2	eggs
1 cup	sour cream
2 tbsp	instant coffee granules
2 tbsp	water, warm
1 tbsp	rum extract
2-3/4 cups	all-purpose flour
1 tbsp	baking powder
1/2 tsp	baking soda
1/2 tsp	salt
1 cup	milk

- Preheat oven to 350˚F. Spray a 9 inch springform pan with cooking spray.

- Make the crumb topping: in a medium bowl stir together instant coffee, brown sugar, cinnamon and allspice. Cut in butter using a pastry blender, or 2 knives until crumbly. Stir in walnuts and chopped white and dark chocolate. Set aside.

- For the cake: in a large bowl beat together using an electric mixer, the butter and sugar until light and fluffy. Add the eggs, one at a time, beating until smooth. Beat in sour cream. Dissolve the instant coffee granules in the warm water, add the rum extract and beat into the egg mixture.

- In a small bowl, stir together the flour, baking powder, baking soda, and salt. With the mixer on low speed, add 1/3 of the dry mixture to the egg mixture, and then follow with half of the milk. Alternate, mixing well after each addition and ending with the flour mixture.

- Spread 1/2 of the batter into the prepared pan and sprinkle with about 1-1/2 cups of the crumb topping. Cover with remaining batter and sprinkle with remaining crumb topping. Bake for 60 minutes or until a toothpick inserted into the centre comes out clean. If the top of the cake browns too quickly, cover loosely with foil.

 Use non-hydrogenated margarine in place of the butter. Use low fat sour cream and skim milk.

 Make the cake a day ahead. Cover with foil or plastic wrap.

trivia clips

This was John Huston's first time in the role of director.
The film was nominated for three Oscars, including Best Picture and Best Screenplay.
Two other previous film versions based on this same novel were made ("The Maltese Falcon", in 1929 and "Satan Met a Lady", in 1936), neither of which was as well received as this 1941 version. Perhaps the magic was in the casting.

the philadelphia story (1940)

Among the top box office hits of the decade is this 1940 romantic comedy. It opens with Philadelphia socialite C. K. Dexter Haven (Cary Grant) being tossed out of his home, precious golf clubs and all, by his wife Tracy Lord (Katharine Hepburn). A year after the break-up, Tracy is about to marry George Kittridge (John Howard), a wealthy aristocrat. Even though Tracy has a new love in her life, C.K. is still pining for her. But this is where the story twists and turns: C.K. learns that the publisher of Spy magazine wants to write an exposé on Tracy's philandering father. To keep a tight lid on the publishing of the story C.K. agrees to smuggle in a Spy reporter, Macauley Connor (James Stewart) and a photographer to cover the elaborate wedding ceremony of his ex and Kittridge. With out giving too much away... we can tell you this: the reporter got more than the story when he laid eyes on the soon-to-be bride, by falling head over heals in love with her. C.K. must pull out all the stops and somehow reclaim his lost love. "The Philadelphia Story" is a bubbly, witty movie tailor-made for Hepburn who shined with two of the most popular leading men of the time.

FEATURED ACTORS
Cary Grant (C.K. Dexter Haven)
Katharine Hepburn (Tracy Lord)
James Stewart (Macauley Connor)
Ruth Hussey (Elizabeth Imbrie)
John Howard (George Kittridge)
Roland Young (Uncle Willie)

DIRECTOR ~ George Cukor

menu
warm soft pretzels • philly cheese steak hoagie • your favourite vegetables and dip • very cherry cheesecake

warm soft pretzels
serves 6 to 8

Anyone who has visited Philadelphia knows that delicious, savoury pretzels are available from street vendors. They are easy to make when using frozen bread dough, and we bet that you eat more than one!

	cooking spray	2 tbsp	water
2 lbs	frozen bread dough, thawed	2 tsps	kosher (coarse) salt
2	egg whites		cheddar cheese, grated (optional)

- Coat two large rimmed baking sheets with non-stick cooking spray. Cut the dough into eight equal pieces. On a lightly floured surface, roll each piece into a 24-inch rope, form into a pretzel shape and place on baking sheet.

- In a small bowl, beat together the egg whites and water, brush over the top of each pretzel. Sprinkle evenly with the salt. Loosely cover with plastic wrap and set aside in a warm, draft-free place to rise for 15 minutes.

- Preheat the oven to 350˚F. Remove the plastic wrap and bake pretzels for 15 to 17 minutes or until golden. If you wish to serve cheese pretzels, sprinkle with grated cheddar at this point, and return to oven for a few minutes until cheese melts. Serve warm.

> **?** Did You Know That... There are 400 million pounds of pretzels made annually in the United States.

trivia clips
Director Cukor also worked with this talented lady who is familiar to us as Dorothy from Kansas in one of her best-loved roles.
Hepburn's love affair with leading man Spencer Tracey sizzled on and off screen.
What was Cary Grant's real name? (Archibald Alexander Leach) Do you think he would have become as famous using his real name?

the philadelphia story (1940)

philly cheese steak hoagies serves 8

Cheese steaks, pretzels, and hoagies: the staples of Philadelphia's blue collar cuisine. Cheese steaks were invented in South Philadelphia in the 1930's at Pat's Steaks, located in the heart of South Philadelphia, hence the addition of "Philly" to the recipe name. They were originally topped with a pizza sauce (now called a pizza steak). Our version adds portobello mushrooms for even more flavour!

2 tsps	olive oil
2	large onions, thinly sliced
2	medium red peppers, thinly sliced
2	medium green peppers, thinly sliced
3	portobello mushrooms, sliced

8	hero-style rolls, each cut horizontally in half
1 lb	thinly sliced deli roast beef, or leftover roast beef, thinly sliced
8	slices Provolone cheese

- In non-stick 12 inch skillet, heat olive oil over medium-high heat until hot. Add onion, peppers, and mushrooms and cook about 12 minutes or until tender and golden, stirring occasionally.

- Meanwhile, preheat broiler. Place rolls, cut sides up, on rack in broiling pan. Top each bottom half with one-eighth of roast beef and a slice of cheese. With broiling pan 5 to 7 inches from source of heat, broil 1 to 2 minutes, until cheese melts and bread is toasted.

- Pile onion mixture on top of melted cheese; replace top halves of rolls. Serve warm along side a platter of fresh vegetables, ready for scooping up your favourite dip (we suggest blue cheese).

 Use low fat cheese.

Did You Know That...
Independence Hall, Betsy Ross House and the Liberty Bell can all be found in downtown Philly. Historic Valley Forge is only 25 miles from the downtown core.

AWARDS WON

Best Actor (James Stewart)	1940 Academy Award
10 Best Films	1940 Film Daily Award
Best Actress (Hepburn)	1940 New York Film Critics Circle Award
Best Picture	1940 New York Film Critics Circle Award
U.S. National Film Registry	1995 Library of Congress Award
100 Greatest American Movies	1998 American Film Institute Award

trivia clips

Hepburn was not the typical Hollywood "glamour girl" she did not wear make-up and never was a pin-up girl like Betty Grable.
"Everybody wants to be Cary Grant. I want to be Cary Grant." Cary Grant (1904-1986) Time Magazine Obituary, 15 December 1986
"It's bloody impractical to love, honour and obey. If it weren't, you wouldn't have to sign a contract"
Katharine Hepburn, Newsweek, 10 November 1969

the philadelphia story (1940)

continued

BEVERAGES

You may wish to try a robust ale such as Well's India Pale Ale or a dark stout like Young's Oatmeal Stout. A wine like Masi Valpolicella would be good, as would be a Mezza Corona Pinot Grigio.

Coffee with dessert.

MUSIC

"High Society", the film and Broadway musical were both based on "The Philadelphia Story". There is a CD with a classic score by Cole Porter (it also features some songs with his lyrics), it is entitled "High Society" (Capital Records). An choice would be a sophisticated jazz CD. Try one of the CD's of ultimate jazz vocalist, Billie Holiday. Her "Songs for Distingué Lovers" is a perfect wind down to a romantic evening!

SETTING THE STAGE

Even though the movie is set in Philadelphia society, the menu is main-stream to suit all lifestyles. If possible, create a pub-style setting, since downtown Philadelphia has a large number of pubs and neighbourhood style restaurant, each with a unique character. Buy a large keg of beer. Use any coasters you may have collected as souvenirs from various pubs and restaurants to add to the atmosphere.

Alternatively, you could easily turn this into a cocktail party by purchasing ready-made appetizers at better supermarkets. Serve a variety of mixed drinks, especially martinis, along with a wide array of wines. Regardless of which culinary approach you take, make the night simple and easy. Use paper plates, or if serving the cheese steaks, serve them in bread baskets lined with butchers paper or thick, paper napkins for an interesting presentation and easy cleanup!

very cherry cheesecake   serves 10

This cheesecake gets its intense flavour from a triple shot of cherries!

For topping:

3/4 cup	dried tart cherries
1	1 lb bag frozen pitted cherries, thawed, drained, juice reserved
1/2 cup	good quality cherry jam (try a European import)
2 tbsp	cherry brandy
1 tbsp	cornstarch

For crust:

1/3 cup	whole almonds
2/3 cup	graham cracker crumbs
1/4 cup	sugar
1/4 cup	(1/2 stick) unsalted butter, melted

For filling:

3	8-ounce packages cream cheese, room temperature
1-1/3	cups sugar
4	large eggs
2 tbsp	fresh lemon juice
1/4 tsp	almond extract
1/4 tsp	salt
1/2 cup	sliced almonds, toasted for garnish

Make topping:

- Combine dried cherries and reserved juice from thawed cherries in medium saucepan. Bring to boil. Remove from heat. Cover; let steep 20 minutes.

- Mix cherry jam, cherry brandy and cornstarch in small bowl to blend. Stir into dried cherry mixture. Add thawed cherries. Stir over medium heat until mixture boils and thickens, about 1 minute. Cool slightly; chill until cold. (Can be prepared 2 days ahead. Keep refrigerated.)

Make crust:

- Finely grind almonds in processor. Add cracker crumbs, sugar and butter. Process until clumps form. Press mixture onto bottom (not sides) of 9-inch-diameter springform pan with sides. Chill 30 minutes.

Make filling:

- Position rack in center of oven; preheat to 350°F. Blend all ingredients except sliced almonds in processor just until smooth, scraping down sides of bowl several times. Transfer filling to crust. Bake until edges of cheesecake are puffed and center is just set, about 50 minutes. Remove from oven. Run knife around pan sides to loosen cake. Chill cake uncovered overnight.

- Release pan sides from cake. Transfer cake to platter. Spoon topping evenly over cake, leaving 1/2 inch border around edge. Garnish edge of cake with sliced almonds.

Begin preparing the dessert a day ahead by making the crust and topping in advance.

the shop around the corner (1940)

menu

tomato and green pepper ragôut • feta cheese (store bought) •hungarian goulash with egg dumplings • country style bread (store bought) • pickled vegetables (store bought) • apricot crêpes

tomato and green pepper ragôut serves 4 to 6

This dish is called Lecs — in Hungarian. It is often served as an appetizer or for lunch with eggs on the side. We suggest serving it with Feta cheese cubes and fresh bread as your first course. The sausage is optional.

3 tbsp	olive oil (lard is traditionally used)	1/2 tsp	salt
1-1/2 cups	onions, finely chopped		freshly ground pepper to taste
1	clove garlic, finely chopped	1/2 cup	tomato paste
2 tbsp	sweet Hungarian paprika	1/2 tsp	sugar
1 lb	green peppers (5 medium sized), seeded, ribbed, and cut in 1/2 inch pieces	1 lb	Hungarian style sausage (we suggest Debreceni) if desired, sliced into 1/8 inch slices
1 lb	tomatoes, peeled, seeded and coarsely chopped		

• In a large, deep skillet or stockpot, heat the oil over medium high heat, When hot, add the onions and garlic. Cook for 8 to 10 minutes or until the onions are a light golden colour. Remove from heat and add paprika, stirring to coat. Stir in the green peppers, tomatoes, salt and pepper. Return to heat and cook for 10 minutes over medium heat. If the tomatoes have not released enough liquid to cover the vegetables, add 1/4 cup or more of the tomato paste. Add the sugar to cut down on the tartness of the tomato paste. Stir and cover the pan, cook for 3 to 5 minutes stirring frequently. If using sausages, add them at this point, then cover and simmer mixture for 1/2 hour. The consistency should be that of a thick, chunky tomato sauce.

Did You Know That...
Budapest is a rare mix of the old and the new, with many reminders of its turbulent past. It is actually two cities, divided by the Danube river. Buda, was named after an Hungarian nobleman and Pest, is actually a Slavic word meaning oven. In Hungary, food and music are inextricably linked. Budapest has a large number of romantic cafés and restaurants that feature live music. Often the musicians perform while moving between tables, offering the diners a "private" performance. Gypsy music has a strong influence in Hungary.

Budapest gift shop clerk Alfred Kralik, played by James Stewart, resents newly hired shop girl Klara Novak, played by Margaret Sullavan. They hate each other almost at first sight. Both clerks are carrying on correspondence with someone they have never met. Love has blossomed for both of them with their "mail sweethearts". Little do they know though, that they have been writing to each other! Will they be as enamoured of each other when they finally meet and discover the other's identity? As you can probably guess, things won't be that simple. "The Shop Around the Corner" is adapted from a Hungarian play written by Nikolaus (Miklos) Laszlo. This delightful romantic comedy was later remade in 1949 as "In the Good Old Summertime", and in 1998 as "You've Got Mail", starring Meg Ryan and Oscar winner Tom Hanks.

FEATURED ACTORS
Margaret Sullavan, (Klara Novak)
James Stewart (Alfred Kralik)
Frank Morgan (Hugo Matuschek)
Joseph Schildkraut (Ferencz Vadas)
Sara Haden (Flora)

DIRECTOR ~ Ernst Lubitsch

AWARDS WON

10 Best Films	1940 National Board of Review of Motion Pictures
U.S. National Film Registry	1999 Library of Congress Award

trivia clips

"Behind every successful man you'll find a woman-who has absolutely nothing to wear.
James Stewart (1908-1997) Film Yearbook, 1990
Margaret Sullavan died at age 49 by overdosing on barbiturates; it is believed that she committed suicide.

continued

BEVERAGES

Hungarian wine, should of course be served! Hungarian Tokaji Furmint, or Leom Beyer Reisling would be suitable to serve with the goulash, as would Tokaji Szamorodi, a popular dry white wine. If you wish to serve red wine, try Szekszárdi Bikavér (Szekszárd Bulls Blood) or Egri Bikavér.

For dessert you must try Tokaji Aszú (5 star), a sweet but full bodied dessert wine. It is reminiscent of the much more expensive ice wines that are popular in North America.

The best liqueurs (likor) are Bon bon meggy (sweet cherry brandy) and Kakao likor, a delicious chocolate liqueur. Alternatively, try Monimpex's Golden Pear liqueur. Don't be misled by the sweetness though, these are also potent brews.

Coffee

MUSIC

In Budapest, an outing to the State Opera House makes for an unforgettable evening. Budapest's citizens love music. For some authentic Hungarian Music seek out anything by Marta Sebestyen, a leading Hungarian singer. She is often backed by Muzsikas, a young group that is comfortable with a number of ethnic Hungarian styles. We suggest the following CD's: "Muzsikas (Hannibal)", "Ketto: Hungarian Folk Music" and "The World of Eastern Europe" (Trace). This last CD features a variety of compositions from this area of the world, including five Hungarian tracks. The "Rough Guide to the Music of Eastern Europe" also offers some tunes from Hungary.

SETTING THE STAGE

For those who are single or for those who are trying to play matchmaker, you may want to try an open letter forum. As the host, send out invitations to your guests with 10 questions for your guest to answer. The questions would require each guest to describe him or herself: hobbies, interests, etc. Provide a self-addressed, stamped envelope to have the personal questionnaires returned back to you. During the evening you could read out the letters and have a "Who Am I?" contest. This could also be a tool for matchmaking. Invite your single friends and proceed as outlined above, but don't play "Who Am I?". Instead, when your guests arrive, allow each guest to view the letters and select the letter of choice. Throughout the evening this will allow guests to strike up conversations with each other to reveal the identity of the writer of each person's chosen letter. You may want to colour code each letter to identify as to male/female. This is a great way of "breaking the ice" but it can also be used for any social get-together.

hungarian goulash with egg dumplings

serves 4 to 6

Known in Hungarian as "Gulyasleves". This recipe is said to be the most authentic version. Some goulash versions have added finely chopped mushrooms and green and red peppers. Feel free to add them if you like.

2 tbsp	cooking oil
2	large onions, chopped
2 lbs	stewing beef cut in 1 inch cubes
1 tsp	salt
2 tbsp	sweet Hungarian paprika
4 cups	water
4	potatoes, peeled and diced
1/4 tsp	black pepper
2	bay leaves
1-1/2 cups	mushrooms, finely chopped (optional)
1	green pepper, finely chopped (optional)
1	red pepper, finely chopped (optional)

Egg Dumplings

1	egg
6 tbsp	all-purpose flour
1/8 tsp	salt

- Heat oil in a large, heavy bottomed pot. Add onions and brown in oil. If using mushrooms and peppers, add at this point. When the onion is translucent and the other vegetables are soft, add beef, salt and paprika. Let beef simmer in its own juice for about 10 to 15 minutes, slowly adding the water. Simmer over low heat, partially covered. Add remaining water, diced potatoes, pepper and bay leaves. Cover and simmer until potatoes are done and meat is tender, about 1 hour.

- <u>Prepare egg dumpling batter:</u> Add flour to unbeaten egg and salt. Mix well. Let stand for 1/2 hour. Drop by teaspoonful into goulash. Cover and simmer 5 minutes after dumplings rise to surface.

apricot crêpes

serves 6

3	eggs
1 cup	milk
1/3 cup	club soda
1 cup	all-purpose flour
3 tbsp	granulated sugar
1/4 tsp	salt
1 tsp	vanilla extract
4 to 6 tbsp	butter or butter-flavoured cooking spray
3/4 cup	good quality apricot jam
1 cup	ground walnuts or hazelnuts
	powdered sugar (garnish)

- In a medium bowl, beat the eggs lightly with the milk, using a whisk. Add the club soda, and then the flour, sugar, salt and vanilla extract. Continue to stir until the batter is smooth.

- Melt a tbsp of the butter (or use cooking spray) in an 8 inch skillet over medium high heat. When the foam subsides and the skillet is heated through, ladle in enough batter to thinly cover the bottom of the skillet; tilt the skillet side to side to spread batter evenly. Cook for 2 to 3 minutes, or until lightly browned on one side and then flip over to brown the other side. When the crêpe is done, spread 2 tsps of jam on one side, roll into a cylinder, and put in a baking dish. Place in a warm oven heated to 200°F to keep warm until all the crêpes are done. Serve this dessert warm, sprinkled with nuts and powdered sugar as garnish.

 Use low fat milk. Grease pan with cooking spray.

yankee doodle dandy (1942)

menu patriotic vegetable platter and herbed dip • hearty new all-american burgers • four star coleslaw • red, white and blue tiramisu

patriotic vegetable platter and herbed dip makes about 2 cups

1	8 ounce package cream cheese	1 tbsp	parsley, chopped
1-1/2 cups	sour cream	1/4 tsp	red paprika
1/4 cup	green onions, finely chopped	1 tbsp	Worcestershire sauce
1/4 tsp	black pepper		a variety of vegetables, cut in small pieces for dipping

- Beat cream cheese to a smooth consistency, blend in sour cream; add the remaining ingredients and blend well. Cover and chill in the refrigerator. Can be made 2 days in advance. On the day of serving, cut up an assortment of your favourite vegetables. Use vegetables in a variety of colours in order to make your platter more appealing (such as both red and green peppers, cauliflower, broccoli, carrots, etc).

- Arrange the vegetables decoratively around the dipping bowl on a large tray or platter if you do not have an actual vegetables and dip serving dish.

hearty new all-american burgers serves 4

1 lb	ground beef	1/4 cup	plain yogurt
1/4 cup	onions, minced	1 tsp	Dijon-style mustard
1/4 tbsp	pepper	4	red onions, thinly sliced
12	spinach leaves, stems removed	2	Portobello mushrooms
4	whole wheat hamburger buns, sliced horizontally	1	avocado, seeded, peeled and sliced into medium wedges

- Combine ground beef, minced onion and pepper thoroughly. Divide mixture into 4 equal parts and flatten into patties. Broil or barbecue over medium heat. Turn over just once.
- Place whole Portobello mushrooms on grill, grill until tender. Remove, slice and set aside.
- Layer 4 spinach leaves on each bun

and add equal amounts of onion and mushroom slices.

Add the burger and top with avocado wedges. In a small bowl, mix the yogurt and mustard top and top off burger with this yogurt mixture. Close with bun top.

❤ You could substitute vegetarian burgers for the beef burgers.

Stepping out of his gangster style roles, James Cagney shines on screen and dances into the hearts of Americans in his portrayal of George M. Cohan, a real-life vaudeville performer. The film is a musical portrait about composer/singer/dancer George M. Cohan. The story is effectively fiction, using only the outline of Cohan's life and some of his songs as reference points. It goes back to Cohan's beginnings through to his comeback and his triumphant moment when he received a medal from the president, Franklin Delano Roosevelt, for his special contributions to the United States of America. Cohan's song, "Over There" became the unofficial anthem of the war. This nostalgic, entertaining film, even though it is a mostly fictional story about the popular Irish-American entertainer, is worth watching for its rip-roaring songs and hilarious comedy.

FEATURED ACTORS
James Cagney (George M. Cohan)
Joan Leslie (Mary Cohan)
Walter Huston (Jerry Cohan)
Richard Whorf (Sam Harris)
Irene Manning (Fay Templeton)
George Tobias (Dietz)
Rosemary DeCamp (Nellie Cohan)
Jeanne Cagney (Josie Cohan)

DIRECTOR ~ Michael Curtiz

trivia clips

Hollywood decided to help out with wartime metal shortages: for the 1942 Academy Awards Ceremony the Oscar statuettes were made out of plaster instead of metal dipped in real gold.
Michael Curtiz directed Casablanca the same year!

BEVERAGES

Boone's Sangria (USA) is a nice light drink, perfect for summer barbecues. For a red wine, try Ernest and Julio Gallo Turning Leaf Cabernet Sauvignon (USA), or their Turning Leaf Sauvignon Blanc (white). Otherwise, choose your favourite American beer.

MUSIC

The Yankee Doodle Dandy (Howard's) original soundtrack is available, as is the album of the same name (Delta) that features various tracks by George Cohan. An excellent alternate choice would be "Movie Box" (Volumes 1 to 3) by Sound of the Movies. These CD's feature vintage pop from the films of the 30's and 40's. The nostalgic songs will add an authentic mood of your film night!

SETTING THE STAGE

Since this movie celebrates the "Fourth of July" in the United States, celebrate outdoors with a backyard or patio barbecue! Find out which of your guests have an upcoming birthday or have had one in the recent past, and surprise them with a mini birthday celebration - cake and all. Decorate the table with red, white or blue tablecloths; balloons, streamers (in red, white and blue of course), silver star confetti scattered on the table add to the celebration of the American melting pot. Buy some small American flags to decorate your dessert, or to use as part of a centrepiece. If some of your guests are of different ethnic origins, purchase small inexpensive flags of their countries as part of your centrepiece. You could suggest that they bring a small sample of their favourite ethnic recipes for all to share.

four star coleslaw

makes about 6 to 8 cups

This coleslaw has more texture and flavour than most and looks very appealing. The raisins are optional. It is always nice however, to spread a little California sunshine nationwide.

1/2	head of medium cabbage	1 tbsp	vegetable oil
2	carrots, peeled and grated	1/4 tsp	white ground pepper
1	small red onion, finely chopped	1 tsp	salt
		1 tsp	sugar
2 tbsp	low fat mayonnaise	1/2 tsp	celery seed
2 tbsp	sour cream	1/2 cup	California raisins (optional)
1 tbsp	white wine vinegar		

- Carefully cut the cabbage in half through the core and then trim core from each piece. Cut the cabbage into the thinnest slices possible. Then chop the slices of cabbage until they are about 2 inches long. Put cabbage into a large bowl. Add the grated carrots and chopped red onion.

- In a small size bowl, combine the mayonnaise, sour cream, vinegar, oil, pepper, salt, sugar and celery seed using a wooden spoon. Mix until well blended.

- Pour the dressing over the cabbage and mix (the best way to mix this all is by using your hands!). Make sure to evenly coat cabbage. Refrigerate. Can be made one day ahead. Before serving mix in the raisins.

red, white and blue
tiramisu serves 10

This delectable dessert has the colours of the American flag. Fitting to serve anytime, but especially for the Fourth of July!

1 pint	strawberries, washed and hulled	1/2 cup	powdered sugar
1 pint	blueberries, washed	3 cups	chilled whipping cream or whipped topping
2/3 cup	sugar, divided		
6 tbsp	brandy or liqueur such as crème de cacao	48	ladyfinger biscuits (imported type such as Savoiardi)
3 cups	mascarpone or ricotta cheese (or a mixture of both)		chocolate shavings or cocoa for garnish

- Using a blender, purée strawberries with 1/3 cup sugar and 2 tbsp brandy or liqueur. Set aside in a separate bowl. Repeat the same steps for the blueberries. Set blueberry purée aside in a bowl.

- In a medium bowl, mix remaining brandy, mascarpone and ricotta cheese, and powdered sugar. In large bowl, whip the whipping cream or whipped topping; fold into cheese mixture.

- To assemble the tiramisu: spoon 2 tbsp of the strawberry purée into the bottom of a 9 X 13 inch glass baking dish and spread to cover the bottom of the dish. Next, dip ladyfingers into strawberry purée and place side by side to cover bottom of baking dish. Spread the remaining strawberry purée over the lady finger layer. Now spread 1/2 of the cheese and whipped cream/topping mixture over the strawberry layer. Next, dip remaining ladyfingers into blueberry purée and add another layer of ladyfingers. Spread remaining blueberry purée over this layer. Top with remaining cheese and whipped cream/topping mixture.

- Refrigerate covered for at least 6 hours or overnight. Garnish with chocolate shavings or dust with cocoa and serve.

 Use reduced fat mascarpone and ricotta. Use reduced calorie or fat whipped topping.

NIFTY 50'S

1950- Kraft launches Deluxe processed cheese slices . Cheese Whiz followed in 1952.

1952- Dr.Jonas Salk develops the polio vaccine.

1954- The first successful kidney transplant is performed.

1955- Captain Kangaroo, with host Bob Keeshan and the puppet character Mr. Moose airs on television.

1956- Crest introduces the first fluoride toothpaste.

1956- Elvis Presley releases "Heartbreak Hotel", which goes on to become his first big record. He went on to dominate the U.S. music scene for years to come . Elvis made rock and roll a household term.

1958- NASA formed

1957- Sputnik:The Space Age began on Oct. 4, 1957, when the Soviet Union launched the first Earth-orbiting satellite Sputnik.

1959- Pantyhose were invented, thus releasing women from sexy, but often uncomfortable garter belts.

1953- Hugh Hefner starts the publication of "Playboy" magazine.

1953- The Chicago Cubs signed their first black player, Ernie Banks.

1955- The first McDonald's franchise restaurant opens, owned by Ray Kroc in Des Plaines, Illinois.

african queen (1951)

Come aboard the "African Queen" for drama, adventure and romance! She isn't a luxury ship, but rather a tramp steamer operated by a jack-of-all trades captain with an appetite for liquid spirits, especially gin. The ship in question is used to supply small African villages during WW I. Charlie Allnut (Humphrey Bogart) rescues the sister of a missionary killed by the Germans (who also decimate the village). Rose Sayer (Katharine Hepburn), is a prim and proper British lady who looks with disdain upon the captain and all his vices. The only thing they have in common at the outset is their being on the same side in the war. They learn to work together to survive the dangerous waterways and they come up with a plan of action to destroy a German gunboat. Surprisingly, these two very different people overcome differences and grow to love each other. Viewers will enjoy the beautiful cinematography, as the film was shot entirely on location in the then Belgian Congo and British Uganda.

FEATURED ACTORS

Humphrey Bogart (Charlie Allnut)
Katharine Hepburn (Rose Sayer)
Robert Morley (Rev. Samuel Sayer)
Peter Bull (Captain of Louisa)
Theodore Bikel (First Officer)

DIRECTOR ~ John Huston

AWARDS WON

Best Actor (Humphrey Bogart)	1951 Academy Award
Best Film- Any Source (John Huston)	1952 British Academy Awards
Best Actress (Katharine Hepburn)	1952 New York Film Critics Circle Award
Best Direction (John Huston)	1952 New York Film Critics Circle Award
Best Film (John Huston)	1952 New York Film Critics Circle Award
U.S. National Film Registry	1994 Library of Congress
100 Greatest American Movies	1998 American Film Institute

menu

ethiopian spicy braised chicken (dorowat) and/or ethiopian beef with peppers • gingered vegetables • injera (ethiopian unleavened bread) • fruit platter with honey-yogurt dip

The countries of East Africa offer a variety of tasty cuisines, but we chose an Ethiopian menu due to its ease of preparation and the availability of ingredients. Ethiopia is an ancient land, well known even before the time of Christ. The Queen of Sheba was from this country and was renowned for her legendary beauty. Ethiopian food is one of the most spiciest on the African continent.

ethiopian spicy braised chicken (dorowat) serves 4

8 oz	tomato sauce
1/4 cup	paprika
1/4 cup	dry red wine
1 tbsp	ginger, grated
1 tsp	red pepper
1/8 tsp	ground cardamom
1/8 tsp	ground nutmeg
1/8 tsp	ground cloves
1/8 tsp	ground cinnamon
1/8 tsp	ground allspice
2 tbsp vegetable oil	
2	onions, chopped
3	cloves garlic, minced
1/2 tsp	ground turmeric
1 tsp	salt
3 lb	broiler chicken, cut into pieces
1/4 cup	dry red wine

• Make the red pepper sauce first: Combine tomato sauce, paprika, 1/4 cup red wine, grated ginger, red pepper, cardamom, nutmeg, cloves, cinnamon, and allspice. Set red pepper sauce aside.

• In a large skillet, heat the vegetable oil, sauté onion and garlic in hot oil until onion is translucent, but not brown. Stir in red pepper sauce, turmeric, and 1 teaspoon of salt.

• Add chicken pieces to skillet. Spoon onion mixture over chicken pieces, and bring mixture to boil. Reduce heat, cover and simmer about 30 minutes. Then stir in 1/4 cup dry red wine and cook uncovered, about 15 minutes turning chicken pieces often. Skim off fat .

• Serve with Ethiopian injera.

african queen (1951)

ethiopian beef with peppers
serves 4 to 6

6	green chili peppers, skinned, seeded and chopped
2 tsp	fresh ginger, peeled and finely chopped
4	cloves garlic, minced
1/4 tsp	ground cardamom
1/4 tsp	ground turmeric
1/4 tsp	ground cinnamon
1/4 tsp	ground cloves
1/2 cup	red wine
6 tbsp	cooking oil
2 lb	sirloin steak, cut in 1/2-inch strips
2 cups	chopped onion
2	red or green bell peppers, chopped

• Purée chilies, ginger, garlic, spices, and wine to a smooth paste. Set aside. Heat the cooking oil in a large skillet and brown the strips of beef. When evenly browned, remove the beef and drain off all but 2 tablespoons of oil. Sauté onion in the oil until soft, but not browned. Add the bell peppers and sauté for an additional 3 minutes. Then add the chile purée and bring to a boil, stirring constantly. Add the beef and mix until strips are coated with sauce.

• Reduce heat and simmer 10 minutes more until the beef is done. Serve with injera.

gingered vegetables
serves 4 to 6

6	small potatoes, peeled and cubed
1/2 lb	green beans
4	carrots, diced
5	green chili peppers, skinned, seeded and chopped
2	onions, quartered and separated
1/2 tbsp	fresh ginger, grated
3	cloves garlic, minced
	salt and pepper to taste
2 tbsp	olive oil

• Place potatoes, green beans, and carrots into boiling salted water, cover, and partially cook for 5 minutes. Remove vegetables and rinse in cold water.

• In a large skillet, heat the olive oil, then sauté the chile and onion in oil until soft, but not brown. Add the ginger, garlic, salt, and pepper and sauté for 5 minutes. Add the partially cooked vegetables, stir well, and cook further over medium heat until vegetables are tender. Serve injera alongside the main dishes.

BEVERAGES

We suggest Harar Beer (Ethiopia) or Tusker beer from Kenya, another East African country, as the flavours of the meal are very complex and spicy.

Serve a dark roast coffee after the meal, or a peppermint tea.

MUSIC

"The Rough Guide to the Music of Africa" (World Music Network) is a wonderful introduction to a variety of African musical styles. "Ethiopia: Falasha & Adjuran Tribal Music" (Smithsonian/Folkways) highlights the ancient musical traditions of these two tribes. The Falasha tribe is known as one of the "lost tribes of Israel". During the 1980's many of them were airlifted out of ravaged Ethiopia and resettled in Israel by the Israeli government. A variety of artists and styles can be found on "Ethiopia, Vol. 2: Gold from Wax" (Lyrichord).

SETTING THE STAGE

A meal in Ethiopia is an experience. Whether you have dinner in an Ethiopian home or restaurant, you eat communally, as is done in many African countries. Tables are usually round in shape to facilitate this style of dining. Ritual hand washing is a must, you may wish to do the following for your guests: Select some brand new washcloths, preferably in white. Wet them, then fold them in half and roll them up. Place on a microwave safe plate and heat them in the microwave for one minute. Place on a silver tray and offer them to your guests prior to the meal (collect them before the meal starts though). Repeat this procedure after the meal. Serve the injera on a large platter or tray alongside the platters with the main dishes. The meal is eaten in the following manner: You tear off a piece of injera about two or three inches square, and then scoop up some of the other foods with it. It takes a bit of doing to accomplish this feat but once you master it, you cannot help but enjoy this sensual way of eating. Everyone eats from the communal serving platters or dishes, but has his part of the dinner in front of him. Provide forks for the uninitiated who

african queen (1951)

may give up before they learn to eat in the traditional way. Dinner is concluded with hand-washing again and with the burning of incense. Coffee in demitasse cups is served right after dinner. Later, you can serve the fresh fruit platter along with the dip.

To create atmosphere, dim the lights and use candles. Have the exotic African music selections playing in the background. Serve dinner on a low table and have guests sit on cushions. Use an interesting wooden or clay figure as a centrepiece, or a simple wooden bowl or platter of fruit will do. Serve the food in clay or ceramic serving dishes. Use a colourful tablecloth that evokes an African theme, perhaps you have a scarf that may do the trick. If the event is planned ahead of time, you could go to a fabric store and purchase some fabric in a leopard or zebra print to top your table with. Alternatively, seek out stores in your city that cater to clientele from this area of the world. You may find some accessories that will add just the right touch to this unusual meal and event!

injera (ethiopian unleavened bread)

serves 6 to 8

For thousands of years in this area of the world this bread has been eaten.

3 cups	warm water		3 tbsp	club soda
2-1/2 cups	self-rising flour			cooking oil

- Put the warm water into a blender or food processor. Add the flour and blend, slowly at first, then with rapid speed. You should probably do this in two batches unless you have a powerful blender. Scrape down the sides of the blender or food processor with a rubber spatula. Place the batter in a medium sized bowl and stir in the club soda. Heat a 12-inch oiled pan or electric skillet to 400°F. Using a ladle, pour 1/4 cup of batter onto the hot pan. Immediately tilt the pan to cover the bottom evenly with the batter. Cook, uncovered, until the top of the bread is filled with holes and no longer wet. The edges should begin to curl just a bit. Remove quickly with your fingers and place the bread on clean kitchen towel. Let it cool for 3 to 4 minutes as you prepare the next piece of bread. Continue until all batter is used up (grease the pan between cooking pieces of bread). Place the cooled bread on a plate. Stack the pieces of bread on top of each other and cover with plastic wrap until ready to serve. Can be made 3 hours prior to serving.

 Use cooking spray to grease the skillet.

fruit platter with honey-yogurt dip

Since the meal is hot and spicy, a light fruit dessert is best suited for this menu. This platter requires a minimal amount of preparation and is both attractive to the eyes and satisfying to the palate!

Buy a variety of fruits that would be found in East Africa such as: citrus fruits, bananas, grapes, pomegranates, figs (both fresh and dried), dates, custard apples (a delectable tropical fruit) as well as pineapple, strawberries, pears and apples. Cut the fruit into slices or bite-size pieces and arrange attractively on a platter, placing the bowl of dip in the centre.

honey-yogurt dip

Yield: About 2 cups

2 cups	vanilla flavoured yogurt		1 tsp	ground cinnamon or 2 tsp grated lime rind
1/2 cup	honey			

- Combine yogurt, honey and cinnamon or lime rind, in small bowl. Stir to blend. Place bowl on a platter and surround with fruit.

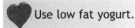 Use low fat yogurt.

all about
eve (1950)

menu	waldorf salad • modern new york style strip loin steak • roasted potato wedges with sea salt and paprika • chocolate-almond grand marnier cheesecake

waldorf salad

serves 6

This simple apple salad got its name from the luxurious Waldorf-Astoria Hotel in New York City. It was invented in 1896, not by a chef, but by the maître d'hôtel Oscar Tschirky. The Waldorf salad was an immediate success. As often happens, many variations have evolved-some with raisins, some with chopped nuts. This one has green apples and red seedless grapes along with walnuts.

2 cups	green apple, diced	1 tbsp	sugar
1 cup	celery, sliced	1/2 tsp	lemon juice
1/2 cup	chopped walnuts		salt to taste
1 cup	red seedless grapes, halved	1 cup	sour cream
1/2 cup	mayonnaise		lettuce leaves (optional)

- In a large bowl, combine apple, celery, walnuts and grapes. In a separate bowl, blend mayonnaise, sugar, lemon juice and salt. Fold sour cream into mayonnaise mixture then fold into the apple mixture. Chill before serving. Serve on a bed of lettuce if so desired.

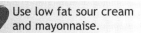 Use low fat sour cream and mayonnaise.

This fifties film garnered 14 nominations at the Academy Awards in 1950. The story is about the competitive, behind-the-scenes world of New York theatre and reveals what people will do to make it to the top. The storyline starts with aspiring actress Eve Harrington (Anne Baxter) showing up in the dressing room of Broadway superstar Margo Channing (Bette Davis), who pities the young girl and takes her under her wing. The so-called naïve young actress, however, is really a conniver who uses the Broadway star, director, director's wife and others to advance her career and to help her make it to the top of the Broadway scene. This entertaining and elegant satire about the world of theatre features some great, unforgettable lines such as the one uttered by character Margo Channing: "Fasten your seatbelts, folks. It's going to be a bumpy ride." Legendary actress, Marilyn Monroe, also appears in a small role as an aspiring actress.

FEATURED ACTORS
Bette Davis (Margo Channing)
Anne Baxter (Eve Harrington)
George Sanders (Addison De Witt)
Celeste Holm (Karen Richards)
Gary Merrill (Bill Simpson)

DIRECTOR ~
Joseph L. Mankiewicz

trivia clips
Bette Davis was quite petite; she was only 5 feet 2 inches tall.
At 50 I thought proudly: Here we are half-century! Being 60 was fairly frightening. You want to know how I spent my 70th birthday? I put on a completely black face, a fuzzy black Afro wig, wore black clothes and hung a black wreath on my door.
Bette Davis (1908-1989) Films Illustrated, December 1979

AWARDS WON

Best Costume Design (Charles LeMaire)	1950 Academy Award
Best Costume Design (Edith Head)	1950 Academy Award
Best Director (Joseph L. Mankiewicz)	1950 Academy Award
Best Picture	1950 Academy Award
Best Screenplay (Joseph L. Mankiewicz)	1950 Academy Award
Best Sound (20th Century Fox Sound Dept.)	1950 Academy Award
Best Supporting Actor (George Sanders)	1950 Academy Award
Best Film- Any source (Joseph L. Mankiewicz)	1950 Academy Award
Best Director (Joseph L. Mankiewicz)	1950 Directors Guild of America Award
10 Best Films	1950 National Board of Review of Motion Pictures
Best Actress (Bette Davis)	1950 New York Film Critics Circle Award
Best Direction (Joseph L. Mankiewicz)	1950 New York Film Critics Circle Award
Best Film (Joseph L. Mankiewicz)	1950 New York Film Critics Circle Award
Best Female Performance (Bette Davis)	1950 New York Film Critics Circle Award
Special Jury Prize (Joseph L. Mankiewicz)	1951 Cannes Film Festival Award
U.S. National Film Registry	1990 Library of Congress Award
100 Greatest American Movies	1998 American Film Institute Award

modern new york style striploin steak serves 6

6	8-ounce New York style strip loin steaks		2 tsp	fresh rosemary, minced
3 tbsp	olive oil		2 tsp	fresh thyme, minced
6	Roma tomatoes		2 tsp	fresh oregano, minced
1/2 cup	pine nuts, toasted		2 tsp	fresh tarragon, minced
3 tbsp	capers, drained and chopped		1/4 cup	dry white wine
2 tbsp	shallots, chopped		2 tsp	fresh lemon juice
2 tbsp	garlic, minced		5 tbsp	butter, cut into pieces

- Heat 1 tablespoon olive oil in skillet; add steak and brown both sides, about 2 to 4 minutes per side or grill on the barbecue. Transfer steak to platter.

- Add remaining oil; sauté tomatoes, pine nuts, capers, shallots, garlic and all herbs for 2 minutes. Add wine and lemon juice; simmer until reduced to a thick sauce. Whisk in butter; pour over steaks.

roasted potato wedges with sea salt and paprika serves 6 to 8

8	large Yukon Gold or russet potatoes, peeled		2 tbsp	sea salt
1/2 cup	olive oil		1/2 tbsp	paprika

- Preheat oven to 450˚F. Cut each potato lengthwise into 8 wedges; toss in bowl with oil, salt and paprika. Arrange in single layer on 2 baking sheets. Bake until tender and golden, turning potatoes and rotating sheets halfway through baking, about 45 minutes. Serve immediately.

trivia clips

The Statue of Liberty, a famous New York City landmark, was a gift from the French in 1886.
The Statue of Liberty stands 151 feet high. Lifts and stairs take visitors to the top.

all about
eve (1950)

chocolate-almond grand marnier cheesecake
Yield: 12 slices

For crust:

20	graham cracker cookies (or 1-1/2 cups graham cracker crumbs)
3 tbsp	unsalted butter, room temperature

For filling:

3	8-ounce packages cream cheese, room temperature
2/3 cup	plus 3 tbsp sugar
1/4 cup	sour cream
5 tsp	cornstarch
3	large eggs

1	large egg yolk
1 tsp	vanilla extract
1/2 cup	Grand Marnier (orange liqueur)
1/3 cup	almonds, toasted, chopped
1 tsp	vanilla extract
4 tsp	unsweetened cocoa powder
	whipped cream for garnish (optional)
	chocolate dipped mandarin orange segments for garnish (optional)
	toasted almonds for garnish (optional)

- Make crust: position rack in centre of oven and preheat to 425°F. Wrap foil tightly around outside of 9-inch diameter springform pan. Finely grind graham cracker cookies in processor. Add butter and process until blended. Press mixture onto bottom only of prepared pan.
Set aside.

- For filling: In a large mixing bowl, blend cream cheese, 2/3 cup sugar, sour cream and cornstarch with an electric mixer. Add eggs, yolk and vanilla; process until well blended, scraping sides of bowl occasionally. Transfer 3/4 cup cream cheese mixture to small bowl; set aside. Add Grand Marnier, almonds and vanilla extract to remaining cream cheese mixture in bowl. Blend well. Spoon 2 cups of Grand Marnier mixture over crust.

- Mix cocoa powder and 3 tablespoons sugar into reserved 3/4 cup cream cheese mixture. Spoon 2/3 cup cocoa mixture over Grand Marnier mixture in pan. Spoon remaining Grand Marnier mixture over cocoa mixture. Drop remaining cocoa mixture over

the Grand Marnier layer by spoonfuls. Run tip of small knife through batter several times to create a marble effect.

- Bake cheesecake 10 minutes. Reduce oven temperature to 325°F and bake cake until perimeter is puffed and centre is set, about 45 minutes. Transfer cake to rack. Using small knife, cut around edge of pan to loosen cake. Cool cake completely in pan. Cover; chill overnight. Remove pan sides from cake. Cut into wedges and serve. Garnish with whipped cream and chocolate dipped mandarin segments and toasted almonds if so desired.

 Use reduced fat cream cheese.

 Prepare the cheesecake a day ahead.

BEVERAGES

The steak calls for a robust wine, try any of the following: Woods End Baco Noir (Ontario), Banrock Station Shiraz Cabernet Sauvignon (Australia), Bersano Barbera D'Asti (Italy) or Cline Zinfandel (USA).

Long Island Ice Tea or a Manhattan would be suitable pre-dinner cocktails (see main beverages page).

Coffee with dessert.

MUSIC

Classic Sinatra (Capital Records) is a good choice if the evening is to be an intimate get together. Otherwise, because of the film's subject matter, Broadway hits fit the bill! Try "Broadway Blockbusters Box" (RCA) or "Greatest Hits: Broadway Songs" (Sony). Both of these compilations feature various tunes from such hit shows as "Fiddler on the Roof", The Sound of Music" and "Phantom of the Opera". Another wonderful compilation is "Broadway Broads: There's Nothin' Like a Dame" (Sony); this collection features classic Broadway hits such as "Diamonds are a Girl's Best Friend" and "The Lady is a Tramp"

SETTING THE STAGE

String white twinkling lights (Christmas lights) throughout the room, wrap around plants or around windows and doors. Tie your place cards on shiny red apples to indicate seating arrangements. Set out any souvenir theatre programmes on your coffee table. Obtain a selection of magazines or promotional items from the state with the "I Love NY" slogan. Go to your local travel agent and get some New York City travel brochures to decorate your table. Attending the theatre is usually a fancy occasion; sometimes a black tie affair. But instead of wearing formal attire, decorate in a black tie style. Use crisp white tablecloths on your table and tie black bows around dining chairs or wrap a bow around the cutlery at each place setting. Use the finest serving pieces you own along with real linen napkins. Make it a special evening. Dine by candlelight with soft music playing in the background. If you live in a highrise, set up your dining area so that you have a view of the city lights.

a streetcar named desire (1951)

Elia Kazan, who directed both the stage and film versions of the Tennessee Williams' plays, said of Tennessee: "Everything in his life is in his plays, and everything in his plays is in his life." The storyline in the film, which is set in colourful New Orleans, involves the volatile relationship between a violent man, his wife and sister-in-law. Blanche DuBois, played by Vivien Leigh, is the emotionally wounded sister-in-law who has, "always relied on the kindness of strangers." She tries to start a new life when she comes to visit her pregnant sister Stella. But her brother-in-law, Stanley, despises her aristocratic nature, and thinks she is holding out on some inheritance money that he believes his wife Stella is entitled to. Stanley and Blanche inevitably clash. Despite her efforts to portray herself as a lady, especially in the presence of Stanley's friend Mitch, to whom she finds herself attracted; she finds cannot escape her torrid past as Stanley does not hesitate to tell Mitch about it. The tension between Stanley and Blanche builds until the final confrontation which negatively affects all three characters.

FEATURED ACTORS
Vivien Leigh (Blanche DuBois)
Marlon Brando (Stanley Kowalski)
Kim Hunter (Stella Kowalski)
Karl Malden (Mitch)
Rudy Bond (Steve Hubbell)

DIRECTOR ~ Elia Kazan

menu

cornmeal cheese fritters • jambalaya or bbq spicy cajun shrimp • cajun caesar salad • tart à la bouie or fresh fruit with amaretto cream

cornmeal cheese fritters
Yield: 24 fritters

1 cup	cornmeal		1 tsp	salt
1 cup	sharp cheese (Cheddar, Swiss, etc.), grated			cayenne, to taste
1/2 cup	onions, grated		3/4 cup	water
1/4 cup	red bell peppers, finely chopped			vegetable oil for frying
				hot sauce

• In a bowl, combine cornmeal, cheese, onions, bell peppers, salt, and cayenne. Stir into boiling water and mix thoroughly. In a deep, heavy pan or deep fryer heat 3 inches of vegetable oil to 350°F.

Drop 6 spoonfuls of the batter into the oil and fry for 2 to 3 minutes or until golden brown. Transfer fritters to paper towels to drain. Season with additional salt if desired. Serve warm with hot sauce.

jambalaya
serves 4 to 6

6	slices bacon, chopped		1/2 tsp	salt
1	onion, chopped		1/2 tsp	pepper
2	green bell peppers, finely sliced		1/4 tsp	paprika
2	garlic cloves, chopped		1/4 tsp	cayenne pepper
1-1/4 cups	long grain white rice		1/4 tsp	onion powder
1	19-ounce can crushed tomatoes, drained		1/4 tsp	garlic powder
			2 cups	chicken broth
1/4 tsp	fresh thyme, chopped		3/4 cup	smoked ham, diced
1/2 tsp	fresh basil, chopped		12	shelled raw shrimp
				fresh parsley, chopped

• In a heavy-bottom casserole, cook bacon over medium heat until crisp. Remove from casserole and reserve.

• Cook onion in bacon drippings until transparent. Add peppers and garlic and sauté for another 3 to 4 minutes. Stir in the rice and continue to cook for another few minutes until the rice becomes slightly opaque.

• Add the tomatoes, bacon, thyme, basil, salt, pepper and other spices, mixing well. Add the chicken broth and bring to boil then reduce the heat to low. Cover and let simmer for about 20 minutes. Add the ham and mix again. Cover the casserole and place on lower rack of oven. Bake for about 10 minutes, then add the shrimp, sinking them in the dish, cook for another 10 minutes or until the rice is tender and the remaining broth has been absorbed. If the rice seems a little dry add more broth. Decorate with fresh chopped parsley.

trivia clips

"They told me to take a streetcar named Desire, transfer to one called Cemeteries, and ride six blocks and get off at Elysian Fields," Blanche DuBois says in the film. The semantics foretell the future!

The Legion of Decency censored about four minutes of film footage, apparently Hunter's Stella was eyeing Stanley with too much desire. It was re-released in 1993.

a streetcar named desire (1951)

bbq spicy cajun shrimp

serves 4 to 6

In this recipe there are no measurements given for the spices-that is up to you! If you can handle the heat, then make your eyes weep!

1/2 cup	butter or margarine
3/4 cup	bottled hickory-flavoured BBQ sauce
2 tbsp	lemon juice
2 pounds	unshelled medium to

	large shrimp
	cayenne pepper to taste
	black pepper to taste
	garlic powder to taste
1/2 cup	dry sherry

- Turn on broiler and melt butter in a 13 x 9-inch broiler pan, or other ovenproof dish.
- Remove pan from oven and stir in BBQ sauce and lemon juice. Add shrimp and toss to coat. Spread out in pan.
- Sprinkle cayenne pepper, black pepper and garlic powder generously over the shrimp, remembering that the shell is

on the shrimp and not all seasoning will be absorbed!
- Broil five inches from the heat source for four minutes. Turn shrimp, add sherry and broil for four minutes longer.
- Let stand for a few minutes in order for shrimp to absorb the spices.

cajun caesar salad

serves 6

1	loaf of day-old Italian bread
3	garlic cloves, mashed
9 tbsp	extra virgin olive oil
1/4 tsp	plus 1 pinch kosher salt
2 heads	romaine lettuce, remove outer leaves

	black pepper to taste
1	lemon, juiced
6 drops	Worcestershire sauce
1/2 tsp	Cajun spice mix
2	eggs
1/4 cup	grated Parmesan cheese

- Heat oven to 350°F. Cut 1/2 to 3/4-inch croutons from the loaf of bread and place on a baking sheet and put into the oven, heat until dry, but not browned. Use a mortar and pestle or food processor to mash the garlic with 4 tablespoons of oil and 1/4 teaspoon kosher salt. Strain the oil into a skillet over medium heat. Add the dried croutons and fry, tossing constantly until all the oil is absorbed and the croutons turn gold. Set aside.

- In a very large bowl, tear lettuce and toss with 3 tablespoons of olive oil. Sprinkle with the remaining kosher salt and the black pepper. Add the remaining 2 tablespoons olive oil. Toss well. Add the lemon juice, Worcestershire sauce and Cajun spice mix. Break in the eggs. Toss until a creamy dressing forms. Toss in Parmesan cheese and serve with croutons.

AWARDS WON

Best Actress (Vivien Leigh)	1951 Academy Award
Best Art Direction (Richard Day / George James Hopkins)	1951 Academy Award
Best Supporting Actor (Karl Malden)	1951 Academy Award
Best Supporting Actress (Kim Hunter)	1951 Academy Award
10 Best Films	1951 National Board of Review of Motion Pictures
Best Actress (Vivien Leigh)	1951 New York Film Critics Circle Award
Best Direction (Elia Kazan)	1951 New York Film Critics Circle Award
Best Film (Elia Kazan)	1951 New York Film Critics Circle Award
Special Jury Prize (Elia Kazan)	1951 Venice Film Festival Award
Volpi Prize for Best Actress (Vivian Leigh)	1951 Venice Film Festival Award
Best British Actress (Vivian Leigh)	1952 British Academy Award
Best Film- Any source (Elia Kazan)	1952 British Academy Award
100 Greatest American Movies	1998 American Film Institute Award
U.S. National Film Registry	1999 Library of Congress Award

BEVERAGES

Try the famous New Orleans Hurricane cocktail (see main beverages page).

As a beer choice. you may wish to try any of the following: Sapporo Draft (Japan), Tiger Beer (Singapore) or Kingfisher Lager (Indian beer brewed in England). All of them would go well with the Jambalaya, and especially with the BBQ Shrimp. Casale Del Giglio Shiraz would be a good choice of red wine, as it can stand up to the intense spicy flavours of the main dishes. Another choice would be Negrar Valpolicella (Italy). If you prefer white wine, then try Pierre Sparr Pinot Blanc Reserve or Trimbach Pinot Blanc (both from France).

trivia clips

New Orleans is best known for its Mardi Gras celebration which starts annually on February 3rd and lasts until March 9th. The celebration known as Carnival came to be associated with Judeo-Christian tradition. It was first recorded in medieval Europe. The Latin word carnelevare, from which "carnival" is derived means "to lift up" or relieve from "flesh" or "meat"; it may have referred to the beginning of the Lenten season of atonement and abstinence rather than to the festive holiday customs that preceded Lent.

continued

MUSIC

Some zydeco music will liven up your evening! Like Cajun music, the dominant instrument is the accordion, but unlike Cajun music, zydeco adds electric bass, horns, and sometimes keyboards. Zydeco is Creole (black) dance music of southwest Louisiana. This style blends Cajun music with rhythm and blues and soul. Try the following CD's: "Zydecajun" (Kajun) by Wayne Toups, "The Rough Guide to Cajun & Zydeco" or "Zydeco on the Bayou" (Enigma) by Terrance Simien. A well balanced compilation CD is "Louisiana Spice: 25 Years of Louisiana Music" (Rounder). This CD features a variety of artists from the state performing nit only Cajun and zydeco, but R & B, country, blues and pop. Alternatively, some New Orleans jazz by the Mills Brothers on "Mills Brothers: The Anthology (1931-1968)", released by MCA, would be nice too.

SETTING THE STAGE

When you are in New Orleans the mood is always festive! Well-known for its famous Creole cuisine and its cultural influences by the French, Spanish, Germans, and Indians, New Orleans has all the right ingredients for a marvelous mix of flavours in both its food and scenery. Since Mardi Gras seems to have become a year-round celebration, this may be the time to bring a little bit of "NuhOrlans" (pronounced as one word) to your home. Set the table with colourful votive candles in clear or smokey glass holders. Streamers, balloons (purple, green, yellow) and party favours could decorate each table. As well, colourful masks could be placed on the walls. You could purchase the masks or make your own with a variety of feathers, sparkles, glow-in-the-dark markers, etc. Make each one different. Better yet, you could send undecorated masks along with your invitation to your guests and let them create their own to wear to the get together! Another recognized symbol of New Orleans is the King Cake. We have taken the basic idea, and made it easier. Purchase about a dozen cinnamon rolls. Put them on a plate, form a circle with the cinnamon rolls. Decorate by piping on more icing sugar, and adding berries, and gold or silver foiled candy. Make it as fancy as you like. In the centre of the King Cake, place a number of small boxes (number them). In one of the boxes, place a coffee bean (spray paint gold or use tinfoil). Have your guests draw for numbers (they should correspond to the numbers on the boxes). During the evening, each guest will have a chance to dance when his or her number is called. After they have danced, they can open their boxes to see if they have the lucky bean. The one who finds it, ends up being the "King or Queen" of luck and chance for the year. Perhaps you could even give the winner some lottery tickets to see how lucky they really are! Don't forget to purchase a number of inexpensive bead necklaces for your guests. Give them away by holding dance or "creative mask" contests (if they've made their own). These contests are a New Orleans tradition and the object is to obtain as many bead necklaces as possible. These necklaces can be purchased at dollar stores or party supply shops.

tart à la bouie

serves 4

This is a custard dessert given to the Cajuns and Creoles in Louisiana by the German settlers, though the French also lay claim to this simple, but delicious custard pie.

4 cups	heavy whipping cream		1/4 cup	melted butter
3	eggs		pinch	of nutmeg
1-1/4 cups	sugar		pinch	of cinnamon
2 tbsp	corn starch		2	9-inch pie shells, uncooked (store-bought or homemade)
2 tbsp	vanilla			

- Preheat oven to 350°F. In a heavy bottom saucepan, heat cream until scalding. In a large mixing bowl, combine eggs, sugar and cornstarch and using a wire whisk, blend ingredients until creamy. Set aside.

- Add vanilla, butter, nutmeg, and cinnamon to cream in saucepan and continue to whip until all ingredients are well-blended. Once cream has come to a low boil, ladle one cup of it into the egg mixture, stirring constantly while pouring. Once well-blended, pour egg mixture into the hot cream and stir continuously. Remove from heat and allow cooling slightly. Pour slightly cooled mixture into one of the pie shells. Using a sharp paring knife, cut the other pie shell into 1/2-inch strips. Lattice the strips across the top of the pie in a decorative fashion. Place pie on center oven rack and bake for 45 minutes or until crust is golden brown.

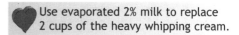 Use evaporated 2% milk to replace 2 cups of the heavy whipping cream.

fresh fruit with amaretto cream

serves 4

This would be an excellent alternate dessert to offer guests, especially those counting calories!

1 1/2 tbsp	Amaretto liqueur		1/2 cup	low-fat sour cream
2 tbsp	packed dark brown sugar		4 to 5 cups	fresh fruit (peeled, hulled etc., if necessary)

- In small mixing bowl combine Amaretto liqueur and brown sugar. Add sour cream and mix well. Prepare at least 2 hours before serving. Stir occasionally to dissolve brown sugar.

Put fruit into sherbet glasses or small soufflé dishes. Drizzle with sauce. Especially good with strawberries, blueberries and green grapes.

ben- hur (1959)

This film made history at the Academy Awards in 1959, winning 11 awards in total. Not until almost 40 years later would the Academy see such a sweep. Karl Tunberg adapted this film version from Lew Wallace's best-selling novel. It is the story of a Jewish prince, Judah Ben-Hur (Charlton Heston), who lives in Judea with his family during the time of Jesus Christ. Ben-Hur's childhood friend, Messala, grows up to become an ambitious Roman tribune, but when Ben-Hur refuses to help him round up local dissidents for the Emperor, Messala frames him, on a charge of attempting to kill the provincial governor; Ben-Hur is banished to the Roman galleys. Much to his dismay, his mother and sister are also imprisoned. During his ordeal as a prisoner, Ben-Hur saves the life of a commander during a sea battle. In gratitude, the commander not only adopts Ben-Hur as his son, but also gives him full control over his stable of racing horses. Though his life has improved, Ben-Hur can't give up trying to find his family and he still has a burning desire to seek revenge for the wrong Messala has done him. The chariot race is a legendary part of this 212 minute biblical epic. Those who enjoy historical drama must see this film!

FEATURED ACTORS
Charlton Heston (Judah Ben-Hur)
Stephen Boyd (Messala)
Jack Hawkins (Quintus Arrius)
Haya Harareet (Esther)
Hugh Griffith (Sheik Ilderim)

DIRECTOR ~ William Wyler

menu

antipasto in a baguette • mediterranean chicken with olives • couscous with dates and almonds • honey-glazed pears with figs and almonds or quince in wine syrup

antipasto in a baguette

Yield: 24 appetizer portions

2	small, thin baguettes
1/4 cup	bottled olive paste or tapenade
4 oz	mild goat cheese
1/4 lb	thinly sliced Italian salami or prosciutto
2 cups	packed arugula leaves or baby spinach, washed well and spun dry

1	7 oz jar roasted red peppers, drained, rinsed, and patted dry
1	7 oz jar roasted eggplant, packed in oil, drained
1	13 to 14 oz can whole artichoke hearts, drained, rinsed, patted dry, and chopped

- Cut top third off each baguette horizontally using a serrated knife. Remove soft crumb from tops and bottoms, leaving shells about 1/2-inch thick. Spread about 1 tablespoon olive paste or tapenade on inside of each bottom shell and top with goat cheese, spreading it evenly. Fold salami or prosciutto slices in half and fit them in an even layer over cheese in each shell. Arrange half of arugula or spinach on each meat layer and top with a layer of roasted peppers and eggplant. Divide artichoke hearts between bottom shells and spread inside of top shells with remaining olive paste.

- Fit top shells over bottom shells and press baguette together, re-forming loaves. Wrap each baguette tightly in foil and chill at least 3 hours or overnight.

- Cut each baguette diagonally into 12 slices using a serrated knife and secure each slice with a wooden pick.

trivia clips

Ben-Hur was one of the top grossing films of 1959. It held the record of the most Academy Awards won until the release of Titanic in 1997. Interestingly, neither film won the Academy for Best Screenplay.

ben-
hur

(1959) right continued

AWARDS WON

Best Actor (Charlton Heston)	1959 Academy Award
Best Director (William Wyler)	1959 Academy Award
Best Art Direction (Hugh Hunt, William Horning, Edward C. Carfagno)	1959 Academy Award
Best Cinematography (Robert Surtees)	1959 Academy Award
Best Picture	1959 Academy Award
Best Score (Miklos Rozsa)	1959 Academy Award
Best Sound (Franklin E.Milton)	1959 Academy Award
Best Editing (John D. Dunning, Ralph Winters)	1959 Academy Award
Best Supporting Actor (Hugh Griffith)	1959 Academy Award
Best Film-Any source (William Wyler)	1959 British Academy Award
Best Film-Any source (Andrew Marton)	1959 British Academy Award
Best Actor (Charlton Heston)	1959 New York Film Critics Circle Award
Best Direction (William Wyler)	1959 New York Film Critics Circle Award
Best Film (Andrew Marton)	1959 New York Film Critics Circle Award
Best Screenwriting (Karl Tunberg)	1959 New York Film Critics Circle Award
Best Director (William Wyler)	1960 Golden Globe Award
Best Supporting Actor	1960 Golden Globe Award
100 Greatest American Movies	1998 American Film Institute Award

BEVERAGES

A light-bodied red wine such as Jaffelin Bourgogne Passetoutegrain (France) would complement the tomato and olive flavours in the main dish. Otherwise, you may wish to serve a Zinfandel such as Fetzer Zinfandel (USA) or a Ruffino Chianti (Italy). Duvel Belgian beer would also be suitable.

mediterranean chicken with olives serves 4

2 tsp	olive oil	4	boneless chicken breast halves
1 cup	onions, chopped	1/2 cup	chicken broth
3 tsp	garlic, minced	1	can (about 14 oz) diced tomatoes, drained
1 tbsp	grated lemon zest	1/3 cup	pitted kalamata olives, halved
1 tsp	dried thyme		
1/2 tsp	salt		
1/4 tsp	pepper		

- In a large skillet, heat oil over medium heat. Sauté onion and garlic until onion is transparent.
- Combine lemon zest, thyme, salt, and pepper; rub over chicken. Move onion mixture to center of skillet and add chicken around the sides. Cook chicken for about 4 minutes per side.

Add half of the broth to keep chicken moist. Add remainder of broth as required so that the skillet is not dry, cover with lid and cook for about 3 to 5 minutes. Remove chicken from skillet; add tomatoes and olives, gently sauté until heated through. Serve tomato and olive mixture over chicken breasts.

couscous with dates and almonds serves 4

2-1/2 cups	chicken broth or water	1/4 tsp	ground cumin
2 tbsp	unsalted butter	1/4 tsp	ground cinnamon
1/4 cup	sliced almonds, toasted	1/2 tsp	salt
1/4 cup	dates, finely chopped	pinch	of cayenne pepper
2 tbsp	chopped fresh mint, parsley, or cilantro	2-1/4 cup	quick-cooking couscous
		1 tbsp	honey (optional)

- In a medium sized saucepan over high heat, bring the chicken broth or water and the butter to a boil. Reduce heat to medium; add the almonds, dates, parsley, cumin, cinnamon, salt, and cayenne pepper. Stir gently, then add the couscous and cover the pan.

Cook according to package directions or until all the liquid has been absorbed. Remove the saucepan from the heat and let stand for 5 minutes. Fluff with fork before serving. Drizzle honey over top if so desired.

trivia clips

What are Vestal Virgins? Traditionally, they consisted of six priestesses from important Roman families who organized the state cult of Vesta, goddess of the hearth. They remained virgins for their period of service (thirty years); they had certain privileges (for example, special seats at games and festivals) and could be very influential, especially the virgo maxima (chief vestal).

ben-hur (1959)

honey glazed pears with figs and almonds serves 4

1/2 cup	almonds, sliced
4	firm-ripe pears preferably Bartlett)
1/2 lb	dried figs (as soft as possible; about 12)
1/2 cup	granulated sugar

1/4 cup	unsalted butter
1	vanilla bean
1 tsp	cinnamon
1/4 tsp	ground allspice
1/2 cup	warmed honey

- Preheat oven to 450°F. In a heavy, ovenproof skillet, toast almonds in one layer over medium high heat on stove until golden, about 5 minute. Transfer to a bowl.

- Halve pears lengthwise and cut each half into 3 wedges, discarding cores. Quarter figs lengthwise. Put aside.

- In the same skillet you used to toast the almonds, melt sugar and butter over moderate heat, stirring occasionally, until sugar is melted completely. Remove skillet from heat. With a knife, halve vanilla bean lengthwise and scrape seeds into melted butter mixture. With a wooden spoon stir in vanilla pod, cinnamon, allspice, pears, and figs until coated. Place skillet in preheated oven, for 20 minutes or until pears are just tender. Remove vanilla pod and lightly brush pears and figs with warmed honey. Sprinkle almonds over the pear and fig mixture and serve.

quince in wine syrup serves 4

This ancient fruit has a flowery bouquet and originates in the Middle East. It usually grows wild in the Mediterranean and it is often served stewed in lamb or chicken dishes. Otherwise, it is used in jams and marmalades, or compote-like desserts such as the one below. Quince can be found in better supermarkets in the autumn.

2 cups	sugar
1/2 cup	water, or as needed
1/2 cup	white wine
2	whole cloves

2	cinnamon sticks
	lemon peel from 1 lemon
2 lbs	quince

- In a saucepan large enough to accommodate the sliced quince, combine the sugar, 1/2 cup water, 1/2 cup wine, cloves, cinnamon sticks and lemon peel. Place over medium heat and bring to a simmer, stirring to dissolve the sugar. Peel, halve, and core the quince. Cut into slices of about 1/2-inch thickness. Add the quince slices and additional water if needed to cover. Simmer over medium heat. Over the course of 3 hours, bring the quince slices to a boil three times in the syrup, boiling them for 5 minutes each time.
Check periodically to ensure that the quince slices do not become too soft. A fork should be able to pierce them with a bit of resistance. Transfer to a serving dish (remove lemon peel, cloves and cinnamon sticks)and refrigerate. Serve chilled.

trivia clips

Charlton Heston portrayed historical figures in two other films. In one of them he played the historical figure who almost became Prince of Egypt and leads his people through the parting of the Red Sea. In the other film, the historical figure he portrays is a well-known Spaniard. Can you name the films?

MUSIC

The late Ofra Haza, a world-renowned singer from Israel, recorded a wonderful album entitled "Yemenite Songs". The album features ancient melodies taught to her by her mother who grew up in Yemen. Traditional instruments and lyrics, some by 16th century poet, Shalom Shabazi, are what make this album unique, as is the fusion of modern instruments with ancient ones found on some of the cuts. The single from this album "Im Nin'alu" reached high up on the Top 20 lists of many European dance charts in the mid to late 80's.

SETTING THE STAGE

Remember that old saying when in Rome ... do as the Romans do. The Roman aristocrats were well-known for their lavish parties. The wealthy host would boast about his wealth and provide the best of everything for his guests. Food was plentiful and so was the wine. It is said that the Romans did not sit at their dinner tables, but instead they would recline on their left elbow and pick the food off the table with their fingers. Arrange to have huge throw pillows on the floor around your coffee table. Move some of the furniture and have a couple of additional low tables surrounded by pillows. Drape the tables with white linens and tie the ends with gold tassels. Use decanters to serve wine or non-alcoholic drinks. Have a variety of fresh fruits: apples, pears, grapes, etc. served on a platter. You could also offer breads with feta cheeses, olives, and pickled red peppers. This is a fun way to watch the movie and enjoy tasty appetizers at the same time. No utensils! Fingers only. If watching the movie with family, the children will certainly love this idea. On your main table, arrange artificial grape bunches and vine leaves along with fancy clear bottles filled with olive oil. Using a fine-tipped marker write your guests' names on each glass and be creative ... look through a Latin book and pick a word or a phrase to go under that person's name. You could play a game by writing out phrases in Latin, and having people try to figure out what they mean. Alternatively, you could make it a costume party-have guests wear togas!

from here to eternity (1953)

Based upon the best-selling novel of the same name by James Jones, this film was eagerly anticipated by those who read the book. The location is hot and steamy Honolulu in the days just before the attack on Pearl Harbour. At Schofield army barracks, the dreams, desires and disappointments of a number of characters are magnified. Living in such a closed community as is found on an army base, people find themselves drawn into the human dramas of those around them. Sergeant Milton Warden becomes a little too friendly with Karen, the bored wife of his commanding officer, which of course create a dilemma for both characters. Then there is "Prew" who has his own way of doing things and who has never really been fully accepted by most of those around him. Prew does have a best friend though, Maggio, who is looked upon with contempt by his sadistic and vicious stockade Sergeant Judson. When Maggio dies due to brutality on the part of Judson Prew sets out on a vengeful course. In the end, he does avenge his friend's death and finds shelter and solace with a prostitute named Alma Lorene. This does not last long though, as Prew tries to return to help his comrades after the Japanese attack.

FEATURED ACTORS

Burt Lancaster (Sgt. Milton Warden), Montgomery Clift (Robert E.Lee Prewitt), Deborah Kerr (Karen Holmes), Donna Reed (Alma Lorene), Frank Sinatra (Angelo Maggio), Ernest Borgnine (Sgt. Judson)

DIRECTOR ~ Fred Zinnemann

menu polynesian pork kebabs with pineapple • cilantro rice • your favourite green salad • hawaiian paradise cake

Pineapple is one of Hawaii's biggest exports. It is a wonderful addition to many foods. Both the main dish and dessert on this menu feature this lovely fruit.

polynesian pork kebabs with pineapple
serves 4 to 6

2 tbsp	red-wine vinegar
1	garlic clove, minced and mashed to a paste with 1/2 teaspoon salt
1 tbsp	dried hot red pepper flakes
1/4 cup	vegetable oil
1-1/2 lbs	boneless trimmed pork shoulder or pork loin, cut into 1-inch pieces
1/4 cup	ketchup
2 tbsp	vinegar
2 tbsp	sugar
2 tsp	soy sauce
1/2 tsp	salt
1/4 tsp	dark sesame oil
1	large fresh pineapple, peeled, cored, and cut into 3/4-inch-thick wedges
ten	10-inch wooden skewers, soaked in water for 30 minutes or metal skewers

- In a large bowl, whisk together the red-wine vinegar, garlic paste, and the red pepper flakes; add the vegetable oil in a stream, and whisk the marinade until it is emulsified. Add the pork, stirring to coat pieces with the marinade, and let it marinate, covered and chilled, for at least 6 hours or overnight.

- In a bowl, whisk together the ketchup, vinegar, sugar, soy sauce, salt, and sesame oil until the sugar is dissolved. Reserve this sweet-and-sour sauce.

- Drain the pork, reserving the marinade. Thread the pork pieces and pineapple wedges, alternating them, onto the skewers. Brush the kebabs with the reserved marinade and grill on a rack set 5 to 6 inches over glowing coals, basting them for the first 10 minutes with the reserved marinade. Turn frequently. Grill until the pork is just cooked through, but still juicy. Brush the kebabs with the reserved sweet-and sour sauce and grill them, turning them once, for 2 minutes more. (Discard any remaining marinade; do not serve it as an accompaniment.)

cilantro rice
serves 4

4 cups	water
2 tsp	salt
1 tsp	olive oil
3	garlic cloves, finely chopped
2 cups	long-grain rice
1/2 cup	fresh cilantro, washed, dried, and chopped
	salt and pepper to taste

- In a saucepan with a tight-fitting lid, add water, salt, oil, garlic and bring to a boil. Stir in rice and cook, covered, over low heat for 20 minutes, or until water is absorbed and rice is tender. Fluff rice with a fork and toss with cilantro and salt and pepper to taste.

hawaiian paradise cake

serves 8 to 10

2-1/2 cups	all-purpose flour		4	eggs
2 cups	sugar		3	ripe bananas, mashed
1-1/2 tsp	baking powder		1	14 oz can unsweetened crushed pineapple
2 tsp	baking soda			
1 tsp	salt		1 tsp	vanilla
2 tsp	ground cinnamon		2 tsp	dark rum
1 cup	vegetable oil			

- Preheat oven to 350˚F. Lightly grease, or spray with cooking spray, a 13 X 9-inch baking pan. Combine flour, sugar, baking powder, baking soda, salt, and cinnamon in a large bowl. Add the rest of the ingredients. Beat with an electric mixer at medium speed for one minute. Pour batter into prepared pan. Bake one hour or until toothpick comes out clean. Cool in pan on wire rack for 5 minutes.

 Use egg substitute for 2 of the eggs called for, and reduce oil to 3/4 cup.

macadamia topping

1/3 cup butter or margarine

1 cup brown sugar

3/4 cup shredded coconut

1/2 cup macadamia nuts

- Preheat broiler. Cream butter or margarine, and sugar together until fluffy. Add coconut and macadamia nuts. Mix well. Spread over hot cake. Place 6 inches below broiler. Broil until topping is bubbly and golden, about 3 minutes. Let cake cool in pan. To serve, cut into squares. If you are feeling decadent, serve the cake with ice cream or whipped cream on top.

 Use non-hydrogenated unsalted margarine instead of butter. It is a healthier type of fat.

AWARDS WON

Best Cinematography (Burnett Guffey)	1953 Academy Award
Best Director (Fred Zinnemann)	1953 Academy Award
Best Picture	1953 Academy Award
Best Screenplay (Daniel Taradash)	1953 Academy Award
Best Sound (John P.Livadary)	1953 Academy Award
Best Supporting Actor (Frank Sinatra)	1953 Academy Award
Best Supporting Actor (Donna Reed)	1953 Academy Award
10 Best Films	1953 National Board of Review of Motion Pictures
Best Actor (Burt Lancaster)	1953 New York Film Critics Circle Award
Best Direction (Fred Zinnemann)	1953 New York Film Critics Circle Award
Best Film (Fred Zinnemann)	1953 New York Film Critics Circle Award
Special Recognition Prize (Fred Zinnemann)	1954 Cannes Film Festival Award
Best Supporting Actor	1954 Golden Globe Award
100 Greatest American Movies	1998 American Film Institute Award

BEVERAGES

Try some tropical cocktails. We suggest: Honolulu Cooler, Mangorita, Cococolada, Melon-Berry Slush, Lemon Blue Dolphin, Mint-Melon Julep or Peachsicle (all drink recipes in main beverages section).

If you want to serve wine, try Balbach Riverside Riesling (Germany); for a red wine try Fleur de Carneros Pinot Noir. Both of these enhance wines enhance this fruit-accented menu. In terms of beer, you may wish to serve Red Stripe (Jamaica).

MUSIC

We suggest the late Hawaiian singer, Israel Kamakawiwo'ole. One of his popular albums is "Facing Future" (Mountain Apple) and it features some songs familiar to us all, such as "Country Roads" and "Somewhere Over the Rainbow". Another Hawaiian music sensation is Keali'I Reichel, who mixes American style pop with traditional Hawaiian chanting. The following albums are worth listening to: "Kawaipunahele" (Punahele) and "E O Mai" (Punahele). For traditional Hawaiian music try "Golden Hawaiian Melodies" (Tropical Music) by the Makaha Brothers.

SETTING THE STAGE

Place bamboo tiki torches outside your home's entrance. If it is dusk or evening, light them to create a magnificent path to your front door. Buy leis for your guests at a party supply store; greet your guests at the door when they arrive by placing one or more around their neck. Create a tropical paradise in your dining area for an Hawaiian luau. Use real or imitation plants. If you have large house plants such as date palms or ficus plants, use them as a backdrop. You could even string tiny lights on them, dim the overhead lights and use only the lights on the plants. Buy a few tropical flowers to use for a dramatic centrepiece. If your budget won't allow for real flowers, use silk ones. They are reasonably priced and almost resemble the real thing except for the scent! Alternatively, buy some tropical fruits such as mango, papaya and coconut and place them decoratively in a basket, intersperse some flowers throughout and you have a practical, yet beautiful centrepiece. Buy helium balloons in the shape of fish, palm trees, etc. place them around your dining area or patio. Top your table in tropical colours. Bring out summer place mats and tablecloths in brilliant hues of pink, yellow and green, etc. Use glassware in summer colours, bring out a pitcher with matching glasses for the drinks. Serve drinks in hollowed out coconuts or other fruits, use colourful straws. Decorate drinks with the bright, little drink umbrellas- and don't forget to garnish with fruit or tropical motif stir sticks. If it is warm out, take your party into the backyard. You can buy scented candles that hint of tropical scents such as coconut and pineapple. For fun have guests do the limbo, make it a contest with prizes for the winner!

rebel without a cause (1955)

This is the landmark movie that the late James Dean is best remembered for. It made him an icon for the era. It is a coming-of-age drama that deals with a group of troubled teenagers. Dean plays the role of Jimmy Stark, a young man who has given his parents much heartbreak as they move the family from place to place, hoping to give their son a fresh start and clean break from his past. The film's action takes place over a 24-hour period. It opens with an appearance in night court by the young Jimmy, who has been arrested for being drunk and disorderly. The next day he starts as a student at a new high school. It does not take long for trouble to come his way as he meets characters such as Judy, who likes to take a walk on the wild side, and Plato, an attention-seeking misfit. Jimmy is also noticed by the local gang leade,r Buzz, who is also Judy's boyfriend. Buzz bullies Jimmy into a reckless test of nerves that will ultimately lead to the deaths of two people and affect forever the lives of those left behind.

FEATURED ACTORS
James Dean (Jimmy Stark)
Natalie Wood (Judy)
Corey Allen (Buzz Gunderson)
Virginia Brissac
    (Jimmy's Grandmother)
Sal Mineo (Plato)
Ann Doran (Jimmy's mother)
Dennis Hopper (Goon)
Jim Backus (Jimmy's father)

DIRECTOR – Nicholas Ray

AWARDS WON

Best Direction (Nicholas Ray)	1955 New York Film Critics Circle Award
Best British Film (Nicholas Ray)	1956 British Academy Award
U.S. National Film Registry	1990 Library of Congress Award
100 Greatest American Movies	1998 American Film Institute Award

menu
spicy california style onion rings • veal or tofu wieners on a sesame roll • patriotic vegetable platter (see index) • malibu sundaes

This is a menu that would appeal to kids and teenagers, as well as those who are still young at heart.

spicy california style onion rings   serves 4

These rings are a tribute to the influence of Latin flavours found in California cuisine. They are great with hotdogs, and with burgers or steak as well.

4 cups	buttermilk
2 large	Vidalia or Bermuda onions (about 2 pounds), cut into 1/4-inch thick rounds, separated into rings
	vegetable oil (for deep frying)

3 cups	all-purpose flour
3 tbsp	ground cumin
3 tbsp	chili powder
1 tbsp	salt
1 tbsp	cayenne pepper

• Place buttermilk in large bowl. Add onion rings and toss to coat. Let stand at room temperature 20 minutes or up to 1 hour, turning onions occasionally.

• Pour enough oil into large, heavy saucepan to reach depth of 3 inches. Heat to 350°F.

• Mix flour, cumin, chili powder, salt and cayenne in large bowl. Remove a handful of onion rings from buttermilk; add to flour mixture and toss to coat. Add onion rings to oil; cook until crisp and golden brown, about 2 minutes. Using tongs, transfer to paper towels and drain. Repeat with remaining onion rings, in batches. Mound in bowl and serve.

trivia clips

Three of the film's stars met with untimely, mysterious deaths. James Dean died prematurely in a car accident on September 30, 1955, shortly after the film was released. Sal Mineo was murdered near his home in Hollywood and the striking Natalie Wood drowned under puzzling circumstances near Catalina Island.
A real life gang member acted as consultant for the fighting scenes.

rebel without a cause (1955)

malibu sundaes

serves 4

The twist to these adult-flavoured sundaes is a simple ginger-flavoured sauce laced with Malibu (a coconut-flavoured rum) and lime. It can be made ahead and rewarmed before you assemble the sundaes.

Malibu Sundae Sauce

1/2 cup	sugar
1/2 cup	firmly packed golden brown sugar
3 tbsp	water
3 tbsp	Malibu (or dark rum + 1 tsp coconut extract)
1/4 cup	strained fresh lime juice
3 tbsp	unsalted butter
2 pieces	crystallized ginger
3 tbsp	minced crystallized ginger

Sundaes

	vanilla ice cream
3 cups	diced peeled tropical fruit such as pineapple, papaya, mango, guava and berries
	toasted sweetened shredded coconut

For sauce:

- Combine first 7 ingredients in heavy, medium saucepan. Stir over medium heat until sugars dissolve. Boil gently until reduced to 1 cup, stirring frequently, about 15 minutes. Cool to lukewarm. Discard ginger pieces and add minced ginger. (Can be prepared 1 day ahead. Cover and store at room temperature. Reheat to lukewarm, whisking occasionally, before serving.)

For sundaes

- Scoop ice cream into dessert or sundae dishes. Spoon lukewarm sauce over. Top with fruit. Sprinkle with coconut and serve.

Rather than offer regular ice cream, serve fat-reduced ice cream or frozen yogurt.

BEVERAGES

Root Beer Floats (see main beverages section), Cola, Milk Shakes (see main beverages section) or your favourite American beer

MUSIC

You must of course listen to some 1950's rock and roll, which was considered rebellious at the time! Remember that during this era censors wouldn't allow Elvis Presley to be filmed below the waist (in case the sight of swiveling hips was too much for the audience) during television appearances. There is a wide variety of 50's compilation albums available, here are a few suggestions: "50's Jukebox Hits" (Universal Special Markets), "Chart Topper: Dance Hits of the 50's" (Priority), and "Classic 50's Hits" (ITC Master). For those making it a romantic evening, we suggest: "Chart Toppers: Romantic Hits of the 50's" (Priority).

SETTING THE STAGE

If you're planning on inviting guests, send them unique invitations; buy some old 45's at a flea market or used record store (or perhaps you have some packed away in storage) and write out the details of the party on the record using silver or gold paint pens that are available at stationery stores. Request that guests wear their favourite 50's style clothes (leather coats and blue jeans, poodle skirts, capri pants, etc.).

You may wish to go to a party supply store for 50's style decorations, some feature cut-outs from the decade, such as guys and dolls signs for the washrooms. Have music from the era playing as your guests arrive. Use stacks of 45's to weigh down helium 50's theme balloons (jukebox or instrument shaped balloons are available) as a centrepiece.

If you have any 50's era vintage dinnerware, use it to set your table. Alternatively, create a diner atmosphere. Use paper place mats (available at party supply stores). Use coloured glassware in shades of blue or green. If you plan ahead, you can scout around for 50's era dinnerware at thrift stores and flea markets.

After watching the film and having dinner, burn some calories by holding a dance contest, or get a hula hoop and hold a contest to see which of your guests can hula the longest! No matter which decade you were born in, you will enjoy a 50's theme party!

trivia clips

Originally the filming was started in black and white, but because Dean's film East of Eden was doing very well, existing footage of Rebel Without a Cause was thrown out and the film was reshot in colour.
Contrary to popular belief, the red jacket James Dean wore in the film was a red nylon windbreaker, and not a red leather jacket.

roman
holiday (1953)

The then young starlet, Audrey Hepburn, stars in this delightful romantic comedy. The captivating actress plays Princess Anne, who is on a diplomatic visit to Rome the Eternal City. Anne is stifled by all of the protocol surrounding her and yearns to explore the city just like any other tourist. She gives her royal chaperones the slip, and begins her exploration of Rome. She quickly meets an engaging American, Joe Bradley, played by the charismatic Gregory Peck, who pretends not to recognize her. He offers to give her a guided tour of the city; little does she know that he is a journalist hoping to get a hot story! To make matters worse, his friend is a photographer who secretly attempts to take photos of the unsuspecting princess. You can guess that Joe falls in love with her, after all, who wouldn't?

FEATURED ACTORS
Audrey Hepburn (Princess Anne)
Gregory Peck (Joe Bradley)
Eddie Albert (Irving Radovich)
Hartley Power (Mr. Hennessey)
Harcourt Williams (Ambassador)

DIRECTOR ~ William Wyler

menu
arugula and blue cheese bruschetta • spaghetti all'amatriciana • four seasons salad • breadsticks (optional and store-bought) • classic zabaglione

arugula and blue cheese bruschetta serves 6

This simple-to-prepare appetizer features a mix of tangy blue cheese, chopped toasted walnuts and peppery arugula.

	butter, room temperature	3 oz	blue cheese such as Gorgonzola, crumbled
18	1/4-inch-thick diagonal baguette bread slices	3 tbsp	finely chopped arugula
6 tbsp	chopped toasted walnuts		pepper to taste
			arugula leaves

• Preheat oven to 400°F. Spread butter over one side of each baguette slice.

• Arrange baguette slices on baking sheet, butter side up. Bake baguette slices until golden, about 12 minutes. Cool.

• Reduce oven temperature to 350°F. In a medium size bowl, mix walnuts,

Gorgonzola and arugula. Spoon the nut and cheese mixture evenly over baguette toasts, pressing to adhere. Season toasts with pepper. Bake toasts just until cheese melts, about 6 minutes. Cool slightly. Arrange bruschetta on platter. Garnish platter with arugula leaves and serve.

spaghetti alla'amatriciana serves 4 to 6

This is one of the most popular and beloved pasta recipes. It is a simple, peasant food originally from Amatrice, a small town near Rome. This dish was the favourite of shepherds, who used to make it, sometimes without tomatoes, as a quick, but filling meal.

1/2 lb	pancetta or bacon, diced	1 lb	spaghetti
1	chili pepper, minced	4 oz	grated pecorino romano cheese
1 tbsp	extra virgin olive oil		
1	28 ounce can of peeled tomatoes, preferably Italian		

• Brown bacon, and the minced chili pepper in a frying pan in one tablespoon of olive oil for 5 minutes at medium heat. Add the tomatoes and leave to cook for about 20 minutes or until sauce thickens. Cook the pasta, until "al dente",

then strain it and mix it with the tomato sauce and the pecorino romano cheese.

♥ Drain off all but 1 tbsp of the bacon fat prior to adding tomatoes.

trivia clips

This was one of the first Hollywood films to be shot almost entirely on location.
Audrey Hepburn influenced style and fashion with her slim, sophisticated, streamlined look.

roman holiday

four seasons salad

serves 4 to 6

2	heads of radicchio	1	small head Boston lettuce
2	heads Belgian endive	4 tbsp	vinaigrette (see index)
1	bunch arugula		

- Wash and strain the different salads, removing the outer leaves. Tear into small pieces and place in a salad bowl, dress with vinaigrette and serve alongside breadsticks.

classic zabaglione

serves 6 to 8

This foamy custard is a traditional Italian dessert. It is delicious on its own, but even better spooned over fresh fruit or served with biscotti.

6	large egg yolks	4 tbsp	dry Marsala wine
1/2 cup	sugar		

- In a metal bowl with a whisk or hand-held electric mixer, beat together all ingredients until well combined. Set bowl over a saucepan of barely simmering water and beat mixture until tripled in volume, about 5 minutes. To ensure that eggs are cooked, beat mixture 3 minutes more.
- Serve zabaglione immediately. Use wine glasses instead of dessert dishes; serve with tall spoons.

BEVERAGES

Campari (Italian aperitif) on ice; before dinner.

Red wine is a must for this zesty pasta sauce, try: Ruffino Chianti or Masi Modello Delle Venezie, both from Italy.

Roman Holiday Punch or Roman Snowball (see main beverages page)

Sambuca (after dinner, or in coffee)

Espresso or cappuccino

MUSIC

Listen to some Italian folk music. Try "Italian Treasury: Folk Music and Songs of Italy"

American singer Connie Francis went back to her roots and recorded in Italian. You may wish to try her two volume CD edition called "The Italian Collection" (PolyGram). It features songs from her previous five Italian albums. There is of course a rendition of "Arrivederci Roma" in the compilation! If you wish to listen to some more modern Italian music we suggest anything by any of the following artists: Umberto Tozzi, Eros Ramazotti or Toto Cotugno.

SETTING THE STAGE

Bring some of the atmosphere of "Bella Italia" and "Bella Roma" into your home. Use streamers or balloons of red, white and green to decorate your entry hall and home. If you have any ceramic serving plates or a pasta set, use them. Create the look of a trattoria in your dining area. Use an old Chianti bottle, or any attractive old wine bottle as a candle holder. Lay out a red and white checker tablecloth or napkins on your table. Place cruets of olive oil and red-wine vinegar on the table. Put on some of the suggested music and enjoy the simple, but delicious meal!

some like it hot (1959)

This hilarious movie is set in the Roaring Twenties during Prohibition. It's about two musicians (Jack Lemmon and Tony Curtis), who have the misfortune to be playing in a jazz band at gangster Spats Columbo's speakeasy, when it is raided by cop Mulligan (Pat O'Brien). Because of the raid, they're left without jobs. Several weeks later, while playing elsewhere, the two struggling musicians witness a St. Valentine's Day massacre between two gangs. Afraid of being next on a mobster's hit list, they try to find a way out of the city. So they dream up a plan that will let them leave incognito. The two dress up as women, Josephine and Daphne, and join an all-female band led by singer Sugar Kane (Marilyn Monroe). While surrounded by attractive women, the two are in a dilemma: they can't hope to act upon their desires while in their female personas. While in Miami, things get even more complicated when gangster Spats Columbo and his entourage appear! In addition to Joe/Josephine falling for Sugar, Jerry, as Daphne, has a rich suitor who will not take "no" for an answer. These elements make for a clever, gender-bending comedy. The acting is superb in this consistently funny and enduring film.

FEATURED ACTORS
Marilyn Monroe (Sugar Kane)
Tony Curtis (Joe/Josephine)
Jack Lemmon (Jerry/Daphne)
George Raft (Spats Columbo)
Pat O'Brien (Mulligan)

DIRECTOR ~ Billy Wilder

menu
artichoke bruschetta • italian style romaine salad • quick and easy chicago style deep dish pizza • simply the best tiramisu

artichoke bruschetta
serves 4 to 6

1	6 oz jar marinated artichoke hearts, drained, patted dry, chopped	2 tbsp	parsley, chopped
		5 to 6 tbsp	mayonnaise
1/4 cup	grated Romano cheese	16	1/3-inch-thick slices French baguette
1/4 cup	grated Parmesan cheese		
1/3 cup	finely chopped red or white onions		

- Place first 5 ingredients in a bowl. Mix in enough mayonnaise to form thick spread.
- Preheat broiler. Top bread slices with spread. Arrange bruschetta on baking sheet. Broil until spread is heated through and begins to turn golden, about 2 minutes.

♥ Use low fat mayonnaise.

italian style romaine salad
serves 4 to 6

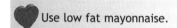

	Italian bread cut into 1/2-inch cubes to measure 1 cup		cheese plus additional for sprinkling, if desired
3 tbsp	olive oil	1/8 tsp	dried oregano, or to taste, crumbled
	salt and pepper to taste	1	large head of romaine lettuce, washed, spun dry, and torn into bite-size pieces
1	small garlic clove, minced		
1 tbsp	balsamic vinegar		
1 tbsp	water	1/2	small red onion, sliced thinly
3 tbsp	freshly grated Parmesan		

- Preheat the oven to 350°F. In a small bowl toss the bread cubes with 1 tablespoon of the olive oil (add salt to taste). On a baking sheet, toast them in the middle of the oven for 10 minutes, or until they are golden.
- Transfer the croutons to a salad bowl and let them cool. In a blender or small food processor blend together garlic, vinegar, water, 3 tablespoons

of the Parmesan cheese, oregano, remaining 2 tablespoons olive oil, salt and pepper to taste until the dressing is well combined. To the croutons add the romaine, onion, and the dressing; toss well. Sprinkle it with the additional Parmesan.

🕐 Use ready-made croutons in place of making your own.

trivia clips

Apparently, Marilyn Monroe required 47 takes to get "It's me, Sugar" correct. She kept saying "Sugar, it's me" or "It's Sugar, me". In the end, the line had to be written on a blackboard for her!

In the film, Columbo (George Raft) sees one of Bonaparte's henchmen flipping a coin, and asks, "Where did you pick up that cheap trick?" In Scarface (1982), Raft played a mafia henchman who is remembered for the fact that he kept flipping a coin.

continued

quick and easy chicago style deep dish pizza
serves 4 to 6

2	28-ounce cans plum tomatoes, drained and coarsely chopped
2	large garlic cloves, pressed
2 tbsp	fresh flat leaf parsley, chopped
1-1/2 tsp	dried oregano, crumbled
1 tsp	dried basil, crumbled
3 tsp	olive oil

	cornmeal
1 lb	(1 loaf) frozen bread or pizza dough, thawed
1 lb	shredded mozzarella cheese (about 4 cups)
7 oz	thinly sliced pepperoni or ham
1/2 cup	grated Parmesan
1	red bell pepper, diced

- Preheat oven to 425°F. Place chopped tomatoes in strainer and drain well. In a bowl, combine tomatoes with garlic, parsley, oregano and basil. Brush 12-inch-diameter deep-dish pizza pan with 1 teaspoon oil. Sprinkle pan with cornmeal. Roll bread dough out to 13-inch round on lightly floured surface. Transfer dough to pan, extending 1 inch up the sides of the pan. Spread 1 cup of the tomato mixture on top of dough. Sprinkle half of mozzarella cheese over tomato mixture. Top with half of pepperoni and remaining tomato mixture.

Sprinkle with remaining mozzarella. Distribute remaining pepperoni atop mozzarella. Sprinkle with Parmesan cheese and red pepper. Drizzle with remaining 2 teaspoons olive oil. Bake until cheese bubbles and begins to brown and crust is golden brown, about 40 minutes.

 Order gourmet pizza from a place that uses a wood burning oven.

simply the best tiramisu
serves 6 to 8

Layers of espresso-soaked pound cake and cream cheese custard come together with chocolate. Tiramisu means "pick me up" in Italian-and this certainly does.

8 oz	(8 squares) semisweet chocolate
1 cup	sugar
4	egg yolks
1-1/2	teaspoons vanilla
4 oz	cream cheese, cut into pieces, room temperature

4 oz	ricotta cheese
1-3/4 cups	chilled whipping cream
1 tbsp	instant espresso powder diluted in 1-1/4 cups hot water, cooled
1	16-oz package lady finger biscuits

- Finely chop chocolate in processor. Set aside. Mix sugar and egg yolks in processor 30 seconds. Add vanilla and process until pale yellow, about 1 minute. Add cheeses in batches and blend until smooth. Transfer to medium size bowl. Cover and chill 1 hour.

- Beat whipping cream until stiff. Fold into cheese mixture. Cover and refrigerate until well chilled, about 1hour. (Can be prepared 2 days ahead.)

- Pour espresso into large shallow dish. Dip lady fingers in espresso, turning to coat all sides lightly. Arrange lady

fingers on bottom of a large, shallow dish, smoothing with fingers to mold together. Sprinkle with half of chopped chocolate, top with chilled cheese mixture. Sprinkle remaining chocolate on top. Cover and refrigerate at least 2 hours. (Can be prepared 1 day ahead.)

 Use low fat cream cheese and low fat ricotta. Rather than use whipping cream, use low fat whipped topping.

Purchase bakery or store-bought tiramisu.

AWARDS WON

Best Costume Design (Orry Kelly)	1959 Academy Awards
Best British Film (Billy Wilder)	1959 British Academy Award
Best Foreign Actor (Jack Lemmon)	1959 British Academy Award
10 Best Films	1959 New York Film Critics Circle Award
Best Actor (Jack Lemmon)	1960 Golden Globe Award
Best Actor in Musical/Comedy	1960 Golden Globe Award
Best Film in Musical/Comedy	1960 Golden Globe Award
U.S. National Film Registry	1989 Library of Congress Award
100 Greatest American Movies	1998 American Film Institute Award

BEVERAGES

For wine choices try: Ruffino Chianti (Italy), Masi Serègo Alighieri Rosso Valpolicella (Italy) or Rothschild Cabernet Sauvignon (France). In terms of beer, Pilsner Urquell (Czech Republic) would best complement the bold flavours on the menu.

MUSIC

For some vintage 20's tunes try "Some Like it Hot" (Contemporary/OJC), with songs such as "I Wanna be Loved by You" and "Sweet Sue". Otherwise, "The Definitive Duke Ellington" (Columbia), who set jazz standards with his music is an excellent choice.

SETTING THE STAGE

Arrange to have a "nightclub" scene with dim lighting. Set out munchies in small bowls on various tables in the area where you will be entertaining (e.g. roasted peanuts, cashews, and pretzels). Also, cut up a variety of different types of breads or use various crackers and serve with dips. Set up an open bar concept with all sorts of glasses, crushed ice, lemon twists, maraschino cherries, straws, and of course the parasols that decorate cocktails. This could also be a non-alcoholic event with different sodas, grenadine syrup and fruit juices. For a group party, you could request that your guests dress up as a member of the opposite sex. Have fun turn it into a contest with awards for the best cross-dressers!

vertigo

(1958)

FEATURED ACTORS
James Stewart
    (John "Scottie" Ferguson)
Kim Novak
    (Madeleine Elster/Judy Barton)
Barbara Bel Geddes
        (Marjorie "Midge" Wood)
Tom Helmore (Gavin Elster)
Henry Jones (Coroner)

DIRECTOR ~ Alfred Hitchcock

AWARDS WON

U.S. National Film Registry	1989 Library of Congress Award
100 American Greatest Movies	1998 American Film Institute Award

menu crispy pita treats • tortellini with mediterranean herbs • fried peppers • feta cheese (optional) • crusty bread or breadsticks (store-bought) • chocolate-mocha surprise ice cream cake

crispy pita treats

serves 4

This makes a perfect casual-occasion appetizer, and you can easily adjust the recipe to serve a crowd.

3 to 4	whole wheat pita bread pockets, split and cut into triangles	1/2 tsp	chili powder
		1/2 tsp	ground cumin
2 tsp	vegetable oil	1/4 tsp	black pepper
1 tsp	garlic salt		salsa or plain yogurt (optional)
1/2 tsp	sweet paprika		

- Preheat oven to 350°F. In medium size bowl, combine pita triangles and oil; toss until coated well. Arrange on baking sheet.
- In small bowl, combine garlic salt, paprika, chili powder, cumin and black pepper. Sprinkle both sides of the pita triangles. Bake for about 10 minutes, until golden brown. Serve with salsa or plain yogurt for dipping, if so desired.

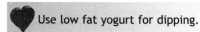 Use low fat yogurt for dipping.

tortellini with mediterranean herbs

serves 4

Try to buy fresh tortellini as opposed to the frozen for this recipe as it tastes so much better.). Tortellini comes in a variety of other flavours such as spinach and tomato, which makes the dish look quite vibrant. Use the colourful tortellini if you can find it.

1	1-lb package tortellini with cheese	1/2 cup	fresh oregano, chopped
1/2 cup	extra virgin olive oil	1/2 cup	fresh rosemary, chopped
4 to 5	cloves garlic, chopped		freshly ground pepper to taste
1 cup	fresh basil, chopped		freshly grated Parmesan cheese
1 cup	flat leaf parsley, chopped		

- In a large stockpot, bring salted water to a boil, add tortellini and cook until almost tender (al dente). Drain pasta when done.
- In a large, no-stick skillet, heat the olive oil over medium heat. Add the garlic and all of the herbs. Sauté for about 1 minute or until fragrant. Pour sauce over the tortellini, sprinkle with freshly ground pepper and grated parmesan cheese; serve on a platter.

trivia clips

The film was unofficially remade by director Brian De Palma in 1975 as Obsession. This federal penitentiary located near San Francisco was nicknamed "The Rock" and it was said to be escape-proof, yet many attempted the life-risking escape. Can you name it?? Hint: It was featured in a film starring Nicolas Cage and Sean Connery.

vertigo

fried peppers

serves 4

1/4 cup	olive or cooking oil
4	Cubanelle or Shepherd peppers (they don't all have to be the same colour or size)

salt and pepper to taste

- Heat the oil in a large skillet with a lid, over medium high heat. When the oil is hot, add the peppers and cover. Fry until peppers are soft and dark golden on all sides. Turn frequently during cooking to ensure that they don't burn, lowering heat if necessary. Place on a plate and sprinkle with salt and pepper.

feta cheese

This tangy cheese is a wonderful accompaniment to many dishes, this one included. Cut feta into cubes or slices and serve alongside the tortellini and peppers.
There are different types of feta cheese as well as reduced-fat versions. Any of them would be suitable.

BEVERAGES

Serve San Francisco cocktails before dinner (see main beverages section).

The flavours and herbs in this menu call out for a red wine! Try Talus Merlot (California), Mouton Cadet Red (France) or Two Oceans Cabernet Sauvignon/Merlot (South Africa). Otherwise, have a variety of different mineral waters for your guests to sample. Serve with a twist of lemon or lime.

MUSIC

Surprisingly, there is a CD that is a compilation from Hitchcock's best films. "Psycho: Essential Alfred Hitchcock" (Silva); this CD would hold a lot of appeal for fans of his films. For something different, try listening to some Brazilian jazz and pop, pick up "A Love Affair-The Music of Ivan Lins" (Telarc/Universal), a tribute album to the Brazilian singer and composer. Some of the featured artists on the CD are Sting, Vanessa Williams and Chaka Khan. Diana Krall's "When I Look In Your Eyes" (Verve/Universal) would be perfect for a romantic get together, as would be Holly Cole's "Romantically Helpless" (Alert Music/Universal Music).

trivia clips

In 1864, Mark Twain was a reporter for the San Francisco Daily Morning Call (from June-October).
"Blondes are the best victims. They're like virgin snow which shows up the bloody footprints." Sir Alfred Hitchcock, Sunday Times, 1 September 1973

vertigo
(1958)

82

continued

SETTING THE STAGE

The movie takes us through various psychological twists and turns and starts off with a focus on the main character's fear of heights. Purchase or borrow a few ladders and place in the corners of the room you will be entertaining in. On every other step of these ladders place a votive candle, for unique lighting. On top of the ladder, place a plant with long trailing stems (such as a spider plant or ivy). Since all in the film is not what it appears to be, have fun with this theme. Write a few messages backwards on mirrors throughout your house relating to the movie. Line the bottom of tall clear glass vase using dark glassy marbles, fill vase with water. Tie a few roses together using decorative curling ribbons and submerge the flowers in this vase upside down with stems up. As strange as this idea sounds, the roses look quite unique and impressive. You could use other kinds of flowers, but make sure the petals are sturdy. Put up some optical illusion posters, or those where you have to search for something in a very busy picture (e.g. Where's Waldo series of books and posters). Play a party game using anagrams that guests must figure out. Exchange stories about the most obsessive thing you've done for love . . .perhaps you have a story of how you spied on a lover and got caught, or how you would call to see if he or she was home and then hang up when they answered. Wasn't life more simple before call display? So spill the beans ... come on, admit it, we have all done something bordering on obsessive at least once!

chocolate-mocha surprise ice cream cake serves 10 to 12

Ice cream for adult palates! A beautiful dessert that layers chocolate and coffee ice creams with mocha sauce in an amaretti cookie crust. The surprise is the chocolate bars in the middle. Don't worry about the amount of servings, as this dessert can be refrozen!

Mocha Sauce

1-1/2 cups	water
1/2 cup	sugar
2-1/2 tbsp	instant espresso powder or double-strength brewed coffee
12 oz	(12 squares) semisweet chocolate, chopped
6 tbsp	(3/4 stick) unsalted butter

Crust

3 cups	amaretti cookie crumbs (Italian almond cookies, found in better supermarkets)
1/4 cup	(1/2 stick) unsalted butter, melted

Filling

2 pints	chocolate ice cream
2 pints	coffee ice cream
3/4 cup	chopped chocolate bar pieces (use chocolate bars that contain nuts or bars such as Skor or Almond Roca)

For sauce:

- Heat water, sugar and espresso in medium, heavy saucepan over low heat, stirring until sugar dissolves. Add chocolate and butter. Stir until chocolate and butter are melted and sauce is smooth. Cool completely.

 Use non-hydrogenated unsalted margarine in place of butter.

 Sauce can be prepared 3 days ahead. Cover and refrigerate. Bring sauce to room temperature before using.

For crust:

- Grease a 9-inch springform pan. Mix 2 cups of cookie crumbs and butter in medium bowl. Press firmly into bottom of prepared pan. Freeze until firm.

For filling:

- Soften chocolate ice cream in refrigerator until spreadable, but not melted. Spread over cookie crumb layer in pan and smooth top. Freeze until firm.

- Spoon 1/2 cup of prepared mocha sauce over layer of chocolate ice cream and sprinkle with remaining 1 cup cookie crumbs. Freeze until firm.

- Soften coffee ice cream in refrigerator until spreadable, but not melted. Spread in pan. Smooth surface and freeze until firm. Spread 1/2 cup mocha sauce over coffee ice cream. Sprinkle with chopped chocolate bar pieces and freeze until firm.

 Can be prepared 3 days ahead. Cover tightly with foil.

Soften cake slightly in refrigerator if necessary. Re-warm remaining mocha sauce over low heat until lukewarm, stirring frequently. Remove pan sides. Cut cake into wedges. Serve, passing warm mocha sauce around separately for those who wish to douse their dessert with more chocolate!

Use low fat ice cream. Omit the butter for the crust and use non-hydrogenated unsalted margarine or cooking spray.

viva
zapata! (1952)

menu mexican peasant soup • guacamole • rice con queso • beef tenderloin with cilantro sauce • deep-fried mexican style ice cream with tortilla fans and berry salsa

mexican peasant soup

serves 6 to 8

This recipe is very easy to make. Serve in small bowls with shredded cheese and tortilla chips.

2 tbsp	cooking oil		Tabasco sauce to taste
3/4 cup	onions, chopped	2 cups	vegetable broth
3/4 cup	celery, chopped	2 cups	(16 ounces) refried beans (store-bought in cans)
1/2 cup	green peppers, chopped		tortilla chips
1	clove garlic, minced		cheddar cheese, shredded
1/4 tsp	ground pepper		
1/4 tsp	chili powder		

- Heat oil in a stockpot over medium-high heat. Sauté vegetables until tender. Add spices, broth, and refried beans. Allow to simmer for 1 to 1-1/2 hours. Serve with tortilla chips and top with cheddar cheese if desired.

 Use low fat refried beans. It is possible to buy baked tortilla chips which are lower in fat than the regular kind. Use low fat cheese.

guacamole

Yiled: About 1-1/2 cups

For those concerned about the fat in avocados, there's a new smooth-skinned avocado from Florida, called the Brooks Lite, which contains 50 percent less fat and 35 percent fewer calories than the dark green pebbly-skinned Hass, the leading California variety. Regardless of which type you choose to make your guacamole, remember that the fat in avocados is monosaturated (the good fat), and avocados contain no cholesterol.

2	medium or 1 large ripe avocado	1/2 tsp	salt
2 tbsp	minced onion	1/4 tsp	coarsely ground black pepper
2 tbsp	chopped fresh cilantro	1	plum tomato, finely chopped or 1/4 cup salsa
1 tbsp	fresh lime juice		
2	serrano or jalapeño chilies, seeded and minced		

- Cut each avocado in half lengthwise; twist halves away from each other and remove seed. With spoon, scoop flesh into medium size bowl.
- Add the next 6 ingredients. With potato masher, coarsely mash mixture. Stir in tomato or salsa. Transfer to small serving bowl.

To increase your intake of vegetables, you may add a half cup of puréed green peas to the guacamole, and then add some low fat sour cream until desired consistency is reached.

This 1952 movie is based on the life of Mexican revolutionary leader Emiliano Zapata. The film follows the life of Zapata from his peasant roots, through to his rise to power in the early 1900s, and to his death. Zapata, the child of tenant farmers, grew up to lead a rebellion against the oppressive rule of then president, Porfirio Diaz. The film romanticizes Zapata somewhat and does not delve into the real reasons for the struggle he waged. He fought to free the land for the peasants of the southern provinces in Mexico. Today's Zapatistas in Mexico are valiantly fighting on for the underdog as they challenge the current political climate in Mexico and fight for the rights of the indigenous peoples.

FEATURED ACTORS
Marlon Brando (Emiliano Zapata)
Jean Peters (Josefa Zapata)
Anthony Quinn (Eufemio Zapata)
Joseph Wiseman (Fernando Aguirre)
and Arnold Moss (Don Nacio)

DIRECTOR ~ Elia Kazan

AWARDS WON

Best Supporting Actor (Anthony Quinn)	1952 Academy Award
Best Male Performance (Marlon Brando)	1952 Cannes Film Festival Award
Best Film (Elia Kazan)	1952 British Academy Award
Best Performance (Marlon Brando)	1952 Cannes Film Festival Award

viva zapata! (1952)

rice con queso

serves 4 to 6

3 cups	cooked brown or white rice, seasoned with salt and pepper	1/2 lb	ricotta cheese (thin the cheese with a little low fat milk or yogurt until spreadable)
1-1/3 cups	cooked black beans or black-eyed peas, or pinto beans	2 cups	shredded Monterrey Jack cheese
3	cloves garlic, minced	1/2 cup	shredded mild cheddar cheese
1	large onion, chopped		garnishes: chopped black olives, onions, and fresh parsley
1/2 cup	canned chilies, chopped		

- Preheat oven to 350°F. Mix together rice, beans, garlic, onion, and chilies. In a casserole, spread alternating layers of the rice-bean mixture, ricotta cheese, and Monterrey Jack cheese, ending with a layer of rice and beans.

- Bake for 30 minutes. During the last few minutes of baking, sprinkle cheddar cheese over the top. Garnish before serving.

 Use low fat cheese.

beef tenderloin with cilantro sauce

serves 4

4	beef tenderloin steaks	2 tsp	garlic, minced
2 tbsp	fresh squeezed lime juice	1/4 tsp	ground cumin
2 tbsp	chili powder	1/4 tsp	red pepper flakes, crushed
2 tbsp	vegetable oil (divided)		

- Place steaks in wide, shallow dish. Combine lime juice, chili powder, 1 tablespoon oil, garlic, cumin and red pepper flakes in small bowl. Pour over steaks and rub to coat.

- Heat remaining oil in large, heavy non-stick skillet over medium-high heat until hot. Add steaks and cook 4 minutes on each side for medium-rare doneness.

- Transfer to serving platter and keep warm. Spoon sauce over steaks.

Did You Know That... The Mexican Bureau of Popular Cultures has identified at least 10,000 fiestas celebrated by different communities in Mexico. Fiestas are an essential part of Mexican culture.

trivia clips

Emiliano Zapata was a revolutionary and a champion of agrarianism, who fought in guerrilla actions during and after the Mexican Revolution (1911-17). Zapata was the son of a mestizo peasant who trained and sold horses. He was orphaned at the age of 17 and had to look after his brothers and sisters.
Zapata adopted the slogan "Tierra y Libertad" ("Land and Liberty").

viva
zapata! (1952)

cilantro sauce

Yield: About 1 cup

1	green chile, chopped
1/2 cup	whipping cream or evaporated skim milk
1/2 cup	sour cream (low fat okay)

1 tbsp	chopped fresh cilantro
	cilantro sprigs (for garnish)
	red or green bell pepper rings (for garnish)

- Place chile in blender and purée until smooth. In a small saucepan over medium-low heat, combine the chile with whipping cream or evaporated skim milk; bring to a gentle boil.

Whisk in sour cream and cilantro. Cook until just heated through.

- Garnish as desired with cilantro sprigs and red or green bell pepper rings.

deep-fried mexican style ice cream with tortilla fans and berry salsa

serves 4

Berry Salsa

2 cups	strawberries, or raspberries or a mixture of berries, chopped

1 tbsp	chopped fresh mint
1/2 tsp	grated lime rind
1 tbsp	lime juice
1-1/2 tsp	honey

- Combine berries, mint, lime rind and juice and honey; cover and refrigerate for 1 hour.

Tortilla Fans

4	flour tortillas
2 tbsp	butter, melted

2 tbsp	granulated sugar
3/4 tsp	cinnamon

- Preheat oven to 375°F. Brush both sides of tortillas with butter. Combine sugar and cinnamon; sprinkle on both sides of tortillas. Bake on lightly greased baking sheet in oven for

about 10 minutes or until crisp and golden. Cut into quarters. Prior to serving, "fan out" the quarters in an ice cream dish.

BEVERAGES

Corona Beer (Mexico) with lime wedges

Frozen Margaritas (see index for drink recipes)

Tequila Sunrise

Spanish Coffee

MUSIC

Listen to some festive Mexican music, such as that found on "The Best of Mexican Music" (Balboa) featuring various artists. If it is a romantic evening for two, we suggest "Serenades" (Balboa). This compilation features an array of serenades such as the well-known Besame Mucho, and other songs. For an interesting re-interpretation of Mexican folk songs we recommend "Los Super Seven" (RCA), by the band of the same name. One of the band members, David Hildago, is a former member of Los Lobos, a band that enjoyed some mainstream success in the 1980's.

trivia clips

Acting, in general, is something most people think they're incapable of but they do it from morning to night.
The subtlest acting I've seen is by ordinary people trying to show they feel something they don't or trying to hide something.
It's something everyone learns at an early age.
Marlon Brando, Newsweek, 13 March 1972

viva
zapata! (1952)

SETTING THE STAGE

Mexicans enjoy celebrating festive occasions; they are noted for their spicy hot foods, and colourful celebrations that often inspire romance. Las Serenatas is a romantic tradition, a serenade to capture the heart of a loved one. Traditionally, a man would hire a mariachi band, or trio, and sing romantic songs under the window sill of his sweetheart, thus "serenading" her. She in return, would not come to her window until a least 3 or 4 songs were played. For those willing to be adventurous and very romantic, surprise your loved one with a serenade on a special occasion such as a birthday or Valentine's Day.

If inviting friends over for a thematic evening, hire a trio of musicians and have them play outside your front door, greeting your guests as they arrive. If your budget allows, you could hire the band for a couple of hours either to start your party or have them play all night. Decorate your front door with a traditional chinchilla blanket or a Mexican flag. Cook using clay pots, wrap your silverware in colourful napkins, set the table in bright colours and use a few cactus plants as a centrepiece. Set out some helium balloons in bright colours or cactus and chili pepper shapes. This fiesta would be ideal for the outdoors; light some citronella candles and patio lanterns. While you're in the mood, don't forget your sombrero. Play some music, keep the rhythm with those souvenir maracas you probably brought back from vacation and maybe even do the Mexican hat dance!

deep-fried mexican style ice cream

1 pint	vanilla ice cream or other flavour	2 tsp	granulated sugar
1/2 cup	crushed cornflakes or cookie crumbs such as graham cracker crumbs	1	egg
			vegetable oil for deep-frying
1 tsp	ground cinnamon		whipped cream (optional)

- Scoop out 4 to 5 balls of ice cream, place in separate bowls and return to freezer. In a medium size bowl, mix cornflake crumbs, cinnamon and sugar. Roll frozen ice cream balls in half of this crumb mixture, and freeze again.

- In a small bowl, beat egg, dip frozen crumb-coated balls in beaten egg, then roll again in remaining crumbs. Freeze once more until ready to use. (For thicker coating, repeat procedure of dipping in egg and rolling in crumbs.) When ready to serve, heat oil to 350°F. Place 1 frozen ice cream ball in fryer basket or on perforated spoon and lower into hot oil 1 minute or until golden. Immediately remove and place in dessert dish.

- Continue to fry balls one at a time. Balls will be crunchy on outside and just beginning to melt inside.

- To assemble dessert for presentation: Place fried ice cream in dish with tortilla fans and drizzle with berry salsa. Top with whipped cream if so desired.

Follow the ice cream recipe up to the point of coating in crumbs the day before serving. Freeze the ice cream balls until you are ready to fry them.

Use low fat ice cream.

SWINGING 60's

1960- The birth control pill is approved by the FDA and revolutionizes relationships between men and women!

1961- Bay of Pigs The United States broke diplomatic relations with the Communist government of Cuba on Jan. 3, 1961, in the last days of the Eisenhower administration. On January 20 John F. Kennedy became president of the United States.

1961- Berlin Wall Its purpose was to keep East Germans from fleeing to the West to escape the oppressive Communist dictatorship of East Germany. Construction of the wall was started on the night of Aug. 12-13, 1961. It began as a barrier of barbed wire and cinder blocks but was eventually turned into a series of concrete slabs 15 feet (5 meters) high and topped with barbed wire and guard towers. It surrounded West Berlin, since the city was itself surrounded by East Germany. In spite of the wall, about 5,000 East Germans managed to escape across it, but 191 persons were killed trying to get away. When the Communist regime in East Germany began collapsing in the autumn of 1989, the wall was opened on November 9. With the unification of the two Germanys in 1990, the wall was demolished. Many people kept pieces of the wall as souvenirs.

1962- First U.S. astronaut orbits the Earth On Feb. 20, 1962, John Glenn became the first American to orbit the Earth. This event happened less than one year after the Soviet cosmonaut, Yuri Gagarin, had orbited the Earth. The space race was going full throttle!

1963- ASSASSINATED President John F. Kennedy in Dallas, Tex., on Nov. 22, 1963.

1964- Civil Rights Act passed in the United States of America.

1965- Buildup of U.S. troops in Vietnam At first, U.S. forces were to advise South Vietnamese troops in their battles against the Communist Viet Cong. As Viet Cong attacks on South Vietnamese citizens and troops increased, and American advisers were killed, more and more American forces were sent to Vietnam. This was the start of what was to become the quagmire for the American government and military.

1969- First man on the moon "Houston. Tranquility Base here. The Eagle has landed." (Message to Mission Control from the lunar module)
"That's one small step for man, one giant leap for mankind." (Statement made by Neil A. Armstrong when he first set foot on the moon, July 20, 1969).
On July 20, 1969, almost eight years after President John F. Kennedy had announced the United States plan to go to the moon, Neil Armstrong became the first man to set foot on the moon. During these eight years, many firsts were recorded by the United States space program, and many benefits for society were developed in medicine, technology, and communications. Five other landings were made on the moon by the Apollo spacecraft in the years 1969-72.

andrei rublev (1966)

This masterpiece medieval epic is based on the life of Rublev, who was a Russian monk and iconographer. The historical backdrop to the film is tumultuous; the first portion of the 15th century saw the Mongol-Tartar invasions and the political intrigues and upheavals which seem to have always plagued mother Russia. The film's protagonist has been commissioned to paint the interior of a cathedral, and on his journey he sees firsthand the brutalities suffered by the common folk as they endure mistreatment by the Mongol hoardes. Rublev's faith and his art is shaken by the difficult life circumstances that affect his countrymen outside of the monastery and he takes a vow of silence after the Mongols burn the cathedral in which he has been painting. A vision from a dead friend inspires him to recoup his strength and his faith. In the film's final section we are introduced to a boy named Boriska who has endeared himself to a group of travelling bell-makers by telling them that he possesses a secret to bell-making passed down to him by his father. Boriska has even convinced himself of this charade, but he hasn't been able to convince Rublev. Though he doesn't quite trust the boy, Rublev is fascinated by his courage and creativity. In the end, Rublev sets aside his vow of silence and acts as confessor to the boy. His own faith in his religion and in art are restored through his contact with Boriska.

The film is shot mainly in black and white with only the final section showing Rublev's exquisite icons in a burst of colour. This is a visual metaphor for the artist's renewed spirituality and faith in art which flourishes even in the midst of social chaos; this renewed spirituality he views as a God-given gift.

menu
russian salad • wild mushroom soup (see index) • chicken kiev • russian style coleslaw • strawberry pavlovas

russian salad
serves 4 to 6 as a side dish or 6 to 8 as an appetizer

Many variations of this salad exist, but they are all based on vegetables and some type of meat mixed in a thick mayonnaise dressing. Serve with baguette slices or dark rye or Russian style bread (purchase at Eastern European bakeries or delicatessens).

4 to 5	potatoes, peeled and diced	2 tbsp	chopped parsley
1-1/2 cups	diced cooked chicken or ham	2	eggs, hard-boiled and diced
1/2 cup	diced cooked carrots		juice of 1 lemon
1 cup	cooked peas		salt and pepper to taste
6	pickles, diced		about 4 cups mayonnaise

• Boil the potatoes and drain. Set aside to cool. Put the meat, carrots, peas, pickles, parsley, and eggs into a mixing bowl. Add the potatoes when they've cooled. Stir to mix using a wooden spoon. Add lemon juice, salt and pepper. Add the mayonnaise to bind the ingredients (the salad will be fairly thick). Put in deep serving dishes (a clear dish looks great with this salad in it). Garnish with more chopped parsley or decoratively cut vegetables.

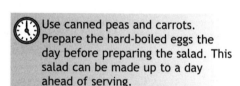 Use canned peas and carrots. Prepare the hard-boiled eggs the day before preparing the salad. This salad can be made up to a day ahead of serving.

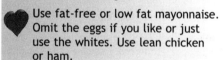 Use fat-free or low fat mayonnaise. Omit the eggs if you like or just use the whites. Use lean chicken or ham.

trivia clips
This epic panorama of medieval life made its debut to the Western world at the 1969 Cannes Film Festival. It wasn't distributed in the U.S.S.R. until 3 years later, as the then Soviet authorities felt that it was too sombre and violent a film for the 50th anniversary celebrations of the October Revolution.

chicken kiev

serves 4

Filling

1/4 cup	butter or margarine, softened
2 tbsp	green onion, chopped
1 tbsp	fresh garlic, minced
1/4 tsp	salt
1 pinch	cracked pepper

Chicken

4	whole boneless, skinless chicken breasts
1/4 cup	butter or margarine
1 cup	breadcrumbs
1/4 cup	fresh parsley, chopped
1/4 tsp	salt
1/4 tsp	thyme leaves
1 pinch	cracked pepper

- To make filling: Stir together all filling ingredients. Divide in four equal portions and freeze portions for at least 30 minutes.
- Preheat oven to 350˚F. Using a meat mallet, flatten each chicken breast, to about 1/4-inch thickness. Place 1 portion of the butter onto each flattened breast. Roll and tuck in edges of chicken; secure with wooden toothpicks.

- In a small saucepan, melt 1/4 cup butter. Set aside.
- Combine remaining breadcrumbs, parsley, salt, thyme and pepper. Dip rolled chicken breast in melted butter, then coat with crumb mixture. Place on baking pan sprayed with cooking spray and bake 55 to 65 minutes or until fork tender. Remove toothpicks before serving

russian style coleslaw

serves 4 to 6

2 cups	red cabbage, shredded
2 cups	green cabbage, shredded
1 cup	carrots, grated
3 tbsp	apple cider vinegar
3 tbsp	water

2 tbsp	sugar
1 tbsp	olive oil or cooking oil
2 tsp	prepared horseradish
	salt and pepper to taste

- In a salad bowl, combine cabbage and carrots. Toss to mix. In a separate small bowl combine vinegar, water, sugar, oil and horseradish. Pour into salad and toss to coat. Add salt and pepper to taste.

FEATURED ACTORS

Anatoli Solonitsin (Andrei Rublev)
Ivan Lapikov (Kiril)
Nikolai Sergeyev (Feofan Grek)
Nikolai Grinko (Danil Cherny)
Nikolai Burlyaev (Boriska)

DIRECTOR ~ Andrei Tarkovsky

BEVERAGES

If you wish to try some Russian beer, here are some brands to seek out: Stepan Razin, Taopin, Baltica and Vityaz. In terms of wine, you may wish to try Pinot Vityazevo (Russia) or any wines from Moldova, a former Soviet republic on the Black Sea, which produces some of the best wine in all of Russia.

MUSIC

"Best of Russian Music" (Le Chant du Monde) features a variety of Russian classical pieces such as "Ruslan and Ludmila" and "Mazurka". "Hymns for the Holy Week in the Russian Orthodox Church" or "Russian Choral Music-Russian Easter" (BMG/Melodiya) would be in line with the spiritual tone of the film. The Orthodox Liturgy features hymns with rich, varied and sometimes haunting tones that are harmonious and melodic even though traditionally no instruments are used in Orthodox churches. Alternatively, "Greatest Russian Composers" (Eclipse), a box set featuring music by Russian greats such as: Rimsky-Korsakov, Prokofiev, Tchaikovsky, Glinka and Rachmaninoff among others, is a wonderful choice for those who would like an introduction to a variety of renowned Russian composers.

andrei
rublev (1966)

continued

Decorate in the traditional Russian colours of red, white and blue or buy an old Soviet flag with a hammer and sickle and use it as a tablecloth. If you have a set of Russian nesting or Matrushka dolls, use them to decorate your table. Perhaps you could use a dark blue or navy tablecloth which will make white or gold rimmed dinner ware look spectacular! Set the table with crystal goblets for both water and wine and use a multi-pronged candelabra. You may wish to tie red, white and blue ribbons around its base.

Wheat is an important symbol in Russian culture. You may wish to create this simple, but beautiful centrepiece: one week prior to your film evening, add some garden soil to a small, decorative bowl filling it almost to the top. Add a handful of whole kernel wheat (available at health food stores), and top off with a small amount of soil. Water and place on a window sill.

In about seven days the wheat will have sprouted. You may trim the wheat with scissors if it has grown too long and is falling over. Place the bowl of wheat in the centre of the table. You could even put a candle in the middle of the wheat and use it in place of a candelabra.

Serve your vodka well chilled in a decorative ice bucket or better yet create your own unique ice bucket... Take a large juice or milk carton and cut off the top portion. Place a

bottle of vodka (and it doesn't have to be a full bottle) in the carton and pour in about 1/2 cup of water. Now add some slices of citrus fruit, strawberries, cranberries, etc. Add greenery such as small boughs of pine or fir. Freeze in the upright position. When the layer is frozen, layer again with water and the decorative garnishes until only the neck of the bottle is visible. Prior to serving, run the carton under warm water and remove the carton to reveal a stunning "ice bucket" around the vodka bottle. Rest bottle on a silver tray or attractive plate surrounded by more greenery or even fresh flowers. This alone would create an exquisite centrepiece.

strawberry pavlovas

serves 6 to 8

12	large egg whites, at room temperature	3 lb	strawberries, halved or quartered if large
1/4 tsp	salt	3 tbsp	fresh lime juice
2-1/2 cups	superfine granulated sugar	1/4 cup	plus 1-1/2 tablespoons granulated sugar
1-1/2 tbsp	cornstarch	2-1/2 cups	chilled heavy cream
1-1/2 tbsp	white vinegar	2 tsp	vanilla

- To make meringues: Preheat oven to 250°F and line 2 large baking sheets with parchment paper.

- Using an electric mixer, beat whites with salt until they hold soft peaks. Beat in 2 cups superfine sugar and continue beating until mixture holds stiff, glossy peaks. Stir together remaining 1/2 cup superfine sugar and cornstarch. Beat into meringue, then beat in vinegar. Spoon 8 (about 1/2 cup each) mounds of meringue (about 2 inches high) 1 inch apart on each lined baking sheet. Divide any remaining meringue among mounds. Bake in upper and lower thirds of oven, switching position of sheets halfway through baking, until meringue is crisp but still soft inside,

- 1 to 1-1/4 hours total. If meringues are still not crisp after 1-1/4 hours, turn off oven and cool in oven 1 hour. Transfer from parchment to racks to cool. (Meringues may stick if cooled completely on paper.)

- Assemble pavlovas: Just before serving, toss strawberries with lime juice and 1/4 cup granulated sugar and let stand, tossing occasionally until sugar is dissolved, 10 minutes.

- Beat cream with vanilla and remaining 1-1/2 tablespoons granulated sugar with cleaned beaters. Tap meringues gently with back of a spoon to create indentations, then mound some whipped cream and strawberries onto each.

2001: a space oddysey (1968)

vegetarian lasagna

serves 6 to 8

1	8-ounce package uncooked lasagna noodles
1 tsp	olive oil
1-1/2 cups	zucchini, sliced
1-1/2 cup	peppers, sliced (red or green)
7 cups	sliced mushrooms (about 2, 8-ounce packages)
1/2 tsp	ground nutmeg
3	garlic cloves, minced
2	15-ounce containers light ricotta cheese
2	10-ounce packages frozen chopped spinach, thawed, drained, and squeezed dry
1/4 cup	grated Parmesan cheese
1 tsp	dried rosemary
1 tsp	dried oregano
1 tsp	pepper
3	large egg whites
1	25.5-ounce bottle good quality tomato sauce
	cooking spray
3 cups	shredded part-skim mozzarella cheese
2 tbsp	grated Parmesan cheese
	fresh oregano leaves, chopped (optional)

- Cook lasagna noodles according to package directions, omitting salt and fat. Drain; set aside 9 noodles. Heat oil in a non-stick skillet over medium heat. Add zucchini and peppers, sauté until soft; remove to a separate bowl and set aside. Add mushrooms to skillet; sauté 3 minutes. Add nutmeg and garlic; sauté 5 minutes. Set aside in a separate bowl.

- Combine ricotta cheese, spinach, Parmesan cheese, rosemary, oregano, pepper, and egg whites; set aside.

- Preheat oven to 375°F. Spread 3/4 cup tomato sauce in bottom of a 13 x 9-inch baking dish coated with cooking spray. Arrange 3 lasagna noodles over sauce; top with half of ricotta cheese mixture, half of mushroom mixture, half of zucchini and pepper mixture, 1-1/2 cups sauce, and 1 cup mozzarella cheese. Repeat layers (until you have used up all the noodles and ingredients), ending with noodles. Spread 1/2 cup sauce over noodles.

- Cover and bake at 375°F for 40 minutes. Uncover; sprinkle with remaining mozzarella cheese and 2 tablespoons Parmesan cheese; bake 10 minutes. Let stand 10 minutes before serving. Garnish with chopped oregano, if desired.

The late Stanley Kubrick's landmark epic deals with the history of humankind. The film is based on renowned writer Arthur C. Clarke's short story "The Sentinel". It is actually four related stories that highlight the mysteries of life and creation and attempt to foretell the destiny of humankind in a thought-provoking manner. At the beginning of the film we see a group of hominids who find a black monolith that inspires an evolution in their thinking process. At the end of this depiction of the era, Kubrick cuts in with a scene millions of years in the future showing a spaceship hovering over the earth. The craft and its occupants are on a mission tracking signals which are being emitted from the moon. It turns out that a strange object buried underneath the moon's soil has been emitting the signals. The object is a black monolith that emits a piercing noise when one of the astronauts attempts to touch it... The galactic journey continues in the next part of the film as astronauts aboard the space ship Discovery (along with colleagues who are in suspended animation) come into conflict with their on board computer HAL 9000. The computer is responsible for running the entire ship, but malfunctions partway through the journey. HAL attempts to murder astronauts to cover up his errors. Astronaut Bowman defends himself and is finally free of HAL. Bowman uncovers a recording made by a scientist, Dr. Heywood Floyd (who was one of the men who travelled to the moon to check out the black monolith), and he discovers the true purpose of the voyage in which he has been a participant.

FEATURED ACTORS
Keir Dullea (Bowman)
Gary Lockwood (Poole)
William Sylvester
　(Dr. Heywood Floyd)
Daniel Richter
　(Moonwatcher, male ape)
Douglas Rain (HAL 9000 voice)

DIRECTOR ~ Stanley Kubrick

trivia clips

The film was nominated for a total of 4 Academy Awards.
HAL stands for Heuristically programmed ALgorithmic computer.
"I'm not going to be asked any conceptualizing questions, right? It's the thing I hate most. I've always felt trapped and pinned down and harried by those questions. Truth is too multi-faceted to be contained in a five-line summary."
Stanley Kubrick (1928-1999) Rolling Stone, 27 August 1986

continued

AWARDS WON

Best Visual Effects (Stanley Kubrick)	1968 Academy Award
Best Art Direction (Ernie Archer, Harry Lange, Tony Masters)	1968 British Academy Award
Best Cinematography (Geoffrey Unsworth)	1968 British Academy Award
Best Film (Stanley Kubrick)	1968 British Academy Award
Best Soundtrack (Winston Ryder)	1968 British Academy Award
10 Best Films	1968 National Board of Review of Motion Pictures
Best Direction (Stanley Kubrick)	1968 New York Film Critics Circle Award
Best Film (Stanley Kubrick)	1968 New York Film Critics Circle Award
Best Screenwriting (Stanley Kubrick and Arthur C. Clarke)	1968 New York Film Critics Circle Award
U.S. National Film Registry	1991 Library of Congress Award
100 Greatest American Movies	1998 American Film Institute Award

BEVERAGES

Robust reds such as: Lindemans Cawarra Shiraz Cabernet (Australia), Merlot Reserve Chateau Aida (Bulgaria), Masi Valpolicella (Italy) or Chianti Ruffino (Italy) would all be suitable to serve along with this menu.

MUSIC

What else but the film's wonderful classical soundtrack "2001: A Space Odyssey" (Sony)!

trio salad

serves 6 to 8

This trio of greens is a powerhouse of vitamins and flavour. Bitter salad greens are a nice complement to the cheese in the lasagna.

1/3 cup	extra-virgin olive oil		2	bunches arugula
2 tbsp	white-wine vinegar		1	small head radicchio
	salt and pepper		2	large Belgian endives

- In a bowl whisk together oil and vinegar and season with salt and pepper.

- Discard coarse stems from arugula. Thinly slice radicchio and cut endives crosswise into 1/2-inch pieces. In a large bowl toss greens with vinaigrette until coated well.

garlic bread with 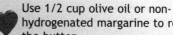romano cheese

serves 6 to 8

1/2 cup	unsalted butter, room temperature		2 to 3	garlic cloves, minced
1/2 cup	grated pecorino Romano cheese (buy a piece of Romano, not the pre-grated type)			pepper
			1	large loaf Italian or French bread, halved lengthwise
1/4 cup	finely chopped fresh flat leaf parsley			

- Mix butter, cheese, parsley and garlic in medium bowl to blend well. Season with pepper.

- Preheat oven to 350°F. Place bread, cut side up, on baking sheet. Spread butter mixture evenly over cut sides of bread. Bake until topping is golden brown and bread is heated through, about 5 minutes.

- Cut bread crosswise into pieces. Serve immediately.

Use 1/2 cup olive oil or non-hydrogenated margarine to replace the butter.

May be prepared 1 day ahead. Cover and refrigerate. Bring to room temperature before using.

2001: a space oddysey (1968)

amaretti baked pears

serves 6 to 8

This easy to prepare dessert looks sophisticated.

5	firm but ripe pears, peeled, halved
2/3 cup	crumbs from amaretti cookies (Italian macaroons)
1	large egg yolk
7 tbsp	sugar

6 tbsp	fresh lemon juice
3 tbsp	unsalted butter
1 cup	chilled whipping cream
2 tbsp	liqueur (Amaretto, Frangelico or even Malibu)

- Preheat oven to 375°F. Butter a 13x9x2-inch glass baking dish. Using a melon baller or a small spoon, core each pear half, leaving 1-1/2-inch-diameter cavity. Arrange 8 pear halves, cut side up, in prepared baking dish. Purée remaining 2 halves in processor. Place 1/2 cup purée in medium bowl (reserve any remaining puree for another use). Mix cookie crumbs and yolk into purée in bowl. Mound filling in pear cavities.

- Combine 6 tablespoons sugar, lemon juice and butter in small saucepan. Bring to boil over medium heat, stirring until sugar dissolves and butter melts. Spoon syrup over pears.

- Bake pears until tender, basting occasionally with syrup in dish, about 40 minutes. (Can be prepared 3 hours ahead; let stand at room temperature.)

- Whip cream with liqueur and remaining 1 tablespoon sugar in medium bowl until soft peaks form. Serve pears with whipped cream.

SETTING THE STAGE

How far away the year 2001 must have seemed when the movie was made! Now that the future is here, we can celebrate with a bit of a futuristic theme to the gathering. Silver is a colour with futuristic connotations, so use a silver tablecloth or table runner. Decorate with Mylar balloons displaying a technological or future theme (spaceships, moon, stars, etc.). Sprinkle some blue and silver stars (available at party stores) on your table. Create a centrepiece using glow sticks (a novelty item available at party and dollar stores) that will gleam as you dim the lights.

Purchase a package of glow-in-the-dark stars. They come in different sizes and are easily removed from most household surfaces. Using a step ladder, affix the stars to your ceiling. There are a number of different types of sticky glow products available. You could purchase dots, and for those of you who are really creative, form different star patterns (Big Dipper, Little Dipper, etc.). Also available is a glow-in-the-dark set of planets from our solar system. The glow products need just a few minutes of exposure of light to glow for quite some time. Surprise your guests: dim the lights, and see if your guests will notice the special effects! Givespace themed novelty headgear to your guests as party favours. You may also wish to ask guests to predict changes or advances in technology for the future. Ask them what they think life will be like in 10 or 20 years. Collect these responses, place them in an envelope, date it ten or twenty years in the future and put it in a safe place. Just think of the fun you'll have in the future reminiscing about your gathering and reading the predictions. You may want to create a small time capsule to open in the future as well. The future is yours, shape it to your liking!

butch cassidy and the sundance kid (1969)

This movie tells the true tale of two likable cowboy criminals who were known for their non-lethal, somewhat suave style. They carry out many train robberies together and end up falling in love with the same woman. While battling over their love interest, they are pursued by an aggressive posse. To outrun the posse they don't just leave town, they leave the country and go to Bolivia. Their love interest, Etta, goes with them but deserts them as the posse closes in. Their luck eventually does run out when they find themselves surrounded in a barn with no possible way of making a run for it. The two main actors, Paul Newman and Robert Redford, made female audiences' hearts throb! Both actors sparkled on screen bringing with them a sense of humour and unique chemistry. This movie is a western with a comic twist. The ending is memorable as is the award-winning cinematography.

FEATURED ACTORS
Paul Newman (Butch Cassidy)
Robert Redford (The Sundance Kid)
Katharine Ross (Etta Place)
Strother Martin (Percy Garris)
Henry Jones (Bike Salesman)

DIRECTOR ~
George Roy Hill and Roy Hill

menu   bolivian cheese empanadas (pukacapas) • grilled tomatoes with pesto • cowboy pork roast with black bean salsa • green salad with vinaigrette dressing (see index) • crusty bread (store-bought) • s'mores squares

bolivian cheese empanadas (pukacapas)
Yield: About 2 dozen large or 3 1/2 dozen small

We just had to include something from the final stomping grounds of Butch Cassidy and the Sundance Kid! These make a tantalizing appetizer. They also freeze well, so you can make them in advance and then reheat them in the oven or microwave.

Dough:

4 cups	all-purpose flour
3 tsp	baking powder
1 tsp	salt
1 tsp	sugar
1/2 cup	butter or margarine
1 cup	milk or water
3 egg	yolks, lightly beaten

Filling:

3 cups	white onion, finely chopped
2 tbsp	paprika
2	chili peppers, seeded and cut into thin strips
2	green peppers, seeded and cut into thin strips
1	small tomato, finely chopped
3	reen onions, cut into small pieces
4 cups	crumbled or grated cheese (a combination of cheeses is okay)
10	black olives, halved and pitted
3 tbsp	flat leaf parsley, finely chopped
1/2 cup	butter or margarine

Glaze:

2 tbsp	paprika
2 tbsp	butter
2 tbsp	water

- Dough: Place all of the dry ingredients in a mixing bowl. Mix in the butter or margarine using a wooden spoon. In a small bowl, beat together the yolks and milk or water. Stir yolk and milk combination into the flour mixture. Knead well until the dough is smooth. Cover and set aside while filling is prepared.

- Filling: In a large bowl, mix all filling ingredients until very well combined. Set aside.

- To assemble: Take a piece of dough (about 1/2 cup) and on a floured surface, knead it and stretch it out until thin. Cut the dough into small round pieces, using a cookie cutter or upside down glass. Place a tablespoon or so of filling in the middle of the round piece.

- Dampen the edge of the piece with water and cover it with another round piece of dough.

- Flute or fold the edges. Repeat the process with each round piece of dough until you have used all the dough up. Do not place the filling too close to the edges as the empanadas will burst while baking. Place the empanadas on a baking sheet sprayed with cooking spray or lightly greased. Set aside. Preheat oven to 400° F.

- Glaze: Mix the paprika with the butter and water in a small saucepan. Cook the mixture over medium heat till warm. Remove from heat. Prior to placing the empanadas in the oven, brush each one with the butter mixture using a pastry brush. Bake until golden. Serve warm on a platter or in a lined basket.

 Use low fat cheese and milk. Use non-hydrogenated margarine.

 You may be able to purchase ready-made empanadas at Latin supermarkets or restaurants.

butch cassidy and
the sundance kid (1969)

grilled tomatoes with pesto serves 4

4	large tomatoes
4 tbsp	prepared pesto sauce

4 tbsp	bread crumbs
	grated Parmesan cheese and/or Romano cheese

- Cut tops off the tomatoes and scoop out a little of the tomato pulp. Discard pulp.
- Combine the pesto and bread crumbs in small bowl. Refill the tomatoes with the pesto mixture and top with grated Parmesan and/or Romano cheese.

- Preheat grill or broiler to 300˚F. Place tomatoes on top of barbecue grill or in oven under the broiler for just a few minutes until cheese is slightly golden and tomatoes have softened slightly.

cowboy pork roast with black bean salsa serves 4

1 tbsp	ground cumin
1 tbsp	garlic, chopped
1 tbsp	red paprika
2 tsp	dried oregano
1/2 tsp	freshly ground pepper
1-1/2	tsp salt
1/2 tsp	cayenne pepper
3 lb	pork loin roast (bone in)

1	avocado peeled, pitted and cut into 1/4-inch cubes
2 tbsp	lime juice
1	19-ounce can black beans, drained and rinsed
2	tomatoes, seeded and chopped
2 tbsp	fresh cilantro, chopped

- Preheat oven to 325˚F.
- In a bowl combine all the spices; place roast in this bowl. Rub the spices all over the roast.
- Spray roasting pan with cooking spray and bake roast, fat side up, in oven

for about 1-1/2 to 1-3/4 hours. Let the roast sit for about 10 to 15 minutes before slicing. Place slices on a platter.

- Toss avocado with lime juice in a small bowl, add the beans, tomatoes and cilantro. Serve with the roast.

AWARDS WON

Best Cinematography (Conrad L. Hall)	1969 Academy Award
Best Original Screenplay	1969 Academy Award
Best Score (Burt F. Bacharach)	1969 Academy Award
Best Song (Burt F. Bacharach & Hal David)	1969 Academy Award
Best Screenwriting (Allan Burns)	1969 New York Critics Film Circle Award
Anthony Asquith Award for Original Film Music (Burt F. Bacharach)	1970 British Academy Award
Best Actor (Robert Redford)	1970 British Academy Award
Best Actress (Katharine Ross)	1970 British Academy Award
Best Cinematography (Conrad L. Hall)	1970 British Academy Award
Best Direction (George Roy Hill)	1970 British Academy Award
Best Editing (John C. Howard)	1970 British Academy Award
Best Editing (Richard Meyer)	1970 British Academy Award
Best Film (George Roy Hill)	1970 British Academy Award
Best Screenplay (William Goldman)	1970 British Academy Award
Best Soundtrack (David Dockendorf & Don Hall)	1970 British Academy Award
100 Greatest American Movies	1998 American Film Institute Award

trivia clips

"All my life I've been dogged by guilt because I feel there's this difference between the way I look, which I suppose is good, and what I feel inside me. I get these black glooms, it's my Scottish-Irish blood." Robert Redford, Sunday Times, 9 March 1980
Steve McQueen was almost cast as the "Kid".
Can you name another movie Newman and Redford were in? Hint: Be careful around bees because they_____!

BEVERAGES

Some Bolivian beers can be found in North America. Among those to try are: TaquiÒa, Astra, Potosina, and La Paz. Otherwise try Red Stripe (Jamaica) or your favourite beer.

The diverse flavours of the menu call for a light-bodied red wine; Rodet Beaujolais Puits d'Amour (France) would be a suitable choice.

MUSIC

Butch Cassidy and the Sundance Kid soundtrack (A & M Records) features a song many of us are familiar with: "Rain Drops Keep Falling On My Head" by B.J.Thomas. The whole soundtrack is quite good. You may also wish to listen to some authentic Bolivian music. We suggest "Bolivia Manta: Music of the Andes" (Ethnic), the melodies on this album are harmonious and very pleasant. "Bolivia: Music of the Calcha" (Le Chant Du Monde) features the music of the Calcha, a people with pre-Colombian roots. The sounds on this album are more complex rhythmically than those on the previously suggested selection, and a wider variety of instruments are used to back lyrics that touch on politics and society.

SETTING THE STAGE

The film is set in the wide, open western frontier. Just picture rolling tumbleweeds, lots of cacti and sitting around an open fire gazing above at the never ending sky filled with shining stars. For those of you lucky enough with outdoor fireplaces enjoy! Otherwise purchase miniature cactus plants at a local nursery or florist. Use as a centrepiece or place around the house. How about recreating the celestial heavens indoors? Check out your local dollar store or party supply store and purchase a package of glow-in-the-dark stars. They come in different sizes and are easily removed from most household surfaces. Using a step ladder, affix the stars to your ceiling. There are a number of different types of sticky glow products available. You could purchase dots, and for those of you who are really creative, form different star patterns (Big Dipper, Little Dipper, etc.). Also available is a glow-in-the-dark set of planets from our solar system. The glow products need just a few minutes of exposure of light to glow for quite some time. Surprise your guests: dim the lights and see if your guests will notice the special effects!

s'mores squares

serves 8

An open campfire usually reminds us of this quintessential childhood treat, which always seemed to taste heavenly! This fun dessert is a rendition, with a twist of sophistication, of that favourite treat from childhood. It is a cinch to make especially if you use a store-bought crust.

8	graham crackers (5 inches by 2-1/2 inches each)
3/4 cup	margarine or butter, softened
1 cup	packed light brown sugar
3/4 cup	granulated sugar
1/2 tbsp	rum extract
1 tbsp	vanilla extract
4	large eggs

1-1/2 cups	all-purpose flour
2-1/4 tsp	baking powder
1 tsp	salt
1 cup	walnuts or pecans, coarsely chopped
1	bar (7 to 8 ounces) semisweet or milk chocolate, chopped
2 cups	mini marshmallows

- Preheat oven to 350°F. Grease a 13 x 9-inch metal baking pan. Line pan with foil; grease and flour foil.

- Coarsely crumble enough graham crackers to equal 1 cup of pieces; set aside. Using a food processor or with rolling pin, crush remaining graham crackers to equal 1/2 cup fine crumbs.

- In a large, heavy saucepan, melt margarine or butter over low heat. Remove saucepan from heat. With spoon, stir in sugars, rum and vanilla extract, then stir in eggs until well blended.

- In a bowl, combine flour, baking powder, salt, and finely crushed graham cracker crumbs; stir into mixture in saucepan just until blended. Stir in chopped nuts.

- Spread batter evenly in pan. Bake 30 minutes or until top is light golden. Remove pan from oven and sprinkle with graham cracker pieces, chocolate pieces, and marshmallows.

- Bake 10 minutes longer or until marshmallows are puffed and golden. Cool completely in pan on wire rack. When cool, cut into squares and serve.

 Use non-hydrogenated margarine.

 These can be made the day before.

trivia clips

Legend has it that Robert Leroy Parker a.k.a. "Butch Cassidy" robbed his first bank in 1896. He later formed his own band called the "Wild Bunch". Harry Longbaugh a.k.a. "Sundance Kid" was a horse thief and apparently got his nickname from his hometown, Sundance, Wyoming. Other members of the Wild Bunch were: "The Tall Texan" Tom, "Peep" O'Day, and Bill Tod Carver (known for his quickdraw).

tandoori chicken on a stick
with yogurt dip
page 30

apricot crêpes
page 56

grilled shrimp salad with
citrus dressing   page 39

simply the best tiramisu
page 79

creamy pecan stuffed mushrooms
page 44

nut encrusted red snapper with south seas salsa
page 18

cioppino
page 50

danish style open-faced
sandwiches
page 41

strawberry pavlovas
page 90

roasted roma tomato tart
page 162

baklava
page 100

middle eastern style grilled
meat on a pita page 99

vanilla cream in puff pastry
page 203

cleopatra

menu baba ghanouj • hummus • marinated feta cheese • middle eastern style grilled meat on a pita* • shepherd's salad • baklava • arabic or turkish coffee or moroccan mint tea • refreshing yogurt drink (*pita bread is store-bought)

How you serve the meal is up to you. If so desired, you may serve the first 3 dishes as appetizers (perhaps during the movie) or serve all of the menu items at once. Just make sure you buy enough pita bread! You will need 1 pita per person for the main dish (Middle Eastern Style Grilled Meat on a Pita) as well as 1 to 2 pitas per person for the appetizers. Enjoy!!

baba ghanouj

Yield: About 3 cups

2	eggplants (about 1 pound each) halved lengthwise
1/4 cup	plain low fat yogurt (Balkan style if possible)
1/4 cup	fresh lemon juice
2 tbsp	tahini
2	large garlic cloves, minced
1	medium tomato (preferably vine ripe), finely diced
1/2 tsp	salt

	freshly ground black pepper to taste
	extra virgin olive oil for drizzling
2 tbsp	fresh flat leaf parsley, minced (for garnish)

Accompaniments:

pita triangles

a selection of fresh olives

• Preheat broiler to 400°F or prepare grill.

• Make 3 to 4 slashes on the cut side of the eggplant, but not through the skin. On an oiled broiler pan or in a shallow baking pan broil eggplants cut side down for 25 minutes or until charred all over and very soft. (Alternatively, grill eggplants on a well-oiled rack set 5 to 6 inches over glowing coals in same manner.) Cool eggplants until they can be handled and peel off and discard skin. Transfer pulp to a colander set over a bowl. Let eggplant pulp drain 20 minutes and discard any liquid in bowl.

• Transfer pulp to bowl. Add yogurt, lemon juice, tahini, garlic, tomato, salt and pepper to taste, and blend until smooth. Transfer baba ghanouj to a shallow bowl and drizzle with oil and sprinkle with parsley. Cover and chill for 30 minutes prior to serving. Serve baba ghanouj with accompaniments.

This spectacular epic follows this life of the legendary Egyptian queen up to the founding years of the Roman Empire. Cleopatra is one of the most fascinating women in all of history. Though not classically beautiful, she was charming, ambitious, full of wit and extremely intelligent. The film highlights her relationships with two very powerful men.

The first, Julius Caesar, is seduced by Cleopatra on order that she may forge an allegiance with Rome and garner solid support in her quest to return to the throne, after having been driven out by her younger brother's guardians. She is deeply in love with Julius Caesar, though he's much older than she is. A son, Caesarion, is produced as a result of the union. Their happiness is short-lived as Julius Caesar is stabbed in the Roman Senate. After the assassination of Caesar, Cleopatra finds herself in a divided Roman Empire, with General Mark Antony responsible for the eastern portion of the empire. Cleopatra sets her sights on him, as she needs a new protector. Cleopatra bears twins for Mark Antony though he ends up marrying Octavia, the sister of Octavian (Octavian later became known as Augustus). Mark Antony realizes he is truly in love with Cleopatra and sends for her while on an eastern expedition. They marry, not realizing that eternal happiness will prove to be elusive and that their bond will lead them both to a tragic end...

FEATURED ACTORS
Elizabeth Taylor (Cleopatra)
Richard Burton (Mark Antony)
Rex Harrison (Julius Caesar)
Pamela Brown (High Priestess)
Roddy McDowall (Octavian)
George Cole (Flavius)
Martin Landau (Rufio)

DIRECTOR ~ Joseph L. Mankiewicz

trivia clips

Cleopatra VII, the last Egyptian royal with that name, is also the best known. She was not actually an Egyptian, rather she was the last sovereign from a Macedonian dynasty that ruled Egypt. Her family line went back to Ptolemy, a marshal of Alexander the Great. Cleopatra is said to have been the only member of the family who actually learned to speak the language of the Egyptians. She endeared herself to them by claiming she was the daughter of Re, the Egyptian sun god.

cleopatra

(1963)

AWARDS WON

Best Art Direction (Walter Scott, Jack Martin Smith, Paul Fox, Maurice Pelling, John De Cuir, Boris Juraga, Elven Webb, Herman A. Blumenthal, Ray Moyer, Hilyard M. Brown)	1963 Academy Award
Best Cinematography (Leon Shamroy)	1963 Academy Award
Best Costume Design (Irene Sharaff/ Vittorio Nino Novarese)	1963 Academy Award
Best Visual Effects (Emil Kosa Jr.)	1963 Academy Award
Best Actor (Richard Burton)	1963 National Board of Review of Motion Pictures

hummus

Yield: 2 cups (as an appetizer serves up to 8 people)

This Middle Eastern dip is very quick and easy to prepare. It is quite versatile and you may use any leftovers to make pita sandwiches or wraps the next day. Just add some of your favourite shredded veggies for a tasty and healthy lunch!

1	19-ounce can chickpeas (about 2 cups)
1/4 cup	fresh lemon juice, or to taste
1/4 cup	tahini (sesame paste)
2 to 3	garlic cloves, minced
	salt and pepper to taste
3	pitted black olives, sliced (for garnish)
1/4 cup	fresh flat leaf parsley leaves, chopped
	extra virgin olive oil (for garnish)

- Drain the chickpeas reserving the liquid. Blend chickpeas with 1/4 cup of the reserved liquid, lemon juice, tahini, garlic, salt and pepper in a food processor or blender until smooth. Add more reserved liquid if necessary to obtain dipping consistency.

- To serve, place in a medium sized bowl. Top with olives, sprinkle with chopped parsley and drizzle with olive oil to lightly cover surface. Heat pita bread until warm, cut in triangles and serve with hummus for dipping.

marinated feta cheese

serves 6 to 8 (as an appetizer)

1 cup	Kalamata olives or other brine-cured black olives
1 cup	cracked green olives
1 cup	extra-virgin olive oil
6 tbsp	fresh lemon juice
5	garlic cloves, thinly sliced
4 tbsp	fresh flat leaf parsley, chopped
2 tsp	grated lemon peel
1-1/2 tsp	dried oregano
2 tbsp	fresh oregano, chopped
1 tbsp	fresh basil, chopped
1 tbsp	fresh rosemary, chopped
	black pepper to taste
1/8 tsp	dried crushed red pepper
1 lb	feta cheese, cut into 1/2-inch-thick slices
	Pita bread, cut into wedges

- Mix all olives, 3/4 cup olive oil, 3 tablespoons lemon juice, garlic, 2 tablespoons parsley, lemon peel, 1/2 teaspoon oregano and red pepper in resealable plastic bag or container.

- Chill overnight. Place feta on platter or serving plate. Drizzle with 1/4 cup oil and 3 tablespoons lemon juice. Sprinkle with fresh chopped parsley, 1 teaspoon dried oregano, fresh oregano, fresh basil, fresh rosemary and black pepper. Chill at least 2 hours or overnight.

- Place olives and marinade in bowl. Serve olives and feta with pita bread.

 Use reduced-fat feta cheese and whole wheat pita bread.

trivia clips

After filming began, Elizabeth Taylor became ill with pneumonia and production was soon suspended as she was scheduled to be in almost every scene. Her illness lasted about 6 months and was quite serious — she fell into a coma at one point! Production was eventually moved from England to Rome, Italy as the weather would hasten her recovery. All of the film footage shot in England was scrapped.

cleopatra

middle eastern style grilled meat on a pita
serves 8

1-1/2 lb	ground beef		1 tbsp	salt
1 tsp	freshly ground black pepper		2	cloves minced garlic
3 tbsp	chopped parsley			Greek style pita bread (store-bought)
3 tbsp	cilantro, chopped		3	onions, diced
1/2 lb	ground lamb			

- Put all of the ingredients except the pita bread, into a large mixing bowl and knead well to bind the meats and spices together.
- Refrigerate for about 2 hours and then take out and knead well again.
- Shape into finger-length shapes (just like small sausages) and cook on a grill or under a broiler at a moderate temperature so that they stay juicy. Turn only once and do not pierce.

- Serve in warmed or grilled Greek style pita bread on a bed of onions.

 You can double the recipe and freeze the meat mixture for next time.

shepherd's salad
serves 6 to 8

Those who are fans of Greek style salads will enjoy this too. The origin of the name is not known, perhaps this tasty mixture made for a light lunch for shepherds tending their flocks on a hot day! It is refreshing as a salad and may even be put in pita bread as a light lunch. Served chilled or at room temperature this dish is typically served as an accompaniment to grilled meat.

2 lb	fresh tomatoes, diced		3/4 cup	crumbled feta cheese
1 lb	fresh peppers, diced		1	hot green pepper or chili pepper (optional)
1	large onion, diced			parsley for garnish
1	cucumber diced			salt and pepper
	extra virgin olive oil			
	vinegar (preferably red-wine vinegar)			

- Put tomatoes, peppers, onion and cucumber into a salad bowl. Pour oil and vinegar to taste over top.
- Crumble the cheese on top and garnish with hot pepper and parsley if so desired. Season with salt and pepper before serving.

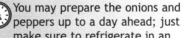 You may prepare the onions and peppers up to a day ahead; just make sure to refrigerate in an airtight container.

 Use low fat feta cheese.

BEVERAGES

Those who adhere to Islam do not consume alcohol, so we suggest the following as drinks: Refreshing Yogurt Drink (see main beverages section) or perhaps your favourite natural fruit juices or mineral water. You may also opt for buttermilk or kefir which would be suitable for the Middle Eastern flavoured dishes on the menu.

There is an interesting beer named Pharaoh's Gold brewed in the United States that you may wish to try. Or if you have money to burn, order some Tutankhamen Ale from Harrod's Department store in London, England. Tutankhamen Ale is a British-made beer supposedly made from a 3,250-year-old recipe of Egyptian beer makers. Only 1,000 bottles were brewed. Archaeologists from Cambridge University's Egypt Exploration Society joined with Scottish and Newcastle Breweries six years ago, after the team uncovered a massive kitchen complex in the Sun Temple of Queen Nefertiti, who was related by marriage to King Tut.

The archaeologists examined grains and seeds left behind by ancient brewers, and the dregs of beer from excavated jars were analyzed to determine how the beer was made.

The quest for the liquid gold of Tutankhamen led to attempts to reconstruct the recipe.

Scottish and Newcastle brew masters used emmer, an ancient wheat grown by the Egyptians, as well as coriander, also known as cilantro, an herb found in the Nile region.

The first bottle sold in England for about $7,200, remaining bottles (if you are lucky enough to snare one) sell for about $75 per bottle. At prices like these you just may have to stick to your regular brand!

trivia clips

Elizabeth Taylor had 65 costume changes in this film! This record was not broken until 1988, by Joan Collins in the television movie "Sins".
Taylor and Burton actually met and fell for each other on the set of Cleopatra.
"I really don't remember much about Cleopatra, there were a lot of other things going on." Elizabeth Taylor, Film Yearbook, 1987

(1963)

MUSIC

Egyptian music is similar to that of other Arabic music traditions, so you may want to listen to "Arabian Classical Music" (Ethnic) or "The Egyptian Music" (Touch and Go).

"Egyptian Nights: Music for Belly Dancing" (Monitor) will set the tone for a romantic evening, with its haunting tones and sexy rhythms. You may even be inspired to try some belly dancing moves for your partner! Well-known for his belly dance music is Hossam Ramzy, an Egyptian percussionist. His "Egyptian Rai" album (rai is a movement to update traditional Arabic music) meshes traditional Arabic instruments such as the lute with instruments from other areas of the world like the accordion, for a unique global musical fusion. It is a good album if you are having a large gathering and anticipate that people may want to dance! Another good choice would be Sting's "Desert Rose" single, especially in its extended version.

baklava

This traditional Middle Eastern treat is a favourite as well in Balkan countries like Greece. The name of the dessert is from the Farsi language spoken in Persia. It means "many leaves," in this case, pastry leaves. Many variations exist but this is the basic recipe. It is very sweet, so serve in small portions!

Syrup:

3 cups	sugar (you may replace 1/3 of the sugar with liquid honey)
1-1/2 cups	water
2 tbsp	lemon juice
2 (optional)	(3-inch) sticks cinnamon
4 to 6	whole cloves, or 1/2 tsp ground cardamom (optional)

Filling:

1 lb	(about 4 cups) blanched almonds, pistachios, walnuts, or any combination, finely chopped or coarsely ground
1/4 cup	sugar
1 to 2 tsp	ground cinnamon
1/4 tsp	ground cloves or cardamom (optional)
1	package (about 1 lb or 24 sheets) phyllo dough
about 1 cup	(2 sticks) melted butter or vegetable oil

- To make the syrup: In a medium size pot, stir the sugar, water, lemon juice, cinnamon sticks, and/or cloves over low heat until the sugar dissolves, about 5 minutes. Stop stirring, increase the heat to medium, and cook until the mixture is slightly syrupy, about 5 to 8 minutes. Discard the cinnamon sticks and whole cloves. Let cool.

- To make the filling: Combine all the filling ingredients.

- Preheat the oven to 350°F. Grease an ovenproof 13-by-9-inch baking pan.

- Place a sheet of phyllo in the prepared pan and lightly brush with butter. Repeat with 7 more sheets. Spread with half of the filling. Top with 8 more sheets, brushing each sheet with butter. Use any torn sheets in the middle layer. Spread with the remaining nut mixture and end with a top layer of 8 sheets, continuing to brush each with butter. Trim any overhanging edges.

- Using a sharp, serrated knife, cut 6 equal lengthwise strips (about 1-3/4 inches wide) through the top layer of pastry. Make diagonal cuts across the strips to form diamond shapes.

- Just before baking, lightly sprinkle the top of the pastry with cold water. This stops the pastry from curling. Bake for 20 minutes. Reduce the heat to 300°F and bake until golden brown, about 15 additional minutes.

- Cut through the scored lines. Drizzle the cooled syrup slowly over the hot baklava and let cool for at least 4 hours. Cover and store at room temperature for up to 1 week. If the baklava dries out while being stored, drizzle with a little additional hot syrup.

 Instead of brushing each layer of phyllo with butter, cut the unbaked baklava into diamonds all the way through, drizzle with 1 cup vegetable oil, and let stand for 10 minutes before baking.

If you are really stuck for time, purchase ready-made baklava at a Middle Eastern supermarket or bakery!

 Reduce the butter called for by half and spray butter flavoured cooking spray between some of the phyllo sheets.

trivia clips

"Elizabeth is a pretty girl, but she has a double chin and an overdeveloped chest and she's rather short in the leg. So, I can hardly describe her as the most beautiful creature I've ever seen."
Richard Burton (1925-84) (on Elizabeth Taylor) Playboy, 1963

baklava

Persian Baklava: Differs from the basic recipe in the use of only the almonds for the nut component and the use of cardamom in the filling and not the cloves. Omit the lemon juice and cinnamon from the basic syrup recipe and add 2 tablespoons rose water or 1 tablespoon orange blossom water after it has cooled.

Variation on baklava: For the filling, use 2 cups blanched almonds, 2 cups unsalted pistachios, 1/4 cup sugar, 1 teaspoon ground cardamom, and 1 teaspoon ground cinnamon. Crush 1/4 teaspoon saffron threads and let steep in 3 tablespoons of the melted butter for 15 minutes and use to brush the top sheet of phyllo.

arabic or turkish coffee   serves 4

This coffee has been compared to espresso in terms of taste and strength. To make this coffee in a traditional manner, you need a small long-handled coffee pot called a dzezva; alternatively, use a small saucepan. The coffee is usually served in small demitasse cups.

Popular folklore states that the grounds that remain at the bottom of the cup reveal one's future! When you have finished your coffee, swirl the grounds around the cup and turn over onto the saucer. Let sit for about 10 minutes and then see what figures and symbols reveal themselves. It is best if someone else "reads" your cup as opposed to doing it yourself.

1-1/2 cups	plus 1 tbsp water
4	heaping tsps Turkish coffee
3	heaping tsp sugar

- In a long-handled coffee pot or a small saucepan, bring 1-1/2 cups of water to a boil.

- While waiting for the water to boil, put the coffee, sugar and 1 tablespoon of water in a cup or mug and stir until well blended and smooth.

- When the water boils, pour in the coffee mixture and bring to a boil again. Remove from heat. With a spoon, remove some froth from the coffee and place in each demitasse cup, and then pour in the actual coffee. Serve with sugar cubes on the side for those who prefer a sweeter brew.

- For an extra special treat, spoon a small amount of whipped cream or whipped topping into the coffee.

moroccan mint tea   see main beverages section

SETTING THE STAGE

In many Arabic countries, dinner is served communal style using a low table with cushions placed all around for diners to sit on (if you have kilim cushions, use them). You may wish to copy this atmosphere. Use a fringed or lace tablecloth, or improvise with a pretty scarf as a table runner. Use brass, copper or silver serving trays to place the appetizer dishes on, as well, use other serving ware made of these materials or use stick looking ceramic or clay pieces if you have them. Dim the lights and use incense or light some candles in brass candleholders or in candelabras. Have one of the music selections playing in the background. If you have a small kilim style rug or Oriental carpet you could hang it on the wall for a beautiful backdrop to your dining area. Perhaps you have some souvenirs from the Middle Eastern countries that you could incorporate into a centrepiece. Alternatively, a tray or fruit bowl of dates, oranges, lemons, pomegranates and figs, interspersed with nuts of various types would make a beautiful, edible centrepiece.

You may wish to make this a costume party whether you're having a crowd or just a few guests... think Thousand and One Arabian Nights, the possibilities are endless! You could even organize a group belly dancing lesson with a local dance studio!

doctor zhivago (1965)

The film is based on Boris Pasternak's novel of the same name that won the 1958 Nobel Prize for Literature. The story is about two star-crossed lovers who endure all to be together. The film is set during the Russian Revolution. The lead character named Yuri Zhivago, played by Omar Sharif, falls in love with a beautiful nurse named Lara, played by Julie Christie. Though the doctor (who is also a poet) is married, he continues his affair with the vulnerable Lara. She is a victim of a rape by a ruthless politician and as she struggles to understand what happened to her, she yearns for true love. Despite the frigid cold weather and the difficult conditions of survival during the Revolutionary battles and civil unrest, passions run hot between the two lovers. Other characters are woven into the story and symbolically represent the good and bad elements of the Bolshevik Revolution.

This epic allows the viewers a glimpse into Russian life during the historic Revolution that swept the country and affected both it, and world events for years to come. Perhaps the film will inspire you to further discover the rich and tumultuous history of Russia. The movie is three hours long, but well worth watching as it features remarkable cinematography.

FEATURED ACTORS
Omar Sharif (Yuri)
Julie Christie (Lara)
Tom Courtenay (Pasha/Strelnikov)
Geraldine Chaplin (Tonya)
Rod Steiger (Komarovsky)
Siobhan McKenna (Anna)
Alec Guinness (Yevgraf)

DIRECTOR ~ David Lean

menu

smoked salmon and caviar (optional) • wild mushroom soup (see index) • russian onion salad (see index) • russian salad (see index) • chicken kiev (see index) • crusty or rye bread (store-bought) • kutia • infused cognac

smoked salmon and caviar
serves 4 to 6 (makes about 30 hors d'oeuvres)

Russian red caviar is considered to be very good, and is highly prized. Its flavour is quite tender and delicate.

1	loaf pumpernickel bread or crackers
1/2 pound	smoked salmon
about 2.5 oz Russian caviar	

1/3 cup	sour cream
	fresh dill (optional)
	lemon slices (optional for garnish)

• Cut pumpernickel into rounds using a cookie cutter. Alternatively, use crackers. Cut salmon lengthwise into 1/2-inch-wide strips and crosswise into 4-inch-long pieces Top each pumpernickel round or cracker, decoratively with salmon, caviar, and sour cream.

• Top with a small sprig of dill if so desired. Place on a serving tray and surround with lemon slices.

trivia clips

The March Revolution of 1917 led to the abdication of Nicholas II and the installation of a provisional government. The last revolution took place in November of the same year. The date was in October on the old Russian calendar; it is usually called the October Revolution. It brought to power the Bolshevik wing of the Communist party, led by Lenin. The Bolsheviks established the Union of Soviet Socialist Republics under the leadership of the Communist party.

doctor zhivago (1965)

kutia

serves 10

This dessert hails from Ukraine, though it is also featured on many Slavic tables such as those in Yugoslavia, Poland and Russia at Christmas time. The wheat represents the staff of life, the honey represents the Spirit of Christ. It is not only delicious, but healthy too (especially because of the fibre in the wheat kernels)!

1 cup	wheatberries (soft wheat kernels)	1/2 cup	walnuts or almonds, chopped
pinch	of salt	1/2 cup	golden raisins
1/2 cup	poppy seeds		whipped cream (optional)
1 cup	liquid honey		

- Set water to boil in a large, deep stockpot. When it comes to a boil, remove from heat and add the wheat kernels. Cover and let stand for about 1 hour. Pour off the water, then add enough cold water to cover kernels by about double. Then add a pinch of salt and cook, covered, over medium-low heat until the kernels are soft, about 3 to 4 hours depending on the type of wheat. Let cool in cooking water. Drain and put in a large mixing bowl.

- While the wheat is cooking, wash the poppy-seeds thoroughly in cold water, scald with boiling water and drain. (Try using a coffee filter set into a small sieve for this.) Place in small saucepan, cover with water and bring to a boil; remove from heat and drain again.

- Set aside.

- Combine the wheat, poppy seeds, and honey. Add the chopped walnuts and raisins. The mixture should be slightly moist. Serve in small dessert bowls with a dollop of whipped cream if so desired.

AWARDS WON

Best Adapted Screenplay (Robert Bolt)	1965 Academy Award
Best Art Direction (Dario Simoni)	1965 Academy Award
Best Art Direction (John Box)	1965 Academy Award
Best Art Direction (Terry Marsh)	1965 Academy Award
Best Cinematography (Freddie Young)	1965 Academy Award
Best Costume Design (Phyllis Dalton)	1965 Academy Award
Best Score (Maurice Jarre)	1965 Academy Award
10 Best Films	1965 National Board of Review of Motion Pictures Award
Best Actress (Geraldine Chaplin)	1965 National Board of Review of Motion Pictures Award
Best Actress (Geraldine Chaplin)	1965 New York Film Critics Circle Award
Best Direction (David Lean)	1965 New York Film Critics Circle Award
Best Film (David Lean)	1965 New York Film Critics Circle Award
Best Screenwriting (Robert Bolt)	1965 New York Film Critics Circle Award
Best Film — Any Source	1966 British Academy Award
Best Actor (Omar Sharif)	1966 Golden Globe Award
Best Film (Drama)	1966 Golden Globe Award
Best Director (David Lean)	1966 Golden Globe Award
100 Greatest American Movies	1998 American Film Institute Award

trivia clips

The Social Democrats were broken into two groups, the Bolsheviks and the Mensheviks. The Bolsheviks, led by Lenin, believed that a revolution should occur right away. The Mensheviks believed that Russia should be industrialized first.

trivia clips

Director David Lean loved to make films in extreme weather conditions. Lawrence of Arabia, with its expansive shots of sand, is quite the contrast to the snowy splendour of Doctor Zhivago.
The actress who played Tonya, had a very famous father who was characterized by his funny mustache and humour. He was well known during the silent picture era. Who is he?
The Bolsheviks became popular in Russia with their slogan "Peace, land, and bread" which appealed to the people's wants. They also promised to take Russia out of World War I.

doctor
zhivago (1965)

BEVERAGES

Before dinner you may wish to serve White or Black Russians (see main beverages page) or the infused cognac. Also, nothing could be more Russian than vodka, it's great to warm you up on a cold winter night. We suggest you try iced vodka, either plain or in a variety of other flavours.

Stolichnaya (Russia), Cristall (Russia) and Finlandia (Finland) make a number of flavoured vodkas such as cranberry.

If you wish to try some Russian beer, here are some brands to seek out: Stepan Razin, Taopin, Baltica and Vityaz. In terms of wine, you may wish to try Pinot Vityazevo (Russia) or any wines from Moldova, a former Soviet republic on the Black Sea, which produces some of the best wine in all of Russia. Otherwise, Domaine Suhidol's Riesling & Muscat (Bulgaria) would suit the flavours in the menu.

MUSIC

"Doctor Zhivago" (Sony/MCA) features the film's entire score. "Lara's Theme" was the biggest hit from the 1965 movie, however other songs such as "Somewhere My Love" turned this into one of the biggest-selling soundtrack albums in history. If you are in the mood for classical music try: "Greatest Russian Composers" (Eclipse), a box set featuring music by Russian greats such as: Rimsky-Korsakov, Prokofiev, Tchaikovsky, Glinka and Rachmaninoff, among others.

For something modern, you may wish to listen to "Very Best of Boney M" (European Import) or "Magic of Boney M" (Musicrama) both feature the hit single "Rasputin" along with other Euro-pop songs by this group who became known internationally during the 1980's.

infused cognac

Yield: 1 bottle

You will need a clean, large glass bottle with a tight sealing lid to make this interesting drink.

1/4 cup	dried figs, chopped	4	cardamom seeds.
1/4 cup	dates, pitted and chopped.		peel of 1/2 lemon
1/4 cup	walnuts.	4 tbsp	sugar
1/8 tsp	cinnamon	1	bottle cognac
1 tsp	vanilla		

- Put all of the ingredients except the cognac in a glass bottle. Slowly pour cognac into bottle.

- Cover tightly and leave in a cool, dark place for 3 weeks. Strain prior to serving.

SETTING THE STAGE

One of the memorable scenes in this movie occurs when the two lovers arrange a tryst at Yuri's rural cabin where they are surrounded by spectacular country landscapes. Perhaps you could plan a weekend get-away at a cottage-style retreat. Even if it is only for an over-night stay, the change of scenery will make for a more exciting atmosphere. Find a location not too far from home. No need to drain your pocket book, look for an inexpensive cabin or motel set in the country, preferably one with a small kitchenette and a television and VCR of course! Bring along the ingredients for your menu. Bring some disposable plates and paper napkins to make clean up easy. If you will be cooking at your rented cabin, verify how well-stocked the kitchen is in terms of pots and pans, utensils etc. The main concept is setting up a romantic mood for two, so you may even wish to dine side by side as opposed to across from each other.

However, if you are enjoying this movie with a group, you may want to decorate your home in a winter-white theme. White tablecloths, clear vases, white roses, and candles. Or decorate in the traditional Russian colours of red, white and blue or buy and old Soviet flag with a hammer and sickle and use it as a tablecloth. If you have a set of Russian nesting or Matrushka dolls, use them to decorate your table. Perhaps use a dark blue or navy tablecloth which will make white or gold- rimmed dinnerware look spectacular! Set the table with crystal goblets for both water and wine and use a multi-pronged candelabra. You may wish to tie red, white and blue ribbons around its base.

Buy some styrofoam eggs at a craft store. Decorate with lace and beaded appliqués to create faux Fabergé eggs, which were popular in the Russian royal court. Use them as decoration at each place setting. You could give one to each guest as a keepsake, or you could even have guests create their own Fabergé egg at the party. Just buy all the supplies required, make sure you have a hot glue gun on hand; then have everyone create their own "eggsquisite" masterpiece!

Wheat is an important symbol in Russian culture. You may wish to create this simple, but beautiful centrepiece: one week prior to your film evening add some garden soil to a small, decorative bowl filling it almost to the top. Add a handful of whole kernel wheat (available at health food stores), and top off with a small amount of soil. Water and place on a window sill. In about seven days the wheat will have sprouted. You may trim the wheat with scissors if it has grown too long and is falling over. Place the bowl of wheat in the centre of the table. You could even put a candle in the middle of the wheat and use it in place of a candelabra.

Serve your vodka well chilled in a decorative ice bucket or better yet create your own unique ice bucket... Take a large juice or milk carton and cut off the top portion. Place a bottle of vodka (and it doesn't have to be a full bottle) in the carton and pour in about 1/2 cup of water. Now add some slices of citrus fruit, strawberries, cranberries, etc. Add greenery such as small boughs of pine or fir. Freeze in the upright position. When the layer is frozen, layer again with water and the decorative garnishes until only the neck of the bottle is visible. Prior to serving, run the carton under warm water and remove the carton to reveal a stunning "ice bucket" around the vodka bottle. Rest bottle on a silver tray or attractive plate surrounded by more greenery or even fresh flowers. This alone would create an exquisite centrepiece.

lawrence of arabia (1962)

menu — cucumber and cumin soup • grilled lamb on a pita with couscous and yogurt • mint iced tea (see main beverages section) • refreshing yogurt drink (see main beverages section) • ricotta stuffed dates • moroccan mint tea (see main beverages section) • orange sorbet (store-bought)

cucumber and cumin soup serves 6

This soup is refreshing and light, especially suited for the summertime! Buttermilk is surprisingly low fat and chock full of calcium! This style of soup is popular throughout the Middle East, Turkey and the Balkans.

1/2 tsp	cumin seed	2 cups	buttermilk
4	medium sized cucumbers, peeled, seeded and chopped		salt and freshly ground pepper
2	cloves garlic, crushed	6	thin slices lemon

• Toast the cumin seeds in a skillet over medium high heat until lightly coloured; be careful not to burn them. Remove from heat and place in a blender or food processor. Add the cucumber, garlic and buttermilk. Process until smooth.

• Pour the soup into a large serving bowl, season with salt and freshly ground pepper to taste and chill in the refrigerator for at least 2 hours.

• Serve in individual bowls, garnished with a lemon slice on top.

Did You Know That...

Any of these drink choices are suitable, but since the Moroccan Mint Tea is served hot, its best consumed after dinner.

This Oscar-winning epic boasts a remarkable, strong cast. The late actor Peter O'Toole, made his film debut playing T.E. Lawrence. Sharing the screen are other notables such as Anthony Quinn, Omar Sharif, Alec Guinness, and Claude Rains. The camera work by Freddie Young is amazing with many beautiful, haunting sweeps of the expansive desert.

This masterful film was shot entirely on location. A definite must see!

This magnificent epic film is based upon the experiences of an enigmatic British lieutenant, T.E Lawrence (1888-1935), serving in North Africa during WW I. This movie presents a fictionalized and romanticized account of the legendary young soldier who operated behind enemy lines during the First World War and incited an Arab revolt against the Turks. Lawrence, an officer of British Intelligence, feeling unsatisfied spending his time colouring in maps, is overjoyed when offered a position as an observer in present day Saudi Arabia. The position of observer gives him the opportunity to work with Prince Faisal, the leader of an Arab tribal army. He establishes an Arab Council, but is later dismayed as the unity of the Council crumbles due to power struggles and political infighting. His adventures, which rewrote the political history of the region, are chronicled in the film by a journalist named Jackson Bentley.

FEATURED ACTORS
Peter O'Toole (T.E.Lawrence)
Omar Sharif
 (Sherif Ali ibn el Kharish)
Anthony Quinn (Auda abu Tayi)
Alec Guinness (Prince Faisal)
Jack Hawkins (General Allenby)

DIRECTOR ~ David Lean

trivia clips

T.E. Lawrence was a student and archaeologist before WW I. His senior thesis was on Crusader forts in the Middle East. He researched by walking more than a thousand miles in what was then the Ottoman Empire. He became familiar with the region, learned Arabic, and became enamoured of Arabian culture. After graduation, he supervised Arab workers on several archaeological digs in the Middle East and made a number of close friends amongst the Arab workers. When Britain needed intelligence officers for the Middle East during the First World War, T.E. Lawrence was an ideal choice.

lawrence of
arabia (1962)

AWARDS WON

1962 Academy Awards:

Best Picture	1962 Academy Award
Best Director (David Lean)	1962 Academy Award
Best Art Direction (John Box/John Stoll/Dario Simoni)	1962 Academy Award
Best Cinematography (Freddie Young)	1962 Academy Award
Best Film Editing (Anne V. Coates)	1962 Academy Award
Best Sound (John Cox)	1962 Academy Award
Best Original Score (Maurice Jarre)	1962 Academy Award
Best Film — Any source; British)	1962 Academy Award
Best British Actor (Peter O' Toole)	1962 British Academy Award
Best Screenplay (Robert Bolt)	1962 British Academy Award
Best Director (David Lean)	1962 Directors Guild of America Award
10 Best Films	1962 National Board of Review of Motion Pictures
Best Director (David Lean)	1962 National Board of Review of Motion Pictures
Best Film — Drama	1963 Golden Globe Award
Best Director (David Lean)	1963 Golden Globe Award
Best Supporting Actor (Omar Sharif)	1963 Golden Globe Award
U.S. National Film Registry	1991 Library of Congress Award
100 Greatest American Movies	1998 American Film Institute Award

BEVERAGES

Skalli Fortant de France Syrah is a red wine that would complement the lamb, as would Angoves Classic Reserve Shiraz and Wolf Blass Yellow Label Cabernet Sauvignon, both from Australia. You may also wish to try Arak, an anise based spirit. For those who prefer non-alcoholic beverages, as many in North Africa do, serve a variety of mineral waters from different countries with twists of lemon or lime. Of course the non-alcoholic suggestions on the menu are suitable too. After dinner you may wish to serve aromatic Arabic coffee (see main beverages section).

grilled lamb on a pita with couscous and yogurt
serves 6

Though the lamb is traditionally barbecued, you may also broil it in the oven if so desired. This dish will appeal to those who may otherwise be reluctant to try lamb. Much of the prep for the meat can be done before hand; it is a great dish for easy warm weather entertaining.

1-1/2 cups	plain yogurt, preferably Balkan style
2 to 3	garlic cloves, pressed
1 tbsp	fresh lemon juice
2 tsp	ground cumin
2 tbsp	freshly chopped cilantro
2-1/4 lb	boneless lamb sirloin, trimmed, cut into 1-inch cubes
1 cup	water
1/4 tsp	salt
2/3 cup	couscous

	half of a cucumber, seeded and chopped
1	ripe tomato, chopped
half	of a small onion, halved and thinly sliced
2 tbsp	olive oil
1/4 cup	black olives
1/4 cup	crumbled feta cheese
2 tbsp	fresh parsley, chopped
6	6-inch-diameter Greek style pita breads

- Set strainer over large bowl. Line strainer with 2 layers of cheesecloth or use coffee filters (do not let strainer touch bottom of bowl). Spoon yogurt into strainer. Let stand at room temperature 1 hour (liquid will drain out and yogurt will thicken; discard liquid).

- Mix yogurt, garlic and lemon juice in small bowl. Season with salt to taste.

- Rub cumin and cilantro over lamb pieces. Thread lamb onto 6 metal skewers.

- (Yogurt mixture and lamb pieces can be prepared 4 hours ahead. Cover these 2 items separately and chill.)

- Combine 1 cup water and 1/4 teaspoon salt in medium saucepan. Bring to boil. Add couscous. Remove from heat. Cover; let stand until liquid is absorbed, about 5 minutes.

- Transfer couscous to large bowl; fluff with fork. Cool to room temperature. Stir in chopped cucumber, tomato, onion, olive oil, olives, feta cheese and fresh parsley. Season with salt and pepper.

- Prepare barbecue (medium-high heat). Grill lamb to desired doneness, turning frequently, about 10 minutes for medium-rare. Transfer to platter. Sprinkle with salt. Grill pitas until heated through and lightly toasted, about 1 minute per side.

- Place 1 pita on each of 6 plates. Spread yogurt mixture evenly over pitas. Spoon couscous down centres of pitas. Slide lamb off skewers onto couscous.

 Use low fat yogurt and feta cheese.

trivia clips

Many incidents in the film are taken from actual events. Lawrence was forced to personally execute a Bedouin who had killed another man. He did this so that the expedition wouldn't disintegrate into a round of revenge killings. Lawrence was so upset after having to do this that he had to be carried onto his camel.

ricotta stuffed dates

serves 6

Medjool dates are the extra large dates that are often bought by the pound. Choose large, plump, intact dates for this simple, but delicious treat. Dates are often consumed to break the period of fasting during Ramadan, an Islamic holy month.

12	plump medjool dates	1 tsp	finely grated orange peel
1/2 cup	ricotta cheese	12	whole almonds (skins on or off, your preference)
1 tsp	superfine sugar		
1 tsp	finely grated lemon peel		

- Carefully slit the dates from end to end, gently pry open and remove the pits. Combine all of the other ingredients, except the almonds, in a small bowl. Mix well, using a wooden spoon. Stuff the dates equally with the mixture using a small teaspoon, pushing it into the cavity and molding the dates around the filling. Place an almond on top of each date and arrange attractively on a pretty serving platter.

Use low fat ricotta for the dates.

Prepare the dates the day before, just cover tightly with plastic wrap so they don't dry out.

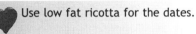
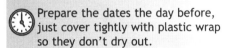

trivia clips

While on a reconnaissance patrol, Lawrence was captured and then flogged and raped by the Turks.
Lawrence was made famous by an American newspaper reporter, Lowell Thomas, who accompanied Lawrence and his Bedouin soldiers for eight days.
Lawrence was killed in a motorcycle accident in 1935.

trivia clips

After the war, Lawrence could have used his popularity to run for office but he refused all of the honours offered to him. He vigorously lobbied the British government to keep their promises of independence to the Arabs.
Lawrence's book The Seven Pillars of Wisdom (1926) describes his wartime experiences and his personal philosophy.

MUSIC

A good choice of music for this event would be the "Rough Guide to North African Music" or "The Rough Guide to World Music Vol.1" (World Music Network)— this compilation boasts 17 tracks representing Africa, Europe and the Middle East. In terms of Moroccan music, try anything by Maroc, especially the CD entitled "Confrerie Des Jilala", a compilation of devotional Islamic music with haunting tones and interesting rhythms. Another good choice is "Arabian Classical Music" (Ethnic) or listen to some mystical sufi music on "Rough Guide to Sufi Music".

SETTING THE STAGE

In many Arabic countries, dinner is served communal style using a low table with cushions placed all around for diners to sit on (if you have kilim cushions, use them). You may wish to copy this atmosphere. Use a fringed or lace tablecloth, or improvise with a pretty scarf as a table runner. Use brass, copper or silver serving trays to place the appetizer dishes on, as well, use other serving ware made of these materials or use stick looking ceramic or clay pieces if you have them. Dim the lights and use incense or light some candles in brass candleholders or in candelabras. Have one of the music selections playing in the background. If you have a small kilim style rug or Oriental carpet you could hang it on the wall for a beautiful backdrop to your dining area. Perhaps you have some souvenirs from the Middle Eastern countries that you could incorporate into a centrepiece. Alternatively, a tray or fruit bowl of dates, oranges, lemons, pomegranates and figs, interspersed with nuts of various types would make a beautiful, edible centrepiece.

You may wish to make this a costume party whether you're having a crowd or just a few guests... think Thousand and One Arabian Nights, the possibilities are endless! You could even organize a group belly dancing lesson with a local dance studio!

my fair lady (1964)

This film is often called one of the all-time great movie musicals. It features classic songs and solid performances by its two top billed stars, Audrey Hepburn and Rex Harrison. My Fair Lady was amongst the top grossing films of 1964 and also at one time the longest-running Broadway musical. Adapted from the George Bernard Shaw comedy, Pygmalion, this same theme would be touched on decades later in the popular 90's hit Pretty Woman. The film is set in the early 1900's, when a rumpled looking flower girl with a Cockney accent, Eliza Doolittle (Audrey Hepburn), captures the attention of linguistic expert Henry Higgins (Rex Harrison). Higgins tells his friend Colonel Pickering (Wilfrid Hyde-White), that he bets he can turn the duckling into a swan in six months by teaching her proper English. The next morning finds a fresher looking Eliza on Higgins' doorstep, offering to pay Higgins to teach her to be a lady. The bet between Higgins and the Colonel is on as Higgins takes up the challenge. A number of surprises occur on the journey of transformation and a stunning finished product blooms in the end. In Higgins' words "irresistible".

FEATURED ACTORS
Audrey Hepburn (Eliza Doolittle)
Rex Harrison (Prof. Henry Higgins)
Stanley Holloway (Alfred P. Doolittle)
Wilfrid Hyde-White (Col. Pickering)
Gladys Cooper (Mrs. Higgins)

DIRECTOR ~ George Cukor

menu
This menu has an English slant to it with some modern twists!
straciatella soup (see index) • easy pot roast • yorkshire pudding • horseradish mashed potatoes (see index) • crusty bread (store-bought) • clementine trifle brûlée (see index)

easy pot roast
serves 6 to 8

1/4 cup	all-purpose flour
1 tsp	salt
1/4 tsp	pepper
5 lb	rump of beef
3 tbsp	cooking oil
2	onions, sliced
2	carrots, peeled and sliced into 1/4-inch rounds
	herbs and seasonings of choice (pepper, bay leaves, parsley, thyme)
1 cup	liquid (wine, bouillon, tomatoes, vegetable broth, etc.)
	vegetables of choice (diced peppers, parsnips, celery, zucchini, etc.)

• Season the flour with the salt and pepper and pound the mixture into the meat with the edge of a plate. Heat the oil in a large Dutch oven over medium heat. Brown meat on all sides in the oil.

• Add the onions, cover and cook over low heat 10 minutes. Add the carrots, herbs, seasonings and liquid. Cover tightly and simmer 3 1/2 to 5 hours, until meat is fork tender. Add desired vegetables during the last 30 minutes of cooking time.

• Variation: For part of the liquid, use 1-1/3 cups of puréed tomatoes. For seasoning, add 1 tablespoon minced parsley, oregano or dill. Once the meat is removed from the pan, add 1 cup sour cream to the sauce.

• Slice the meat and serve on a platter surrounded by the vegetables. Drizzle the meat with sauce. Serve extra sauce on the side .

trivia clips
Julia Andrews did not get cast for the role of Eliza as she was considered "not bankable". However, that same year she beat out Audrey Hepburn at the Oscars, and won the award for Best Actress for her role in Mary Poppins.
This singer was nicknamed "Ghostess with the Mostess". Marni Nixon was one of Hollywood's talented singers who dubbed Hepburn in My Fair Lady, Natalie Wood in West Side Story and Deborah Kerr in The King and I.

my fair lady (1964)

yorkshire pudding

serves 6

1 heaping cup	all-purpose flour	2	eggs
1/4 tsp	salt	4 to 5 tbsp	melted butter or cooking oil
1 cup	milk		

- To make the batter: In a bowl, combine flour, salt, and milk until well blended. Add eggs and blend together until you have a smooth liquid batter. Let batter stand at room temperature for 1 hour.

- You have two options for baking: the muffin pan method or the roasting pan method. We prefer using the muffin pans as the individual puddings hold their shape better and make for a nicer presentation.

- To bake in a 9 x 13-inch ovenproof roasting pan: Preheat oven to 450°F. Place roasting pan in oven and heat for 10 minutes. Place the butter or oil into the pan and continue heating for 10 to 15 minutes. Next pour in the prepared batter and bake for 20 to 25 minutes or until golden brown. Serve immediately.

- To bake in a large 6 muffin pan: Preheat oven to 375°F. Place pan in oven and heat for 10 minutes. Place equal amounts of the fat into each muffin mold and continue heating in oven for 10 to 15 minutes. Pour equal amounts of prepared batter into each muffin mold and bake for 15 to 20 minutes or until golden brown. Serve immediately.

BEVERAGES

With dinner, a robust red is required; try Woods End Baco Noir (Ontario), Stoney Ridge Bench Cabernet Franc (Ontario) or even Talus Zinfandel (USA).

Pink Lady, Kir Royale, Champagne Cocktails, Cappuccino Punch (see main beverages page)

MUSIC

"My Fair Lady: Original Soundtrack" (Sony/Columbia) is available. Alternatively, celebrate female musicians by having each guest bring to the get together their favourite album by a female performer. Play each guests' musical choice during the spa sessions (see below) or during dinner.

SETTING THE STAGE

Since this movie deals with transformation or makeover, it would be a perfect time to have a spa dinner with your female friends. Invite your guests to a fun-filled evening where they would be pampered. Contact your local beauty salon and ask to have a stylist come to your home for a couple of hours to do either up-dos or sets. Salons will often give great group rates. You could also arrange for an esthetician to come along to provide facials, manicures, the works! All in the comfort of your home! Also, go to your local upscale retail store and ask for their professional wardrobe consultant and make arrangements to have the stylist come to your home during your party for at least an hour. The consultant could bring clothing samples from their store and make professional assessments of your guests, advising them of the best colours and styles suitable for them. As well, clothing companies that sell clothing through home parties also offer wardrobe consultations. Meanwhile arrange a comfortable place in your home and transform it into a spa-like setting. Place fresh cut flowers in pretty vases in several locations. Roll up colourful towels and place in baskets, you'll need them. Tell your guests to bring their housecoats. Purchase inexpensive flip-flops or slippers (dollar stores are a good source) for your guests. Fill the room with scented candles and bowls of sample soaps. Bring out a tray of nail polish in the latest colours for guests to try. An excellent idea to suggest to your guests is to bring outfits they no longer wear or like and exchange with other guests at the get together. Any unwanted clothing could be donated to charity. Pamper your guests and set a formal table using proper place settings (just like in the film). Use your best china, silver and crystal and a damask tablecloth. Serve a variety of herb teas that the ladies could sip while getting pampered, and don't forget every woman's favourite treat—chocolate! Splurge on some fancy, good quality chocolates and serve them on doily lined silver trays for an extra special touch. Indulge yourselves fair ladies!

AWARDS WON

Best Actor Rex Harrison)	1964 Academy Award
Best Art Direction (George James Hopkins)	1964 Academy Award
Best Art Direction (Cecil Beaton)	1964 Academy Award
Best Art Direction (Gene Allen)	1964 Academy Award
Best Cinematography (Harry Stradling Jr.)	1964 Academy Award
Best Costume Design (Cecil Beaton)	1964 Academy Award
Best Director (George Cukor)	1964 Academy Award
Best Picture	1964 Academy Award
Best Score (Andre Previn)	1964 Academy Award
Best Sound (George R. Groves)	1964 Academy Award
Best Director (George Cukor)	1964 Directors Guild of America Award
10 Best Films	1964 National Board of Review of Motion Pictures Award
Best Actor (Rex Harrison)	1964 National Board of Review of Motion Pictures Award
Best Actress (Audrey Hepburn)	1964 New York Film Critics Circle Award
Best Direction (George Cukor)	1964 New York Film Critics Circle Award
Best Film	1964 New York Film Critics Circle Award
Best Film — Any Source	1965 British Academy Award
Best Actor — in Musical/ Comedy (Rex Harrison)	1965 Golden Globe Award
Best Director (George Cukor)	1965 Golden Globe Award
Best Film — in Musical/ Comedy	1965 Golden Globe Award
100 Greatest American Movies	1998 American Film Institute Award

the sound of music (1965)

This enduringly popular old-fashioned musical is suitable even for children. Julie Andrews plays Maria, a young nun with both a talent and penchant for singing, so much so that she sometimes misses her morning prayers! Her Mother Superior feels that Maria should experience more of the real world prior to taking her final vows and finds her a position as governess to the seven children of widower Captain Von Trapp. Maria, who is the latest in a long line of governesses, brings a sense of fun and genuine warmth to the normally cold, stoic atmosphere of the Von Trapp household. She wins the hearts of the children, particularly the oldest daughter Liesl. Maria soon realizes that she is falling in love with Captain Von Trapp and decides to return to Nonnberg Abbey. Interestingly enough, she is encouraged to return to Von Trapp by her Mother Superior. Upon her return, Von Trapp breaks off his engagement to the wealthy Baroness Schrader and weds the women he really cares for: Maria. Alas, their carefree honeymoon period is shattered by the Nazis' insistence that Captain Von Trapp to report for naval duties. He refuses and comes up with a plan to escape with his family to Switzerland using the cover of a music festival.

FEATURED ACTORS
Julie Andrews (Maria)
Christopher Plummer
   (Captain Von Trapp)
Eleanor Parker (the Baroness)
Richard Haydn (Max Detweiler)
Peggy Wood (Mother Abbess)

DIRECTOR ~ Robert Wise

menu
continental style veal cutlets • twice-cooked potatoes • green salad with austrian style lemon-sour cream dressing • crusty or rye bread (store-bought) • sacher torte

continental style veal cutlets
serves 6

A great dish for company; this is continental cuisine at its finest. Serve with a good Riesling wine and you'll impress your guests.

1/2 cup	cream cheese	1/4 cup	grated caciocavallo cheese (Swiss cheese may be substituted)
1	small onion, minced		
1/2 cup	minced flat leaf parsley		cooking oil
1/2 tbsp	hot pepper, chopped (optional)	6	veal cutlets
5	eggs	6	slices prosciutto
	salt and pepper to taste		flour for dredging
1/4 cup	dry curd cottage cheese or ricotta cheese		fine bread crumbs for dredging

- In a small bowl, mix together the cream cheese, onion, parsley, hot pepper (if using), 2 beaten eggs, salt and pepper, cottage and caciocavallo cheese. Set aside.

- Heat cooking oil in a skillet or a deep fryer to medium-high heat. Pound the cutlets with a meat mallet and sprinkle with salt. Place a spoonful of the cheese filling on one half of the cutlet, place a slice of prosciutto on top of the cheese, and fold the other half of the cutlet over this. Secure with toothpicks so that the filling won't come out.

- Beat the remaining 3 eggs in a bowl. Put flour and bread crumbs into separate bowls suitable for dredging. Dredge cutlets first in flour, then in

eggs and finally in bread crumbs. Fry until golden on both sides.

- Another option would be to roll the meat once the filling has been placed on top, just secure with toothpicks and ensure that the roll is golden on all sides before removing from the skillet.

 Make the cheese filling the day before.

 Use low fat cheese. Reduce the eggs in the filling to one whole egg plus one egg white.

trivia clips
The film was shot in Austria, in and around Salzburg.
Julie Andrews earned $225,000 for her role in the film.
The front and the back of the Von Trapp estate were actually two different locations.

continued

twice-cooked potatoes

serves 4 to 6

In this recipe the potatoes are first boiled and then sautéed with onions and paprika. This simple side dish goes especially well with schnitzels and pork chops.

2-1/2 lb	potatoes
	salt
2	onions, sliced
1/4 cup	olive or canola oil

1 tbsp	ground paprika (or to taste)
	salt and pepper to taste
	parsley, chopped for garnish (optional)

- Boil the potatoes in their skins in salted water. While the potatoes are cooking, sauté the onions in the oil in a large skillet over medium heat. Set skillet aside when the onions are soft and beginning to caramelize. Peel the potatoes when done and quarter them. Put the potatoes in the skillet with the onions. Over medium heat sauté briefly, then sprinkle with paprika and salt and pepper. Sprinkle with parsley if so desired, serve hot.

 Use a non-stick skillet and reduce the oil to 2 tablespoons.

green salad with austrian style lemon-sour cream dressing

1	head Boston lettuce or other delicate greens
1 cup	sour cream
2 tbsp	lemon juice
2 tsp	sugar

1 tsp	salt
	freshly ground pepper
	fresh dill, chopped (optional)

- Wash lettuce, spin dry and tear into small pieces. Set aside.

- In a separate small bowl, combine the sour cream with the lemon juice, sugar, salt, pepper and dill. Whisk until all of the ingredients are combined. Toss salad with dressing and transfer to serving bowl or platter.

AWARDS WON

Best Director (Robert Wise)	1965 Academy Award
Best Editing (William H. Reynolds)	1965 Academy Award
Best Picture	1965 Academy Award
Best Score (Irwin Kostal)	1965 Academy Award
Best Sound (James Corcoran)	1965 Academy Award
Best Sound (Fred Hynes/ Todd AO Sound Dept)	1965 Academy Award
Best Director (Robert Wise)	1965 Directors Guild of America Award
10 Best Films Board	1965 National of Review of Motion Pictures
Best Actress (Julie Andrews)	1965 New York Film Critics Circle Award
Best Actress in Musical/Comedy (Julie Andrews)	1965 Golden Globe Award
Best Film in Musical/Comedy	1965 Golden Globe Award
100 Greatest American Movies	1998 American Film Institute

(1965)

BEVERAGES

What else but beer! If you wish to serve from a keg we suggest Bitburger Keg (Germany) or for individual bottles try Rieder Dunkle Weisse, Gösser Heller Bock, Haydn-Bräu Pils, Stiegl Gold Spezial, or Zipfer Pils (all from Austria). If you can't find any of these, use a German or Dutch imported beer. Perhaps you could try a variety of beers from these areas. Cheers to you the Austrian way, "Prost"!

Weingut Undhof Riesling-Spätlese Kremser Kögl (Austria) is a good choice if you wish to serve wine, as is Daruvarski Rizling (Croatia).

MUSIC

There is of course the soundtrack entitled "The Sound of Music". Otherwise, listen to some classical music composed by famous Austrians such as Mozart or Haydn.

SETTING THE STAGE

Though one could try and emulate the setting of fine Viennese hotels or restaurants, because this is a family film we suggest going for more of a casual atmosphere. Perhaps one that could be found in small, family run restaurants in the Austrian Alps. Use some simple flowers, such as wild flowers or daisies and place them in a vase, or better yet arrange them in an old teapot or cup. Place some greenery, such as pine boughs on the table for a touch of colour. Use a simple white tablecloth or one with a conservative print such as gingham. Serve the salad in a wooden salad bowl and place the bread on a wooden platter. Serve the schnitzels on one side of a large tray or platter with the potatoes on the other side. Serve beer in frosted beer mugs (frost by placing in freezer for at least 15 minutes) or from a cask. Pour the children's drinks into frosted mugs too, they'll think it's quite neat.

sacher torte

Yield: 1 cake (serves 8 to 10)

This torte was invented in 1832 by a master baker named Franz Sacher to win the favour of well-known Austrian statesman, Prince Klemens von Metternich, who had a sweet tooth. Sacher's descendants operated the famous Sacher Hotel in Vienna for many years. The cake was of course a featured item on the menu and the recipe was closely guarded for a long time. As with all good things, it was meant to be shared, so eventually the recipe became public knowledge. Now a number of versions of this renowned torte exist; here is an especially good one.

Cake:	
1/4 lb	sweet butter
1/2 cup	sugar
4	eggs, separated
4	squares (4 ounces) dark chocolate, melted and cooled
2/3 cup	all-purpose flour
2 tbsp	good quality apricot jam (preferably imported European)

Ganache:	
5	squares (5 ounces) dark chocolate, chopped
1/4 cup	heavy cream
	whipped cream for garnish (optional)

- Cake: Preheat oven to 350°F. Grease a 9-inch round cake pan with oil or cooking spray and set aside. In a medium sized bowl, beat butter and sugar with an electric mixer until light and creamy. Add yolks one at a time, mixing well between each addition. Next, add the chocolate and beat until well combined. Using a wooden spoon, fold in the flour.

- In a separate small bowl, beat the egg whites with an electric mixer until soft peaks form (make sure the beaters are clean and dry). Using a wooden spoon fold the egg whites into the chocolate mixture, until evenly combined. Spoon mixture into prepared cake tin, smooth the surface of the cake using a rubber spatula. Bake for 40 minutes, or until a toothpick inserted in the centre comes out clean. Let the cake cool in the pan for 15 minutes prior to turning out onto wire rack to cool.

- Warm jam in a microwave or in a small saucepan over medium-low heat until it turns to liquid. Strain through a small sieve. Place cake upside down on a wire rack so that the base is on

top; brush evenly with jam. Set aside and make ganache.

- Ganache: Combine chocolate and cream in a small saucepan. Stir over low heat until the chocolate has melted and the mixture is smooth. Remove from heat, cool slightly.

- Set the wire rack with the cake on it into a jelly roll pan (this will facilitate clean-up after glazing the cake). Reserve 2 tablespoons of the ganache and place into a small piping bag or small self closing sandwich bag, set aside. Hold the saucepan about 2 inches away from the cake and slowly pour ganache over the cake, spreading evenly. Next, with the reserved ganache in the piping bag, write the word Sacher in the middle of the torte.

- Serve with a dollop of whipped cream on the side if so desired.

 This cake may be prepared several days in advance if stored in an air tight container.

viva las vegas (1963)

Las Vegas is known for its sumptuous buffets. Serve the meal buffet-style and offer any of the following suggested main dishes based upon the number of guests you will be having. Feel free to add your own favourite items to the buffet. You could also purchase some ready- made appetizers and other menu items.

menu
peanut butter & banana sandwiches • patriotic vegetable platter and herbed dip (see index) • sweet & sour meatballs • cilantro rice with peas and corn • oven barbecued chicken (see index) • roasted potato wedges with sea salt and paprika (see index) • green salad with vinaigrette dressing (see index) • sweet potato pie

peanut butter & banana sandwiches
serves 6 to 8

This is said to have been one of the "King's" favourite treats. It is worth a try and most definitely a great way to get your guests in a fun mood! This would also appeal to children...

1/4 cup	creamy peanut butter	10	slices bread, preferably whole grain
2	very ripe bananas, mashed with a fork	3 tbsp	sugar mixed with 1 tsp cinnamon
	butter		

- Blend the peanut butter with the banana until creamy. Spread the mixture over 5 slices of the bread. Top with the remaining bread.

- In a skillet, melt enough butter to coat the bottom of the pan. Place the sandwiches in the butter and grill them until the bread is lightly toasted. Flip to grill the other side. Drain on paper towels.

- Cut sandwiches into triangles to serve as a fun finger food; sprinkle with cinnamon sugar and arrange on serving plate.

Use reduced fat peanut butter and light butter. Grill in a non-stick skillet.

Elvis never received an Academy Award for any of his films, but to his many fans he is still "The King". We thought that we would include one of his films for his fans to enjoy. For those of you who don't know much about the man or his music, this movie will motivate you to learn more about this American music legend who shook the music world with his swiveling hips and good looks. In the early 1950's he broke out onto the music scene and "Shook, rattled and rolled" in his "blue suede shoes". Elvis made a number of movies in the 60's, none of which were huge commercial hits, but it is still his movies many of us remember him by. In this movie , Elvis plays, Lucky Jackson, a racecar driver competing in the Las Vegas Grand Prix opposite his main rival Count Elmo Mancini played by Cesare Danova. Luck Jackson takes a job as a casino waiter to earn enough money to pay for his entry fee in the race. He also ends up singing at the casino, and of course he is a magnet for women, whether they be co-workers or patrons of the casino! Somehow though he attracts the wrong kind of women and is oblivious at first to the one who would be most suitable for him. In the end, this dream girl, Rusty Martin (played by Ann-Margret), manages to finally snag her man. With two beautiful stars in their prime, and a whopping twelve songs on the soundtrack you can't go wrong with this film!

FEATURED ACTORS
Elvis Presley (Lucky Jackson)
Ann-Margret (Rusty Martin)
Cesare Danova
        (Count Elmo Mancini)
William Demarest (Mr. Martin)
Nicky Blair (Shorty Farnsworth)

DIRECTOR ~ George Sidney

trivia clips

"Yogurt and vegetables — I don't know ... What's good for the body ain't always good for the taste buds." Elvis Presley on Food
"Ain't nowhere else in the world where you can go from driving a truck to driving a Cadillac overnight. Nowhere." Elvis Presley on "The American Dream"

continued

BEVERAGES

Offer a variety of alcoholic and non-alcoholic choices. Some mixed drinks to try are: "Leaving Las Vegas," "Sex Machine," "Banana Sandwich," "Between the Sheets," "Blue Hawaii," "Acapulco Gold" and "Strawberry Blonde" (see main beverages page). Citrus Mint Punch would be a refreshing non-alcoholic choice (see main beverages page).

Otherwise, offer a variety of international beers and mineral waters to go with the buffet theme.

MUSIC

"Elvis: The Legendary Performer Series" (RCA) is an amazing collection of Elvis Presley's songs from the 50's, 60's and 70's.

SETTING THE STAGE

You can have fun with this theme. Hire an Elvis impersonator to make an appearance at your party or have guests come as "The King". Set up card tables to use as dining tables, and use your dining room table for the buffet. Ask your guests to arrive dressed to the nines — after all, high rollers have to look good. Set up a stage or performing area for entertainment, using a shiny, shimmering curtain (improvise with a tablecloth or an inexpensive piece of fabric, or even foil covered cardboard as a backdrop would do).

Borrow or rent a karaoke machine and belt out your favourite Elvis tunes. Cover your buffet table with a green tablecloth. There is no need to use very fancy plates as you will be stacking them on the buffet table. String a few twinkling lights across the ceiling and decorate with a few large fuzzy dice and playing cards. Bring out the lava lamps and mirror balls. Set out any kitschy souvenirs you may have from Las Vegas or any other gambling havens. Provide your guests with lottery tickets as favours and don't forget to tell them that "Elvis has left the building"!

sweet & sour meatballs
Makes 4 dozen

These meatballs are perfect for entertaining and are a hit with guests of all ages.

1/3 cup	bread crumbs
1/2 cup	water
1/2 cup	light cream
3 tbsp	cooking oil
2 tbsp	onion, finely chopped
3/4 lb	ground beef
1/4 lb	ground pork
3/4 tsp	salt
3/4 tsp	sugar
1/4 tsp	freshly ground pepper

Sweet and Sour Sauce:

2 tbsp	cornstarch
1/2 tsp	salt
1/4 cup	packed light brown sugar
1/4 cup	vinegar
1 cup	pineapple juice

- In a large mixing bowl combine the bread crumbs, water and cream. Set aside.

- In a heavy skillet, heat 1 tablespoon of oil and sauté the onion until transparent. Transfer the onion to a separate mixing bowl and add the ground beef, ground pork, salt, sugar, pepper, and bread crumb mixture, blending well. Shape the meat into balls about 3/4-inch in diameter.

- In the same skillet, heat 2 tablespoons of oil over medium heat. Brown the meatballs, turning frequently to brown evenly. Reduce the heat and cover. Continue to cook for about 10 minutes, turning frequently, adding more oil if necessary.

- In a saucepan, blend together the remaining ingredients. Cook over medium heat until thick, stirring constantly. Pour the sauce over the cooked meatballs.

 Use lean ground beef and pork. Broiling the meatballs on a rack in a baking pan will drain off the fat. Use a non-stick skillet to fry the meatballs. Use evaporated skim milk in place of light cream.

 Make the meatballs up to 2 days before, reheat gently in sauce prior to serving.

cilantro rice with peas and corn
serves 4 to 6 as a side dish

2 tsp	cumin seeds
1 tbsp	vegetable oil
3 cups	chilled cooked long grain white rice
1 tbsp	seasoned rice vinegar

1 tbsp	soy sauce
1 cup	fresh cilantro, chopped
4	scallions, chopped
1 cup	frozen peas
1 cup	frozen corn kernels

- In a large, non-stick skillet, sauté cumin seeds in oil over moderately high heat, stirring until fragrant, about 1 minute. Add rice and fry, stirring occasionally, until heated through, about 3 minutes.

- Add vinegar and soy sauce, stirring to coat rice and stir-fry until liquid is evaporated. Stir in cilantro, scallions, peas and corn and continue to stir-fry until heated through, about 2 minutes, seasoning with salt if necessary.

viva
las vegas (1963)

sweet potato pie

This Southern specialty is also known to have been one of Elvis' favourites.

2	small sweet potatoes
1	medium russet or Yukon Gold potato
1/2 cup	sweet butter
1 cup	packed brown sugar
1/2 tsp	grated nutmeg
3	large eggs, beaten

1-1/4 cups	evaporated milk
1/2 tsp	vanilla extract
1	9" unbaked pie crust (store-bought or homemade — see recipes for "It Happened One Night")
	whipped cream for garnish (optional)

- Place all of the well-scrubbed potatoes in a 3-quart saucepan. Cover with cold water and bring to a boil. Reduce heat to a simmer and cook until potatoes are very soft, about 20 to 30 minutes. Drain, and when cool enough to handle, peel. In medium bowl, combine potatoes, butter, brown sugar and nutmeg. Using a potato masher, cream the potatoes until very smooth. In small bowl, beat eggs, 1 cup evaporated milk and vanilla together.

- Beat this mixture into the potatoes. Mix thoroughly. Pour into piecrust and drizzle the remaining 1/4 cup of milk on top. Bake 15 minutes in a preheated 450°F oven then turn heat to 325°F and continue baking for 30 minutes or more until the filling is set. Serve with a dollop of whipped cream if so desired.

 Use egg substitute to replace 1 of the eggs and use evaporated skim milk.

trivia clips

Elvis' favourite soda pop was Pepsi.
Elvis' only child, a daughter, married and then divorced which famous rock/pop sensation?
Graceland is still one of the most popular tourist sites in Memphis. Elvis named his estate after his mother, whom he adored.

west side story (1961)

This film is a twist on the classic story of Romeo and Juliet. It has been updated and set in New York City. This Oscar-winning musical landmark was adapted from the Broadway musical of the same name by Ernest Lehman. In the movie, two rival street gangs, the Jets, second-generation American teens, and the Sharks, Puerto Rican immigrant teens, are in a tense relationship. The tension increases as the Jets' leader, Riff (Russ Tamblyn), challenges the Sharks to one last rumble. The Sharks' leader, Bernardo (George Chakiris), and Riff decide to meet to talk things out. Riff brings along his good friend and Jets co-founder Tony (Richard Beymer). But Tony has a secret, his heart and mind are elsewhere... beyond the boundaries of his own turf. Tony has fallen for the rival gang leader Bernardo's sister, Maria (Natalie Wood). The circumstances classify this as a forbidden love affair, thus it is inevitable that complications will ensue and that tragedy is written in the stars for the two young lovers.

Unlike many film adaptations of Broadway scores, West Side Story incorporates all of the songs from the stage production with only minor changes to satisfy censors. The choreography is stunning and it is easy to see why this film received numerous accolades and awards!

FEATURED ACTORS
Natalie Wood (Maria)
Richard Beymer (Tony)
Russ Tamblyn (Riff)
Rita Moreno (Anita)
George Chakiris (Bernardo)

DIRECTOR ~ Jerome Robbins
Director / Choreography

Robert Wise Producer / Director

menu
fried plantain chips • black bean soup • spicy puerto rican style chicken • cilantro rice with peas and corn (see index) • vanilla flan

fried plantain chips
serves 4 to 6

4   green plantains
     salt

vegetable oil for frying

• Peel the plantains and slice crosswise as thinly as possible. Drop into salted ice water and let stand for 30 minutes. Drain and dry on paper towels.

• Heat oil in a skillet or deep fryer to 370˚F (the oil should be at least 1-inch deep). Fry plantain slices until golden. Drain on paper towels, sprinkle with salt and serve as an accompaniment to drinks.

black bean soup
serves 6 to 8

3 tbsp	Caribbean or Jamaican jerk seasoning blend
6	(15- to 16-ounce cans) black beans, drained
3-3/4 cups	canned vegetable broth
6 tbsp	olive oil

6 tbsp	fresh lime juice
	plain yogurt (for garnish)
1	red or green onion, chopped (for garnish)
	lime wedges

• Heat a medium, heavy saucepan over medium heat. Add the seasoning blend to the saucepan, and stir until fragrant and slightly darker in color, about 4 minutes. Transfer seasoning to food processor. Add black beans, vegetable broth and olive oil to processor and purée until mixture is almost smooth. You may need to scrape down sides of bowl occasionally. Transfer purée to same saucepan. Bring to a gentle boil, stirring occasionally. Mix in lime juice.

Season soup to taste with salt and pepper. Garnish the soup with yogurt and chopped red or green onions. Serve with lime wedges.

 Use low fat plain yogurt. Reduce olive oil by half and use a non-stick saucepan.

trivia clips
Director Robert Wise and co-director Robbins feuded on the set which delayed production time. Robbins insisted on extra rehearsals to get the choreography just right. Wise tired of him and had him removed from the set!
Natalie Wood was married to Robert Wagner up until her tragic drowning in 1981. Her real name was Natasha Nicholaevna Gurdin, she was of Russian descent.

west side story (1961)

continued

spicy puerto rican style chicken

serves 4

1	4 to 5 lb chicken, cut in pieces
8	garlic cloves, peeled
1 tsp	kosher or rock salt
1 tbsp	chopped fresh oregano
1 tsp	black peppercorns
4	small hot chili peppers, chopped
1 tsp	minced fresh ginger root
1/4 tsp	saffron threads
1/2 tsp	ground cumin seeds

1/2 cup	olive oil
2 tsp	paprika
3	green onions, chopped
2	medium tomatoes, chopped
1/2 cup	red wine
1/3 cup	brandy
1/3 cup	chicken stock
2 tbsp	chopped fresh cilantro
	lemon wedges for garnish

- Wash the chicken parts, pat dry and remove the skin. Place in a deep square pan and set aside. In a food processor, combine garlic, salt, oregano, and black peppercorns. Process until garlic is crushed and peppercorns are cracked, then add the chili peppers, minced ginger, saffron threads and cumin seeds. Process until a paste forms and then incorporate the oil slowly.

- Spread the mixture evenly over the chicken parts, lifting the chicken pieces to ensure distribution of the marinade to the bottom of the chicken parts. Sprinkle all parts with paprika.

- Cover and refrigerate overnight.

- Preheat a deep skillet over medium heat. Arrange marinated chicken pieces side by side and brown the chicken on all sides. Spread the chopped onions, chopped tomatoes, and drizzle the wine, brandy and chicken stock over the chicken parts.

- Cover and finish cooking on low heat for approximately 35 minutes. Remove from heat and sprinkle chopped cilantro on the chicken prior to serving.

Use low fat chicken stock.

Use chicken thighs or breasts, or a mixture of the two.

AWARDS WON

Best Art Direction (Victor A. Gangelin)	1961 Academy Award
Best Art Direction (Boris Leven)	1961 Academy Award
Best Cinematography (Daniel L. Fapp)	1961 Academy Award
Best Costume Design (Irene Sharaff)	1961 Academy Award
Best Director (Jerome Robbins/ Robert Wise)	1961 Academy Award
Best Editing (Thomas G. Stanford)	1961 Academy Award
Best Picture	1961 Academy Award
Best Score (Saul Chaplin, Sid Ramin, Johnny Green, Irwin Kostal)	1961 Academy Award
Best Sound (Gordon Sawyer /Fred Hynes)	1961 Academy Award
Best Supporting Actor (George Chakiris)	1961 Academy Award
Best Supporting Actress (Rita Moreno)	1961 Academy Award
Best Director (Robert Wise/ Jerome Robbins)	1961 Directors Guild of America Award
Best Direction (Robert Wise/ Jerome Robbins)	1961 New York Film Critics Circle Award
Best Film (Robert Wise)	1961 New York Film Critics Circle Award
Best Screenwriting (Ernest Lehman)	1961 New York Film Critics Circle Award
Best Film — Any Source and British (Robert Wise/Jerome Robbins)	1962 British Academy Award
Best Supporting Actor (George Chakiris)	1962 Golden Globe Award
Best Supporting Actress (Rita Moreno)	1962 Golden Globe Award
U.S. National Film Registry	1997 Library of Congress Award
100 Greatest American Movies	1998 American Film Institute Award

west side story (1961)

BEVERAGES

"Cerveza, por favor", as beer can handle the spices in the dish! If you can't find a Puerto Rican beer like Medalla, try: Carib Lager (Trinidad), Corona (Mexico), Red Stripe (Jamaica), or even Tiger Beer (Singapore)

MUSIC

"West Side Story: The Original Soundtrack" (Sony/Columbia) is available. Alternatively, listen to something with a Latin beat like "Latin Dance Party Vol. 1-5" (Premium Music) with music by various artists. Or "Salsa" (International) featuring Celina Gonzale, Malena Burke and Nglabanda. The album has 9 tracks that will have you up and moving to the beat! "Salsa Mundo" is an interesting album as it features salsa played by musicians from all over the world. It is a testament to how the Afro-Cuban sound has influenced music cross-culturally. "Luis Mario and Cimarron" (La Fiesta) is an album which is a fusion of Cuban and Puerto Rican salsa by an Havana born tenor. You could also listen to "Buena Vista Social Club" (Electra/Asylum) by the group of Cuban musicians of the same name who play a Latin Jazz type music. Another good choice would be Santana's "Supernatural" (Arista) CD featuring the song "Smooth".

To listen to some traditional Puerto Rican plena music try "Puerto Rico, Puerto Rico" (Shanachie) by the band named Los Pleneros de la 21/Los Conjunto. This vibrant type of music proves that Puerto Rico has more to offer than salsa.

SETTING THE STAGE

Since this is a romantic movie the setting would be ideal for a couple. The choreography in the movie is fabulous, especially with the Latin-beat of the music. The cha-cha, and mambo are dances that are fun to learn. Check out your local dance studio and learn some of these dances prior to your dinner, or have the instructor come to your home for a lesson or two. Clear a large area in your home to make room for a dance floor, and have a go at dancing to a Latin beat with your partner.

vanilla flan

serves 6

1/4 cup	water		1	14-ounce can low-fat sweetened condensed milk
1/2 cup	sugar		1-1/2 cups	skim milk
3	large eggs		1 tbsp	vanilla

- Preheat oven to 325˚F.

- In a small, heavy saucepan bring water and sugar to a boil, stirring until sugar is dissolved. Boil this syrup, without stirring, until it is a golden caramel. Pour caramel into a 1-1/2-quart soufflé or other glass dish such as a deep pie plate. Tilt the dish to coat the bottom and some of side with caramel.

- In a large bowl, whisk together eggs, condensed milk, skim milk, and vanilla until smooth. Pour mixture through a fine sieve into soufflé dish. Put dish in a baking pan and add enough hot water to pan to reach halfway up side of dish. Bake flan in middle of oven 1-1/4 hours, or until it is just set, but still trembles slightly. (Flan will set as it cools.)

- Remove flan from pan and cool in dish on a rack. Chill flan, covered, until cold, at least 4 hours and up to 1 day. To remove from baking dish: dip dish in a baking pan of hot water for 3 seconds. Run a thin knife around edge of dish and invert flan onto serving plate.

Did You Know That...

Use real vanilla extract for enhanced flavour.

Vanilla beans are actually the pods of a wild climbing orchid native to the rainforests of southern Mexico.

The beans are ripened, cured and fermented to bring out their intense, delicious flavour.

SETTING THE STAGE - CONTINUED

Latin music has become wildly popular, especially with today's Latino entertainers and their domination of the pop charts and the movie screens!

Since this movie takes place in the 1960's you may choose to decorate your home with 60's paraphernalia : peace symbols, unique ceramic bowls or plates, use some of the macramé, plant hangers or place mats you've been hanging on to. Another idea is to use red and blue bandannas as your place mats or napkins. Bandannas are often used by "gangs" to identify and distinguish themselves.

1970's

1970-   The first Earth Day was celebrated.

1971-   Soft contact lenses are introduced.

1971-   Texas Instruments introduced the first electronic calculator. It was portable but not small enough to be a pocket calculator.

1972-   Berenice Gera first female umpire in pro baseball.

1972 -   Mark Spitz an American, becomes the first athlete to win 7 Olympic gold medals.

1973-   Emily Warner becomes the first female commercial airline pilot in the US. (Frontier Airlines)

1974-   Mia Farrow appeared on the cover of the first People Magazine.

1974-   Richard Milhous Nixon, first and only U.S. president to resign from office.

1975-   the first personal computer, the Altair 8800, went on the market. It used an Intel 8800 microchip. This machine was followed within two years by a personal computer from Tandy Corporation, sold through its Radio Shack outlets. Soon after came the Apple Computer, designed by Stephen Wozniak and Stephen Jobs.

1976-   Commercial supersonic transport becomes a reality. Supersonic airplanes are those that fly faster than the speed of sound, or about 740 miles (1,190 kilometers) per hour. The first commercial supersonic plane to go into regular service was the Concorde, built in Europe by a French-British consortium. The Concorde began regular service in Europe on Jan. 21, 1976.

1977-   "Saturday Night Fever" premieres fueling discomania.

1978-   Test-tube baby Louise Brown is born. Her birth was the first known birth of a baby conceived outside its mother's womb. This miracle took place in Lancashire, England, on July 25, 1978.

1979-   Invention of the compact disc. A new technique, invented in 1979, for recording sound and playing it back, revolutionized the recording industry in the 1980s. The compact disc, or CD, has since replaced the older style long-play (LP) records in most music stores. Music CDs became available in Japan in 1982 and in North America and Europe in 1983.

fiddler on the roof (1971)

Fiddler on the Roof was a long-running Broadway musical before it was adapted to the screen by Canadian director Norman Jewison. The film is set in the Ukrainian village of Anatevka. The main character is Tevye (played by Topol, the same Israeli actor who had the role on the London stage). He is the village milkman, a man blessed by no less than five daughters. His day-to-day existence is constantly challenged by poverty, prejudice and the romantic escapades of his daughters. Tevye is a god-fearing man and when the going gets tough he carries on lengthy conversations with God, who is at least a better listener than Tevye's wife. Looking to secure the future of his eldest daughter Tzeitel, he arranges a marriage for her to wealthy butcher Lazar Wolf. Complications ensue when she falls in love with poor tailor Motel Kamzoil. But it does not end there. Tevye finds out that his other daughter Chava, has fallen in love with and wants to marry Fyedka, a non-Jew. "Tradition, tradition" is all Tevye has and all that he can really hold on to. His life is thrown into further turmoil as pogroms against the Jews are carried out by the Czar's followers. Tevye and his fellow villagers are forced to leave their village as their lives take an unexpected turn. This was one of the last successful Hollywood-financed movie musicals. It is spirited, funny and features some wonderful music! The cinematography is Oscar-winning and the set is amazing. A must-see film that is suitable for young and old alike!

FEATURED ACTORS
Topol (Tevye), Norma Crane (Golde)
Leonard Frey (Motel)
Molly Picon (Yente)
Paul Mann (Lazar
Wolf), Rosalind Harris (Tzeitel)
Stanley Fleet (Farcel)
Stella Courtney (Shandel)
Jacob Kalich (Yankel)

DIRECTOR ~ Norman Jewison

menu golden potato latkes • brisket with root vegetables • kasha varnishkes • green salad with vinaigrette dressing (see index) • rye bread (store-bought) • noodle kugel

golden potato latkes
serves 6 to 8

This version of potato latkes uses both Yukon Gold potatoes and sweet potatoes for an extra special flavourful touch.

3	small onions, quartered
5 to 6	Yukon Gold potatoes (about 2-1/2 pounds)
2	sweet potatoes (about 1-1/2 pounds)
4	eggs, beaten

1/3 cup	all-purpose flour
1 tsp	baking powder
1-1/4	tsp salt
1/2 tsp	pepper
	vegetable oil for cooking
	sour cream (for topping)

• Peel onions, Yukon Gold and sweet potatoes. If using a food processor, cut vegetables lengthwise into quarters. By hand or in food processor using shredder blade, alternately shred onions and potatoes. Transfer to colander; squeeze out as much moisture as possible, discarding liquid. Transfer to large bowl. Mix in eggs, flour, baking powder, salt and pepper.

• In a large skillet, heat an inch of vegetable oil over medium-high heat until hot but not smoking.

• Add 1/4 cup mixture per latke, leaving space between each; flatten slightly. Cook for 3 minutes or until browned and crisp around edges; turn and cook for 3 to 5 minutes longer, or until crisp and golden. Transfer to paper towel-lined racks to drain well. Repeat with remaining mixture, stirring to reblend, removing any cooked bits from skillet and adding more oil as necessary. Serve with sour cream for topping.

 Use low fat sour cream.

 Make the latkes ahead of time; cover and refrigerate for up to 3 hours; re-crisp in 450°F oven for about 5 minutes.

trivia clips

The movie wasn't filmed in Ukraine, it was actually filmed in the beautiful country of former Yugoslavia. Former Yugoslavia has a Jewish population now scattered mainly throughout Serbia, Croatia and Bosnia.
Twenty-nine percent of the total world population of Jews live in Israel, 45% in the United States and Canada, 10% in the Soviet Union and 8% in Europe.
Fiddler on the Roof was the second highest-grossing movie of the year (after The Godfather).

fiddler on the roof (1971)

brisket with root vegetables serves 8

3 tbsp	oil
3	medium onions, chopped
4	large cloves garlic, minced
2 tbsp	tomato paste
1 tbsp	Hungarian paprika
3-1/2	cups beef stock
1-1/2	cups dry red wine
3	whole bay leaves
2 tsp	dried thyme
4-1/2 lb	beef brisket
	paprika, to taste

2 lb	potatoes, cut into 1-inch pieces
2 lb	rutabagas or turnip, cut into1-inch pieces
4	large carrots, cut into 1-inch pieces
4	large parsnips, cut into 1-inch pieces
1	small squash, peeled and cut into 1-inch pieces
	salt and pepper to taste
	minced fresh parsley, for garnish

- Preheat oven to 350°F. Heat vegetable oil in large, heavy saucepan over medium heat. Add chopped onions and minced garlic and cook until they begin to brown, stirring often, about 20 minutes.

- Add tomato paste, and 1 tablespoon paprika. Stir 20 seconds. Add beef stock, red wine, bay leaves and thyme. Boil 10 seconds to blend flavours. Transfer broth mixture to large roasting pan.

- Sprinkle brisket with paprika and rub in. Arrange brisket fat side up in roasting pan. Cover and bake 1 hour.

- Arrange potatoes, rutabagas or turnip, carrots, parsnips, and squash around brisket. Cover and bake until brisket is tender when pierced with fork, about 2-1/2 hours longer. Cool 20 minutes.

- Transfer brisket to cutting board. Drain cooking liquid from pan into heavy, medium saucepan and de-grease. Purée cooking liquid in blender or processor. Return to saucepan and boil over high heat until reduced to 3-1/2 cups, about 10 minutes. Season sauce to taste with salt and pepper.

- Thinly slice brisket across grain. Place on serving platter and arrange the vegetables around brisket.

- Spoon sauce over meat. Sprinkle with parsley and serve. To serve, thinly slice brisket across grain.

- Arrange in shallow baking dish. Surround with vegetables

Can be prepared 2 days ahead. After reducing sauce, but before slicing brisket, cover brisket, vegetables and sauce separately. Cover with foil and reheat in oven at 350°F for about 40 minutes. Transfer to platter. Reheat sauce and spoon over brisket. Sprinkle with parsley.

AWARDS WON

Best Cinematography (Oswald Morris)	1971 Academy Award
Best Score (John Williams)	1971 Academy Award
Best Sound (Gordon K. McCallum)	1971 Academy Award
Best Sound (David Hildyard)	1971 Academy Award
Best Actor (Topol)	1971 New York Film Critics Circle Award
Best Direction (Norman Jewison)	1971 New York Film Critics Circle Award
Best Film (Norman Jewison)	1971 New York Film Critics Circle Award
Best Actor — in Musical/ Comedy (Topol)	1972 Golden Globe Award
Best Film — in Musical/ Comedy	1972 Golden Globe Award

trivia clips

Jewish law requires one ring, given by the groom to his bride. However, double-ring ceremonies are now the norm. The ring must be made of plain metal, usually gold, with no precious stones and of one piece. The ring to be given to the bride must belong to the groom. After reciting the marriage proposal aloud, the groom places the ring on the index finger of the bride's right hand and recites the appropriate betrothal formula: "HARAY AT M'KUDESHET LI B'TABAAT ZO K'DAT MOSHEH V'YISRAEL" Which translates as : by this ring you are consecrated unto me as my wife in accordance with the law of Moses and the people

continued

BEVERAGES

Try some red kosher wines: Carmel Merlot Vineyard Selections (Israel), Alfasi Cabernet Sauvignon

(Chile) or Kesser Red Seventy Seven (USA).

MUSIC

If you have never listened to klezmer music, we strongly suggest you give it a go! Klezmer is a Yiddish term for musician, and refers to a tradition of Jewish folk music with German and Eastern European roots. The violin and the clarinet are two of the most important instruments in this tradition.

Klezmer music is being revived in North America by bands such as The Flying Bulgar Klezmer Band from Canada, whose album of the same name is found on the Agada label. You could also listen to "Yiddish American Klezmer Music" (Yazoo) by Dave Tarras. Of course, there is also the original movie soundtrack of Fiddler on the Roof by United Artists.

SETTING THE STAGE

Create a village or peasant atmosphere. Use a traditional looking tablecloth for your table, perhaps a crocheted lace or embroidered one. Decorate with baskets of fresh fruit and nuts interspersed with greenery. Serve the food in ceramic, wood or rustic looking bowls and platters. Set the table with simple, traditional dinnerware. Serve wine out of a pitcher. If it is warm and you have a patio, take the meal outdoors and enjoy your nature-filled backyard. And of course don't forget the music in the background!

kasha varnishkes

serves 6 to 8

These make an interesting accompaniment to the brisket.

2	large onions, sliced in rounds
2 to 3 tbsp	butter or margarine (traditionally chicken fat was used)
1	large egg or egg white, slightly beaten
1 cup	medium or coarse kasha
2 cups	water or bouillon
	salt and freshly ground pepper to taste
1 package	(about 3/4 lb) small bow tie-shaped noodles
2 tbsp	fresh parsley, chopped

- Sauté the onions in 2 tablespoons of the butter or margarine in a heavy frying pan, covered until golden. Remove to a plate.

- Beat the egg in a small mixing bowl and stir in the kasha. Mix, making sure all the grains are coated.

- Put the kasha in the same frying pan, set over a high heat. Flatten, stir, and break up the egg-coated kasha with a fork or wooden spoon for 2 to 4 minutes or until the egg has dried on the kasha and the kernels are brown and mostly separate. Add the water or bouillon, salt, and pepper to the frying pan and bring to a boil. Add the onions, cover tightly, and cook over low heat, steaming the kasha for 10 minutes. Remove the cover, stir, and quickly check to see if the kernels are tender and the liquid has been absorbed. If not, cover and continue steaming for 3 to 5 minutes more.

- Meanwhile, bring a large pot of water to a boil. Cook the bow-tie noodles according to the directions on the package. Drain.

- When the kasha is ready, combine with the noodles. Adjust the seasoning, sprinkle with the parsley.

- If desired, add a bit more margarine or butter for flavour.

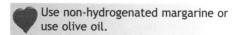 Use non-hydrogenated margarine or use olive oil.

noodle kugel

serves 4 to 6

This is a frugal dessert that could be made by almost anyone using pantry staples. It is simple, but tasty!

4 to 6 cups	cooked wide flat egg noodles
3	eggs
1-1/2 cups	cottage cheese
3/4 cup	sour cream
8 oz	cream cheese
1/2 tsp	vanilla extract
2 tsp	cinnamon
1/4 cup	honey
2	medium cooking apples, chopped
1 cup	white raisins and/or grated orange peel (optional)
1 tbsp	butter
1/2 tsp	salt
1 cup	cornflake crumbs
1/4 cup	butter, melted
	whipped cream (optional)

- Boil noodles in salted water until tender, drain and butter. Combine all other ingredients (except for cornflakes and melted butter), mix, and then add to greased baking pan.

Top with cornflake crumbs, then melted butter. Bake uncovered at 350°F for 45 to 60 minutes. Serve warm or cold, topped with whipped cream, if so desired.

the french connection (1971)

menu french onion soup • veal and mushroom crêpes • green salad with french farmhouse herb dressing (see index) • chocolate fondue

french onion soup
serves 4

This is a relatively simple recipe. But the most important feature is using the authentic individual bowls and making sure the cheese melts over it just right. Appearance is everything.

2 tbsp	butter	6 cups	chicken or beef broth
6	cooking onions, thinly sliced	4	slices of French crusted bread
1 tbsp	vegetable oil	1 clove	garlic halved
1 cup	Beaujolais wine	1-1/2 cup	Gruyere cheese, grated

- Preheat oven to 400°F. Heat butter and vegetable oil in a large saucepan. Sauté onions until transparent, then cover with Beaujolais and broth. Allow to simmer for about 5 minutes over medium setting. Set aside.

- Cut bread slices into 4 circles and place on baking sheet. Broil in oven until golden and rub with garlic halves. Pour soup into soup bowls. Top with the toasted bread slices and sprinkle with grated cheese. Broil in oven for about 2 to 3 minutes until cheese is melted.

veal and mushroom crêpes
serves 4

Crêpes: This batter makes 16 crêpes
For this recipe use only 8 crêpes

1-1/4 cup	all purpose flour	1 cup	milk
1/2 tsp	salt	4 tbsp	water
3	large eggs	1-1/2 tbsp	melted unsalted butter
			cooking oil

- Sift flour and salt into a mixing bowl. Make a well in the centre. Add eggs and beat in the surrounding flour using a wooden spoon. When egg mixture starts to thicken, gradually add half of the milk and mix until the batter is smooth.

- Stir in remaining milk and water. Use a fine sieve and pour batter through into another bowl. Now add the melted butter to the batter. If not using the batter immediately, cover bowl and chill in the refrigerator for up to 2 hours before use.

- Apply light coating of vegetable cooking oil over the cooking surface of a non-stick frying pan and allow to heat at a medium-high setting. When the pan is hot, pour crêpe batter onto pan, swirling the pan to evenly distribute the batter. Cook the crêpe until edges turn golden brown, flip over and cook the other side. Be careful not to overcook. Set crêpes aside until ready to fill.

Tough guy cop, Jimmy "Popeye" Doyle, played by Gene Hackman, attempts to bust an international heroin smuggling ring bringing the drug from Europe to New York. He has a tough attitude, and sometimes breaks the rules of conduct for a cop. Alain Charnier, a slick foreign drug smuggler, is the "bad guy." His character is in contrast to the rude and crude cop played by Hackman. Charnier is the French drug lord who is the main connection, supplying most of the heroin to New York City. On a hunch, Doyle becomes suspicious of a couple who draws attention to themselves with their wealthy standard of living. They own a small corner variety store which hardly rakes in enough money to keep them afloat. Gritty cop Doyle's hunch pays off when he discovers the couple are agents for Charnier. This movie set the standard for many good cop-bad cop movies that followed in the years to come. One of the most memorable scenes in the movie occurs when Doyle chases a hitman in a high-speed action-packed car chase. The film was inspired by a true story and will appeal to those who like action films.

FEATURED ACTORS
Gene Hackman (Jimmy "Popeye" Doyle)
Fernando Rey (Alain Charnier)
Roy Scheider (Buddy Russo)
Tony Lo Bianco (Sal Boca)
Marcel Bozzuffi (Pierre Nicoli)

DIRECTOR - William Friedkin

trivia clips

Eddie Egan and Sonny Grosso were real life New York police officers whose experiences in the battle against international drug smuggling became the basis of the movie The French Connection. Both Egan and Grosso had small parts in the movie.
Friedkin was the youngest director at that time to receive the Oscar; he was 32 years old.

veal and mushroom crêpes   continued

Filling:

2 tbsp	butter or margarine
1	small onion, chopped
1/2 cup	sliced button mushrooms
1 1/2 cups	minced veal
2 tbsp	light cream
1 tbsp	tomato paste

salt
white pepper
pinch of red paprika
sour cream for topping
parsley for garnish

- Melt butter in a small frying pan and gently fry onion and mushrooms for a few minutes. Add the veal and stir in well, allowing the meat to brown. Add the cream, tomato paste and seasoning. Stir this mixture for about 5-10 minutes.

- Place about 2 tbsp of filling in the centre of each crêpe, roll up.

- Place crêpes in a greased ovenproof dish and heat through in oven set at 350°F for about 15 minutes.

- Serve immediately topped with sour cream and sprinkled with parsley.

 Use lean ground meat, and low fat sour cream. Evaporated skim milk can replace the light cream.

The secret to mastering the skill of making authentic crêpes is to invest in a good crêpe pam, and remember practice does make perfect, so don't get discouraged. A French steel pan is ideal, and the best size to get is 15 - 18 cm diameter. The first crêpe does not count; it is always the practice one. Did you know old English recipes call crêpes hearth cakes?

trivia clips

He was known by such names as Johnny "Pops," "Canada's Capone", "Godfather" and the "Enforcer". Johnny Papalia was arrested for his involvement in the real-life French Connection heroin smuggling ring. Author Adrian Humphrey's book entitled The Enforcer published by HarperCollins, details the life of Canada's infamous mob boss.

continued

chocolate fondue

serves 4

7 oz	(7 squares) semi-sweet chocolate, chopped into small pieces
1 cup	whole or 2% milk, warmed

<u>Fruit for dipping:</u>

1	banana, peeled and sliced
3 to 4	kiwis, peeled and sliced
2	Anjou pears, sliced
1	star fruit, sliced
2	peaches, sliced
1	red apple, sliced
1 pint	strawberries, whole

- Use a double boiler to melt the chocolate or use a saucepan, but make sure to melt over low heat. Be patient so as not to burn the chocolate. Slowly pour in the warm milk and mix well.

- Pour the chocolate sauce into a fondue pot. Use long-handled dessert forks to facilitate dipping. Dip the fruit into the rich sauce and enjoy. Experiment with this and add your favourite liqueur: Amaretto, Grand Marnier, or brandy.

BEVERAGES

Before dinner serve Bronx cocktails (see main beverages page).

In terms of wine, serve a French white such as Rothschild Sauvignon Blanc or Skalli Chardonnay Fortant. A Gewurztraminer would also be a good choice for those who prefer something drier. Try Pierre Sparr Gewurztraminer or Kuhlmann Gewurztraminer, both from France.

MUSIC

Try some French music from the era — perhaps Yves Montand's "En Balade" (Sony) or "By Request" (CBS). Anything by Gilbert Montagne would be suitable as would "French Café Songs" (Gallerie) which features various artists.

SETTING THE STAGE

Since the focus is on French cuisine, dine French style. Bring out your best plates and cutlery. Use linen napkins or very fancy paper ones that are colourful and unusually shaped. Buy some elegant, long-stemmed flowers and place them in a crystal vase or place one flower by each table setting for a simple, yet graceful impact. Dim the lights and set out various candles — put some mysterious French music on the stereo and enjoy a long drawn out French style meal! You may want to use a round table as the setting is more intimate, and seat couples beside each other as the French do!

Since this movie became a pinnacle of organized crime films in Hollywood, it would be an interesting evening to further extend this theme. Mobsters, gangs and the lifestyles they depict on the silver screen have often been romanticized by Hollywood for a number of years. Take this opportunity to have a true-crime night. Invite friends to bring true crime books they have read and have a book talk and a book exchange. Allow each person to give a brief description of the book with interesting background information that doesn't totally give everything away. Maybe you will be inspired to start a book club, you could focus on true crime stories for one month and then extend it to include different titles or genres of your choice.

the godfather (1972)

This movie is about family ties and loyalties as much as it is about crime. The dialogue is great and the acting is wonderful. The depth of character development is rarely seen in today's Hollywood blockbusters. It is a movie that you will want to watch more than once.

Don Vito Corleone is the traditional head of a New York Mafia "family". He is content to stick with conventional sources of income for the "family" such as gambling, protection rackets, etc. Other crime families want a slice of the ever increasing profits to be made in the drug market. Corleone abhors the idea of getting involved with anything to do with drugs. He is an obstacle to the expansion of "business" interests of the other crime families who collaborate with each other, so an attempt is made on his life by the Sollozzo family. This creates an unprecedented crisis for both his immediate and extended "family" members. Michael Corleone, the youngest son of the Don, thwarts an attempt on the life of his father, thus putting him in the thick of the "disagreement" with the Sollozzo family.

To avenge the attempt on his father's life, Michael kills Sollozzo and ends up fleeing to Sicily with his oldest brother, Sonny, to hide. While in Sicily, he forgets about his American girlfriend, Kay Adams, and ends up marrying a Sicilian girl. After mafia violence erupts in Sicily, Michael is left a widower and his brother Sonny is murdered. Michael returns to America and assumes leadership of the Corleone family and marries his old flame Kay Adams. His leadership leads the family to unparalleled wealth and prosperity, but as his wealth grows, Michael's moral downfall becomes more obvious as he exacts revenge on those who tried to decimate the Corleone family.

menu

marinated bocconcini • antipasto platter (see index) • variety of italian breads (store-bought) • italian wedding soup • pasta with pesto sauce • osso bucco with mushroom sauce and polenta • adriatic octopus salad • triple delight tomato salad • four seasons salad (see index) • fruit and cheese platter (recipe not included) • cappuccino cheesecake brownies • sicilian cassata

This menu is quite extensive. Feel free to choose the items which suit your get together the best! This menu applies to both The Godfather I and The Godfather, Part II.

marinated bocconcini

2 to 3 pieces	of bocconcini cheese per person
2 to 3 tbsp	each of fresh chopped basil, oregano, parsley and rosemary
1/2 cup	extra virgin olive oil
pinch	of freshly ground pepper
pinch	of red hot pepper flakes (optional)

• Place the cheese in a serving dish with sides of at least one inch high. Chop the herbs and sprinkle over the cheese. Pour the olive oil on the cheese and sprinkle with the freshly ground pepper and the red hot pepper flakes if so desired. Allow to marinate for at least 2 hours in the refrigerator. Take out of the refrigerator and let sit for 1 hour prior to serving to allow olive oil to come to room temperature.

• For a nice effect, serve on lettuce lined plates.

trivia clips

Warren Beatty, Jack Nicholson, and Dustin Hoffman were all offered the part of Michael Corleone, but they all turned down the role.

During rehearsals, a false horse's head was used for the bedroom scene. For the actual shot, a real horse's head was used. This would most likely not be possible today as the rules on the treatment of animals for film use have become stricter.

the godfather (1972)

italian wedding soup

serves 4 to 6

This soup is popular at Italian weddings. A number of versions exist, but they all feature a bitter green and meatballs.

For soup:

2	, finely chopped
1 1/2 tsp	chopped fresh rosemary leaves or 1 tsp dried rosemary, crumbled
2 tbsp	olive oil
1 lb	escarole (about 1 head), cut crosswise into1/2-inch strips, washed well, and spun dry (about 12 cups packed)
7 cups	low-salt chicken broth
1/2 cup	orzo (rice-shaped pasta) or other small pasta

For meatballs:

1/2 lb	ground beef (or chicken)
6 tbsp	fine fresh bread crumbs
2	large egg yolks
2	green onions, minced
2 tbsp	freshly grated Parmesan cheese
	salt and pepper
2 tbsp	olive oil
2	garlic cloves, minced and mashed to a paste with 1/2 tsp salt
2 tsp	fresh lemon juice

- To make the soup: In a large, heavy saucepan cook onion and rosemary in oil over moderate heat, stirring, until onion is softened. Add escarole, stirring to coat with oil, and cook, covered, 1 minute.

- Add broth and orzo and simmer, partially covered, stirring occasionally, 10 minutes.

- Make meatballs while soup simmers: In a bowl, combine well first 5 meatball ingredients; season with salt and pepper.

- Form mixture into meatballs about 1-inch in diameter. In a medium size, heavy skillet heat oil over moderately high heat until hot but not smoking, and brown meatballs about 3 minutes (meatballs will not be cooked through).

- Add meatballs to soup and simmer, partially covered, for 5 minutes. Stir in garlic, salt, and lemon juice. Taste and adjust salt and pepper if required.

 Use lean ground meat and fat-free chicken broth.

pasta

serves 4 to 6

Cook your favourite pasta shapes in boiling, salted water until al dente. Rotini or fettuccine both work well. Pour pesto sauce over pasta, toss and serve.

pesto sauce

Yield: about 1-1/2 cups

2 cups	fresh basil leaves
3	cloves garlic
1 cup	parsley (optional)
1/2 cup	grated Parmesan cheese

2 tbsp	grated pecorino Romano (optional)
2/3 cup	pine nuts or walnuts
3/4 to 1 cup	extra virgin olive oil

- Blend all ingredients in a blender, or food processor until they form a soft paste. The amount of oil used depends on the method. If you use the blender, it is best to make the pesto in two batches, using enough oil each time to cover the blades of the blender — about 1/2 cup. To store unused portion of pesto, place in a jar and cover the surface with a film of olive oil. Wrap in foil or plastic wrap. Keep in refrigerator or freeze in ice cube trays and put cubes in freezer bags once frozen. Use 2-3 cubes per person for pasta sauce.

You could buy prepared pesto sauce. The fresh homemade version though has much more depth of flavour! It is so easy to make too!

FEATURED ACTORS
Marlon Brando (Don Vito Corleone)
Al Pacino (Michael Corleone)
Diane Keaton (Kay Adams)
Robert Duvall (Tom Hagen)
James Caan (Sonny Corleone)
Sterling Hayden (McCluskey)
Talia Shire (Connie Corleone Rizzi)
Abe Vigoda (Tessio)
Richard Conte (Barzini)
Sofia Coppola (baby)

DIRECTOR ~ Francis Ford Coppola

AWARDS WON

Best Supporting Actor (Robert Duvall)	1972 New York Film Critics Circle Award
Best Actor (Al Pacino)	1972 National Society of Film Critics Award
Best Supporting Actor (Al Pacino)	1972 National Board of Review of Motion Pictures Award
Best Drama Adapted from Another Medium (Francis Ford Coppola and Mario Puzo)	1973 Writers Guild of America
Best Actor (Marlon Brando)	1973 Academy Award
Best Picture (Albert S. Ruddy)	
Best Writing, Screenplay Based on Material from Another Medium (Francis Ford Coppola and Mario Puzo)	1973 Academy Award
Best Costume Design (Anna Hill Johnstone)	1973 Academy Award
Best Director (Francis Ford Coppola)	1973 Academy Award
Best Film Editing (William Reynolds II and Peter Zinner)	1973 Academy Award
Anthony Asquith Award for Film Music (Nino Rota)	1973 British Academy Award
Best Actor (Marlon Brando)	1973 British Academy Award
Best Costume Design (Anna Hill Johnstone)	1973 British Academy Award

the godfather (1972)

Outstanding Directorial Achievement in Motion Pictures (Fred C. Caruso — unit production manager), (Francis Ford Coppola-director), (Fred Gallo and Steven P. Skloot — assistant directors)	1973 Directors Guild of America
Best Director — Motion Picture (Francis Ford Coppola)	1973 Golden Globe Award
Best Motion Picture — Drama	1973 Golden Globe Award
Best Motion Picture — Actor (Marlon Brando)	1973 Golden Globe Award
Best Original Score (Nino Rota)	1973 Golden Globe Award
Best Screenplay (Francis Ford Coppola and Mario Puzo)	1973 Golden Globe Award
Best Original Score written for a Motion Picture or T.V. Special (Nino Rota)	1973 Grammy Award
10 Best Films	1972 National Board of Review of Motion Pictures Award
U.S. National Film Registry	1990 Library of Congress Award
100 Greatest American Movies	1998 American Film Institute Award

osso bucco with mushroom sauce and polenta serves 6

6 to 8	2-inch-thick veal shanks (5 lb total), each tied securely with kitchen string to keep meat attached to bone
3 tbsp	olive oil
3 tbsp	unsalted butter
4	medium onions, thinly sliced
2	red peppers, diced
2	celery ribs, thinly sliced
	salt and pepper
1/2 lb	fresh cremini or white mushrooms, tough stem ends trimmed
1/2 lb	fresh chanterelle mushrooms, stems discarded
1/2 lb	fresh Portobello mushrooms, stems discarded
3/4 tsp	dried thyme, crumbled
1/2 cup	dry white wine
1 tbsp	fresh lemon juice
1/2 to 3/4 cup	water
1 to 2 tbsp	balsamic vinegar, or to taste
1 tbsp	fresh rosemary, chopped
1/4 cup	fresh parsley leaves, washed well, spun dry, and minced

- Preheat oven to 275˚F. In a heavy, ovenproof kettle large enough to hold veal shanks in one layer, heat 1 tablespoon each of oil and butter over moderately high heat until foam begins to subside. Sauté onion, red pepper and celery until they begin to turn golden.

- Pat shanks dry between paper towels and season with salt and pepper. Arrange shanks on onion mixture and roast, covered tightly, in middle of oven 3 hours. (Meat will give off juices as it cooks.) Shanks may be prepared up to this point 1 day ahead and cooled, shanks uncovered, before chilling, covered. Reheat before proceeding.

- Cut mushrooms into 1/4-inch-thick slices. In a large skillet, heat remaining 2 tablespoons each of oil and butter over moderately high heat until foam begins to subside. Sauté mushrooms with thyme and salt and pepper to taste, stirring until mushrooms begin to give off their liquid. Stir in wine and lemon juice and cook, stirring, until all but about

1/3 cup liquid is evaporated. Mushrooms may be made 1 day ahead and cooled completely before chilling, covered.

- Transfer shanks to a platter and keep warm. Transfer onions, red peppers,celery and pan juices to a blender with 1/2 cup water and purée until smooth, adding more water if necessary to thin sauce to desired consistency. Pour sauce into a saucepan and stir in mushroom mixture, vinegar, and salt and pepper to taste. Heat sauce over moderate heat until heated through and stir in rosemary and parsley. Arrange shanks on polenta (recipe below) and spoon sauce over them.

 Use non-stick cookware and reduce the amount of oil and butter by a tablespoon.

trivia clips

During the scene where Sonny (James Caan) beats up Carlo (Gianni Russo), Caan actually broke a few of Russo's ribs (ouch)! Author Mario Puzo and director Coppola deliberately avoided using the word "Mafia" in their screenplay.
The presence of oranges in all of the "Godfather" movies indicates that a death or a close call with death will soon occur. Vito Corleone is shot after buying oranges, and dies with an orange in his mouth. Tessio is tossed an orange at the wedding reception and is then later executed as a traitor.

basic polenta

serves 6 to 8

Polenta is a staple in much of Northern Italy. It can be eaten in almost any course, alone with some butter and cheese, fried, broiled, grilled, or sliced and baked; or used as an accompaniment as it is here. Polenta is quite versatile, and you should experiment. Prepare it in various ways to fully appreciate it, you'll never call it just cornmeal mush again!

8 cups	water
2 tsp	salt
2 cups	polenta (coarse cornmeal)

- Combine 8 cups water with salt in heavy, large saucepan. Bring to a boil.

- Gradually add cornmeal, whisking until smooth. Reduce heat to low. Cover and cook until polenta is thick and creamy, stirring frequently with a wooden spoon, for about 30 minutes.

Get an extra dose of calcium — add some skim milk powder to the water prior to adding the cornmeal. Whisk until blended and then add the cornmeal. this well also give the polenta a creamier taste.

adriatic octopus salad

serves 4 to 6

This is a salad that seafood lovers will enjoy. A trick we learned from a friend, who is a native of Split in Dalmatia, is to boil the octopus with a few wine corks in order to help make it tender. Strange, but true; it really works.
Serve with crackers or breadsticks.

1	large octopus, cleaned and rinsed		juice of 1 lemon	
			salt and pepper to taste	
2 to 3	wine corks, if at all possible	1	clove garlic, minced	
		2 to 3 tbsp	chopped parsley	
1	red onion, thinly sliced	2 tbsp	capers (optional)	
	olive oil		lettuce leaves (optional, for garnish)	
	wine vinegar			

- Pound the octopus with a meat mallet. Place in a saucepan with water to just cover the octopus, add the wine corks. Simmer over medium heat for about 3 hours until completely tender. Let cool in its cooking water, then chop or slice the octopus and place in salad bowl. Add the sliced onion. Season with olive oil, wine vinegar, lemon juice, salt, pepper, garlic and parsley.
Add capers and garnish with lettuce leaves if desired.

 Buy fresh, cleaned octopus at quality supermarkets and fish markets. You may also find octopus that is cleaned and frozen, just thaw it and cook.

 Use fat-free or low fat Italian dressing instead of the olive oil and vinegar.

trivia clips

Sofia Coppola (daughter of director) appears as Michael Corleone's baby nephew in the christening scenes.
The name of the traditional Sicilian hat worn, by Michael's bodyguards is "coppola."
Marlon Brando refused the Oscar in 1973 because he felt that America and especially Hollywood, discriminated against the Indian people. Brando did not show up at the ceremony, but sent a phony Indian woman named Sacheen Littlefeather who later turned out to be Maria Cruz, a little known Californian actress.

the godfather (1972)

triple delight tomato salad
serves 4 to 6

Sliced tomatoes in two colours are topped with sun-dried tomatoes, olives and capers. This is a very Mediterranean salad that is sure to become a hit!

4	large red tomatoes, sliced			salt and pepper
4	large yellow tomatoes, sliced		1/2 cup	Kalamata olives (preferably imported), quartered lengthwise
1/4 cup	chopped, drained, oil-packed sun-dried tomatoes (reserve 2 tablespoons oil)		2 tbsp	drained capers, chopped
			2 tbsp	chopped fresh marjoram
1 tbsp	extra virgin olive oil		2 tbsp	chopped fresh oregano
1 tbsp	balsamic vinegar or red-wine vinegar		2 tbsp	chopped fresh thyme

- Arrange tomatoes decoratively on platter or serving plate. Combine reserved sun-dried tomato oil and 1 tablespoon olive oil in small bowl. Mix in vinegar. Drizzle over tomatoes. Sprinkle with salt and pepper. Top with sun-dried tomatoes and all remaining ingredients

- Fruit and Cheese Platter: Set up a large platter with a variety of cheese. Don't slice the cheese, just set out the wedges of cheese and provide a cheese knife. Next to the cheese platter place another platter or even a basket with a variety of fruit. Peel and/or slice those fruits that may need to be served that way such as pineapple. Garnish platters with sprigs of fresh rosemary.

cappuccino cheesecake brownies
Yield: About 2 dozen squares

For the brownie layer:

8 squares	(8 ounces) fine-quality European bittersweet chocolate, chopped
3/4 cup	unsalted butter, cut into pieces
2 tbsp	instant espresso powder dissolved in 1 tbsp boiling water
1-1/2 cups	sugar
2 tsp	vanilla
4	large eggs
1 cup	all-purpose flour
1/2 tsp	salt
1 cup	walnuts, chopped

- Make the brownie layer: In a metal bowl set over a pan of barely simmering water, melt the chocolate with the butter and espresso mixture, stirring until the mixture is smooth. Remove the bowl from the heat, let the mixture cool to lukewarm, and blend in the sugar and the vanilla. Add the eggs, 1 at a time, stirring well after each addition, blend in the flour and the salt, stirring until the mixture is just combined, and mix in the walnuts. Pour the mixture into a buttered and floured 13- by 9-inch baking pan, smooth the top, and bake the brownie layer in the middle of a preheated 350°F oven for 22 to 25 minutes, or until a toothpick inserted in the centre comes out clean. Let the brownie layer cool completely in the pan, on a rack.

- Make the cream cheese frosting: In a bowl, using an electric mixer, cream together the cream cheese and the butter until the mixture is light and fluffy, add the confectioners' sugar, sifted, the vanilla, and the cinnamon, and beat the frosting until it is well combined.

For the cream cheese frosting:

8 oz	cream cheese, softened
6 tbsp	unsalted butter, softened
1-1/2 cups	confectioners' sugar
1 tsp	vanilla
1 tsp	cinnamon

For the glaze:

6 squares	(6 ounces) fine quality European bittersweet chocolate
2 tbsp	unsalted butter
1/2 cup	heavy cream
1-1/2 tbsp	instant espresso powder dissolved in 1 tbsp boiling water

- Spread the frosting evenly over the brownie layer and chill the brownies for 1 hour, or until the frosting is firm.

- Make the glaze: In a metal bowl set over a pan of barely simmering water, melt the chocolate with the butter, cream, and espresso mixture, stirring until the glaze is smooth. Remove the bowl from the heat, and let the glaze cool to room temperature. The brownies keep, covered and chilled, for 3 days.

 Use low fat cream cheese and non-hydrogenated margarine in place of the butter.

 If you don't have time to bake, buy ready-made plain brownies at a good bakeshop and serve them with a scoop of cappuccino flavoured ice cream.

BEVERAGES

Set up a buffet table to use for the bar. Make sure you have an ice bucket, tongs, and a variety of glasses and garnishes such as lemon twists, maraschino cherries, olives, etc. Perhaps have on hand some milk or cream for those who wish to make some cocktails. Don't forget to include Brio Chinotto, an Italian cola style beverage, as well as a variety of Italian mineral waters like San Pellegrino. Buy a number of Italian red and white wines so that guests can choose their favourite or sample something new. In terms of red, we suggest the following: Ruffino Chianti, Negrar Valpolicella, Sartori Villa Mura Cabernet, and Fazi-Battaglia Sangiovese. For a selection of Italian white wines we recommend: Collavini Pinot Grigio, Masi Soave Classico, and Fazi-Battaglia Verdicchio. Of course, feel free to add favourites of your own.

You could also serve Godfather and Godmother cocktails (see main beverages page).

MUSIC

Since the menu is based on an Italian wedding feast, just as the opening scenes of the movie are, we suggest "Italian Wedding Favourites" (Polygram) by Luciano Pavarotti or Emilio Pericoli's "Italian Golden Hits" (Orfeon). You may wish to listen to some Italian folk music. Try "Italian Treasury: Folk Music and Songs of Italy" American singer Connie Francis went back to her roots and recorded in Italian. You may wish to try her two volume CD edition called "The Italian Collection" (PolyGram). It features songs from her previous five Italian albums. You can't go wrong with anything from Andrea Bocelli. If you wish to listen to some more modern Italian music, we suggest anything by any of the following artists: Umberto Tozzi, Eros Ramazotti or Toto Cotugno.

the
godfather (1972)

SETTING THE STAGE

Bring some of the atmosphere of an Italian wedding into your home or better yet into your courtyard or backyard. Use streamers or balloons of red, white and green to decorate your entry hall and home. Have vases of fresh flowers located in the entrance hall. Decorate with small pots of flowers or potted Mediterranean herbs like rosemary. Set up a "welcoming table", use your best tablecloth. Set glasses of various Italian liqueurs such as Amaretto, Frangelico, etc. on a silver tray for guests to help themselves to as they arrive, just as is customary at Italian weddings. Have a small, crystal bowl full of candied almonds on this table as well. You may wish to offer champagne and strawberries at this welcome table. Sprinkle some gold and silver stars on the table to add to the festive appearance. You could also place small candles in votive holders at a number of places on the table or even hollow out some artichokes and use them as votive holders. Use crisp, white tablecloths, cloth napkins folded in a fancy manner, your best dinnerware and silver and real crystal glasses. Dress up chairs with slipcovers or bows tied to the back rests.

In terms of the main meal, you could serve it formally, or set up a buffet, do what suits the circumstances best. No matter which style you choose, create an air of elegance and sophistication, as it suits the wedding themed mood. Play our suggested music selections softly in the background during dinner. This get together is sure to be a hit!

sicilian cassata

serves 8 to 10

1/4 cup	milk
2 tbsp, plus 2 tsp	butter
8	eggs
2 cups, plus 2 tbsp	sugar
1 cup	flour
1 tsp	baking powder
1/2 tsp	salt
1 tsp	vanilla
2 cups	ricotta cheese
1 cup	confectioners' sugar
1 tbsp	pure vanilla extract
3 tbsp	rum

3 tbsp	candied lemon peels, finely chopped
3 tbsp	candied orange peels, finely chopped
4 tbsp	chopped pistachio nuts
1/4 cup	heavy cream, whipped until stiff
1/4 cup	Grand Marnier or Cointreau, or other orange liqueur
1-1/2 cups	sweetened whipped cream
3 cups	semi-sweet chocolate, chopped into pieces
1/2 cup	cold espresso coffee
1/2 lb	cold butter, cut into cubes

- Preheat the oven to 350° F. In a small saucepan, heat the milk and 2 tablespoons of butter together. Using an electric mixer, combine the eggs and sugar together. Beat at medium-high speed for about 8 minutes, or until the mixture is pale yellow, thick and has tripled in volume. With the machine running, slowly add the heated milk and butter.

- In a mixing bowl, sift the flour, baking powder and salt together. Fold the flour mixture into the egg mixture and mix thoroughly, so that there are no lumps and the mixture is smooth. Fold in the vanilla.

- Grease a 13 by 9-inch baking pan with 2 teaspoons of butter. Sprinkle with 1 tablespoon of sugar.

- Pour the cake batter into the pan and bake for about 25 minutes, or until the cake springs back when touched. Cool for about 2 minutes. Using a thin knife, loosen the edges of the cake and flip onto a wire rack. In a mixing bowl, whisk the cheese, powdered sugar, vanilla and 2 tablespoons rum. Blend well. Add 2 tablespoons each of the candied citrus and 2 tablespoons of the nuts. Mix well. Fold the whipped cream into the mixture. Mix well. Cut the cake lengthwise into 4 equal pieces. Trim the edges of the cake pieces to fit a 10-inch loaf pan. Brush the tops of each cake with the orange liqueur. Line the bottom of the loaf pan with parchment paper.

- Place one piece of the cake on the bottom of the pan. Spread 1/3 of the cheese filling evenly over the piece of cake. Repeat the layering with the remaining cake sections and cheese filling. Cover with plastic wrap and refrigerate for 2 hours. Remove from the refrigerator and unmold the cake. Place the cake on a wire rack with a sheet pan underneath. Spread the top and sides of the cake with the sweetened whipped cream. Place the cake in the refrigerator and chill for 1 hour. In a saucepan, over medium heat, add the chocolate and coffee. Stir until the chocolate is melted. Stir in the 1/2 pound of butter and remaining tablespoon of rum. Mix well. Cool the mixture until it is spreadable. Pour the chocolate frosting over the entire cake. Place the cake back in the refrigerator and chill for 2 hours, until the cake sets. Remove the cake from the refrigerator. Using a long spatula, carefully lift the cake from the rack and place on a serving plate.

- Garnish with a sprinkle of the remaining nuts and candied citrus. Slice and serve.

the godfather
part II (1974)

For the Menu, Beverages and Setting the Stage see the preceding pages for The Godfather.

AWARDS WON

Best Adapted Screenplay (Francis Ford Coppola/Mario Puzo)	1974 Academy Award
Best Art Direction (Dean Tavoularis /Angelo P.Graham/ George R. Nelson)	1974 Academy Award
Best Director (Francis Ford Coppola)	1974 Academy Award
Best Picture	1974 Academy Award
Best Score (Carmine Coppola/Nino Rota)	1974 Academy Award
Best Supporting Actor (Robert De Niro)	1974 Academy Award
Best Director (Francis Ford Coppola)	1974 Directors Guild of America
Best Director (Francis Ford Coppola)	1974 SOC
Best Actor (Al Pacino)	1975 British Academy Award
U.S. National Film Registry	1993 Library of Congress Award
100 Greatest American Movies	1998 American Film Institute Award

This film is both prequel and sequel to The Godfather; it examines the rise and fall of the father and son in parallel stories. The story of Vito Corleone begins in his Sicilian village with the killing of his family by the Mafia, which causes the young Vito to flee to America. He settles in Little Italy, in the urban sprawl of New York, where he struggles to eke out an existence for wife and increasing family.

Vito is determined to support his family regardless of whether the money he brings home was made legally or by other means. He has ties to the "cosa nostra", and his stature in the organization grows after he does away with Black Hand Fanucci, who hesitated to give him a cut of his business. Even with his involvement in the cold, brutal underworld, Vito remains a staunch, family man. His family is his most prized possession. The film also tells the story of Vito's youngest son, Michael, who as he becomes very ambitious and deeply entrenched in the family business, loses both his sense of self and his appreciation of family. This damages his marriage and relationship with his brother, Fredo. Michael is an instrument of his own demise as he becomes paranoid and corrupt.

This film is one of the rare sequels that matches the quality of its predecessor.

FEATURED ACTORS
Al Pacino (Michael)
Robert Duvall (Tom Hagen)
Diane Keaton (Kay Adams)
Robert De Niro (Vito Corleone)
John Cazale (Fredo Corleone)
Talia Shire (Connie)
Lee Strasberg (Hyman Roth)
Giuseppe Sillato (Don Francesco)
James Gounaris (Anthony Corleone)

DIRECTOR ~ Francis Ford Coppola

trivia clips

Sofia Coppola appeared again in the film as a child.
The film was nominated for a total of 10 Academy Awards.
The Godfather and The Godfather, Part II were later cut together in chronological order for television viewing and aired under the name The Godfather Saga.

grease

(1978)

Grease became the highest grossing movie musical ever, and the third most popular film of the new blockbusters of the 1970's after Star Wars (1977) and Jaws (1975). "Grease,was the word." The setting of the story in this long-running Broadway hit was Chicago, but it was changed to sunny California for the screen version. The film features a teen opposites-attract story line. Danny (John Travolta) and transplanted Australian student Sandy (Olivia Newton-John) spend the "Summer Nights" falling in love despite their obvious differences. Fall arrives and it's back to school at Rydell High. There, Sandy finds out that her summer love Danny, belongs to the bad boy club at school, known as the T-Birds. His friends do not accept his new girl because of her clean cut image, even though she has been befriended by some of the Pink Ladies (the cool girls at school). Sandy and Danny go through a series of break-ups and make-ups before deciding they really do want each other. The summer of 1978 definitely belonged to Grease as crowds packed the theatres and the many hit singles spawned by the film rose up the charts! John Travolta was still riding the crest of popularity that he attained in Saturday Night Fever, and other actors in the film such as Frankie Avalon, Eve Arden and Sid Caesar also attracted many fans into the theatres during the summer nights of 1978. This humourous, nostalgic film with great music is a sure hit for all generations.

FEATURED ACTORS
John Travolta (Danny Zuko)
Olivia Newton-John (Sandy)
Stockard Channing (Rizzo)
Jeff Conaway (Kenickie)
Didi Conn (Frenchy)
Eve Arden (Principal McGee)

DIRECTOR ~ Randal Kleiser

AWARDS WON
Best Film   1979 PEO

menu
spicy california style onion rings (see index) • veal or tofu wieners on a sesame roll (store-bought) • patriotic vegetable platter (see index) malibu sundaes (see index)

BEVERAGES

Root Beer Floats (see main beverages section)

Cola

Milk Shakes (see main beverages section)

Your favourite American beer

MUSIC

"Grease Original Soundtrack" (RSO), featuring Olivia Newton-John, John Travolta, Frankie Valli, Sha-Na-Na, and Peter Frampton on guitar.

You must of course also listen to some 1950's rock and roll, which was considered rebellious at the time! Remember that during this era censors wouldn't allow Elvis Presley to be filmed below the waist (in case the sight of swivelling hips was too much for the audience) during television appearances. There is a wide variety of 50's compilation albums available, here are a few suggestions: "50's Jukebox Hits" (Universal Special Markets), "Chart Topper: Dance Hits of the 50's" (Priority), and "Classic 50's Hits" (ITC Master). For those making it a romantic evening, we suggest: "Chart Toppers: Romantic Hits of the 50's" (Priority).

SETTING THE STAGE

If you're planning on inviting guests, send them unique invitations; buy some old 45's at a flea market or used record store (or perhaps you have some packed away in storage) and write out the details of the party on the record using silver or gold paint pens that are available at stationery stores. Request that guests wear their favourite 50's style clothes (leather coats and blue jeans, poodle skirts, capri pants, etc.). Alternatively, they could come dressed as one of the main characters from the film or as one of the other T-Birds or Pink Ladies from Grease.

You may wish to go to a party supply store for 50's style decorations; some feature cut-outs from the decade, such as guys and dolls signs for the washrooms. Have music from the era playing as your guests arrive. Use stacks of 45's to weigh down helium 50's theme balloons (jukebox or instrument shaped balloons are available) as a centrepiece.

If you have any 50's era vintage dinnerware, use it to set your table. Alternatively, create a diner atmosphere. Use paper place mats (available at party supply stores). Use coloured glassware in shades of blue or green. If you plan ahead, you can scout around for 50's era dinnerware at thrift stores and flea markets.

After watching the film and having dinner, burn some calories by holding a dance contest, or get a hula hoop and hold a contest to see which of your guests can hula the longest! No matter which decade you were born in, you will enjoy a 50's theme party!

trivia clips

Olivia Newton-John was a big international pop star during the 1970's. Although she was considered a little old for the part, she was believable to audiences, spurring tons of look-alike contests nationwide.
He had a small part in the movie and later went on to star in a popular 1980's evening soap opera called Falcon Crest. Who is he? Hint: Billy Crystal use to portray this actor's father on Saturday Night Live by saying "You look marvelous". (Answer: Lorenzo Lamas)

jaws

menu   lobster fondue dip • citrus shark kabobs • cilantro lime rice • green salad with vinaigrette (see index) • grilled pineapple or hawaiian paradise cake (see index) • tropical flavoured white sangria

A seafood menu is called for! Seafood is very healthy and though some types contain cholesterol, they have very little saturated fat! For those who are reluctant to eat fish; we believe you just have not met the right fish!

lobster fondue dip

Yield: 1-1/2 cups dip

Serve this hot cheese dip with a variety of crisp crackers.

2 tbsp	butter	1/3 cup	dry white wine
2 cups	sharp cheddar cheese, shredded	5 oz	lobster, cut into small pieces (you can use canned, but drain well)
1/4 tsp	red pepper sauce		

- Melt butter in pan over low heat. Gradually stir in cheese until cheese is melted. (Cheese butter mixture may appear separated.) Add red pepper sauce; slowly add wine, stirring until mixture is smooth. Add lobster; stir until heated. Serve while hot.

citrus shark kabobs

serves 4

4 tbsp	butter	2	medium zucchini, cut in 1-1/2 inch pieces
2	large shallots, minced	12	pearl onions, blanched
1 tbsp	orange peel, grated	2	oranges, peeled and quartered
1/4 cup	orange juice		peanut or canola oil
2 lb	shark steaks, cut in 1-1/2 inch pieces	4 tbsp	dried thyme, crumbled
	milk		

- Make sauce: Melt butter in a saucepan over medium heat. Add shallots and sauté until tender, stirring occasionally. Whisk in orange peel and juice. Bring mixture to a boil, stir, and remove from heat.
- Reheat sauce when ready to serve.

- Grill shark kabobs: Soak shark cubes in milk for 1 hour before grilling. Drain fish and pat dry with paper towels. Thread four 10-inch skewers with fish, zucchini, onions and orange quarters. Brush with peanut oil and sprinkle with 1 tablespoon of the thyme. Sprinkle remaining thyme over hot coals. Grill kabobs, rotating every 3 minutes until shark cubes begin to flake when tested with a fork. Serve on individual platters and pass around the warm orange sauce at the table.

trivia clips

What does an ichthyologist actually do? (Hint: Studies a creature we associate with the sea.) Sharks have existed as a group for over 350 million years!
The great white shark (Carcharodon carcharias) is found in temperate waters throughout the world's oceans, and it is an important, though not common, predator in California`s coastal habitats.

Its theme was terror in the water, but for film studio officials it first appeared that it might end up as a scary box office flop as the movie was well over budget and production time was doubled from the original estimate. It ended up becoming one of the 20 top grossing films of all time! It landed the then 27-year old director Steven Spielberg, the title of "wunderkind" and became that year's blockbuster summer hit. The film is set in a fictional, popular tourist resort along the Atlantic coast. The first scene shows a female going into the ocean for a little moonlight swim as her friends continue to party on the beach. The audience is soon introduced to the pounding, crescendo of the music that signifies that a shark attack is imminent. The music becomes a significant part of the film and later recognizable in pop culture. We are given a view of the shark as it draws closer to its prey. With her feet dangling in the water, the young women is suddenly yanked underneath never to be seen again.

Police soon draw the appropriate conclusion and want to post warnings to the tourists and close the beach. It ends up becoming a battle, between the police and the mayor of the town who refuses to comply. Roy Scheider plays the chief of police, who becomes the hero of the story. He teams up with an ichthyologist Hooper (Richard Dreyfuss), together they join forces to capture the great white shark. Their struggles are not only with the unseen shark in the water, but with a greedy mayor on land that refuses to close the beaches and co-operate with them. Instead, the mayor continues to promote the town's beautiful beach location to generate money for the town. Most of the money from tourism is generated in the summer and he isn't prepared to see the town coffers dwindle just because of a shark! Everyone is under stress with one of the summer's biggest holidays approaching...the Fourth of July. What will happen is anybody's guess. Will the shark take more victims? Who will win the battle of wills, and most importantly, will the public be protected? At the time, this was considered a frighteningly believable movie. Most of us can probably remember seeing the film and being afraid to go into anything but a pool for quite sometime afterwards! For those who haven't seen the film, it may still make you think twice about what may be lurking underneath the waters of the deep blue seas!

jaws

(1975)

FEATURED ACTORS
Roy Scheider (Chief Martin Brody)
Robert Shaw (Quint)
Richard Dreyfuss (Matt Hooper)
Lorraine Gary (Ellen Brody)
Murray Hamilton
(Mayor Larry Vaughan)

DIRECTOR – Steven Spielberg

AWARDS WON

Best Editing (Verna Fields)	1975 Academy Award
Best Score (John Williams)	1975 Academy Award
Best Sound (Roger Heman)	1975 Academy Award
Best Sound (Robert L. Hoyt)	1975 Academy Award
Best Sound (Earl Madery)	1975 Academy Award
Best Sound (John N. Carter)	1975 Academy Award
Anthony Asquith Award for Original Film Music (John Williams)	1975 British Academy Award
Best Film (Steven Spielberg)	1975 British Academy Award
Best Film	1976 PEO
100 Greatest American Movies	1998 American Film Institute

continued

cilantro lime rice

serves 4

2 tbsp	butter		1/4 cup	fresh lime juice
1	onion, peeled, finely chopped		3 tsp	grated lime peel
				salt and pepper to taste
2 cups	long grain white rice		1/4 cup	fresh cilantro, chopped
3-3/4 cups	vegetable or chicken stock			

- Melt butter in in a large, heavy saucepan over medium heat. Add onion and saute until tender, about 10 minutes. Add rice and stir to coat. Add stock, lime juice and lime peel. Bring to boil, stirring occasionally. Reduce heat to low, cover and cook until rice is tender and liquid is absorbed, about 20 minutes. Remove from heat and let stand covered 5 minutes. Season to taste with salt and pepper.

- Add fresh chopped cilantro. Toss to combine. Transfer rice to serving bowl.

grilled pineapple

serves 4

1	ripe pineapple		1 tsp	ground cinnamon
1/2 cup	melted sweet butter		1/8 tsp	ground cloves
3/4 cup	granulated sugar			whipped cream
1 tsp	grated lime zest		1/2 cup	dark, strong rum for flambéing (optional)

- Preheat the grill to high. Oil the grate.

- Cut the rind off the pineapple, leaving the green leaves intact. Cut the pineapple in half lengthwise through the leaves as well as the fruit to obtain 8 slender wedges of pineapple with leaves intact. Trim the core off each pineapple wedge. Have the melted butter in one shallow bowl; mix the sugar, lime zest, cinnamon and cloves in another bowl.

- Dip each wedge of pineapple first in melted butter, then in the sugar mixture, shaking off the excess.

- Grill the pineapple wedges until browned and sizzling, 5 to 8 minutes per side. Transfer the pineapple wedges to plates or a platter. Serve with whipped cream.

- If using the rum, heat it in a small saucepan until very warm, but do not let boil. Touch a match to the rum and pour it over the pineapple. Serve at once.

trivia clips

The great white lives in tropical and temporal waters around the world and can be recognized by its large size, conical snout, black eyes, and large arrowhead-shaped teeth. It is generally gray, bluish, or brownish in colour, with a white or grayish belly that is the source of its name. Adult specimens can grow up to 36 feet (11 meters) in length and weigh more than 4,500 lb (2500 kg)! The great white shark is a member of the Lamnidae family of sharks, a group of fast-swimming sharks often referred to as mackerel sharks.

tropical flavoured
white sangria serves 4

2 bottles	dry white wine	3/4 cup	passion fruit, mango or guava fruit purée
3/4 cup	brandy	3	oranges, sliced into thin rounds
1/2 cup	triple sec	3	green apples, cored and sliced thin
3/4 cup	simple syrup (equal parts of sugar and water, heat until sugar dissolves and cool)	2	lemons, sliced into thin rounds

- Combine all ingredients in a large pitcher. Refrigerate covered, 3 hours or up to 2 days. Serve over ice.

jaws
(1975)

BEVERAGES

The sangria would probably suit the tastes of most of your guests. However, if they prefer white wine on its own, try: Stoney Ridge Bench Chardonnay (Ontario) or Baron Phillipe De Rothschild Chardonnay (France).

MUSIC

Any of the following would suit the beach party theme of the evening! Try: "Beach Boys Greatest Hits" (Springboard), "Beach Party" by Chubby Checker (Parkway), "Beach Music Vol. 1" (Beachbag), or "Beach Party Classics" (EMI). The latter two compilations feature a variety of different artists.

SETTING THE STAGE

This movie is mostly set on the beach. You could bring the beach indoors and invite guests to wear beach attire or their best "tacky tourist" shirts, shorts, etc. Decorate tables with vibrant summer colours. Set out beach towels, bring in the lawn chairs and blow up water tubes, rings, etc. Designate a sand area (preferably outdoors, unless you are brave enough to bring some sand indoors) as your entertainment spot.

If the weather does not permit a little bit of outdoor play, then fill some plastic or tin pails with sand and use as your table setting with a few colourful citrus candles in interesting shapes and sizes.

On your dining table, use lifesavers candies as decorations. Place seashells by each place setting. Use a plastic or rubber shark in a sand pail as a centrepiece. Decorate the room with nautical flags and nautical balloons, and nautical tablecloths as well. Hang mini and regular sized beach balls from the ceiling and in doorways. You might hang lights and string plastic sand shovels around the room or patio.

love story (1970)

This movie was not a favourite with the critics, but it was a huge hit at the box office. Based on the best-seller by Eric Segal, this opposites attract storyline soon becomes a tearjerker when it is discovered that one of the characters is diagnosed with a disease which offers no chance of survival. Ryan O'Neal, in his prime, plays Oliver Barrett IV, an Ivy League pre-law student who falls in love with music student Jenny Cavilleri (Ali MacGraw), a free-spirited, tough talking girl from a blue-collar Italian-American family. Oliver's father (Ray Milland) disapproves of the pending marriage and cuts off his son from any financial support. The happy couple ties the knot anyway, and despite financial problems and the fact that he must now work, the duo is ecstatically happy. Their happiness is shattered however, when Jenny is diagnosed with a life-threatening disease. Will their love fall apart? The plot is simple, yet the two charismatic characters are brought to life by the actors, and believable chemistry is created on screen.

FEATURED ACTORS
Ali MacGraw (Jenny)
Ryan O'Neal (Oliver Barrett IV)
John Marley (Phil)
Ray Milland (Oliver Barrett III)
Russell Nype (Dean)

DIRECTOR – Arthur Hiller

AWARDS WON

Best Score (Francis Lai)	1970 Academy Award
Best Actress — in Drama (Ali McGraw)	1971 Golden Globe Award
Best Director (Arthur Hiller)	1971 Golden Globe Award
Best Film — in Drama	1971 Golden Globe Award
10 Best Films	1971 National Board of Review of Motion Pictures Award

menu
bruschetta bread • shepherd's pie • green salad with vinaigrette (see index) • crusty bread (store-bought) • brownie ice cream sandwiches

bruschetta bread

serves 4

4	slices Italian bread		2 tbsp	fresh oregano, finely chopped
1	clove garlic		1 dash	ground pepper
1 tsp	olive oil		4 tsp	Parmesan cheese
2 tbsp	onion, minced			
1	large tomato, diced			

• Toast bread. Rub one side of hot toast with cut side of garlic. Heat oil in non-stick skillet over medium-high heat; add onion and cook, stirring until tender. Add tomato, oregano and pepper, stir.

• Spoon tomato mixture over garlic side of hot toast; sprinkle with Parmesan and serve immediately.

trivia clips
Ryan O'Neal was the long time love of a former Charlie's Angel. Who is she?
Tatum O'Neal, Ryan's daughter, married and then divorced which " bad boy" of tennis?
Ali MacGraw made the film The Getaway with this actor, who she then fell in love with during filming and ended up marrying later. Who is he? (Steve McQueen).

love story (1970)

shepherd's pie

serves 4 to 6

This is considered a comfort food, loved by many, and it is very simple to make. Add a side of your favourite vegetables to complete this meal if you so desire.

2-1/2 lbs	potatoes		3/4 tsp	salt
1/4 cup	butter		1 tsp	black pepper powder
1 tsp	salt		1	chicken stock cube dissolved in 1 cup of hot water
2 tbsp	milk			
1/2 tsp	pepper		1-1/2 tbsp	dark soya sauce
Filling:			1	carrot, diced
2 tbsp	vegetable oil		2 tbsp	corn flour mixed with 2 tbsp water
2	large onions, peeled and chopped finely		1-1/2 tsp	Worcestershire sauce
1-3/4 lb	ground beef sirloin		2 tbsp	vegetable oil

- Wash potatoes; place in a large pot and cover with water. Bring to a boil and continue to cook over high heat till potatoes are soft, about 30 minutes. Drain water from pot and peel potatoes while they are still hot. Add butter, salt, milk and pepper. Mash well with a potato masher or an electric mixer (do this while the potatoes are still hot and soft). Set aside.

- Preheat oven to 350°F.

- To make filling: heat a medium size pan over medium heat, and add the vegetable oil. Add chopped onions and stir-fry for about 4 minutes. Add beef; stir-fry till color changes. Add salt, pepper, chicken stock and dark soya sauce. Sauté all this for about 5minutes, stir in Worcestershire sauce. Add diced carrots if desired. Add cornflour mixture and blend well into the mixture. Remove from heat. Place filling at the bottom of an ovenproof glass bowl; layer with the mashed potatoes and run a fork across the surface to create "ripples". Bake in an oven for 30 to 40 minutes, or until Shepherd's Pie is golden brown on top.

BEVERAGES

Try American micro-brewery beer such as: Samuel Adams Boston Lager, Hempen Gold, Mississippi Mud Beer, Pete's Wicked Ale, or St.Ides Strong Beer.

MUSIC

There is a great soundtrack to the film, "Love Story" (Prism), otherwise listen to soft rock artists that topped the billboard charts of the early 1970's such as Carly Simon. Try "The Best of Carly Simon" (Electra) featuring her former husband James Taylor. Anything by Paul McCartney and his group Wings or anything by Fleetwood Mac would be great, as would compilation albums of 70's hits. You could have guests bring their favourite music from the decade.

SETTING THE STAGE

This film makes us realize that despite the plans many of us have set for our lives, sometimes life's journey hands us many hurdles to jump. Take this opportunity to sponsor a charity of your choice by collecting funds to donate. Invite guests to bring their contribution in a sealed envelope, then donate as a group. The amount of money does not matter. You could donate to a larger national foundation or look within your own community for worthy organizations. Seniors homes, schools, day care centres, hospitals, or perhaps a struggling family in your community would welcome the support. The ideas are endless and any contribution will be appreciated by the charity of your choice. This movie is emotional, you could suggest for your guests to bring along one of their favourite "comfort" foods if you are hosting this as a event, and turn it into a potluck dinner.

love story (1970)

brownie ice cream sandwiches

serves 4 to 6

Brownie layer:

1/2 cup	unsalted butter
2 oz	(2 squares) unsweetened chocolate
1 cup	granulated sugar

- Preheat oven to 350°F.
- Melt the butter and chocolate together in a medium saucepan over very low heat. Stir together and remove from heat. Add sugar, eggs and vanilla. Mix well. Stir in the flour and salt. Add nuts.

2	large eggs
1/2 tsp	vanilla extract
1/3 cup	all-purpose flour
1/8 tsp	salt
1 cup	nuts, chopped (optional)

Spread the mixture into a greased 8-inch square pan. Bake until set, about 40 minutes.
Cool before cutting.

Ice Cream Sandwiches: Serves 4

4	brownie squares
1 pint	vanilla ice cream

- Place a brownie in the centre of each of 4 plates. Top each brownie with a scoop of ice cream. Drizzle chocolate sauce over ice cream. Garnish with raspberries or strawberries and mint sprigs.

4 tbsp	chocolate sauce
1/2 cup	raspberries or strawberries
4	mint sprigs

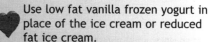 Use low fat vanilla frozen yogurt in place of the ice cream or reduced fat ice cream.

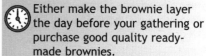 Either make the brownie layer the day before your gathering or purchase good quality ready-made brownies.

trivia clips

Ali MacGraw briefly joined the cast of a popular mid-eighties evening soap? Hint: The cast included Linda Evans and Joan Collins. The 1970 Academy Awards presentation was a year of big gaps between first and second statue winners. Helen Hayes won for best supporting actress in Airport, 39 years after her win in The Sin of Madelon Claudet. And Ring Lardner Jr. won for M*A*S*H, 29 years after his win for Woman of the Year.

m*a*s*h

(1970)

menu   quick kimchi • korean grilled beef • sesame fried rice • persimmon punch • green tea ice cream

Korean cuisine is famous for its variety of pickled vegetables. Kimchi is usually made a few days prior to serving and allowed to pickle. We offer a quick, but no less tasty version. Grilling is a favourite preparation method for meat, especially beef. Should you not have the time to make the Sesame Fried Rice, just serve plain steamed or boiled white rice (preferably jasmine).

quick kimchi

serves 4 to 6

1	small head Napa cabbage
1	small head Romaine lettuce
8	green onions, thinly chopped on the diagonal
1 tsp	red pepper flakes, or more to taste
1 tsp	grated ginger

1	clove garlic, crushed into a paste
3 tbsp	sesame oil
4 tbsp	rice wine vinegar
3 tbsp	soy sauce
2 tbsp	sesame seeds, toasted

• Tear Napa cabbage into bite size pieces. Cut Romaine lettuce into 1/3-inch strips. Toss in large bowl with green onions. In a small bowl combine red pepper flakes, ginger, garlic, sesame oil, vinegar and soy sauce. Pour over greens and toss well. Sprinkle with sesame seeds. Serve alongside the main dish.

korean grilled beef

serves 4 to 6

1 lb	beef tenderloin, boneless
1 tbsp	sesame seeds
3	green onions, chopped
2	garlic cloves, minced
2 tsp	rice wine vinegar
1-1/2 tsp	water
3 tbsp	soy sauce
1 tbsp	sugar
1 tbsp	sesame oil

1/2 tsp	pepper
2 tbsp	cooking oil
1 tbsp	fresh ginger, minced
1 tbsp	garlic, minced
3	carrots, peeled and sliced on diagonal
1/4 cup	water
1/4 lb	snow peas

• Wrap beef in plastic wrap and freeze until firm (but not frozen solid). Once firm, slice beef thinly across the grain. Place in baking dish. In a small skillet toast sesame seeds. To create marinade, in small bowl combine scallions, garlic, vinegar, water, soy sauce, sugar, sesame oil and pepper. Stir well. Pour marinade over beef. Let sit for 30 minutes

• In separate skillet, heat oil. Add ginger and garlic and cook until aroma is released. Add carrots and 1/4 cup water. Simmer until carrots are tender, about 2 minutes. Add snow peas and simmer until tender, about 2 minutes.

• Preheat indoor grill or grilling pan to medium-high heat. Remove beef from baking dish and grill until brown around edges, about 30 seconds per side. Add vegetables to beef. Stir and sprinkle with sesame seeds. Serve with rice.

This was one of the top grossing films of 1970 and it spawned the long-running television series of the same name. The television series is still in syndication. This film is a black comedy and is one of the first Hollywood films to treat the military and war from a humourous perspective. An anti-war and anti-establishment stance is obvious throughout the film as well. M*A*S*H focuses on a group of military doctors and nurses stationed in Korea at an American Mobile Army Surgical Hospital (hence the acronym, M.A.S.H.) during the Korean War. The characters at first appear to be a mismatched bunch, yet they all manage to get the job done and have fun while they're at it! The two surgeons, who are real jokesters, band together to get under the skin of a bible thumping Major and a good-looking army loyalist, whom they call "Hot Lips". They make light of a fellow soldier's transient sexual inadequacies and play hard when they are not on duty! M*A*S*H shows draftees brought together with regular military personnel, and when they clash there is always a story to tell.

The film satirizes the character types one might find on a military base. Gritty humour often allows people to get through tough situations and its use in the plot line is quite evident in this film. An enjoyable film, even for those who have never watched the television series.

FEATURED ACTORS
Elliott Gould (Trapper John)
Donald Sutherland (Hawkeye)
Tom Skerritt (Duke)
Sally Kellerman (Major Hot Lips)
Jo Ann Pflug (Lieutenant Dish)
Robert Duvall (Major Frank Burns)

DIRECTOR ~ Robert Altman

AWARDS WON

Best Film (Robert Altman)	1970 British Academy Award
United Nations Award (Robert Altman)	1970 British Academy Award
Golden Palm (Robert Altman)	1970 Cannes Film Festival
Best Direction (Robert Altman)	1970 New York Critics Film Circle Award
Best Film (Robert Altman)	1970 New York Critics Film Circle Award
U.S. National Film Registry	1996 Library of Congress Award
100 Greatest American Movies	1998 American Film Institute

sesame fried rice

serves 4 to 6

2 tbsp	canola or peanut oil	6 cups	cooked jasmine or white rice, cooled and broken up (can be made one day ahead)
4	large whole eggs		
1 tbsp	garlic, minced		
1 tbsp	ginger, minced	1/2 lb	bean sprouts
2 tbsp	chopped green onions	2 tbsp	soya sauce
		1 tbsp	sesame seed oil
			salt and black pepper to taste

- In a hot wok coated with canola or peanut oil, quickly scramble the eggs to soft stage. Remove and set aside.

- In the same hot wok coated with oil, add garlic, ginger and scallions. Cook until soft then add rice, bean sprouts, soya sauce and sesame oil; toss to combine. Season with salt and pepper and add the eggs. Heat thoroughly, taste and adjust for seasoning.

♥ Use egg substitute in place of real eggs.

🕐 Make the plain rice required for the recipe the day before and refrigerate until using.

persimmon punch
(soo jeung ga)

serves 6 to 8

This punch is often served in the winter time in Korea due to its hefty quota of vitamin C! This should be made the day prior to serving.

8 cups	water	1-1/2 cups	sugar
1/2 cup	fresh ginger, thinly sliced	1 cup	dried persimmons, sliced
3	cinnamon sticks	1/2 cup	pine nuts (for garnish)

- In a large saucepan, combine the water, ginger, and cinnamon and let simmer for 1/2 hour. Remove from heat and strain the liquid. Stir in the sugar and persimmons. Cool first, and then let sit in the refrigerator overnight. Serve well chilled with a teaspoon of pine nuts floating in each cup for garnish.

 Cultivated Japanese persimmons can be found in California. they are large, heart-shaped and deep orange in colour. Persimmons contain lots of beta-carotene and Vitamin C.

trivia clips

M*A*S*H was the third most popular film in 1970, after Love Story and Airport.
"My only enemy is me" Elliot Gould, Photoplay, April 1979
I was up for a wonderful part but I was told: "Sorry, you're the best actor for the role, but this calls for a guy-next-door type. You don't look like you've ever lived next door to anyone.' Donald Sutherland, Playboy, October 1981

green tea ice cream

serves 4 to 6

This is a very rich tasting, premium quality ice cream. Serve in small portions. You will need an ice cream maker to make this dessert.

2 cups	heavy cream	9	egg yolks
2 cups	half and half	3/4 cup	sugar
1/2	vanilla bean, split lengthwise	2 tbsp	green tea powder

- In a large saucepan over medium heat, combine the cream, half-and-half, and vanilla bean, stirring occasionally to make sure the mixture doesn't scorch on the bottom. When the cream mixture reaches a simmer (do not let it boil), set aside to infuse for 10 to 15 minutes. In a medium bowl, using an electric mixer, blend together the egg yolks and sugar. Next, slowly pour the still-hot cream mixture into the egg yolk mixture and use a whisk to blend. Return the mixture to the saucepan and cook over medium heat, stirring constantly with a wooden spoon. At 160˚F, the mixture will give off a puff of steam. When the mixture reaches 180˚F it will be thickened and creamy, like eggnog. If you don't have a thermometer, test it by dipping a wooden spoon into the mixture.

Run your finger down the back of the spoon. If the stripe remains clear, the mixture is ready; if the edges blur, the mixture is not quite thick enough yet. When it is ready, quickly remove it from the heat and whisk in the green tea powder. Meanwhile, half-fill a large bowl with ice water. Strain the mixture into a smaller bowl to smooth it and remove the vanilla bean. Rest the smaller bowl in the ice water and let the mixture cool, stirring often, then continue according to the directions of your ice cream maker.

 Use evaporated 2% milk instead of the half and half.

 You may purchase green tea ice cream at Asian supermarkets.

 If you can't find powdered green tea (usually found in Asian supermarkets), then grind regular green tea in a coffee or spice grinder until powdered.

BEVERAGES

If you wish to try Korean beer, the OB Lager is a good choice. Otherwise, serve Japanese Sapporo Draft or Tsingtao beer from China.

Green tea may also be served, it even comes in familiar flavours such as Earl Grey.

MUSIC

Should you wish to listen to some authentic Korean music then play "Korean Traditional Music Ensemble: Traditional Music From Korea" (ARC Music). The music is distinctly Asian with some Chinese and Japanese influences. The Koreans also have their own form of opera which would appeal to fans of this musical genre. You may also wish to listen to music from the 70's. Have guests bring their favourite music from that decade and play some various selections. It will be fun to listen to the songs and think back to where you were at that time in your life.

SETTING THE STAGE

Perhaps you could go to a fabric store and buy some fabric with a military motif to create a tablecloth or table runner. This is in keeping with the film's theme. Use camping style dinnerware and serving pieces if you have them. Ask guests to come dressed as their favourite characters from the M*A*S*H film or the TV series. Depending on the age range at your party, you could also ask guests to bring photos of themselves during the 70's; display them and have guests try to guess who's who...

Otherwise, go for an Asian look. Purchase some inexpensive paper lanterns at Korean or other Oriental stores. Decorate with red and gold. Create a simple centrepiece with a bonsai tree or with one of the now popular indoor miniature fountains. Use chopsticks at place settings and square shaped serving pieces if you have them.

saturday night fever

(1977)

Before MTV or any other music videos flashed across TV screens, Saturday Night Fever made music history and turned John Travolta into an idol and pop cultural phenomenon of the late 1970's. Disco dancing and music were considered an underground movement by some, but with this film they were brought to the forefront of mainstream society. This movie is gritty and has a lot of attitude and it begins as soon as Travolta does his strut down a Brooklyn street to the background sounds of mega hit single "Stayin' Alive" by the Bee Gees. Tony Manero, a middle class Italian-American, works as a clerk at a Brooklyn paint store during the day, but at night he is transformed into king of the dance floor at Manhattan nightspots. Tony struts his stuff and attracts a female following, but his main dance partner is a secretary, Stephanie, who enjoys the glamour of the night life. Tony dreams of escaping his mundane life and pursues this dream at a contest at the local disco club, all in hopes of a better life. The movie's best-selling soundtrack became a goldmine, grossing over $100 million. A number of movies that were hits on the screen and the pop charts simultaneously followed suit, such as Grease, which also starred Travolta. Later in the 80's we had Flashdance. Even though the disco culture was short-lived, nostalgia still remains for this popular, glamorous era that is remembered by many, some of whom may still have polyester clothes and platform shoes tucked away in their closets!

FEATURED ACTORS
John Travolta (Tony Manero)
Karen Gorney (Stephanie)
Barry Miller (Bobby C.)
Joseph Cali (Joey)
Paul Pape (Double J.)

DIRECTOR ~ John Badham

menu

farinata • a variety of olives and cheese (store-bought) • stuffed celery stalks • modern new york style strip loin steak (see index) • fried peppers (see index) • roasted potato wedges with sea salt and paprika (see index) • caesar salad • seventh heaven

farinata

serves 6 to 8

This is an easy-to-prepare appetizer that goes over well in both winter or summer

3-3/4 cups	water		4 tbsp	extra virgin olive oil
2-1/3 cups	chickpea flour			pinch of pepper
1 tsp	salt		1	medium onion

- In a large bowl, pour in the water then slowly add the chickpea flour, mix together with a wire whisk.

- Add salt to the mixture and let it stand at room temperature for 3 hours, or even better, overnight.

- Remove the foam from the top. Grease a baking pan, about 16" x 12", with oil; once greased add another 2 tablespoons of oil. Then add the chickpea mixture. Use a fork to combine the oil and chickpea mixture. Sprinkle generously with pepper.

- Meanwhile slice the onion thinly. Put 2 tablespoons of oil in a medium non-stick pan and when the oil is hot, add the onion. Cook on medium heat for about 10 minutes or until soft but not golden.

- Preheat the oven to 400°F. Top the farinata with the onion slices and bake for 20 to 25 minutes.

- Remove from the oven and let it cool for about 10 minutes before cutting. Serve with the olives and cheese.

stuffed celery stalks

serves 8

8	crisp tender celery stalks		1 tbsp walnuts, finely chopped
1 cup	creamy Italian Gorgonzola cheese or blue cheese		

- Trim the stalks and cut them into 4-inch pieces.

- In a bowl combine the Gorgonzola cheese with the walnuts. Stir the ingredients together until smooth and well blended. Fill the celery sticks with the cheese mixture and chill before serving.

trivia clips

The 90's saw a revival of 70's nostalgia in terms of fashion and music.
Do you know who directed the sequel to Saturday Night Fever called Stayin' Alive in 1983? He also had a brief cameo in the film. Hint: In one of the first films that made him a star he was known as the Italian Stallion. His mother is an Astrologist and he has been married a number of times.

saturday night fever (1977)

caesar salad

serves 6

1	loaf of day-old Italian bread
3	garlic cloves, mashed
9 tbsp	extra virgin olive oil
1/4 tsp	plus 1 pinch kosher salt
2 heads	romaine lettuce, remove outer leaves

	black pepper to taste
1	lemon, juiced
6 drops	Worcestershire sauce
2	eggs
1/4 cup	grated Parmesan cheese

- Heat oven to 350°F. Cut 1/2 to 3/4-inch croutons from the loaf of bread. Place on a baking sheet and put into the oven; heat until dry, but not browned. Use a mortar and pestle or food processor to mash the garlic with 4 tablespoons of oil and 1/4 teaspoon kosher salt. Strain the oil into a skillet over medium heat. Add the dried croutons and fry, tossing constantly until all the oil is absorbed and the croutons turn gold. Set aside.

- Tear lettuce and place in a very large bowl, and toss with 3 tablespoons of olive oil. Sprinkle with the remaining kosher salt and the black pepper. Add the remaining 2 tablespoons olive oil. Toss well.

- Add the lemon juice and Worcestershire sauce. Break in the eggs. Toss until a creamy dressing forms.

- Add the Parmesan cheese, toss again, and serve with croutons.

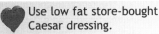 Use low fat store-bought Caesar dressing.

AWARDS WON

10 Best Films	1977 Board of Review of Motion Pictures Award
Best Actor (John Travolta)	1977 Board of Review of Motion Pictures Award
Best Actor (John Travolta)	1977 New York Film Critics Circle Award
Best Actress (Donna Pescoe)	1977 New York Film Critics Circle Award

BEVERAGES

The steak calls for a robust wine, try any of the following: Woods End Baco Noir (Ontario), Banrock Station Shiraz Cabernet Sauvignon (Australia), Bersano Barbera D'Asti (Italy) or Cline Zinfandel (USA).

Long Island Ice Tea or a Manhattan would be suitable pre-dinner cocktails (see main beverages page).

Coffee with dessert and a selection of liqueurs like Amaretto, Frangelico, Limoncello, etc.

trivia clips

One of the trendiest hot spots during the disco era was Studio 54 in New York City.
The 1977 Academy Awards were somewhat of a political platform for some actors. Vanessa Redgrave reacted to protest made by the Jewish Defense League about her nomination. And Woody Allen refused to attend at all, calling the awards, "meaningless".
Travolta is married to this actress who co-starred with Tom Cruise in Jerry McGuire. Who is she?

saturday night
fever (1977)

continued

MUSIC

Listen to the original soundtrack "Saturday Night Fever" (Polydor), featuring The Bee Gees, Kool and the Gang, as well as K.C. and the Sunshine Band. You may wish to have a compilation album on hand too. Try "Disco Dance Hits: 1977-1997" (Popular), or "Disco Classics" (K-Tel). The latter choice features 12 original tracks like Blondie's "Heart of Glass" and "Get Up and Boogie" by Silver Convention. You could also have guests bring their favourite music from the era. Donna Summer, The Bee Gees, Earth Wind and Fire, Gloria Gaynor, Lionel Ritchie, Peaches & Herb, and The Village People are all good choices. The great thing about the 1970's music scene is that it was full of variety and great music.

SETTING THE STAGE

Create a dance floor! Your guests will want to "get down on it" and "boogie" after this movie. Whether or not you remember how to disco dance, 70's nostalgia is definitely back and so is the dancing. No more wall flowers! Make this a fun get-together with friends. Dig out your favourite polyester shirts. Everyone has at least one pair of hot pants and an item of tie-dyed clothing hiding in their closet. For those of you who have teenagers you will blend in with them, especially with today's fashion stars like platform shoes. Rekindle old dance moves or learn something new. Give party favours to guests as they arrive to get them into a 70's frame of mind; perhaps a happy face pendant or metal mood ring to get them in a funky mood. Your younger guests may appreciate toys like slinkies. To decorate your "pad" you could hang a beaded curtain at the front door to welcome all of your guests in 70s style. Inside, at the party, set up black lights and lava lamps around the room. You know bean chairs are a must, whether tye-dyed or denim. Hang mini disco balls in all colors from the ceiling for an added cool illusion. Have a lip-sync/karaoke contest — Sing or lip sync (mouth the words along with the music) to your favourite tunes from the disco days. Award a prize to the best act. You could also award prizes to the best dressed in 70's attire! Don't forget to have a groovy time and let your hair down!

seventh heaven

serves 10

4	eggs, separated		4 tbsp	instant coffee (black)
1 cup	granulated sugar		1 cup	unsalted butter, softened
2 tbsp	all-purpose flour		1 cup	powdered sugar
1 tsp	baking powder		1	egg yolk
1/2 cup	ground walnuts		2 tbsp	chopped walnuts
1	torte wafer sheet (square crispy wafers available at European grocers)			

- Preheat oven to 375˚. Beat the 4 yolks and 1/2 cup of the granulated sugar together until frothy.

- Blend in the flour and the baking powder. In a separate bowl, beat the egg whites until stiff peaks form, gradually adding the remaining 1/2 cup granulated sugar. Combine the ground walnuts with the yolks and fold egg whites into the yolk mixture.

- Grease a baking dish and trim the wafer to the size of the dish (lay wafer in the dish, waffle side up).

- Pour in the egg and walnut mixture and bake for about 15 minutes or until a toothpick inserted in the centre comes out clean.

- Dissolve the coffee in 1 cup of hot water. Allow to cool completely. Cream the butter and powdered sugar at high speed with the electric mixer. Add 1 egg yolk and then add the cooled black coffee, tablespoon by tablespoon, until the filling is that of a thick cream (you will not use up all of the coffee).

- Allow the cake to cool before spreading the coffee mixture on top. Garnish with the chopped walnuts.

 Use light butter for the topping.

 Make the day before.

---

trivia clips

One of Travolta's passions is flying; he is a licensed pilot and has even named his son Jett.
The Bee Gees have had a hit single every decade.

the last picture show (1971)

guacamole (see index) • layered mexican dip • flank-steak fajitas with spicy summer vegetables • tex-mex confetti salad • deep-fried mexican style ice cream with tortilla fans and berry salsa (see index)

layered mexican dip

serves 8 to 10

1	14 ounce can refried beans	2 tbsp	lime juice
1-1/4 cups	light sour cream	1/4 tsp	hot pepper flakes
1/2 tsp	each ground cumin and salt	2 cups	shredded cheddar cheese
1/4 tsp	hot pepper sauce	2	tomatoes, chopped
2	avocados	1/3 cup	sliced green onions
1/3 cup	finely chopped onion	1/2 cup	sliced pitted black olives

• In bowl, stir together refried beans, 1/4 cup of the sour cream, cumin, 1/4 tsp of the salt and hot pepper sauce; spread in 12-inch round serving dish that is at least 1-1/2 inches deep. Peel and pit avocados. In bowl, mash together avocados, onion, lime juice, hot pepper flakes, 1 cup of the sour cream and remaining salt; spread over refried bean layer. Top with remaining sour cream. Starting at outside, garnish with concentric rings of shredded cheese, tomatoes, green onions and olives. (Make-ahead: Cover and refrigerate for up to 24 hours.)

trivia clips

Cybill Shepherd and Peter Bogdanovich began a relationship on the set. They were a couple for eight years.
She is mother of 3 children (including twin boys).
Cybill dated Elvis Presley.

trivia clips

At one time she was known as the _____ Girl (a brand of shampoo), and she also graced the cover of Seventeen magazine a number of times during her modeling career. The sequel to The Last Picture Show called Texasville (1990), did not enjoy the same success as its predecessor.

It's 1951, and it seems like not much is happening in Anarene, a Texas one-horse town, where generation after generation of town folk lead what appears to be mundane lives. They go through the same rites of passage, and dream the same unrealized dreams, and all of them, some more than others, feel the claustrophobia of small-town life. The story follows two high school seniors, Sonny and Duane, whose world consists of football, going to the movies at the town's Royal Theatre and hanging out at the local pool hall. They both even lust after the same girl, Jacy, who happens to be blessed with good looks and the luck of being born into a wealthy family. Jacy is a flirt and she knows that both boys are attracted to her. As senior year passes, Sonny is quickly initiated into the complex adult world through an affair with his coach's wife, Ruth, while his friend Duane pursues the elusive and fickle Jacy who in turn has set her sights on rich Bobby Sheen. After the death of their friend, Sam the Lion, who was the owner of the pool hall, things begin to take a turn for the worse in their lives. Duane decides to enlist and go to Korea after he tires of Jacy's fickle and flirtatious nature. Jacy then toys with Sonny's emotions and there is an altercation between the boys when Duane returns from the army. Duane and Jacy resume their relationship and decide to elope, but are prevented from doing so by her parents. Duane spends his last night in town with his friend Sonny, viewing the final scheduled performance at the cinema. This closing of the theatre serves as evidence of the town's decay and fraying of the community. This bittersweet, at times funny and reflective film is worth watching for its snapshot view of American small-town life during the 1950's.

FEATURED ACTORS
Timothy Bottoms (Sonny Crawford)
Jeff Bridges (Duane Jackson)
Cybill Shepherd (Jacy Farrow)
Ben Johnson (Sam the Lion)
Cloris Leachman (Ruth Popper)
Ellen Burstyn (Lois Farrow), Randy Quaid (Lester Marlow)

DIRECTOR ~ Peter Bogdanovich

the last
picture show (1971)
continued

BEVERAGES

Serve your favourite Mexican beer (like Corona) with wedges of lime, or serve a variety of American beer. If you are lucky enough, you may be able to track down some beers from Texas micro-breweries such as Yellow Rose Brewing Co. or Saint Arnold.

Frozen Margaritas (see index for drink recipes)

Tequila Sunrise

Spanish Coffee

flank-steak fajitas with spicy summer vegetables serves 6

The marinade is the secret to these spectacular fajitas. If you wish you may substitute chicken in equal amounts to the steak.

Marinade:

1/3 cup	fresh cilantro, minced
1/3 cup	fresh lime juice
1/3 cup	water
4 tsp	dried oregano
1 tbsp	ground cumin
1/2 tsp	salt
1/4 tsp	black pepper
1/4 tsp	crushed red pepper
5	garlic cloves, minced

Fajitas:

1 cup	vertically sliced onion
1 lb	flank steak, cut into strips
	cooking spray
1	red bell pepper, cut into strips
1 cup	yellow squash, julienne-cut
1 cup	zucchini, julienne-cut
1 cup	frozen corn kernels
6	(10-inch) flour tortillas
2 cups	chopped tomato
2 tbsp	low-fat sour cream

- Prepare the marinade by combining all the ingredients in a small bowl.

- Prepare fajitas: Combine 1/3 cup marinade, onion, and steak in a large zip-top plastic bag; seal.

- Marinate in refrigerator 1 hour, turning occasionally. Remove steak mixture from bag; discard marinade. Place a large non-stick skillet coated with cooking spray over medium-high heat until hot.

- Add the steak mixture, and stir-fry 5 minutes. Place the steak mixture in a large bowl, and keep warm. Add bell pepper, squash, zucchini, corn, and remaining marinade to skillet; stir-fry 5 minutes or until vegetables are crisp-tender. Add to steak mixture; toss gently.

- Warm tortillas according to package directions. Arrange 1 cup steak mixture, 1/3 cup tomato, and 1 teaspoon sour cream down centre of each tortilla; roll up.

continued

tex-mex confetti salad

serves 6 to 8

This salad will complement the flavour of the fajitas. It will also satisfy vegetarian guests as it can be eaten as a main course on its own.

Salad:

2 cups	drained canned whole-kernel corn
2 cups	canned black beans, rinsed
1	cucumber, peeled, seeded and diced
3	jicama, peeled and diced
8	large red radishes, trimmed, thinly sliced
2	red bell peppers, diced
2	serrano chilies, seeded, minced
4 tbsp	fresh lime juice
1	large red onion, sliced
2	large ripe avocados, peeled, diced
	salt and pepper to taste

Chunky Yogurt Dressing:

4 cups	plain low-fat yogurt
2	cucumbers, peeled, seeded and diced
2 cups	chopped fresh cilantro
4 tbsp	fresh lime juice
	salt and pepper to taste

- Combine ingredients for salad in large bowl. Season with salt and pepper. Mound salad on platter.

- Serve chunky yogurt dressing in a separate bowl alongside.

- To make chunky yogurt dressing: Blend all ingredients in processor using on/off turns just until cucumber is finely chopped. Season with salt and pepper. Transfer to small bowl. (Can be prepared 1 hour ahead. Cover and chill.) Makes 3 cups.

MUSIC

Play some down home Texas Blues which is a geographical subgenre. It features a more relaxed, swinging sound than other styles of blues. You could try "Johnny Guitar Watson: Very Best of Johnny Guitar Watson" (Rhino) or "Blind Lemon Jefferson: King of the Country Blues" (Yazoo), who is credited with founding Texas Blues. Another Texan musical genre is Tex-Mex, which is a unique genre that is a fusion of rock, country, and Latin music. Some interesting compilations to seek out are: "Doug Sahm: Best of Doug Sahm (1968-1975)" (Rhino) and "Johnny Rodriguez: Greatest Hits" (K-Tel). You could listen to music from the 1950's since the film was set in this decade. Try "50's Jukebox Hits" (Universal Special Markets), "Chart Topper: Dance Hits of the 50's" (Priority), and "Classic 50's Hits" (ITC Master).

For those making it a romantic evening, we suggest: "Chart Toppers: Romantic Hits of the 50's" (Priority).

If you have a gregarious group, you may wish to try some good old-fashioned square dancing to really hoe-down! Two excellent albums, both by one of the most influential musicians in this genre, the late Tommy Jackson, are: "Popular Square Dance Music" (Dot) and "Good Old Fiddle Music" (MCA).

SETTING THE STAGE

It is best to set up this meal as a buffet. Place a gingham tablecloth on your buffet table. Use terracotta or ceramic serving dishes for the food. Place ice in a large decorative tin bucket or washbasin and use as your beer cooler. If you're making Margaritas for a crowd, make a large quantity and serve from a tin bucket. Should you have cowboy boots and a cowboy hat lying around, incorporate them into your decorating theme. Create a scarecrow; stuff a pair of jeans and a plaid shirt, as well as a white plastic bag. Using markers draw a face on the bag and top this Texas scarecrow with a cowboy hat. Buy a small bale of hay and place the scarecrow in a sitting position on the bale of hay. This sight could greet your guests outside your home! Place miniature cacti at each place setting with place cards for each guest. You could also place simple flowers such as daisies in old glass milk jugs or in small coloured bottles such as those used for mineral water. This is a gift for your guests to take home. Buy some bandannas to use as dinner napkins; you could also buy some "sheriff badges" at a dollar or party store and use them as napkin rings. Place some small figurines of cows and horses on your buffet table and create some romantic lighting with tin lamps.If you are setting up outside, track down the equipment for a game of horseshoes. You could even arrange to go for a horseback ride prior to watching the film and making dinner, it is an experience that everyone should try at least once!

EXTRAVAGANT 80'S

EXTRAVAGANT 80'S

1981-   MTV arrives as a basic cable television station that features popular music videos and shows, including comedy showcases and series. Its initials stand for music television, it began broadcasting in 1981; "I want my MTV" became a catch phrase by 1982. MTV Japan launched in 1984.

1981-   On April 12, 1981, the shuttle Columbia was launched into space, and between then and July, 1982, it was relaunched three times to test its ability to maneuver and carry payloads. During the 1980's, three other shuttles were put into space: Challenger, Discovery, and Atlantis. In January, 1986, the Challenger blew up less than two minutes after launch, killing all seven astronauts aboard. This disaster halted the shuttle program for several years. The Soviet Union meanwhile, began its space shuttle program in 1988 with an unmanned flight.

1981-   AIDS diagnosed. A new fatal, infectious disease was diagnosed in 1981. Called Acquired Immunodeficiency Syndrome (AIDS), it began appearing in major cities among homosexual men and intravenous drug users.
For a number of years, people mistakenly believed it wasn't present in the heterosexual community.

1983-   Vanessa Williams becomes the first black Miss America. Williams relinquished her crown during her reign when nude pictures of her were published in "Penthouse" magazine. She has since earned respect as a talented actress and singer.

1986-   Chernobyl nuclear accident — The worst accident in the history of the nuclear power industry occurred on April 25-26, 1986, at the Chernobyl station in what was then the Ukrainian Soviet Socialist Republic (now independent Ukraine).

1987-   Stock market crash — The largest stock market crash in the history of the United States securities industry took place on Monday, Oct. 19, 1987. The Dow Jones Industrial Average fell more than 508 points, representing more than half a trillion dollars in equity losses on one day. About 604 million shares traded hands, a huge volume of trading for one day. This day has since come to be known as Black Monday.

1989-   Collapse of Communism in Eastern Europe — One of the most significant events in modern history began to unfold slowly during the summer of 1989. After more than four decades of living under Communist totalitarianism, the peoples of eastern Europe were getting restless. They watched their poor quality of life get even worse, as the free nations of the West got ever more prosperous. Sadly, life for the average citizen in many of these countries has worsened in some respects with the rise in the crime rate that has come with open borders and social changes.

a fish called wanda (1988)

deep fried broccoli & carrots in scallion & caper beer batter
serves 4 to 6

Beer makes for a particularly crisp batter here, and the capers add piquancy. Use your favourite vegetables, adjusting the deep-frying time as necessary.

1-1/2 cups	all-purpose flour			vegetable oil for deep-frying
12-ounce	bottle of beer (not dark)			
6	scallions, finely chopped		1	head of broccoli, cut into 1-1/2-inch florets
2 tbsp	drained bottled capers, finely chopped		3	carrots, cut into 1/2-inch-thick sticks
1-1/2 tsp	salt			

- In a bowl, whisk together the flour, beer, scallions, capers, and salt. In a heavy deep pot or a deep fryer heat at least 1-1/2 inches of oil to 375˚F.
- Working in batches, dip the broccoli and carrots in the batter, and fry in the oil for about 3 minutes, or until golden, transferring it as it is fried to paper towels to drain.

- If you are counting calories try using raw vegetables with a low-fat dip instead of deep-frying them, or steam and serve them with a little bit of olive oil and herbs.

coleslaw
serves 6

1 cup	mayonnaise		12 cups	lightly packed shredded green cabbage (about 2 small heads)
6 tbsp	cider vinegar			
6 tbsp	barbecue sauce			salt and pepper
3 tbsp	sugar			

- Mix first 4 ingredients in large bowl. Mix in cabbage. Season with salt and pepper. Chill at least 1 hour.

 Use low or no fat mayonnaise for the coleslaw.

A tale of murder, lust, greed, revenge, and of course a fish. This is one of the funniest films ever! The film is so well put together, you will want to see it more than once. This movie is perfectly cast and well directed. Kevin Kline's performance alone was quoted as being one of the best comedic performances.

Sexy American diamond aficionado and con artist, Wanda, is in England to use her charms to obtain some valuable jewelry stolen by her swindler lover George, played by Tom Georgeson. To accomplish this, she seduces his accessory, Otto (Kevin Kline). To facilitate her getaway she even plays upon the heartstrings of George's lawyer, Archie (John Cleese). Though she plans her getaway with Otto, she finds herself falling for Archie. Will she get the jewels? Who does she end up with? Well, you will just have to watch this hilarious and quirky film featuring British and American actors to find out.

FEATURED ACTORS
John Cleese (Archie Leach)
Jamie Lee Curtis
   (Wanda Gerschwitz)
Kevin Kline (Otto West)
Michael Palin (Ken)

DIRECTOR ~ Charles Crichton

AWARDS WON

Best Supporting Actor (Kevin Kline)	1988 Academy Award
Best Actor (John Cleese)	1988 British Academy Award
Best Supporting Actor (Michael Palin)	1988 British Academy Award

trivia clips

John Cleese was most famous in Monty Python sketches, "The Ministry of Silly Walks"; he found himself continually pestered by admirers to do silly walks for them.
John Cleese's family name was Cheese, but was changed to Cleese before his birth.
John Cleese's character is called "Archie Leach", which is Cary Grant's real name.
Cary Grant and John Cleese are both from the same hometown, Weston-Super-Mare.

a fish called
wanda (1988)

continued

BEVERAGES

Nothing else but a pint, a pint of British ale or lager, will do! Try: Boddington's Pub Ale, Black Sheep Ale, Fiddler's Elbow Ale, John Smith's Pub Draught, Newcastle Brown Ale, Kingfisher Premium Lager and Wells Premium Lager.

MUSIC

The 1980's was a time when British groups and solo artists dominated the charts! Listen to any of the following for a blast from the past: Duran Duran, Genesis, Queen, Sade, Culture Club, The Police, Wham and David Bowie. Or perhaps a compilation album like "The 80's" (K-Tel) would be suitable.

SETTING THE STAGE

Make this into a "Pub Night." Serve plenty of dark ale in frosty mugs or pints. The movie is funny, and the evening should be a carefree one. Serve the fish and chips in baskets lined with parchment paper—clean up will be a breeze. Have condiments such as tartar sauce, vinegar and a variety of ketchup on hand. Use red and white checker tablecloths, or perhaps just some new plaid tea towels as place mats. Dim the lights and enjoy the movie!

CRÈME FRAÎCHE

This matured, thickened cream has a slightly tangy, nutty flavour and velvety rich texture. The thickness of it can range from that of commercial sour cream to that of room-temperature margarine. A very expensive facsimile of crème fraîche is sold in some gourmet stores.

classic fish and chips
serves 4 to 6

	vegetable oil (for deep-frying)
3/4 cup	all-purpose flour
1/2 cup	water
1/2 cup	dark ale
1-1/2 lb	halibut or cod fillets (about 3/4 inch thick), cut crosswise into 1-1/2-inch-wide strips
	salt and pepper
1 lb	potatoes, peeled, cut lengthwise into 1/2-inch-wide strips
	Malt vinegar or apple cider vinegar

- Pour enough oil into large, heavy skillet to reach depth of 1/2 inch. Heat oil over high heat to 360°F.

- Meanwhile, whisk flour, and water and beer in medium bowl until smooth batter forms; add more flour if required in order to make it thick enough to coat the fish. Sprinkle fish with salt and pepper. Add fish to batter and stir to coat. Add potato to skillet; fry until golden brown and crisp, stirring often, about 7 minutes. Using tongs, transfer potato to paper towels. Sprinkle with salt and pepper.

- Add fish to skillet; fry until coating is golden and crisp and fish is just opaque in center, about 3 minutes per side. Transfer fish to paper towels. Sprinkle with salt and pepper.

- Serve with vinegar.

 Pick up an order of fish and chips at your local favorite fish & chip restaurant.

english lemon tart
serves 4 to 6

For crust:

1/3 cup	almonds
1-1/4 cups	all-purpose flour
3 tbsp	sugar
1/4 tsp	salt
6 tbsp	chilled unsalted butter, cut into 1/2-inch pieces
2 tbsp	(or more) ice water

For filling:

2/3 cup	fresh lemon juice
1/2 cup	sugar
3 tbsp	crème fraîche or sour cream
4	large eggs
	lemon slices (optional)

- Make crust: Finely grind almonds in processor. Add flour, sugar and salt and process until blended. Add butter and process until mixture resembles coarse meal. With machine running, add ice water, 1 tablespoonful at a time, and blend until moist clumps form, adding more water if dry. Gather dough into ball; flatten into disk. Wrap in plastic; chill at least 1 hour and up to 1 day.

- Preheat oven to 375°F. Roll out dough on floured surface to 12-inch round. Transfer to 9-inch-diameter tart pan with removable bottom. Fold dough overhang inwards, pressing dough together to form double-thick sides. Pierce dough all over with fork. Freeze 20 minutes.

- Bake crust until set and light golden about 30 minutes, piercing with fork if crust bubbles,. Cool crust on rack 15 minutes. Maintain oven temperature.

- Make filling: Whisk lemon juice and sugar in medium bowl to blend. Whisk in crème fraîche. Whisk in eggs 1 at a time until well blended. Pour mixture into crust.

- Bake tart until filling is set, about 35 minutes, covering crust edges with foil if browning too quickly. Cool tart completely in pan on rack. Refrigerate until cold, about 2 hours.

- Remove pan sides. Garnish tart with lemon slices, if desired. Cut into wedges and serve.

 For those watching what they eat, serve a lemon sorbet or granita instead.

amadeus

(1984)

liptauer cheese dip

Yield: About 3 cups

This easy-to-make cheese dip tastes great! Feel free to adjust the amount of herbs and spices to your liking.

1 cup	butter, softened
1 lb	quark (or softened cream cheese if you can't find quark)
1 tbsp	grated onion
1-1/2 tsp	Dijon mustard
1 to 1-1/2 tsp	ground caraway seeds

2 tsp	fresh parsley, chopped
2 tsp	fresh chives, chopped
2 tsp	capers, chopped
1 tbsp	sweet paprika
1/4 tsp	salt
	freshly ground pepper to taste

- Mix all ingredients well. Shape into mound. Sprinkle extra parsley or chives on top if so desired. Serve with Melba toast or a variety of crackers and bread.

 Use low fat quark or cream cheese.

 Make this dip the day before, store in a tightly sealed container and garnish with fresh herbs prior to serving.

Quark may be found at European delis. It can be described as a cross between ricotta and cream cheese, but a bit sharper. It is made with skim or partly skimmed milk. the low fat versions are just as good as the full fat.

This film is yet another successful adaptation of a Broadway hit. This musical drama attempts to expand on a Viennese rumour surrounding the death of musical genius and legend, Wolfgang Amadeus Mozart. The story is told from the viewpoint of an aging, mad composer of the Austrian Royal court, Antonio Salieri. The rivalry between Salieri and Mozart began as soon as the young Mozart came to the attention of Austrian Emperor Joseph II. Salieri was resentful of the young prodigy and did all he could to place obstacles along Mozart's career path. He used his numerous connections at the Royal court to accomplish this. Salieri viewed Mozart as a vulgar and obnoxious person who had perhaps been given his musical gift by a divine accident. In the end, Salieri helps to bring about Mozart's demise by posing as a rich and enigmatic benefactor who commissions the laborious "Requiem". Composing this work eventually costs Mozart all that he has; his wealth, health and life. This film is a treat for fans of classical music and will perhaps even encourage those who have not adequately explored this musical genre to do so—they may even become aficionados of classical music, a music that stirs the soul unlike any other.

FEATURED ACTORS
F. Murray Abraham (Antonio Salieri)
Tom Hulce
   (Wolfgang Amadeus Mozart)
Elizabeth Berridge
   (Constance Mozart)
Simon Callow (Emanuel Schikaneder)
Roy Dotrice (Leopold Mozart)

DIRECTOR ~ Milos Forman

trivia clips

With the filming of this movie, Milos Forman returned to Prague for the first time since he'd left due to the Russian invasion of Czechoslovakia in 1968.
Wolfgang Amadeus Mozart was born in Salzburg, Austria on January 27, 1756. He died on December 5, 1791 in Vienna.

amadeus

(1984)

austrian vegetable cheese soup
serves 6 to 8

3/4 lb	root vegetables, finely diced (celery stalk, carrots, parsley, etc.)
1	small kohlrabi, trimmed, peeled and finely diced
1	small cauliflower, separated into small florets
10	brussels sprouts, trimmed
1/2 lb	green beans, trimmed, halved
2 tbsp	butter
pinch	sugar
4 cups	beef broth
	salt and pepper
1-1/2 cup	sliced mushrooms or whole peas (frozen peas are okay)
3 tbsp	bacon, coarsely chopped
	oil
1	slice white bread per serving (an Italian or French bread works best)
	a sharp or tangy cheese
	chopped parsley (optional for garnish)

- Boil all of the vegetables, except the mushrooms (or peas) briefly in salted water—vegetables should remain crispy. Drain vegetables, reserving the water and set aside. Melt butter in a large stockpot, stir in sugar and let brown slightly. Add a small amount of beef broth along with the vegetables and sauté 5 to 10 minutes. Now stir in the mushrooms (or peas) and again allow the vegetable mixture to cook briefly for about 5 minutes. Add remaining beef broth and as much of the reserved water as needed to cover vegetables by 1-inch. Let ingredients cook thoroughly over medium heat. Season with salt and pepper. In the meantime, fry the chopped bacon in hot oil until crisp. Top the slices of white bread with cheese and brown lightly in oven. Ladle soup into small bowl, sprinkle the crisped bacon over the cheese-covered bread slices and carefully lay them in the soup. Serve immediately. Sprinkle with a small amount of chopped parsley if so desired.

wiener schnitzel
serves 4

4	veal cutlets, about 4 ounces each
	salt
	freshly ground black pepper
1 cup	all-purpose flour
2	eggs, beaten with 2 tbsp milk
2 cups	fine, dried bread crumbs
1/2 cup	vegetable oil
1 tbsp	finely chopped fresh parsley leaves

- Place each piece of veal between 2 large pieces of plastic wrap or parchment paper.

- Using a meat mallet, pound the veal until very thin. Season both sides of the veal with salt and pepper. Also, season the flour with salt and pepper as well as season the egg wash and bread crumbs with salt and pepper.

- Heat 1/4 cup of the oil in a large skillet over medium heat. Dredge each piece of veal in the seasoned flour. Next, dip pieces in the egg wash, letting the excess drip off and finally dredge them in the bread crumbs, coating completely. Place the piece of veal directly into the hot oil. Repeat the above process with the remaining pieces of veal. Pan-fry until golden brown and crispy, about 2 to 3 minutes on each side. Remove and drain on paper towels. Season with salt and pepper. Garnish with chopped parsley.

trivia clips

Mozart is considered the greatest musical genius of all time. His musical legacy, especially in view of his short life, was enormous. It includes 16 operas, 41 symphonies, 27 piano and five violin concerti, 25 string quartets, 19 masses, and other works in every form popular in his time.

Mozart's middle name, Amadeus, means "beloved of God".

amadeus

austrian style fried potatoes serves 4

1-3/4 lb	potatoes (Yukon Gold is a suitable choice)		4 tbsp	cooking oil
1 tsp	salt		1	small onion, finely chopped
			2 pinches	caraway seeds

- Cook potatoes in salted water. Drain. Peel and slice them into 1/4-inch thick slices. Heat cooking oil in a large skillet over medium heat. Fry chopped onions until soft and golden,

add potatoes and fry until golden; turn often. Sprinkle with salt and crushed caraway seeds. Serve alongside schnitzel.

opera torte

serves 6 to 8

We won't kid you—this fabulous torte is labour intensive, but the dramatic and exquisite results are worth it! The cake has multiple alternating layers of chocolate Bavarian cream, coffee buttercream and chocolate ganache that separate thin layers of rum-soaked almond sponge cake. The recipe also requires that you weigh the ingredients. Use a kitchen scale made for this purpose.

Almond Sponge Cake

5	egg whites
4 oz	sugar
2 oz	ground almonds
1/2 tsp	baking powder
2-1/2 oz	cake flour
2	whole eggs

Coffee Buttercream

1-1/2 oz	water
10 oz	sugar
6	egg yolks
1 lb	unsalted butter, cooled to room temperature
1-1/2 tbsp	espresso or very strong black coffee

Crème Anglaise

2 cups	milk
6 oz	sugar
1/2	vanilla bean pod, split
6	egg yolks

Chocolate Bavarian

1	packet unflavored gelatin
2 tbsp	cold water
12 oz	bittersweet chocolate, chopped
1 cup	crème anglaise (above)
3 cups	heavy (whipping) cream

Ganache

12 oz	semisweet chocolate, chopped
8 oz	heavy (whipping) cream

Rum Syrup

2 cups	water
4 oz	sugar
1 tbsp	rum
6 oz	semisweet chocolate, chopped

additional 1/2 recipe of crème anglaise (at left)

fresh raspberries

- To make the sponge cake: Line two 1/2-inch-deep sheet pans with parchment paper.

- Preheat the oven to 400˚ F. In a deep bowl, beat the egg whites with one half of the sugar until stiff peaks form and the mixture is glossy.

- Transfer to a clean bowl. Sift the ground almonds, baking powder and cake flour together onto parchment paper. In a deep bowl, beat the whole eggs and remaining sugar until the mixture thickens and turns pale

yellow. Gently fold one-half of the whites into the yolk mixture.

- Fold in the dry ingredients. Very gently fold in the remaining whites. Spread into the prepared pans and bake 7 to 10 minutes, until the cake springs back when touched.

- Remove from the oven and cool in the pan for 10 minutes. Then remove from pan and cool completely on a rack.

BEVERAGES

Serve some Austrian wines and/or beer with dinner. In terms of wine we suggest a Grüner Veltiner, a somewhat tart wine. Try any of the following producers Malat, Prager or Salomon. A Riesling would also be suitable. Some names to look for are: Hardegg, Hirsch, Knoll and Loimer.

If you wish to serve beer, try: Rieder Dunkle Weisse, Gösser Heller Bock, Haydn-Bräu Pils, Stiegl Gold Spezial, or Zipfer Pils (all from Austria). If you can't find any of these, try a German or Dutch imported beer. Cheers to you the Austrian way, "Prost"!

MUSIC

Falco's 1986 hit "Rock Me Amadeus" on his "Greatest Hits "(Buddha) album is a neat, modern dance song that could be playing while your guests arrive. During dinner we suggest anything by Mozart. His works are so diverse that we are sure you will find something that you like. We suggest buying a number of his works; everything from symphonies, sonatas and piano concertos. You are guaranteed to find something that will move you!

(1984)

Since much of the film is centred around happenings at the royal court, we suggest you make it a black-tie affair. Since the dinner will be formal, grace the table with a crisp white tablecloth, and add fancy plates with chargers (a large, usually ornate metal or glass decorative base for dinner plates). Place white floating candles with flowers in a crystal bowl and sprinkle a few silver or gold sparkles on the table. Use formal place settings with music note motif place cards. Fold napkins in a creative way. Use the best serving pieces and dinnerware you own. This includes crystal goblets, real silverware, linen napkins, etc. Place an ornate candelabra on your table. If you have a German or Austrian delicatessen near by see if you can find some Mozart chocolates. Pack them individually into small chocolate boxes (available at party supply stores), or wrap in pretty cellophane and give out as favours at the end of your event.

opera torte

continued

- To make the coffee buttercream: Mix the water and sugar together in a heavy saucepan and heat over medium heat until the mixture reaches 242°F on a candy thermometer (soft ball stage). Do not stir. Wipe away any crystals that form on the side of the pan with a damp brush. In a deep bowl, beat the egg yolks until they thicken and turn pale yellow.

- Continue beating and slowly add the sugar mixture in a small stream. When all the sugar has been added, continue beating until the mixture has cooled and is light and fluffy. Beat in the butter, a tablespoon at a time. When all the butter has been added, beat in the coffee extract. Store the buttercream in the refrigerator until ready to use.

- To make the crème anglaise: Put the milk and sugar in a heavy saucepan. Scrape out the seeds from the vanilla bean pieces with the point of a sharp knife and drop into the milk and sugar. Drop the pods into the mixture. Bring the mixture to a boil over medium-high heat. Remove from heat and take out the vanilla bean pods. Lightly beat the egg yolks in a small bowl to break them up. Whisk in a large spoonful of the hot milk mixture to temper the eggs. Return the saucepan to the stove; reduce the heat under the milk mixture to medium-low and slowly whisk in the egg-milk mixture. Cook until the mixture coats the back of a spoon.

- To make the Chocolate Bavarian: Sprinkle the gelatin into the water and let soak. Melt the chocolate in the top of a double boiler over barely simmering water. Remove from heat. In a heavy saucepan over medium-low heat, warm the crème anglaise and stir in the gelatin mixture, continuing to stir until it has completely dissolved. Stir the crème anglaise into the chocolate. In a deep bowl, beat the cream until it stands in soft peaks. Gently fold a large spoonful of the cream into the chocolate mixture, then fold in the remaining cream.

- To make the ganache: Melt the chocolate in the top of a double boiler over barely simmering water. Remove from heat. Bring the heavy cream to a boil over medium heat.

- Blend the hot cream into the chocolate.

- To make the rum syrup: Bring the water and sugar to a boil in a heavy saucepan over medium-high heat. Boil for 1 minute. Let cool to room temperature and stir in the rum.

- To assemble: Cut each sponge layer into 4 strips lengthwise (20 strips total). Place the first of these layers on a long platter or a piece of heavy cardboard cut to fit and covered with foil. Brush with rum syrup. Spread with a thin layer of coffee buttercream. Add a second layer of sponge, pressing down gently, and paint with rum syrup (paint each successive layer of sponge with rum syrup as you build the torte). Put the Bavarian in a pastry bag fitted with a large flat tip and pipe a layer of chocolate Bavarian on the sponge.

- Add the next layer of sponge, brush with rum syrup and spread with ganache. Top with another layer of sponge, brush with rum syrup and top with coffee buttercream. Top with a final layer of sponge, brush with rum syrup and a final layer of coffee buttercream.

- Spread the top with ganache, smoothing the ganache. Chill until set, 30 to 40 minutes.

- To serve: In the top of a double boiler over barely simmering water, melt semisweet chocolate.

- Put the chocolate in a pastry bag with a small plain tip. Slice the torte into serving portions with a very sharp serrated knife. Place slightly off-centre on serving plates. Pipe a row of chocolate scrolls diagonally across the top of each portion. Put a spoonful of crème anglaise on each plate. Pipe 3 chocolate music notes in the crème anglaise on each plate. Pipe chocolate scrolls on the plates at the forward edge of the crème anglaise (closest to edge of plate) and place raspberry in centre.

- Any leftover sponge may be used to make mini versions of the torte.

Go to an Austrian or French bakery and purchase individual slices of opera torte to serve at your dinner.

coal miner's daughter (1980)

menu down home vegetable stew • crusty bread (store-bought) • chili pot pie • green salad with vinaigrette (see index) • rhubarb-strawberry cobbler

down home vegetable stew serves 6

This is an economical recipe that has fed many folks in bluegrass country!

4 cups	water	1	clove garlic, finely chopped
4	chicken bouillon cubes	1	10-ounce box frozen green beans
2	cans crushed tomatoes	1	can white kidney beans
1	onion, chopped		salt to taste
1/2	cabbage head, chopped	2 tbsp	parsley, chopped
3	carrots, peeled and sliced into rounds		hard cheese (optional for garnish)
3	zucchini, sliced into rounds		

• Dissolve the bouillon in water in a big pot; add tomatoes, then all the fresh vegetables and garlic. Simmer until vegetables are tender; add the green beans, then the kidney beans. Simmer for an hour or so until the soup thickens and the flavours blend.

Adjust salt to taste. The soup should be fairly thick. Sprinkle chopped parsley on top prior to serving. Serve with crusty French or Italian bread and a little hard cheese to grate on top of the soup.

Most people had never even heard of Butcher Hollow, Kentucky, until one of Nashville's first female country superstars, Loretta Lynn, belted out her heart wrenching melody and sang about her life story on stage. Her autobiography entitled Coal Miners Daughter was made into a movie starring Sissy Spacek in the title role. Loretta was one of eight children born into a family which was held together on a shoestring budget. She was only 13 years old when she married, and a mother of four children at age twenty. Her husband Doolittle "Mooney" Lynn was a tough-talking, controlling husband who was credited for steering Loretta's singing career. She would strum on her guitar and play old honky-tonk bars on the weekends. Mooney encouraged her to cut her own demo tape, which was the starting point for Loretta's unforgettable journey in which she made Nashville history. Loretta was considered a pioneer of women's liberation. She sang about cheating husbands and their wives who were not going to take it. The road to success was not easy for Loretta. Her rags to riches success meant dealing with stress, sorrow and a marriage on the verge of a break-up. Spacek played Loretta with such natural grace and was awarded a well-deserved Academy Award for her portrayal of the country legend.

FEATURED ACTORS
Sissy Spacek (Loretta Lynn)
Tommy Lee Jones (Doolittle "Mooney" Lynn)
Beverly D'Angelo (Patsy Cline),
Levon Helm (Ted Webb)
Phyllis Boyens (Clara Webb)

DIRECTOR ~ Michael Apted

trivia clips

Loretta and Mooney made a long road trip through the American South in which they stopped at every country radio station they could find. Their efforts paid off, Loretta's first single, "Honky Tonk Girl," hit the charts and earned her a spot at the Grand Ole Opry.

coal miner's
daughter (1980)

chili pot pie

serves 4 to 6

1/2 lb	lean ground beef
1	onion, chopped
1 cup	each, chopped celery and carrot
1	sweet green pepper, diced
1/4 cup	raisins
2	cans beans (28 ounces total) (any kind)
1	14-ounce can diced tomatoes, undrained
2 tbsp	chili powder
1/4 tsp	hot pepper flakes
1/2 tsp	each, salt and pepper

- In large non-stick skillet or saucepan, brown beef over medium-high heat about 8 minutes, breaking up with back of spoon. Drain off fat. Add onion, celery, carrot, green pepper and raisins; cook for 5 minutes. Add beans, tomatoes, chili powder and hot pepper flakes; cover and simmer for 30 minutes. Stir in salt and pepper. Spoon into deep square 12-cup (3 L)casserole.

- Cornmeal Crust: In bowl, mix together flour, cornmeal, sugar, baking powder and salt.

- Cut in butter until mixture is crumbly. Mix in cheese (if using). In another bowl, beat egg with milk and stir into flour mixture just until blended. Spread evenly over chili. Sprinkle with parsley.

Cornmeal Crust:

2/3 cup	all-purpose flour
1/3 cup	cornmeal
2 tsp granulated sugar	
1 tsp	baking powder
1/2 tsp	salt
1 tbsp	butter, softened
1/4 cup	shredded light Cheddar-style cheese (optional)
1	egg
1/2 cup	skim milk
1 tsp	fresh parsley, chopped

- Bake in 375˚F oven for about 25 minutes or until crust is golden brown.

 Use low fat cheese.

Make the chili can be made the day before and refrigerate, then the day of serving make the crusty cornmeal topping and add just before baking. You can use a variety of canned beans: kidney, pinto, chickpeas.

coal miner's
daughter (1980)

rhubarb-strawberry cobbler serves 6 to 8

This winning combo makes for both a sweet and tart taste that is sure to please!

Filling:

1-1/4 cup	granulated sugar
3 tbsp	all-purpose flour
1-1/2 tsp	cinnamon

1-1/2 tsp	orange rind
6 cups	rhubarb, coarsely chopped
3 cups	strawberries, sliced

• Preheat oven to 400˚F. In large bowl, combine sugar, flour, cinnamon and orange rind.

• Add rhubarb and strawberries; toss well. Spread mixture in 13" x 9" pan. Bake in oven for about 10 minutes. Remove from oven and add topping.

Topping:

1-1/2 cups	flour
3 tbsp	sugar
1-1/2 tsp	baking powder

1/2 tsp	baking soda
1/4 tsp	salt
3 tbsp	butter or margarine
1 cup	buttermilk

• In a large bowl, combine flour, sugar, baking powder, baking soda, and salt. Using fingers or two knives cut in butter or margarine until mixture resembles small peas. With fork, stir in buttermilk just until soft dough

forms. Drop by tablespoons to form 12 mounds on top of hot fruit filling. Bake at 400˚F for about 25 minutes or until topping is golden brown. For an extra special treat serve with whipped cream or vanilla ice cream.

trivia clips

Ernest Tubb makes a cameo appearance as himself in the movie.
Loretta Lynn also sang a duet with which county superstar? (Conway Twitty)
Loretta appeared in a number of commercials promoting which product?
Hint: It makes crispier chicken and flakier pies.

BEVERAGES

Try some Kentucky brewed beer: Blue Grass Brewing Company's Altbier is a good choice as are the following from

Lexington Brewing Company: Limestone 1897 Original Amber Ale, Limestone Dark Ale, Limestone Pale Ale.

Otherwise, serve your favourite American beer or non-alcoholic beverages such as apple cider or lemonade.

MUSIC

For some classic Loretta Lynn, listen to "The Coal Miner's Daughter" (MCA) soundtrack, "Loretta Lynn's Greatest Hits Vol. 1 & 2" (MCA), "Best of Loretta Lynn" (MCA) or her "All Time Gospel Favourites" (Madacy). Otherwise, listen to anything by Patsy Cline, Garth Brooks, Trisha Yearwood or any of today's country stars (remember even Shania Twain qualifies as "country" these days!).

SETTING THE STAGE

Recreate a humble country setting. Use a gingham tablecloth and grace it with fresh daisies or wildflowers in a simple vase. Carve out gourds, pumpkins, apples and use as unique candleholders. Husk some fresh corn, place around a glass so that you can't see the glass, and tie the corn around the glass with a pretty gingham ribbon. Use the glass as a simple, country- theme vase. Enjoy the evening, listening to country crooners. The music genre has changed over the years, especially the last decade. Try square dancing or line dancing, this is a perfect way to break the ice with guests and get everyone up onto their feet. No formal dancing skills are required. If you have plenty of room, or are outdoors, set the scene with barrels or haystacks, they make great additional seating.

Have your own country contests, ranging from a pie-eating contest to singing and dancing. Who knows, maybe the next big country crooner is on your guest list!

children of a lesser god (1986)

The movie is set in a small New England school for the deaf. A speech teacher played by William Hurt (James Leeds) falls in love with a beautiful deaf girl he meets at the school. He is an unconventional teacher who is warned by the school director to keep his creative teaching strategies to himself. But he has his own teaching plans and goals in mind. He plays loud rock music so that his students can feel the vibrations and he attempts to get them to use their voices to learn how to speak. When Sarah (Marlee Matlin), an attractive custodian at the school, attracts his attention, James pursues the beautiful deaf girl only to find her bitter and somewhat in a self styled world of seclusion. Sarah, a graduate of the school she works at, finds it safer to be amongst her own peers and in her silent world.

Although she only communicates with James through sign language, she is able to speak a little and understand lip-reading. Sarah has had some painful experiences in the past and is reluctant to trust outsiders. James discovers why Sarah is so wary of forming a relationship and eventually finds a way to get through to her. The two fall in love and discover new ways to communicate with each other.

FEATURED ACTORS
William Hurt (James Leeds)
Marlee Matlin (Sarah Norman)
Piper Laurie (Mrs. Norman)
Philip Bosco (Dr. Curtis Franklin)
Allison Gompf (Lydia)

DIRECTOR ~ Randa Haines

AWARDS WON

Best Actress (Marlee Matlin)	1986 Academy Award
Best Actress— in Drama (Marlee Matlin)	1987 Golden Globe Award
Special Silver Bear Award (Randa Haines)	1987 Berlin International Film Festival

menu
new england boiled dinner • horseradish (store-bought) • crusty bread (store-bought) • strawberry and almond creme roll

new england boiled dinner serves 6 to 8

This meal is simple, yet hearty. It is great winter comfort food, though it may be prepared any time of year as the ingredients are always readily available.

5 lbs	beef brisket (ham may be substituted instead)	8	small white onions, peeled
6	peppercorns	6	medium potatoes, quartered
	cold water to cover	4 to 6	wedges green cabbage
1/2 cup	dry white wine	1/2 cup	parsley, chopped
3	parsnips, cubed	2 tbsp	melted butter
6	carrots, scraped and cubed		horseradish (optional)
2 cups	cubed rutabaga, or 6 small white turnips, peeled		

- Place the beef in a large stockpot, add the peppercorns and cold water to cover. Cover the stockpot with a lid, bring to a boil and simmer 4 to 5 hours or until the meat is tender, skimming occasionally. Remove meat and keep in a warm place. Add the parsnips, carrots, rutabaga or turnips, onions and potatoes. Cook 30 minutes.

Add cabbage wedges during the last 10 to 15 minutes and cook just until tender. Place the meat on platter and surround with the vegetables.

- Blend parsley with melted butter and spoon over vegetables. Delicious served with horseradish on the side.

trivia clips
Actress Camryn Manheim, of ABC's popular TV drama "The Practice," actually worked as an interpreter for the deaf. Before she landed her role on "The Practice," Manheim used her signing skills on the TV-drama; "Law and Order" where she played an attorney who signed for her accused deaf client on an episode of that television series.

trivia clips
William Hurt and Marlee Matlin had a real-life romance during the filming of the movie but eventually broke up. It was reported that Hurt had some "hurt" feelings over Marlee's nomination and win at the Academy Awards.
Sign Language is not universal, as there is no universal spoken language.

trivia clips
Marlee Matlin can be seen on the popular drama The West Wing. She is married and has two children. She also writes a column for Rosie magazine in which she gives parenting advice.
American Sign Language or ASL is a language that primarily uses hands and facial expressions to communicate grammatically.

continued

strawberry and almond creme roll
serves up to 10 people

Fresh-picked strawberries and almond-flavoured whipped cream make a mouth watering filling for this cake roll dessert. You can make the cake ahead of time, refrigerate, and fill an hour or so before serving.

Cake:

	butter or margarine to grease pan
3	eggs
1 cup	granulated sugar
1/3 cup	water
1 tsp	almond extract
1 cup	cake flour
1 tsp	baking powder
1/4 tsp	salt
	confectioner's sugar (to dust cake)

shaved chocolate (for garnish optional)

slivered almonds (for garnish optional)

Filling:

2 cups	sliced strawberries
1 cup	heavy cream
2 tbsp	confectioner's sugar (plus extra for dusting)
1/2 tsp	almond extract
	Chill bowl and beaters before preparing whipped cream filling.

- Preheat oven to 375°F. Line jelly roll pan (15 1/2"x10 1/2"x 1") with aluminum foil and generously grease foil with margarine.

- Beat eggs in bowl at high speed for at least 5 minutes until thick and the colour of lemons. Gradually add sugar, then reduce to low speed and add water and almond extract.

- Combine remaining dry ingredients except for sugar and add to mixture slowly.

- Beat at low speed until batter is smooth. Pour into greased, foil-lined pan. Bake 12 to 15 minutes until toothpick inserted in centre comes out clean. Remove immediately from pan and carefully invert onto towel that has been dusted abundantly with confectioners sugar. Carefully remove foil and trim any hard edges. Lightly dust cake bottom with additional powdered sugar.

- While still hot, carefully roll cake and towel to form a 10 1/2" roll. Cool 30 to 40 minutes on wire rack.

- While cake is cooling, slice strawberries and prepare almond whipped cream by beating remaining filling ingredients at medium speed until stiff. Unroll cake, remove towel, and spread cake with half of whipped cream.

- Arrange sliced strawberries on top and re-roll. Dust with powdered sugar, cover with plastic wrap and refrigerate about an hour before serving.

- Slice and top with additional whipped cream. Shaved chocolate or toasted sliced almonds are excellent as additional toppings.

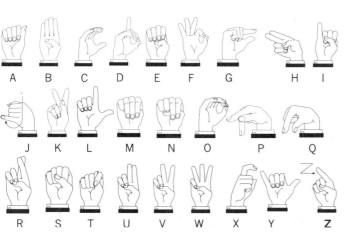

A B C D E F G H I
J K L M N O P Q
R S T U V W X Y Z

A little history... Nathaniel Hawthorne, author of numerous short stories and great works of literature including "The Scarlet Letter", was one of New England's literary greats.

MUSIC

Now that you have learned an interesting fact about Beethoven, perhaps you will listen to his dramatic compositions with a new ear and renewed appreciation for his artistic ability and determination. He must have had a lot of drive and determination to overcome the obstacles in his way.
We suggest anything by this late, great composer!

SETTING THE STAGE

Learning something new is valuable, enriching and entertaining. Sign language is a unique and expressive language communicated by the use of your hands, and facial expressions. This would be a great opportunity to learn a language, which to the hearing world is silent; but to the Deaf is a vivid, colourful language that is rich in history and culture. Start with learning how to finger spell the alphabet below. You can then finger spell any word. Practice this with a group of people so that each of you can communicate using your hands. Select a few library books prior to your dinner and make copies of phrases, or words you'll want to learn for the evening to share with your guests. Start with simple phrases such as "hello, how are you," "dinner," "what would you like to drink," etc. Make a few copies of these words and phrases and glue on to coloured construction paper and place face down all around the dinner table. Allow each guest to select a few of the cards, review them and then using sign language share with someone else. This is the best way to learn a new language, and you can guarantee that your guests will at least memorize the ones they selected to share with others.

cinema paradiso (1988)

This nostalgic comedy-drama is based upon the real life experiences of the film's director and screenwriter, Giuseppe Tornatore. The film reflects on the impact that the cinema, or movie theatres, can have upon us. The film starts in the present day, showing a mother yearning for her son, who left his small Sicilian village years ago to become a hot-shot film director in Rome. The son, Salvatore, receives word that his one-time surrogate father and mentor, the town's former film projectionist, has passed away. He returns to his home village for the funeral, and we as viewers are transported back in time... A time when the cinema was an escape from the dismal reality of post-war Italy and the poverty found in the south of the country. A time when censors still edited out any kissing or sexual connotations found in films. But nevertheless, as a boy Salvatore, learned much about love and life at the cinema. He developed a very close emotional bond with the projectionist who took the boy under his wing and taught him the tricks of his trade. The bond between the two becomes even closer when the boy saves the life of the projectionist after a fire in the projection room is ignited by the silver nitrate filmstock. The projectionist is left blind after the tragic accident, and Salvatore must fill his shoes.

Love comes into his life, but his heart is broken as the object of his affection does not wait for him to complete his military service. Salvatore decides to seek a world beyond the confines of his village, and he finds the kinds of things that he has only seen on screen. He has become successful and happy in many facets of his life, but as we all learn we must never forget where we come from. His childhood friend and mentor has left him a final gift, one that will clarify outstanding issues in his life. He realizes this as he is sitting in the Cinema Paradiso and relishing his final moments in this relic from his past, before it is demolished forever.

menu straciatella soup (see index) • roasted roma tomato tart • four seasons salad (see index) • sicilian cannoli

roasted roma tomato tart serves 6

This simple to make, yet elegant tart, doesn't require any baking (except for the pastry crust). It can be assembled several hours ahead and served at room temperature—it's a great a dish for summer entertaining.

tarte shell

For tarte shell:

1/2 cup	chilled, unsalted butter
1/4 cup	lard or vegetable shortening
2-1/4 cups	unbleached flour
1 tsp	salt
6 tbsp	ice cold water

- Cut the chilled butter and lard or vegetable oil shortening into 1/4" cubes.
- Mix the first 4 ingredients together in a mixer or with the back of a fork until crumbly.
- Do not overwork the dough. Mix it just enough to incorporate the butter and Crisco into the flour.
- Gradually add the water and mix only until the water has been absorbed. Do not over mix at this stage. If you do, the gluten in the flour will become elastic and your tart shell will not have a flaky texture.
- Form the dough into a round flat disk, wrap tightly in plastic wrap and refrigerate for at least 1 hour to let the dough rest.
- Preheat oven to 425˚F.
- Roll out 2/3 of the dough for a 12" tart and fit it into a French-style tart ring (i.e.one with fluted straight sides and a removable bottom). (Keep the remainder of the dough for another tart. This dough freezes very well and can be used by simply defrosting and rolling out.)

- Gently mold a sheet of aluminum foil over the unbaked shell, easing the foil onto the bottom and up the sides of the entire shell. Fill the unbaked, foil-covered tart shell with heavy beans or marbles. (This keeps the sides upright until they are baked enough to stand up on their own.)
- Bake the shell in this way for about 10 minutes, then remove the foil (along with weighting beans). Prick the bottom with a fork in several places (to allow air to escape from the underside) and bake for an additional 10 to 15 minutes until the shell is a nice golden brown.
- Remove from the oven. Remove the outer ring and cool.

trivia clips

The first real steps toward motion pictures were the result of experiments in the persistence of vision. Investigation of the subject was stimulated by a scientific paper presented in London, England, by Peter Mark Roget in 1824. Roget's paper, "Persistence of Vision with Regard to Moving Objects", led investigators to try to build devices that would test his theory.

cinema
paradiso (1988)

roasted roma tomatoes

8 to 10   Roma tomatoes

- Preheat oven to 450°F. Wash the tomatoes. Cut off just enough of the stem end to remove the stem and then cut the tomatoes in half (lengthwise). Place the cut side down on a flat baking sheet lined with parchment paper.

- Bake in oven until the skins "pop" up off the flesh (should take about 20 minutes).

- Remove the baking sheet from the oven. Using tongs, pluck the skins off the flesh, while the tomatoes are still hot. Discard the skins and let the flesh cool on the baking sheet until ready to use.

goat cheese mixture

3/4 cup   fresh, mild goat cheese
1/2 cup   crème fraîche or sour cream

1   small clove garlic, minced
           salt and pepper

- Mix the goat cheese and crème fraîche or sour cream together and blend in garlic. Season lightly with salt and pepper. Refrigerate until ready to use.

basil oil

6   large, fresh basil leaves
1/4 cup   olive oil

           salt to taste

- In a very deep saucepan, fry 6 fresh basil leaves for a few seconds in 1/4 cup olive oil.

- Remove immediately from the saucepan. This must be done quickly because the leaves burn easily. While

the leaves are still crispy and hot, put them into a mini small food processor and blend with the frying oil until the leaves are very finely chopped and almost emulsified into the oil. Salt to taste.

assembly:

- Assembly: When ready to serve, spread a thin layer of the goat cheese mixture over the bottom of the baked (cooled) pastry crust and top with a layer of roasted Roma tomato halves. Decorate with fresh basil leaves.

- The tarte could be assembled several hours before serving with out serious deterioration of the crust. Just before serving, drizzle the deep-fried basil oil over the tomatoes.

FEATURED ACTORS
Philippe Noiret (Alfredo)
Salvatore Cascio
        (Salvatore as a child)
Marco Leonardi
   (Salvatore as an adolescent)
Antonella Attili (young Maria)
Jacques Perrin
        (Salvatore as an adult)
Agnese Nano (adolescent Elena)
Pupella Maggio (older Maria)

DIRECTOR ~ Giuseppe Tornatore

AWARDS WON

Best Foreign Film	1989 Academy Award
Special Jury Prize (Giuseppe Tornatore)	1989 Cannes Film Festival Award
Special Jury Award (Giuseppe Tornatore)	1989 European Film Academy Award
Best Actor (Philippe Noiret)	1990 British Academy Award
Best Foreign Language Film	1990 British Academy Award
Best Original Screenplay (Giuseppe Tornatore)	1990 British Academy Award
Best Score (Andrea and Ennio Morricone)	1990 British Academy Award
Best Supporting Actor (Salvatore Cascio)	1990 British Academy Award
Best Foreign Film	1990 Golden Globe Award

trivia clips

By 1870, inventors in the United States and England had developed devices in which posed photographs of motion, mounted on a revolving disk, passed between a light source and a lens for projection for an audience.
By 1877, increased speed of photographic emulsions and improved camera shutters made it possible to photograph rapid motions.

cinema
paradiso (1988)

BEVERAGES

San Ripolo Chianti if you prefer red is a good choice as is Bonera, a Sicilian wine. However, whites such as Salento Chardonnay, again from Sicily, or Ruffino Orvieto Classico would also be suitable.

MUSIC

"La Nostra Italia" (European import) features a number of artists and songs. If you wish to listen to some Italian folk music, try "Italian Treasury: Folk Music and Songs of Italy" American singer Connie Francis went back to her roots and recorded in Italian. You may wish to try her two volume CD edition called "The Italian Collection" (PolyGram). It features songs from her previous five Italian albums. You can't go wrong with anything from Andrea Bocelli. If you wish to listen to some more modern Italian music, we suggest "Le Mie Canzoni: The Best of Umberto Tozzi" (Alex) "Stile Libero" (RCA) by Eros Ramazotti or anything by Toto Cotugno.

SETTING THE STAGE

Create the look of a trattoria in your dining area. Use an old Chianti bottle, or any attractive old wine bottle as a candle holder. Lay out a red and white checker tablecloth or napkins on your table. Place cruets of olive oil and red-wine vinegar on the table. Use rustic or ceramic looking serving pieces. Set out side plates for chunks of Italian bread and small bowls with extra virgin olive oil for dipping. Use small pots of herbs like rosemary, basil, oregano and sage for table decoration. Put on some of the suggested music and enjoy the simple, but delicious meal!

sicilian cannoli

Yield: About 10 to 12 cannoli

Shells:

2 cups	flour
1 tsp	ground cinnamon
2 tbsp	shortening
1 tsp	sugar
1/4 tsp	salt
3/4 cup	Marsala wine
1	egg white
	vegetable oil, for deep frying

- Combine the flour, cinnamon, shortening, sugar and salt, and wetting gradually with the wine, knead together with fingers until rather hard dough or paste is formed. Form into a ball, cover with a cloth and let stand for about 1 hour. Cut dough in half and roll half of the dough into a thin sheet about 1/4-inch thick or less and cut into 4-inch ovals. Place a metal tube diagonally across each oval lengthwise. Wrap dough around tube by overlapping the 2 sides, sealing the overlapping sides with a little egg white.

- Meanwhile heat vegetable oil in a large deep pan for deep frying. Drop 1 or 2 of the tubes at a time into the hot oil, fry gently on all sides until dough turns a golden brown color.

- Remove from pan, let cool a little, gently remove shell from the metal tube. Set shells aside to become cold. Repeat procedure until all shells are made.

Filling:

1-1/2 lb	ricotta cheese
1/2 cup	confectioner's sugar
1/2 cup	chocolate chips or finely chopped chocolate
1-1/2 tsp	vanilla
3 tbsp	citron peel, chopped
3 tbsp	candied orange peel, chopped

- Mix the ricotta thoroughly with the confectioner's sugar. Blend in the chocolate. Add two drops of vanilla and chopped fruit peel. Mix and blend well. Chill mixture before filling shells. Fill cold shells with prepared mixture and smooth evenly at each end of the shell.

- Sprinkle the shells with confectioner's' sugar. Refrigerate until ready to serve.

trivia clips

The first people generally credited with using Celluloid film for motion pictures were the American inventor Thomas A. Edison and his assistant William K.L. Dickson, who were trying to provide visual illustrations to supplement the sound recordings of the phonograph. By 1890 they had developed the Kinetograph, a motion-picture camera using Eastman film.

ghandi

(1982)

menu — samosas (store bought) • vegetable mulligatawny soup • spicy lamb patties • tandoori chicken on a stick with yogurt dip (see index) • indian tomato salad • passage to india rice (see index) • naan (see index) • chai crème brûlée • kulfi (see index)

vegetable mulligatawny soup

serves 4 to 6

1 tsp	whole black peppercorns
2 tbsp	whole coriander seeds
1 tsp	whole cumin seeds
1/2 tsp	whole fennel seeds
1/2 tsp	ground turmeric
1/4 tsp	cayenne
1-1/2 tbsp	chickpea flour
4 to 5 cups	vegetable stock (bouillon cubes may be used here)
2	small potatoes, peeled and diced
2	medium carrots, peeled and sliced
2	small turnips, peeled and diced
12	fresh curry leaves or 8 fresh basil leaves
2	garlic cloves, peeled and coarsely chopped
1	medium onion, coarsely chopped
1 tbsp	fresh ginger, peeled and finely chopped
1	14-ounce can coconut milk
1-1/4 tsp	salt, or to taste
	Lime wedges for serving

• Put the peppercorns, coriander seeds, cumin seeds, and fennel seeds in a small cast-iron frying pan and set over medium-high heat. Stir and roast until the spices emit a roasted aroma and some turn a shade darker. Empty into a plate to cool, then grind in a clean coffee grinder or other spice grinder. (It is a good idea to sift the ground spices through a fine sieve, stirring them about with a spoon as they pass slowly through the mesh. This is not absolutely necessary, but it makes for a finer soup.) Add the turmeric and cayenne to the spice mixture. Put the chickpea flour in a bowl. Slowly add 2 tablespoons of the stock, mixing as you go. Now add 4 cups of stock and mix. Combine the chickpea flour mixture, spices, all vegetables, curry leaves, garlic, onion, and ginger in a large pan and bring to a boil.

• Cover, turn the heat down to low, and simmer for about 50 minutes, or until all the vegetables are tender. Blend the soup in a blender in several batches, if necessary, and then press through a coarse sieve. Return the soup to the soup pan, add the coconut milk and salt, and bring to a simmer. Simmer gently for 2 to 3 minutes to blend the flavours; thin out with more stock, as needed. Serve hot with lime wedges.

This extravagant Oscar-winning film, is about the late Indian political and spiritual leader, Mahatma Gandhi. The film begins in the early part of the 20th century with Mohandas K. Gandhi working as a British trained lawyer. Though his life is comfortable and stimulating, his spirit is restless. He decides to give up his worldly goods and privilege to fight for Indian independence. Gandhi did not believe in violence even though the British government was more than willing to use weapons and force to crush the Indian independence movement. Gandhi embraced a policy of "passive resistance".

He was a devout, gentle man and almost mystical Hindu. He was a man with lots of determination and conviction. Some observers called him a master politician. Others believed him to be a saint. To millions of Hindus he was their beloved Mahatma, meaning "great soul." To the rest of humanity, his life story provides inspiration and reaffirms all that is positive about the human spirit. Don't miss watching this film!

FEATURED ACTORS
Ben Kingsley (Mahatma Gandhi)
Candice Bergen
   (Margaret Bourke-White)
Edward Fox (General Dyer)
John Gielgud (Lord Irwin)
Trevor Howard (Judge Broomfield)

DIRECTOR ~ Richard Attenborough

trivia clips

Mahatma Gandhi (1869-1948). Throughout history most national heroes have been warriors, but Gandhi ended British rule over his native India without striking a single blow. A frail man, he devoted his life to peace and brotherhood in order to achieve social and political progress. Tragically, less than six months after his nonviolent resistance to British rule won independence for India, he was assassinated by a religious fanatic.

ghandi

(1982)

AWARDS WON

Best Actor (Ben Kingsley)	1982 Academy Award
Best Art Direction (Bob Laing/Michael Seirton/Stuart Craig)	1982 Academy Award
Best Cinematography (Billy Williams)	1982 Academy Award
Best Costume design (John Mollo/Bhanu Athaiva)	1982 Academy Award
Best Director (Richard Attenborough)	1982 Academy Award
Best Editing (John Bloom)	1982 Academy Award
Best Original Screenplay (John Briley)	1982 Academy Award
Best Picture	1982 Academy Award
Best Actor (Ben Kingsley)	1982 British Academy Award
Best Direction (Richard Attenborough)	1982 British Academy Award
Best Film (Richard Attenborough)	1982 British Academy Award
Best Supporting Actress (Rohini Hattangady)	1982 British Academy Award
Best Director (Richard Attenborough)	1982 Directors Guild of America Award
Best Actor (Ben Kingsley)	1982 New York Film Critics Circle Award
Best Film (Richard Attenborough)	1982 New York Film Critics Circle Award
Best Actor—in Drama (Ben Kingsley)	1982 Golden Globe Award
Best Director (Richard Attenborough)	1982 Golden Globe Award
Best Foreign Film	1982 Golden Globe Award

spicy lamb patties

serves 4

For cucumber raita:

1	cucumber, peeled and grated
1 cup	plain yogurt
1 tsp	salt
1 tsp	diced red onion
1 tsp	fresh lime juice

For lamb patties:

2 lb	ground lamb
1	small red onion, chopped
1/4 cup	mango chutney (store-bought)
7 tbsp	chopped fresh coriander
1/2 tsp	ground cumin
1/2 tsp	ground coriander seeds
1/4 tsp	paprika
1/2 tsp	curry powder
	salt and pepper to taste
2 tbsp	vegetable oil

Make raita:

- Once grated, the cucumber should be salted and placed in a colander. Allow to drain for one hour. In a small bowl, stir together all raita ingredients, add cucumber and season with salt and pepper.

Make patties:

- In a large bowl mix together all patty ingredients except oil until combined well and season with salt and pepper. Form mixture into 4 to 6 patties about 1 inch thick. In a large, heavy skillet heat the oil on medium high heat, until hot but not smoking and cook patties until just cooked through, about 3-1/2 minutes on each side.

- Serve lamb patties with raita on the side.

indian tomato salad

serves 4

1/4 cup	vegetable oil
2 tbsp	wine vinegar
1 tbsp	lime or lemon juice
1	clove garlic, minced
1 tsp	Dijon mustard
1/4 tsp	ground cumin
1/4 tsp	each salt and pepper

1/4 cup	chopped fresh mint
2	large tomatoes, sliced
1	onion, thinly sliced
1	piece English cucumber, thinly sliced
	Fresh mint leaves

- In large bowl, whisk together oil, vinegar, lime juice, garlic, mustard, cumin, salt and pepper.

- Stir in mint. Add sliced tomatoes, onion and cucumber; toss gently. Garnish with mint leaves.

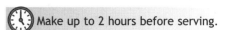 Make up to 2 hours before serving.

trivia clips

Mohandas Karamchand Gandhi was born on Oct. 2, 1869, in Porbandar, near Bombay. His family belonged to the Hindu merchant caste Vaisya. His father had been prime minister of several small native states. Gandhi was married when he was only 13 years old.

ghandi

continued

chai crème brûlée

serves 6

Chai, or Indian style tea is a beverage that has become quite popular in North America. Most coffee shops now have Chai on their beverage lists.

1 cup	Darjeeling tea leaves
12	extra large egg yolks, beaten
1 cup	brown sugar
4 cups	heavy cream
1 tbsp	chai spice powder (see recipe below)
1 cup	light brown sugar

Chai spice powder:

1 tsp	cardamom
1	stick cinnamon
1/2 tsp	black pepper corns
1/4 tsp	whole cloves

- Steep 1 cup Darjeeling tea leaves in 4 cups boiling water for 7 minutes. Strain tea leaves and reduce to 3/4 cup. Grind chai spice ingredients in a spice mill to form powder.

- Preheat the oven to 325˚F. In a large heat-proof mixing bowl, whisk together the egg yolks and sugar. Place the cream in a heavy bottomed saucepan over medium heat. Warm just until bubbles form around the edge. Remove from heat and, whisking constantly, pour into the egg and sugar mixture. Add the spice powder and the reduced tea liquid. Continue whisking until the sugar has dissolved and the mixture is well combined. Pour the mixture through a very fine sieve into 6 crème brûlée dishes, filling them only half full. Place the dishes in a shallow baking dish large to hold them without crowding. Place the dish on the middle rack in oven. Working quickly to preserve the heat, finish filling the dishes with the custard mixture, making sure that it comes right to the top of each dish. Then carefully fill the baking dish with very hot tap water so it comes halfway up the sides of the filled dishes. Bake for about 25 minutes, or until the custard is set in the centre. Remove the custards to a wire rack to cool.

Refrigerate for at least 3 hours, or until ready to serve. When ready to serve, preheat the broiler. Pass the brown sugar through a fine sieve to eliminate all lumps. Generously sprinkle the top of each chilled custard with an equal portion of the brown sugar, taking care to cover all of the custard, so that it gives an even finish. Place the chilled crème brûlée dishes under the preheated broiler and broil for about 2 minutes, or until the tops are crackling brown.

- Remove from the broiler and serve immediately.

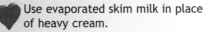 Use evaporated skim milk in place of heavy cream.

trivia clips

In 1891 Gandhi returned to India. In 1893 he went to South Africa as he did not meet with success in Bombay. At Natal he was the first so-called "coloured" lawyer admitted to the supreme court. He then built a large practice.

BEVERAGES

A dry Reisling such as Leon Beyer Reisling (France) would be a solid choice as would be Banrock Station Unwooded Chardonnay (Australia), if you wish to serve white wine. Red wines are more difficult to match with the spices in Indian cuisine, but a safe bet would be Periquita (Portugal) or a Beaujolais such as Duboeuf Beaujolais Brouilly (France).

Beer is always a good match for Indian food, we recommend Kingfisher Premium Lager (England) or an authentic Indian beer like Kalyani Export Special.

MUSIC

For classical Indian music we suggest: Ravi Shankar "Ragas" (Fantasy) or anything by Anindo Chatterjee. Another solid, classical Indian music selection is "Call of the Valley" (EMI), by classical musicians Shivkumar Sharma, Brijbushan Kabra and Hariprasad Chaurasia.

For those who prefer something more modern, we suggest "The Rough Guide to Bhangra" (World Music Network). Bhangra is an updated folk music style that originated in West Punjab. The music is great for dancing and has nuances of other world music styles. The music has received mainstream play in Europe, especially in the U.K.

SETTING THE STAGE

People have always been drawn to India and its culture because it seems so much more exotic when compared to our own "Western" culture. Capitalize on this to set the mood for the evening. If you are lucky enough to be close to a large cosmopolitan centre (as we are, being close to Toronto), then find out where there are authentic shops catering to Indian clientele. Pick up some incense and vibrant fabrics to use to turn your home into a more exotic locale. Use tableware and fabrics in gold, silver, bronze and jewel tones to create a rich, mysterious atmosphere. Drape sheer organza fabrics over doorways, or use beaded curtains. Buy colourful children's bangles at an Indian store to use as napkin rings or use jewel tone organza ribbons to tie up napkins. Splurge and buy a few exotic flowers, such as orchids, and use them as a centrepiece, or float them in a crystal bowl along with some floating candles—the candles will disperse the scent of the flowers. Be adventurous in your style of dress, perhaps you could pick up a sari for yourself—and be more daring with your makeup.

the color purple (1985)

Adapted to the screen from author and Pulitzer Prize winner Alice Walker's novel of the same name, the movie did not find favour at the Academy Awards that year even with 11 nominations. Even so, it was a box-office hit! The story is based on a young black girl growing into maturity and eventually achieving hard won independence. The setting is in rural Georgia between the years 1909 to 1947. The movie examines the hardships oppressed Celie (Whoopi Goldberg) must face. She struggles to understand her role as a woman and seeks to find her sister whom she thought had died. She finds out her sister is alive and begins to confide in her sister through letters. Her abusive husband Albert (Danny Glover), sees no point in his wife corresponding with her sister and conceals the letters of reply. But after gaining the compassion and friendship of her husband's mistress Shug (Margaret Avery), as well as gaining a dose of self-confidence, she soon recovers the lost letters and reunites with her sister. Celie also finds a kindred spirit in the wife of her husband's son from a previous marriage, Sofia (played by Oprah Winfrey). Racism rears its ugly head when Sofia is beaten by some white folks. But even through difficult circumstances the characters celebrate and appreciate the qualities of kindness, love and compassion. In the end, Celie is transformed with the help of those around her and is able to leave her husband to begin a new independent life. A good way to describe this film: a drama that will stay with you for a long time.

FEATURED ACTORS
Danny Glover (Albert)
Whoopi Goldberg (Celie)
Margaret Avery (Shug Avery)
Oprah Winfrey (Sofia)
Willard E. Pugh (Harpo)

DIRECTOR ~ Steven Spielberg

menu
fried okra • black-eyed peas and ham • corn pudding • pineapple upside-down cake

fried okra
serves 4 to 6

1 lb	okra	2 tsp	salt or to taste
1/2 cup	vegetable oil	2 tsp	freshly ground black pepper

• Wash the okra in cold water and drain. Remove the stems and cut it into 1/2-inch slices. Heat half the oil (1/4 cup) in a large heavy skillet over medium heat. Add half the okra and spread it into an even layer with a spatula. Sprinkle with salt and pepper.

Fry the okra, turning with a spoon to cook evenly, until the okra is tender, crispy, and well browned, about 10 minutes. Drain on paper towels. Repeat with remaining oil and okra and serve hot.

black-eyed peas and ham
serves 4 to 6

2 cups	water	3	crushed garlic cloves
1-1/2 cups	dried black-eyed peas	1/2 tsp	red pepper sauce
2/3 cup	chopped fully cooked smoked ham	2 tbsp	vegetable oil
2 cups	sliced okra	4 tsp	chopped fresh cilantro
2	small onions, chopped	2	small tomatoes, seeded and chopped
1 tsp	salt		

• Heat water and peas to boiling in 4-quart saucepan. Boil uncovered 2 minutes; reduce heat. Add ham. Cover and simmer 30 to 40 minutes, stirring occasionally, until peas are tender (do not boil or peas will burst); drain. Cook okra, onion, salt, garlic and red pepper sauce in oil in saucepan about 5 minutes or until onion is softened. Stir in cilantro, tomato and peas. Heat until mixture is hot.

trivia clips

The term "soul food" originated from the cuisine developed by the African slaves, who mainly lived in the American South. It was a period in the history of the United States that resulted in a cuisine fashioned from the limited amount of ingredients available to the slave and sharecropper black families. The meats used were usually from the least desirable cuts and only small amounts of vegetables were available for use.

trivia clips

All ten of the Best Actor/Actress nominees were American-born, a first time in Oscar history.
The Color Purple was Whoopi Goldberg's first film.
Quincy Jones was producer / composer of the music score for this movie.
All of the nominees in the Best Supporting Actor and Actress categories were first-time nominees.

the color purple (1985)

corn pudding

serves 4

	corn oil	1	16-ounce can creamed corn
2	large eggs	1	tsp salt
1	can evaporated milk	1/4 tsp	freshly ground black pepper
1/4 cup	sugar	1 tbsp	unsalted butter or margarine
1 tbsp	cornstarch		

• Preheat the oven to 350˚. Lightly grease a 7 x 7-inch baking dish with corn oil. Beat the eggs and evaporated milk in a small bowl until blended. In another bowl, stir the sugar and cornstarch together in a small bowl. Add them slowly to the egg mixture, beating constantly, until blended. Fold in the corn, salt and pepper. Pour the mixture into the greased baking dish and dot with the butter.

• Bake until the pudding is set and golden brown on top, about 1 hour. Serve hot alongside the main dish.

 Use evaporated skim milk.

It was Africans who brought okra to the American South. They knew it could be used to thicken soups and impart a hint of flavour. Okra can be described as a cross between asparagus and eggplant. It is also used in Creole and Cajun cuisine. In fact, gumbo, is taken from the Angolan word ngombo, which is the word for okra. It is best used fresh, though frozen may be used in soups and stews. Okra contains substantial amounts of vitamin C, iron and calcium, plus it is low in calories (68 calories per 7-3/4 oz). Fibres of mature okra are used to make paper.

AWARDS WON

Best Actress (Whoopi Goldberg)	1985 National Board of Review of Motion Pictures Award
Best Actress— Drama (Whoopi Goldberg)	1986 Golden Globe Award

BEVERAGES

Once again beer is the beverage of choice for this menu. Try some beers from the American South or Africa. In terms of American beer try: Surly Boy's Scotch Ale (Texas), Red Mountain Beer (Alabama). Black Sheeo Light Lager (Georgia), Steve and Clark's Bulltown Brown and Melon Head Red (North Carolina) and Weidman's Hell on the Border Porter (Arkansas).

Tusker beer from Kenya is a good choice. Nigeria has a Guinness brewery that produces Guinness Nigerian Foreign Extra Stout in accordance with local brewing laws. It is unlike any of the other Guinness' products. Other Nigerian beers that are worth a try are: Star Lager and Legend Extra Stout. Mamba Lager from the Ivory Coast and Castle Club from Ghana are also complementary choices.

MUSIC

Music was an outlet for pent up emotions for the black community. It provided tremendous relief for them. The slaves had their songs, and they would play their instruments and their music to keep their hearts and souls alive through nearly two hundred and fifty years of slavery in the New World. They liked to dance, sing, and play the banjo, drums or fiddle. Blues, jazz, and rock' n' roll have roots deeply embedded in black culture. Many white performers and groups, from Benny Goodman, Frank Sinatra to the Beatles and Elvis and even Rod Stewart and Boy George have said that they owe their biggest debt to black music.

trivia clips

Ragtime became popular around 1900. It was highly syncopated music, usually played on the piano, the left hand played the rhythm and the right hand played a bright and cheerful melody. The best known ragtime writer was Scott Joplin, whose fame came from such songs as "The Entertainer" and "Maple Leaf Rag."

trivia clips

Oprah Winfrey and Danny Glover teamed up once more in her world premier Beloved which did not do well at the box office. Back in the days of slavery, slaves were often forced to eat the scraps that their slave masters did not want. They turned these scraps into delicious dishes. Some of these foods are black-eyed peas, cornbread, bread pudding, greens, sweet potato pie, and chitlins.

the color
purple (1985)

MUSIC - CONTINUED

You may wish to listen to the blues, if so try: anything by Bessie Smith, Muddy Waters, Johnny Lee Hooker or W.C. Handy (also known as the father of the blues because he brought the world's attention to blues music). "Blues 1923-1933" (Fremeaux and Associates) is a great classic blues album featuring a number of artists like Bessie Smith and Louis Armstrong. Other good choices in various genres are: "Blues and Ragtime" (Shanachie) by Rev. Gary Davis, "Blues and Gospel: Mississippi Field Recordings 1934" (Document) and Duke Ellington's "Blues and Ballads" (Varese). For jazz lovers, anything by Billie Holiday or Count Basie is suitable.

SETTING THE STAGE

North America is a cultural mosaic that mirrors the rest of the world's cultures. We should be open to learning more about other cultures. Food, music and love are an international means of communication! Make your next family dinner unique. Take the opportunity to enjoy the tastes and flavours of different cultures and traditions. Make the recipes listed above to share with your family. Bringing down barriers and absorbing a different ethnic culture sets the stage. African-Americans and Aboriginal or Native peoples have played a significant role in the development of North America. It is time that we appreciated this a bit more than we have in the past. We can do this by learning not only about their cultures, but also by sampling their cuisines.

Share with fellow diners the historical notes at the beginning of the section preceding the menu. Perhaps you will be able to add to each other's knowledge. An important part of this setting is the music. Play a variety from early ragtime, blues and jazz to rhythm and blues. The lyrics in the music often contain heartfelt stories of tragedies and triumphs. Enjoy the menu's "soul" food in combination with this music for the soul.

pineapple upside-down cake

serves 8 to 10

1/2 cup	brown sugar		1/4 cup	shortening
2 tbsp	butter or margarine		1 cup	sugar
1	can pineapple slices		1	egg, beaten
10	maraschino cherries		1 tsp	vanilla
2 cups	cake flour, sifted		3/4 cup	milk
2 tsp	baking powder			vanilla ice cream (optional)
1/4 tsp	salt			whipped cream (optional)

- Preheat oven to 350°F. Sprinkle brown sugar in bottom of 9-inch round well-greased cake pan. Dot with butter. Drain pineapple. Place slices in pan with cherry in centre of each pineapple slice. In a medium bowl, sift together flour, baking powder and salt. In another medium to large bowl, cream shortening. Gradually add sugar to shortening and beat until fluffy. Then add egg and vanilla and beat well. Add flour mixture, a little at a time, alternating with milk. Pour batter over fruit. Place in oven and bake until golden brown (about 50 to 60 minutes). Turn out on to a serving plate so that pineapples are on top.

- Serve with vanilla ice cream or whipped cream if so desired.

 Use non-hydrogenated margarine and skim milk.

trivia clips

The Underground Railroad was composed of volunteers who would hide slaves travelling north to Canada. Slaves were hidden during daylight hours at stops along the route, and using the North Star, they moved in the dark to the next location 10 or 15 miles north. Until they reached Canada, they were never completely safe. If a slave catcher or United States marshal caught them, they would be returned to their master by force.

trivia clips

On April 6, 1909, history was made when two men, one Black and one White, planted the American Flag at the North Pole. Thus, Matthew A. Henson, a Black man, became one of the first Americans to reach the top of the world. Yet, undoubtedly due to his race, he was for years denied recognition of his role in this historic trek.

the princess bride (1987)

cinnamon wine soup

serves 4 to 6

This recipe, which is more like a beverage than a soup, originated in Istanbul during the 15th century. It makes for an unusual starter!

3 cups	dry red wine	3 tbsp	cornstarch
1	stick cinnamon, about 7 cm. long	3 tbsp	sugar
peel	of 1/2 lemon, in 2 or 3 pieces	2	egg yolks, beaten lightly

- In a saucepan, simmer together the wine, cinnamon stick and lemon peel for 10 minutes.

- In a mixing bowl, blend together the cornstarch and 3 tablespoons of cold water. Stir this into 3 cups of water, transfer to a separate saucepan and simmer gently for 5 minutes.

- Strain the cornstarch mixture into the wine mixture and add the sugar, stirring well (may add more sugar to taste). Slowly spoon about 1 cup of the hot wine soup into the egg yolks, beating constantly.

- Pour the mixture back into the soup slowly, beating constantly. Heat through but do not boil. Taste and correct the flavouring with sugar if necessary. Serve either hot or chilled.

This enchanting fairytale will capture the hearts of young children, yet provide comical one-liners for adults, making this movie enjoyable for the entire family. The movie is based on the satirical novel by William Goldman and directed by one of Hollywood's most notable directors and producers, Rob Reiner, who has been involved in the making of a number of comedy hits. Actor/comedians Billy Crystal and Mandy Patinkin spice up the film enough to make it enjoyable for adults. The story is told as a bedtime story by a grandfather (Peter Falk) to his grandson played by Fred Savage. It is about a young stable boy who falls in love with a beautiful princess. The main problem for him at the outset is that Princess Buttercup (Robin Wright Penn) sees him as nothing but a farm boy. Soon though, because of his many efforts at winning her heart, she realizes to her surprise that she is falling in love with him. But a poor commoner cannot marry the princess. So stable boy Westley, goes off in search of riches so that he may be worthy of marrying his heart's desire, the princess. While he is gone, Buttercup receives news that his ship has sunk and she automatically assumes the worst. In the midst of all this, Prince Humperdinck (Chris Sarandon) arrives on the scene, and he wants to marry Buttercup even though he knows she does not love him. The Princess comes into danger during an awesome adventure and she is rescued from the evil villains by her true love Westley. The happy ending is no surprise as the stable boy eventually wins the hand of his princess. This updated fairytale will delight the whole family!

trivia clips

Though the film received positive reviews, it didn't win any awards. It did receive an Academy Award nomination however, in 1987 for Best Song.
Robin Wright is married to actor Sean Penn.

the princess bride (1987)

FEATURED ACTORS
Cary Elwes (Westley)
Robin Wright Penn
   (Princess Buttercup)
Mandy Patinkin (Inigo Montoya)
Chris Sarandon (Prince Humperdinck)
Christopher Guest (Count Rugen)
Wallace Shawn (Vizzini)
Peter Falk (The Grandfather)
Fred Savage (The Grandson)
Andre the Giant (Fezzik)

DIRECTOR ~ Rob Reiner

BEVERAGES

If there are children at your party, serve them mocktails like: Shirley Temple or Ice Castle Fantasy (see main beverages section).

For the adults, we suggest Mead, a wine made from honey. It's an authentic drink, most lords of the manor made it in-house. Luckily, commercial mead is now available. You'll pay a little bit more than you would for an average bottle of wine, but it will add an old-world quality to the evening. Try Moniack Mead from Scotland.

In November or December two nice, light wines to try are Beaujolais Nouveau Georges Duboeuf Beaujolais or Pisse-Dru, both from France. This is the time of year that these light and delicate wines are available. They are released a few weeks after the harvest, usually the third Thursday of November. Beaujolais is meant to be consumed before Christmas. Italy also has its own version of Beaujolais Nouveau, called vino novello.

At any other time of year you may wish to serve a Chardonnay such as: Gallo of Sonoma (California), Banrock Station Unwooded Chardonnay (Australia) or Fortant De France Chardonnay (France).

MUSIC

Mark Knopfler, of Dire Straits, produced the The Princess Bride (Warner Brothers) soundtrack; he was hand picked by Director Reiner for this task. You could also listen to some Celtic music as its haunting tones suggest the mystery of long forgotten times. For a new age blend of Celtic music you might try anything by Enya, or Canadian sensation, Loreena McKennitt. She also has a wonderful array of songs that incorporate Celtic, folk and ethnic sounds.

crunchy chicken wings
serves 4

These will appeal to any of your pint-sized guests! These wings are easy to prepare as no frying is involved!

3 lbs	chicken wings	1 tsp	dried basil
1 cup	dry bread crumbs	1/2 tsp	each salt and black pepper
1/2 cup	grated Parmesan cheese	1/4 tsp	paprika
1/3 cup	sesame seeds	1/2 cup	butter, melted
1 tsp	dried oregano		

- Preheat oven to 375°F. Remove tips (if desired), excess skin and fat from chicken wings.

- In shallow dish combine bread crumbs, Parmesan cheese, sesame seeds, oregano, basil, salt, pepper and paprika. Dip wings into butter; roll in bread crumb mixture to coat completely.

- Arrange wings, meaty side down, on well-greased rimmed baking sheet. Bake for 40 to 45 minutes, turning halfway through, until golden crisp and no longer pink on the inside.

Want to feel like royalty?

Rent or purchase a castle in Europe. Weekly rentals range from $11,000 to $14,000 in U.S. funds. It is also possible to buy "royal titles", though of course, the ones for sale do not carry any weight in real royal circles!

trivia clips

Long before the written word, during primitive times, stories were passed on from generation to generation by word of mouth. Many of the fables and fairytales we know today are based on those old stories. Since the invention of the printing press, these stories have become an integral part of childhood for generations.

chocolate explosion cakes serves 6

9 oz	(9 squares) bittersweet chocolate, chopped
1/2 cup	butter
1/2 cup	granulated sugar
2 tsp	vanilla
4	eggs, separated

1/4 tsp	cream of tartar
3/4 cup	all-purpose flour

Ganache:

3 oz	(3 squares) bittersweet chocolate, chopped
1/3 cup	whipping cream

- Preheat oven to 350°F. Line small baking sheet with plastic wrap; set aside.

- Ganache: Place chocolate in bowl. In small saucepan, heat cream over medium heat just until steaming and bubbles form around side of pan. Pour over chocolate, whisking just until melted.

- Refrigerate, stirring often, for 30 minutes or until think enough to hold shape. Spoon ganache onto prepared pan in 6 mounds, each about 1-1/2 inches (4 cm) high. Cover loosely with plastic wrap and freeze for at least 4 hours or until firm. (Make ahead: Freeze for up to 1 week.)

- Generously grease six 3/4-cup (175 mL) soufflé dishes or ramekins. Line bottoms with parchment or waxed paper. Set aside. In large heat proof bowl set over a saucepan of hot (not boiling) water, melt chocolate with butter, stirring.

- Remove bowl from over hot water, and let cool for 30 minutes or until chocolate reaches room temperature. Beat in 1/3 cup of the sugar and vanilla. Beat in eggs yolks, 1 at a time, scraping down sides of bowl after each addition, until mixture is slightly thickened.

- In separate bowl and using clean beaters, beat egg whites with cream of tartar until soft peaks form. Beat in remaining sugar in thin steady stream until stiff peaks form. Fold one-third each of egg white mixture and flour into chocolate mixture just until blended; repeat twice.

- Divide half of the chocolate mixture among prepared soufflé dishes; place frozen ganache mound in centre of each. Cover with remaining chocolate batter, smoothing top. (Make ahead: Cover with plastic wrap and refrigerate for up to 8 hours.)

- Bake on baking sheet in centre of oven for 22 minutes or until top is puffed and edge is set but centre is still soft. Let cool on rack for 2 minutes. With fingertips or knife, gently loosen from dishes. Unmould onto dessert plates. Serve immediately.

the unbearable lightness of being (1988)

This lush and erotic film, much of it filmed on location in Prague, is a successful adaptation of Czech author Milan Kundera's best-selling novel of the same name. The main characters, even with all of their human foibles are likeable. Tomas, a doctor in Prague, is a womanizer who doesn't see the point of changing his ways even after he marries Tereza, a sensitive and loyal soul. She is a bit naïve, and most of her life experience has consisted of small town living with the occasional foray into the city of Prague. Sabina, the mistress Tomas can't let go of, is a free spirit who willingly shares her life with more than one man. Much to her surprise and Tereza's, end up forming a friendship. This story of bittersweet love and existence is further complicated by the fall of the Dubcek government and the 1968 Russian invasion of Prague. The political circumstances they find themselves in affect the characters and their philosophy of life.

Those who enjoyed the sweet satisfaction that comes after a good read, upon completing Kundera's novel, will not be disappointed by the film. Perhaps those who have not read anything by this excellent author will be inspired to do so after viewing this movie.

FEATURED ACTORS
Daniel Day-Lewis (Tomas)
Juliette Binoche (Tereza)
Lena Olin (Sabina)
Derek de Lint (Franz)
Erland Josephson (Ambassador)

DIRECTOR ~ Philip Kaufman

menu sheep's cheese spread • rye or brown bread (store-bought) • czech beer soup • braised mushrooms and yogurt on a bed of noodles • green salad with vinaigrette (see index) • vanilla crescents or plum dumplings

sheep's cheese spread
serves 4

This tangy spread is sure to be a hit! It is easy to make and will keep for several days when in a container with a sealed lid.

2 tbsp	butter		salt to taste
1-1/2 cups	sheep's milk cheese	1/2 tsp	caraway seeds, crushed
1	small onion, finely chopped	1/8 tsp	sweet paprika
4 tsp	capers, chopped	1 tbsp	fresh dill, chopped
1	gherkin pickle, finely chopped		

• Cream butter with sheep cheese. Add onion, capers, gherkin and salt to taste. Blend in caraway seeds, paprika and dill. Spread on slices of brown bread.

 Select low fat cheese. Use light butter or non-hydrogenated margarine.

czech beer soup
serves 4

2	slices bread, cubed	1/2 cup	butter
4 cups	light coloured beer	pinch	of salt
pinch	of caraway seeds	4	egg yolks
2/3 cup	sugar	1 cup	cream

• Combine bread cubes, beer, a pinch of caraway seeds, sugar, butter and salt. Boil well and collect foam. Next, in a small bowl mix the egg yolks with the cream, slowly add to soup, stirring to blend: heat thoroughly.

 Reduce butter to 1/4 cup to keep the flavour and cut some of the fat.

trivia clips

The nation of Czechoslovakia split peacefully into two countries on Jan. 1, 1993. The western provinces of Bohemia and Moravia became the Czech Republic, while the eastern section became Slovakia. Of the two new countries, the Czech Republic was the larger, with a land area of 30,441 square miles (78,842 square kilometres), compared to Slovakia's 18,919 square miles (49,000 square kilometres).

the unbearable
lightness of being (1988)

braised mushrooms and yogurt on a bed of noodles
serves 4

1 lb	wide egg noodles (store-bought)		1 cup	plain yogurt
1-1/2 lb	mushrooms, sliced		1 tsp	lemon juice
1/4 cup	butter		1 tbsp	parsley, chopped
	salt		1 tbsp	chives, chopped
	pepper		1 tbsp	dill, chopped
			1 tbsp	chervil, chopped

- Prepare noodles according to package directions. Sauté the mushrooms in butter. Add salt and pepper to taste and place in a dish. Drain noodles when done, set aside. Heat the yogurt and add lemon juice and chopped herbs. Pour yogurt and herb sauce over mushrooms, blend and serve on a bed of noodles.

Use low fat yogurt and yolk-free noodles.

AWARDS WON

Best Adapted Screenplay	1988 British Academy Award
Best Director (Philip Kaufman)	1988 SOC Award
Best Film	1988 SOC Award
Best Cinematography	1989 Independent Spirit Award

vanilla crescents
Yield: About 36 crescents

This is a traditional Czech Christmas cookie, though it is also served during the year. It goes well with tea and coffee.

1/2 lb	sweet butter, softened		1 tsp	vanilla extract
1/2 cup	sugar		1/2 tsp	salt
2 cups	sifted all-purpose flour			confectioner's sugar
1-1/4 cups	ground unblanched almonds			

- Cream the butter and sugar together by beating them against the sides of a bowl with a wooden spoon (or with an electric mixer at medium speed) until light and fluffy. Beat in the flour 1/2 cup at a time, then add the almonds, vanilla extract and salt, continuing to beat until the mixture becomes a slightly stiff dough. Shape the dough into a ball, wrap it in wax paper and refrigerate it for about an hour.

- Preheat the oven to 350˚F. Lightly butter two 12" x 15" baking sheets. Pinch off walnut sized pieces of the chilled dough and place them on a floured board; roll each one into a strip an inch wide and 1/2 inch thick. This will make it about 2 1/2 inches long. Shape each piece into a crescent by pulling it into a semi-circle.

- Arrange the crescents at least 1/2 inch apart on the baking sheet. Bake for 15 to 20 minutes. Remove and leave to cool for 5 minutes, then transfer them to a cake rack. Dust with confectioner's sugar.

Make the crescents up to 2 days prior to serving. Store in a cookie tin.

trivia clips

The Czech republic's population was almost twice as large: 10,314,000 compared to Slovakia's 5,297,000. Economically, too, the Czech Republic was better off, with a much higher gross domestic product, less unemployment, and greater success in returning former state industries to private hands.

The earliest recorded settlement in Prague dates from the 9th century. Two castles were built, one at Hradcany and the other on the hill of Vysehrad on the east bank, south of the present city centre.

BEVERAGES

You must try some Czech beer. They have a very old brewing tradition and beer is the national drink. The Czechs mainly produce pilsners, though there are a few good dark beers. Any of the following would complement the menu: Black Lion lev Czech Premium Dark Beer, Lion Lev Export Lager, Radegast Premium, Golden Pheasant, Pilsner Urquell or Kozel Beer.

MUSIC

The Unbearable Lightness of Being (Fantasy) soundtrack is available. You may wish to listen to a historical snapshot of what rock and roll sounded like behind the Iron Curtain... If so, try "Czechoslovakian Beat 65-68 Vol.1" (Reverendo Moon). For some authentic ethnic music, listen to: "Czechoslovakian Song and Dance Ensemble" (Monitor) or "Czech Ethnic Music" (Lotos).

SETTING THE STAGE

The Czechs enjoy their pints in beer halls which have an atmosphere similar to that of a pub (there is a beer hall scene in the movie). So use red and white checker tablecloths, or perhaps just some new plaid tea towels as place mats. Light some candles. Dim the lights and enjoy the country style food and excellent movie!

plum dumplings

serves 4

These are delicious whether served as a hearty dessert or as a sweet meal on their own.

1/3 cup	plus 2 tbsp butter	12 to 15	prune plums, pitted
2	eggs	1/4 cup	cinnamon sugar
	salt	1 cup	fine bread crumbs
2 cups	sifted flour (all-purpose)		
2 cups	boiled potatoes, riced or pressed through a metal colander		

- Cream 2 tablespoons butter, beat in eggs and salt. Gradually beat in flour and riced potatoes. Knead thoroughly, dough should be stiff enough to be rolled. On floured board, roll out dough to 1/4-inch thickness, then cut into 3-inch squares. Lay 1 plum on each square, sprinkle with little cinnamon sugar and fold edges over plum. Shape with hands into a ball. The wall of dough should be very thin. Drop dumplings into boiling salted water, cover and simmer for about

15 minutes. Drain. Brown bread crumbs in 1/3 cup hot butter. Roll dumplings in buttered bread crumbs, sprinkle with cinnamon sugar.

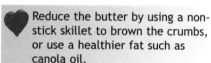 Reduce the butter by using a non-stick skillet to brown the crumbs, or use a healthier fat such as canola oil.

trivia clips

Nearly 95 percent of the population in the Czech republic consists of Bohemians or Czechs and Moravians. The other major ethnic groups are Hungarians, Slovaks, and Gypsies. The Gypsy population may be the largest in Eastern Europe, but they have no legal standing as a recognized ethnic group.

trivia clips

Prague, the capital, exceeds 1 million in population. The second largest city, Brno, has a population of only about 390,000, however. Ostrava, in the northeast, and Pilsen, in the southwest, are the other major cities. The latter is one of the most famous beer-brewing centres in the world.

time of the gypsies (1989)

zigeuner schnitzel

serves 4 to 6

The name of this dish translated into English is "gyspy schnitzel"; the reason as to why has been lost or forgotten. This schnitzel is great with potatoes or rice. You may also purchase German style spaetzle noodles at European delicatessens (cook according to package directions) and serve in place of potatoes or rice.

6	3-ounce veal cutlets		1	red bell pepper, thinly sliced
	salt and pepper		1	onion, thinly sliced
2 tbsp	butter			pitted ripe olives
1/4 lb	smoked ham or prosciutto, thinly sliced			paprika
1/4 lb	mushrooms, thinly sliced			cayenne
1	green bell pepper, thinly sliced		1/4 cup	dry white wine

- Season veal with salt and pepper. Melt butter in a large skillet over medium-high heat.

- Add veal and sauté until browned, turning once, about 8 to 10 minutes. Transfer the veal to a heated platter and keep warm. Add ham, mushrooms, peppers, onion and olives to the same skillet. Sauté over medium-high heat until tender — about 4 minutes. Season to taste with paprika and cayenne. Blend in wine, simmer until mixture thickens slightly.

- Spoon over veal and serve immediately. Serve with potatoes along side.

This film received many accolades when it was shown at the Cannes Film Festival. The main character is a somewhat nerdy, Romany teenager named Perhan, who is not very streetwise, in fact he's fairly naïve. Perhan is drawn into a relationship of sorts with a sleazy crook who is looking for someone to take under his charge and train to be a partner in crime. Perhan is on the road to becoming a man, but not necessarily one whom his family envisioned. While learning the tricks of the trade he also searches for his sister, who allegedly left home for a leg operation and has not yet returned. Perhan, like any young male, is preoccupied with fantasies about the object of his affection, a young woman from his village. His visions during these flights of fancy are quite amusing.

FEATURED ACTORS
Davor Dujmović (Perhan)
Bora Todorović (Ahmed)
Ljubica Adžović (grandmother)
Husnija Hasimović (Uncle Merdžan)
Sinolička Trpkova (Danira)

DIRECTOR ~ Emir Kusturica

AWARDS WON
Best Director   1989 Cannes
(Emir Kusturica)   Film Festival Award

BEVERAGES
As Emir Kusturica is from the former Yugoslavia, we thought we would feature some white wines from this region. Try Badel's Daruvarski Rizling (Croatia), and Navip's Riesling Fruska Gora (Yugoslavia).
Alternatively, serve your beer of choice or try Karlovacko Pivo (Croatia), BIP (Yugoslavia) or Nisko Pivo (Yugoslavia).

trivia clips

This is the first feature movie to be filmed with the entire dialogue in Romany, the language of the gypsies, who prefer to have their ethnicity described as Romany. Romany, an unwritten language of the Roma peoples of Europe, is spoken by probably a few million individuals.

MUSIC

Nothing else but an international array of gypsy music will do! In first place we recommend the soundtrack which has been released under the name "Erdelezi" (Mercury) and features the amazing compositions by Yugoslav music legend Goran Bregovic. If you like the "Gypsy Kings", try some other gyspy music from Spain: "Gypsy Flamenco" (Vanguard) by Maritas de Plata, will definitely have you out of your chair and up dancing! Eastern Europe has a long tradition of appreciating gypsy music, so there are many albums to choose from. We suggest: "Imre Magyari and his Gypsy Band" (Hungaroton) from Hungary, and "Gypsy Music from Eastern Europe" (Isba) which features performers and songs from several countries. A few great albums from the former Yugoslavia are: Jovica Nikolic's "Gypsy Holiday" (Pro Arte), "Djelem" (Orange Music) and "Gypsy Esma" (Monitor)

SETTING THE STAGE

How about a fun costume party! Have guests dress up in gypsy costume, this is especially easy for the women as almost everyone must have some ruffled skirts or off-the-shoulder tops in their clothes closets. Play some of the enchanting gypsy music, bring out some toy tambourines (or the real ones if you have them) and other musical instruments. Dance and have a good time! Many people equate gypsies with fortune-telling—hire a person to do tarot card or psychic readings for the get-together. Everyone loves the idea of knowing about their future! If you can't afford to hire someone, just buy the cards and try it yourself. There are many books on the market that will explain the method of laying out the cards as well as the symbols and meanings of the cards. We all have a bit of a gypsy soul—now is the time to let it out!

crêpes with chocolate and walnuts
serves 6

3	eggs
1 cup	milk
1/3 cup	club soda
1 cup	all-purpose flour
3 tbsp	granulated sugar
1/4 tsp	salt
1 tsp	vanilla extract

4 to 6 tbsp	butter or use butter-flavoured cooking spray
3/4 cup	chocolate spread such as Nutella
1 cup	ground walnuts or hazelnuts
	powdered sugar (garnish)

- In a medium bowl, beat the eggs lightly with the milk, using a whisk. Add the club soda, and then the flour, sugar, salt and vanilla extract. Continue to stir until the batter is smooth.

- Melt a tablespoon of the butter (or use cooking spray) in an 8-inch skillet over medium high heat. When the foam subsides and the skillet is heated through, ladle in enough batter to thinly cover the bottom of the skillet; tilt the skillet from side to side to spread batter evenly. Cook for 2 to 3 minutes, or until lightly browned on one side and then flip over to brown the other side.

When the crêpe is done, spread 2 teaspoons of chocolate spread on one side, roll into a cylinder, and put in a baking dish. Place in a warm oven heated to 200°F to keep warm until all the crêpes are done. Serve this dessert warm, sprinkled with nuts and powdered sugar as garnish.

 Use low fat milk. Grease pan with cooking spray.

 If you don't have chocolate spread, just grate some good quality chocolate to sprinkle on the crêpe before rolling up.

trivia clips

There are more than twelve million Roma located in many countries around the world. There is no way to obtain an exact number since they are not recorded on most official census counts. Many Roma themselves do not admit to their true ethnic origins for economic and social reasons.

trivia clips

The Roma are a distinct ethnic minority, distinguished by Rom blood and the Romani, or Romanes, language, whose origins began on the Indian subcontinent over one thousand years ago. No one knows for certain why the original Roma began their great wandering from India to Europe and beyond, but they dispersed worldwide, despite persecution and oppression through the centuries.

1990-   Unification of Germany
         Once the Berlin Wall was opened in November, 1989, it was only a matter of
         time until the two halves of Germany were united again. The period turned
         out to be much shorter than most people expected. Despite other countries'
         concerns about a large, powerful Germany once more at the heart of Europe,
         the Germans sped up the unification process.

1991-   End of the Soviet Union

1992-   The "Comeback Kid" Bill Clinton regains the popular vote and sets George
         Bush and the Reagan era to an end as he becomes the next U.S. President.
         The 90's have Clinton trying to come back in many different ways and leave a
         legacy other than the scandal dealing with "that woman" (Lewinsky).

1996-   Dolly the sheep is cloned at the Roslin Institute in Scotland

1993-   For the first time, a female is Prime Minister of Canada: Kim Campbell

1993-   The first woman to pilot the Concorde (March 25th.) is Barbara Harmer

1997-   The streets of London were packed with crowds bigger than any other since
         V-E Day in 1945, up to 2 million was one estimate. Worldwide, an estimated
         audience of 25 million was glued to their TV sets, as Londoners and the world
         said their sad farewell to the "People's Princess" Diana, Princess of Wales,
         who was killed in a car crash in Paris.

new age 90's

braveheart

(1995)

There are a selective number of actors who after years of performing on screen or stage, discover their own talents for working behind the scenes, producing or directing. But only a small handful is talented enough to reach such a high level of achievement and be recognized for their work on-screen and behind the scenes. Australian born heartthrob and well loved actor, best known for his action-packed dramas has made his mark on Hollywood in this way. It was with this movie, Braveheart, that Hollywood recognized one of their own for multi-faceted achievement, and justifiably so. The story is based on the legend of Scotland's own national hero, William Wallace. Even prior to the film, a number of loyal fans dedicated web-sites to celebrating and recognizing one of Scottish history's best known figures. William Wallace's life as depicted in this movie by Mel Gibson is based on the poem entitled "Life of Wallace" by "Blind Harry," a 15th century minstrel. It is the story of a medieval Scottish patriot, William Wallace, who struggles to unify his nation against its English oppressors. The story begins with the young Wallace, whose father and brother have been killed fighting the English. Wallace is taken away by a nationalist uncle, and returns twenty years later, an educated man versed in the classics as well as the art of war. Upon his return, he finds his childhood sweetheart and the two fall in love. There are rumours of a revolt against the English, but Wallace decides to keep his distance choosing to live in peace. Wallace and his bride marry secretly, so that the local English lord can not exercise his right of "prima nochae," which means his right to spend the first night of marriage with the bride usurping the right of the groom to his spouse. Tragedy ensues as his new bride is killed by the English the day after their romantic secret ceremony. In his rage, Wallace single-handedly slaughters a whole platoon of foot soldiers. His fellow villagers join him in destroying the English garrison, and thus commences a revolt; which in turn becomes a full-fledged war. Wallace leads the Scots in a number of battles causing serious damage to the English. He becomes both an omnipresent threat and a thorn in the sides of his oppressors. He also finds love again, though it is complicated as the object of his desire is none other than the Princess of Wales played by beautiful French actress, Sophie Marceau who was hand picked by Gibson for the role. The film has a tragic, moving ending. The cinematography is gorgeous and the battle scenes are well played out. You will want to see this film more than once and you will have a better understanding of how rich Scottish history truly is.

menu | scones • "auld reekie" cock-a-leekie soup • shepherd's pie (see index) or steak and kidney pie • green salad with vinaigrette (see index) • crusty bread (store-bought) • drambuie flavoured oranges

scones

makes 1 dozen

This could be served with alongside the soup or with tea or coffee. If serving with tea or coffee serve some butter, jam and honey with the scones.

4 tbsp	butter or margarine		pinch of salt
2-1/2 cup	all-purpose flour	3/4	cup 2% or whole milk
1 tbsp	baking powder		

- Preheat oven to 450˚F.
- Cut the butter or margarine into the flour and add baking powder and salt. Slowly mix in the milk until the mixture forms a dough.

- Divide into about 12 heaps and place on a floured cookie sheet. Bake for about 12 minutes, or until slightly browned. Serve warm with butter and jam.

"auld reekie" cock-a-leekie soup

serves 4 to 6

The "Auld Reekie" does not refer to the soup being "smoky" but to the origins of the recipe in Edinburgh, which used to be called Auld Reekie in the days of coal fires.

3 lb	stewing chicken (giblets removed)	1/2 cup	Scotch whisky
3	slices of bacon, diced	4 pints	water
1lb	shin of beef	1 tbsp	dried tarragon
2 lbs	leeks		salt and pepper
1	large onion	8	pre-soaked prunes (optional but traditional!)

- Mix the whisky, tarragon and sugar in the water. Place the chicken, bacon, and beef in a large bowl and pour over the whisky marinade. Leave to soak overnight. Place the chicken, bacon, and beef in a large soup pot. Add the leeks (reserve 1 cup) to the pot along with the onions.
- Salt and pepper to taste.

- Bring to the boil, cover and simmer for two hours, removing any skimming off the top as required. Remove the chicken from the pot, remove skin and bones. Chop the meat into small pieces and return to the pot. Cut up the shin of beef, if required. Add the prunes and the last of the chopped leeks and simmer for 10 to 15 minutes.

trivia clips

A number of the major battle scenes had to be reshot because some of the extras were seen wearing modern things like sunglasses and wristwatches.
What was the first film that made Mel Gibson popular in North America?
Hint: He wasn't really mad!

braveheart

steak and kidney pie

serves 4 to 6

Versions of this pie are found all over Scotland and Britain. If you don't using veal kidneys, just add more steak.

Pastry:

1-1/3 cups	flour
1/2 cup	(1 stick) cold, unsalted butter, cut into 1/2 inch cubes
1/4 tsp	salt
1	egg
2 to 3 tbsp	iced water

Filling:

5 tbsp	oil
1 lb	marbled steak, cut into 1 inch cubes
3/4 lb	trimmed veal kidney (about 2 kidneys), cut into 1 inch cubes
	salt and freshly ground black pepper
10 oz	mushrooms, quartered
3	onions, chopped
3 tbsp	flour
2 tbsp	Worcestershire sauce
2 cups	hot water
	milk, for brushing pastry
	sea salt
	freshly cracked black pepper

- Prepare the pastry: In a large bowl, combine flour with butter and salt. Mix lightly with your fingertips until butter forms pea sized pieces. Whisk together egg and 1 tablespoon of the water. Add to flour mixture all at once, mixing gently with your fingertips. You should be able to see chunks of fat, and the pastry should be moist enough to begin to stick together. If the pastry is too dry, add up to 2 more tablespoons of water.

- Turn the pastry out onto a lightly floured work surface, dust with flour, and knead it until the pastry is smooth, about 3 to 4 times. Transfer to a plastic bag and form pastry into a disk.

- Refrigerate a minimum of 30 minutes, or as long as 3 days.

- Meanwhile, heat 2 tablespoons of the oil in a casserole or Dutch oven. Add the steak and kidneys, season with salt and pepper, and cook, stirring, until just browned, about 3 minutes.

- Remove to a plate and reserve. Add 1 more tablespoon of oil to casserole, and add mushroom quarters. Cook over high heat, stirring, until light brown. Reserve on plate with meat.

- Add the remaining oil to the casserole, and add onions. Cook until well browned, about 5 minutes.

- Sprinkle the flour over the onions and stir so that the juices soak up the flour. Cook, stirring constantly, about 1 to 2 minutes.

- Stir the Worcestershire sauce into the hot water, and pour over the hot onion mixture while whisking. Add the reserved meats and mushrooms, and any juices that have collected, and season with salt and pepper. Reduce the heat to low and simmer 3 to 4 minutes or until slightly thickened.

- Preheat oven to 400° F. Roll out the pastry to a thickness of 1/4 inch. Fill a 9-inch pie dish with the steak and kidney mixture. Dampen the edges of the dish with water, then fit the pastry on top, pressing it down well all around the edge to seal. Make a steam hole in the center, brush the top with milk and sprinkle with sea salt and freshly cracked black pepper. Bake for 25 minutes, or until pastry is golden.

trivia clips

The battle scenes are spectacular showing many actors and horses on the battle ground. Despite using fake horses director/producer Mel Gibson was investigated by the RSPCA, who thought the fake horses were real. It turns out that digital computer special effects made the fakes seem very real!

MUSIC

The "Brave Heart Soundtrack" (Polygram), is a good choice with composer James Horner and the London Symphony Orchestra. Horner was also one of the composers for James Cameron's movie, Titanic. Other suitable alternatives are: "Celtic Celebration" (Legacy), "Scottish Songbook" (Moidart), or "Scottish Traditions" (Greentrax).

SETTING THE STAGE

This movie is set during the 13th century, medieval time period. To replicate that use brocade or tapestry type prints for setting the table. Tall candles are compulsory, the more the better; especially in silver or brass candelabra. Bring out your silverware and silver goblets if you have them, otherwise use crystal. A large fruit bowl full of various fruits and nuts in the shell, surrounded by some greenery makes a nice centrepiece. Add some touches of tartan to your table, whether with a tablecloth, runner or napkins.

Scots around the world celebrate Robbie Burns Day. You may wish to become familiar with the works of this Scottish poet. Here are some suggestions for this thematic evening : Obtain copies of his poems. Have guests gather and mingle, and peruse through the poems. The chairman or host may make some introductions among the guests, assign some readings, or deliver a few opening remarks. Each guest should choose a poem that "speaks" to their heart and recite it aloud. Everyone will come away from this evening knowing a bit more about Scottish history and literature.

drambuie flavoured oranges

An easy recipe that uses a well-known Scottish product; Drambuie liqueur!

1	large orange for each person	Drambuie liqueur
	brown sugar	fresh mint leaves as garnish

- Cut the oranges in half and use a grapefruit knife to cut the flesh away from the skin. Cut the orange segments into bite-size pieces. Place in small oven-proof ramekins. Spoon a shot of Drambuie onto the oranges. You can leave the oranges at room temperature until you are ready to go on to the next stage. Prior to serving, sprinkle brown sugar on the top of the oranges and broil in the oven until the sugar starts to bubble. Decorate with a sprig of mint before serving.

> **?** Drambuie is a scotch whisky-based liqueur flavored with heather and honey.

trivia clips

How many sequels was there to Lethal Weapon?
Name another historical movie that Mel was in?
Braveheart was filled mostly in Ireland.
Monster of Loch Ness mythical creature or real beast? Nessie was first seen by St Columbia in 565 A.D.

trivia clips

Scotland is the only part of the UK that has a statutory public holiday on the 2nd January as well as the 1st January.
Famous Scots: Sir J M Barrie (1860-1937), was the Author of Peter Pan and The Admirable Crichton.
Alexander Graham Bell (1847-1922), a Scot who lived out the latter portion of his life in Canada, was inventor of the telephone. He was also involved in genetics and phonetics.

il postino

(1994)

menu crusty bread with extra virgin olive oil dip • arugula and blue cheese bruschetta (see index) • layered mediterranean pie (pita rustica) • four seasons salad (see index) • chilean caramel apples or chocolate-almond grand marnier cheesecake (see index)

crusty bread with extra virgin olive oil dip
serves 6 to 8

This is one of the simplest appetizers you will ever make. It is often served in Italian restaurants.

1	loaf crusty bread (store-bought), cut into thick slices or chunks	2 tbsp	fresh oregano, chopped
3/4 cup	extra virgin olive oil	2 tbsp	fresh parsley, chopped
3	cloves garlic, chopped	2 tbsp	fresh basil, chopped
2 tbsp	fresh rosemary, chopped	1/2 tsp	salt
			freshly ground pepper to taste

- Place extra virgin olive oil in a ceramic or rustic looking bowl. Add other ingredients, stir to blend.

Serve bread in a basket lined with a red and white checkered tea towel or napkin.

This sweet, romantic comedy is set in 1950's Italy. The focus of the film is the relationship between Chilean Nobel Prize-winning poet Pablo Neruda who is seeking peace and quiet on an island off the Italian coast. Mario, is the local postman who is a poet at heart. Mario tries to win over the somewhat aloof Neruda, eventually he becomes successful and Neruda starts to warm to him. They have conversations and Neruda shares some philosophies on love, politics and life with Mario. He even helps Mario write some poetry to send to Beatrice, the object of Mario's affections. Neruda leaves the island but Mario, still inspired by him continues with his poetry even though ties with Neruda have been severed and his letters to the poet are unanswered. Even so his relationship with Neruda has changed Mario's life for the better.

FEATURED ACTORS
Massimo Troisi (Mario Ruoppalo)
Philippe Noiret (Pablo Neruda)
Maria Grazia Cucinotta
  (Beatrice Russo)
Linda Moretti (Donna Rosa)
Renato Scarpa (telegrapher)

DIRECTOR ~ Michael Radford

AWARDS WON

Best Original Dramatic Score (Luis Enriquez Bacalov)	1995 Academy Award
Audience Award	1995 São Paulo International Film Festival Award
Best Film—not in English Language	1996 British Academy Award
David Lean Award for Direction (Michael Radford)	1996 British Academy Award

trivia clips

Writer/co-director/star, Massimo Troisi, postponed heart surgery so he could complete the film. Unfortunately, he did not live long enough to receive accolades for his part in the making of the film. The day after filming was completed, he suffered a fatal heart attack.

il postino

BEVERAGES

Serve a variety of red wine from Italy and Chile. Try: Folonari Valpolicella Classico, Collavini Merlot, and Ruffino Chianti. From Chile try: Santa Carolina Merlot, Chicureo Merlot, Concha Y Toro Sunrise Merlot, or Santa Rita "120" Cabernet Sauvignon.

MUSIC

"La Nostra Italia" (European import) features a number of artists and songs. If you wish to listen to some Italian folk music, try "Italian Treasury: Folk Music and Songs of Italy" American singer Connie Francis went back to her roots and recorded in Italian. You may wish to try her two volume CD edition called "The Italian Collection" (PolyGram). It features songs from her previous five Italian albums. You can't go wrong with anything from Andrea Bocelli. If you wish to listen to some more modern Italian music, we suggest "Le Mie Canzoni: The Best of Umberto Tozzi" (Alex) "Stile Libero" (RCA) by Eros Ramazotti or anything by Toto Cotugno.

For some Chilean music try: Poncho Sanchez's "Chile con Soul" (Concord Picante), this album is a Latin Jazz and Tito Puente is a guest on some of the tracks. A compilation CD with various artists is "Chile Con Sus Mas Grandes" (Orfeon)

layered mediterranean pie (pita rustica) serves 6 to 8

This dish really is a feast for the eyes! The multi-coloured layers look so appetizing when the pie is cut into wedges. Serve warm, or at room temperature.

Pastry:

1-3/4 cups	all-purpose flour
1 tsp	salt
1 tsp	baking powder
1/3 cup	olive oil
1/3 cup	milk
2	eggs

Filling:

1/4 cup	olive oil
2	zucchinis, cut crosswise into 1/2-inch thick slices
2	onions, cut crosswise into 1/2-inch thick slices
1	eggplant, cut crosswise into 1/2-inch thick slices
1 tsp	salt
1	head garlic

3	roasted red peppers, peeled and sliced
1/4 cup	black olives, pitted and chopped
1 cup	shredded Fontina or mozzarella cheese (or 1-1/2 cups ricotta mixed with 1 egg)
4	marinated artichoke hearts, drained and sliced
2 to 3	small pieces of bocconcini cheese, sliced
2 tbsp	pine nuts or walnuts
2 tbsp	homemade or prepared pesto sauce
1/4 cup	fresh oregano, chopped
1/4 cup	fresh basil, chopped
1/2 tsp	pepper

- Preheat oven to 425˚F.

- In large bowl, stir together flour salt and baking powder. In separate bowl, whisk together oil, milk and 1 of the eggs; add to dry ingredients all at once. Using fingers or in mixer using dough hook, blend until liquid is absorbed and dough is smooth. Turn out onto lightly floured surface; knead for about 2 minutes or until velvety smooth. Transfer to bowl; cover and refrigerate for 30 minutes. (Make-ahead: Wrap in plastic and refrigerate for up to 5 days.)

- Filling: Brush two large baking sheets with 2 teaspoons of the oil. Place zucchini, onions and eggplant in single layer on prepared sheets. Brush with 2 tablespoons of the oil; sprinkle with 1/2 teaspoon of the salt. Without peeling, separate garlic into cloves and place in small bowl; add remaining oil and toss to coat. Add garlic to sheets, reserving oil in bowl. Roast in oven, rotating pans once, for about 40 minutes or until vegetables are tender and garlic is softened.

- Let cool. (Make-ahead: refrigerate in airtight container for up to 12 hours.) Squeeze garlic from skins in to reserved oil in bowl; mash with fork and set aside.

- On lightly floured surface or pastry cloth, roll out pastry to 18-inch circle; transfer to large baking sheet. Spread garlic in 9-inch circle in center of pastry. Top with one-third of the vegetable mixture and one-third of the red peppers; sprinkle with one-third of the cheese, oregano, basil, pepper, black olives and remaining salt. Repeat layers twice. To the final layer add the artichoke hearts, bocconcini slices, dot with pesto sauce and sprinkle with pine nuts.

- Fold pastry border over filling to form attractive irregular edge, leaving 2-inch opening on top.

Lightly beat remaining egg; brush over pastry to seal folds. Bake in lower third of 375˚F oven for about 30 minutes or until pastry is golden and filling is steaming. Let stand on sheet on rack for about 5 minutes before cutting into wedges.

Variation: Add a layer of thinly sliced black forest ham or roast turkey on top of the Fontina, mozzarella or ricotta cheese.

 Use low fat cheese in the filling and skim milk for the pastry crust.

il postino

chilean caramelized apples

serves 4

Since one of the characters in the film was Chilean, we included this easy to prepare, but delicious dessert!

1/3 cup	sweet butter	2 tbsp	Calvados or cognac
1/2 cup	brown sugar	1/2 tsp	cinnamon
4	large green apples, peeled, cored and sliced	pinch	of nutmeg
			whipped cream for garnish

- In a large skillet, melt the butter over medium heat. Add the sugar and stir until mixed. Next, add the apples to the skillet and stir until the apples are coated with the butter mixture.

Add the rest of the ingredients and bring to a simmer. Cook for 3 minutes. Serve hot with a dollop of whipped cream!

SETTING THE STAGE

Create the look of a small town Italian trattoria in your dining area. Use an old Chianti bottle, or any attractive old wine bottle as a candle holder. Lay out a red and white checker tablecloth or napkins on your table. Place cruets of olive oil and red-wine vinegar on the table. Use rustic or ceramic looking serving pieces. Set out side plates for chunks of Italian bread and small bowls with extra virgin olive oil for dipping. Use small pots of herbs like rosemary, basil, oregano and sage for table decoration. Put on some of the suggested music and enjoy the simple, but delicious meal!

trivia clips

Over the next decades Neruda traveled widely and continued writing poetry. Among his other books were 'Residence on Earth' (1933), written while he was in South Asia; General Song (1950), one of the greatest epic poems written in the Americas; and One Hundred Love Sonnets (1959). During the Marxist regime of Salvador Allende, Neruda was Chile's ambassador to France (l971-72). He died in Santiago on Sept. 23, l973.

trivia clips

Pablo, Neruda (1904-73) Was a Latin American poet with an international reputation. He was also committed to politics and social reform. Often referred to as the "poet of enslaved humanity," he was awarded the Lenin Peace Prize in 1953 and the Nobel Prize for Literature in 1971.

trivia clips

Neruda was born Neftali Ricardo Reyes Basoalto, on July 12, 1904, in Parral, Chile. His mother died soon after. He completed his secondary schooling in 1920, the same year he began using the name Pablo Neruda. In 1921 he went to Santiago to continue his education but soon became so devoted to writing poetry that his schooling was abandoned. Neruda's first book, Crepusculario, was published in Spanish in 1923. The next year he published Twenty Love Poems and a Song of Despair..

like water for chocolate (1993)

There is an old saying that states "that the way to a man's heart is through his stomach". It is also said that those who cook well are very passionate people. Most people would agree that there seems to be some truth to these sayings after all, and this movie plays with these ideas.

This evocative movie is based on the best-selling novel by Laura Esquival. It is about a young Mexican woman named Tita, and the magical effects of her cooking. The youngest of three daughters in a traditional Mexican family, Tita, as is customary, remains unmarried as she is taking care of her mother who is getting on in age. But fate has other plans, and Tita falls in love with a handsome man named Pedro who also has his eye on her. The two fall in love, but Tita's family disapproves of Pedro as a choice of mate for her. He ends up marrying Tita's oldest sister instead. Heartbroken, Tita becomes so sad that it ends up affecting her cooking.

Anytime someone eats something she cooks, they end up feeling the same heartbreak and despair she does. Regardless of circumstance, Pedro and Tita no longer can hide their love for one another and commence a secret love affair. This romantic fable used magical realism in its approach towards cooking and romance. The film was very popular in Mexico. It was also one of the highest grossing foreign films in the United States.

FEATURED ACTORS
Lumi Cavazos (Tita de la Garza)
Mario Leonardi (Pedro Muzquiz)
Regina Torne (Mama Elena)
M. Martinez (John Brown)
Ada Carrasco (Nacha)

DIRECTOR ~ Alfonso Arau

menu   mayan dip • chicken mole in tortillas • rice con queso (see index) • churros

mayan dip

1-1/4 cups	canned black beans	1/2 tsp	cayenne pepper
2	cloves garlic, thinly sliced	1/2 tsp	chili powder
pinch	of salt		salt and pepper to taste
2 tbsp	Dijon mustard	2-3	green onions, thinly sliced
1/2 cup	cream cheese		tortilla chips

- Drain beans and puree in a food processor, adding garlic, pinch of salt, Dijon mustard, cream cheese, cayenne pepper, and chili powder. Season with salt and pepper to taste.

- Pour pureed mixture into serving bowl and garnish with green onions. Serve with tortilla chips.

trivia clips

"Love and gluttony justify everything" - Oscar Wilde
Another movie with chocolate in the title is "Chocolat", starring Academy Award winner Juliet Binoche and Johnny Depp.

like water for chocolate (1993)

chicken mole in tortillas   serves 4

Here is a quick and easy version of chicken with mole sauce!

2	medium size onions, finely chopped
2	cloves garlic minced
2 tbsp	olive oil
2	large tomatoes, chopped
1 cup	chicken broth
1/4 cup	canned green chilies, chopped
2 tbsp	each sesame seeds and dry roasted unsalted peanuts
1/4 tsp	each of ground cinnamon, cloves
1 tsp	each of ground cumin and dried oregano

2 tbsp	ground chili powder
1/4 cup	golden raisins
1/2 lb	boneless skinless chicken breasts cut into 2-inch long by 1/3-inch strips
1/2 lb	smoked skinless chicken breasts, cut into 2-inch long by 1/3-inch strips
1/2 oz	(1/2 square) unsweetened chocolate, grated or cut into fine pieces
8	large flour tortillas
	sour cream, and chopped cilantro for garnish, optional

- Sauté the onions and garlic in the oil for about 10 minutes or until tender. Add the tomatoes, chicken broth and green chilis and simmer, uncovered for 15 minutes, stirring frequently.

- Meanwhile, in a dry iron skillet toast the sesame seeds and peanuts for a few minutes or until they begin to smell roasted, then add the cinnamon, cloves, cumin, oregano and chili powder and toast for a few seconds. Remove and cool slightly, then purée with the raisins to form a paste.

- Add the chicken to the sauce and simmer 3 minutes to cook through; add the smoked chicken and simmer another 3 minutes to warm through. Add the chocolate and simmer a minute until melted. Stir in the paste and simmer until thickened to the proper consistency. Meanwhile warm the tortillas on the oven.

- To assemble, put some spoonfuls of chicken and sauce in the middle of a warm tortilla and roll up, top with more spoonfuls of sauce, and sour cream and cilantro.

Use whole wheat tortillas.
Use low fat sour cream and no-fat chicken broth.

What is it?
Mole, pronounced (MOH-lay) is from the Nahuatl molli, meaning "concoction, or mixture". Red mole is from central Mexico in the Pueblo and Oaxaca regions, also known as the Land of Seven Moles. Other mole colors include brown, black, green and yellow. This red mole is a rich, dark, reddish brown sauce usually served with poultry. Generally, mole is a smooth sauce blended of onion, garlic, several varieties of chilies, ground seeds and a small amount of chocolate. It is important to note that not all moles contain chocolate. The traditional mole is usually served over turkey.

trivia clips

Chocolate contains a small amount of theobromine, which is an alkaloid similar to the caffeine found in tea and coffee. The stimulant properties of theobromine may account for some of chocolate's popularity. In some sensitive people the theobromine content can produce the same effects as caffeine alertness, elevated mood, depression of appetite, and increased mental and physical energy. Too much consumption of chocolate can cause insomnia and tremors.

AWARDS WON

Best Film (Alfonso Arau)	1992 Golden Ariel (Mexico)
Best Actor (Mario Iván Martínez)	1992 Golden Ariel (Mexico)
Best Actress Regina Torné)	1992 Golden Ariel (Mexico)
Best Cinematography (Emmanuel Lubezki)	1992 Silver Ariel (Mexico)
Best Direction (Alfonso Arau)	1992 Silver Ariel (Mexico)
Best Production Design (Emilio Mendoza II/ Ricardo Mendoza II/Gonzalo Ceja	1992 Silver Ariel (Mexico)
Best Screenplay (Laura Esquivel)	1992 Silver Ariel (Mexico)
Best Actress (Lumi Cavazos)	1992 Tokyo International Film Festival
Best Artistic Contribution Award (Steven Bernstein I/ Emmanuel Lubezki)	1992 Tokyo International Film Festival

BEVERAGES

Chocolate Liqueurs

Mexicola (see main beverages section)

Mexican Spice Coffee (see main beverages section)

MUSIC

The "Like Water for Chocolate" (Milan) soundtrack is available. With its romantic orchestral music, it is a good choice if you are making it a quiet evening for two. Otherwise, listen to some festive Mexican music, such as that found on "The Best of Mexican Music" (Balboa) featuring various artists. If it is a romantic evening for two, we suggest "Serenades" (Balboa). This compilation features an array of serenades such as the well-known Besame Mucho, and other songs. For an interesting re-interpretation of Mexican folk songs we recommend "Los Super Seven" (RCA), by the band of the same name. One of the band members, David Hildago, is a former member of Los Lobos, a band that enjoyed some mainstream success in the 1980's.

Mexicans enjoy celebrating festive occasions; they are noted for their spicy hot foods, and colourful celebrations that often inspire romance. Las Serenatas is a romantic tradition, a serenade to capture the heart of a loved one. Traditionally, a man would hire a mariachi band, or trio, and sing romantic songs under the window sill of his sweetheart, thus "serenading" her. She in return, would not come to her window until a least 3 or 4 songs were played. For those willing to be adventurous and very romantic, surprise your loved one with a serenade on a special occasion such as a birthday or Valentine's Day.

If inviting friends over for a thematic evening, hire a trio of musicians and have them play outside your front door, greeting your guests as they arrive. If your budget allows, you could hire the band for a couple of hours either to start your party or have them play all night.

Decorate your front door with a traditional chinchilla blanket or a Mexican flag. Cook using clay pots, wrap your silverware in colourful napkins, set the table in bright colours and use a few cactus plants as a centrepiece. Set out some helium balloons in bright colours or cactus and chili pepper shapes. This fiesta would be ideal for the outdoors; light some citronella candles and patio lanterns. While you're in the mood, don't forget your sombrero. Play some music, keep the rhythm with those souvenir maracas you probably brought back from vacation and maybe even do the Mexican hat dance! For fun, you could also ask guests to bring a sampling of their favourite chocolates to share with others at the get together. After all, you can never have too much chocolate!

churros

These Mexican fritters are very common and quick and simple to make. They are often served at outdoor festivals throughout Mexico.

1 cup	water
2 tbsp	plus 1-1/2 tsp white sugar
1/2 tsp	salt
2 tbsp	vegetable oil
1 cup	all-purpose flour

8 cups	oil for frying
1/2 cup	confectioner's sugar, or to taste
1 tsp	ground cinnamon

- In a small saucepan over medium heat, combine water, 2-1/2 tablespoons sugar, salt and 2 tablespoons vegetable oil. Bring to a boil and remove from heat. Stir in flour until mixture forms a soft ball.

- Heat oil for frying in deep-fryer or deep skillet to 375°F. Pipe strips of dough into hot oil using a pastry bag. Fry until golden; drain on paper towels. Combine 1/2-cup confectioner's sugar and cinnamon. Roll drained churros in cinnamon and sugar mixture.

What is it?
Tequila is distilled from pulque. This milky fermented liquor is derived from a cactus-like plant. Spanish settlers in Mexico first discovered it. Apparently this cactus is becoming difficult to find... some people have started to stockpile Tequila!

trivia clips

Annual world consumption of cocoa beans averages approximately 600,000 tons, and per capita chocolate consumption is greatly on the rise. Chocolate manufacturing in the United States is a multi billion-dollar industry. Other important manufacturing countries are Germany, The Netherlands, Great Britain, and France.

trivia clips

Chocolate for eating is made by adding cocoa butter to chocolate liquor. For sweet, or dark, chocolate finely powdered sugar is added. For milk chocolate a third ingredient, milk, is included. Various flavorings may also be added.
Cocoa butter is sold separately for other purposes. When solid, it is white and pleasant tasting. Baking firms may use it instead of regular butter. It is also an ingredient of soaps and complexion creams.

mediterraneo

(1991)

menu white bean dip with pita crisps • mediterraneo pizza • greek shrimp with feta cheese • four seasons salad (see index) or italian style romaine salad (see index) • baklava (see index)

white bean dip with pita crisps   Yield: 2 cups

1/3 cup	extra virgin olive oil	1/4 cup	fresh lemon juice
3	large cloves garlic, minced	1 tbsp	tahini
1/2 tsp	each salt and pepper	1/2 tsp	ground cumin
3	Pita breads	1/2 tsp	hot pepper sauce
1	19 ounce can white kidney beans, drained and rinsed	1/4 cup	fresh cilantro, chopped

- Stir together 2 tablespoons of the olive oil, one-third of the garlic and pinch each of the salt and pepper. Cut pitas into 6 rounds; cut into triangles and place on baking sheet. Brush triangles with olive oil mixture. Bake in 350°F oven for 8 to 10 minutes or until crisp.

- Meanwhile, in food processor, purée together remaining olive oil, garlic, salt and pepper, kidney beans, lemon juice, tahini, cumin and hot pepper sauce. Stir in fresh cilantro. Serve with pita crisps.

 The spread can be refrigerated in airtight container for up to 2 days before serving.

This foreign flick is a comic anti-war story with a bit of romance to spice it up! It deals with a group of Italian soldiers, led by Lieutenant Montini, who are marooned on what they deem to be a deserted island on the Aegean after the British sunk their ship. The island is not as it appears—upon sighting the ragtag group of Italian soldiers, the residents go into hiding, thinking their island is under attack from the Germans. They assume this because the young men of the island's village have already been imprisoned by the Germans. The Italian brigade is soon accepted by the Greek villagers and they settle into the daily routines of the island hamlet. They even help repaint frescoes in the local church, organize soccer tournaments and win the hearts of the women in the village. They have no news from the outside world until an Italian pilot lands on the little Aegean paradise and fills them in on how the war has played out.

The British arrive and bring back the men from the island that were taken prisoners, and offer to take the Italians back to their home country. Montini goes home, but some of the men stay. He re-joins them four decades later on the little island that won a place in all their hearts.

FEATURED ACTORS
Diego Abatantuono (Nicola Lorusso)
Claudio Bigagli (Raffaele Montini)
Giuseppe Cederna (Antonio Farina)
Claudio Bisio (Corrado Noventa)
Gigio Alberti (Eliseo Strazzabosco)

DIRECTOR ~ Gabriele Salvatore

AWARDS WON

Best Foreign Film	1991 Academy Award

trivia clips

The Greek islands are very picturesque. The contrasts between the deep azure blue of sea and sky, the white of limestone crags and whitewashed buildings, and the burnt-orange of tiled roofs contribute dramatically to what strikes all visitors as a quality of light that is unique and not found anywhere else.

BEVERAGES

Arabic or Turkish Coffee (see index)

Sambuca (Italian anise and botanical flavoured liqueur)

Ouzo, an anise based spirit, is the national drink of Greece. It has a distinctive licorice flavour.

Ouzo can be presented dramatically. Pour into small serving glasses, put 2 to 3 coffee beans on top; then strike a match and bring it down to the surface of the liqueur. Serve to guests who must blow out the flame and make a wish! Remember to tell the guests to give the liqueur a moment to cool off before drinking.

The Greeks have been producing wine for centuries! Sample a variety, you are sure to find a number of them to your liking. With the main meal serve Greek white wines made with retsina such as: Kourtakis Retsina of Attica or Malamatinas Retsina. Kourtakis Apelia, or Kourtakis Patras Kouros are also good choices for white wine. If you would like to try some Greek red wine we recommend: Boutari Red or Kourtakis Vin de Crete Red.

MUSIC

There are lots of choices for Greek music. Here are a few to get you started: "Greek Folk Dances and Songs" (Orata), "Greek Archives Vol. 1-6" (FM), "Greek Dance-Along" (Rainbow), and "Greek Folk Favourites" (Tradition), this latter compilation features a variety of songs and traditional Greek instruments such as the pipiza, defi, dulcimer, and lute. One of the most popular singers in Greece is George Dalaras, his "Greek Voice" (Tropical Music) is a good starting point for a foray into more modern Greek music.

mediterraneo pizza

Yield: 6 to 8 slices

This pizza is in line with the film's setting and characters. What could be more Italian than pizza? In honour of the film's setting, we've developed a pizza with a Greek flair!

pizza dough

Yield: 1 12-inch crust

This recipe produces a European style thin crust pizza. If you are short of time you may use ready-made pizza dough. Most supermarkets now carry pizza dough, try to buy the fresh dough rather than the frozen kind. The dough recipe is easily doubled if you are using a larger pizza pan. You may also freeze the dough for later use.

1/2 cup	water		1 tsp	quick-rising (instant) dry yeast
1-1/2 tsp	olive or canola oil		1/2 tsp	salt
1-1/2 cups	all-purpose flour			

- In small saucepan, heat water with oil until at 120°F. In large bowl, combine flour, yeast and salt. With wooden spoon, gradually stir in water mixture until dough forms (you may need to use hands). Turn out dough onto lightly floured surface; knead for about 8 minutes or until smooth and elastic. Place in greased bowl, turning to grease all over. Cover with plastic wrap; let rise in warm draft-free place (an oven with the interior light turned on is ideal) until doubled in bulk, about 1 hour. Turn out dough onto lightly floured surface; and shape into disc. Roll out into 12-inch (30 cm) circle, letting dough rest, covered, if too elastic to roll. Sprinke a 12-inch (30 cm) pizza pan with cornmeal; center dough on pan. Let rest for 15 minutes. Press all over to form slightly raised rim.

mediterraneo pizza topping

2 tbsp	olive oil		3	tomatoes, thinly sliced
1 tbsp	fresh oregano, chopped (or 1 tsp dried)		1/3 cup	black olives, pitted and sliced (do not use canned)
1 tbsp	fresh basil, chopped		1 tbsp	capers, chopped
1	recipe pizza dough (see above)		1	green pepper, diced
2 cups	grated mozzarella cheese		1 cup	crumbled feta cheese

- Brush oil over pizza base. Sprinkle with mozzarella cheese. Arrange tomatoes in overlapping concentric circles over mozzarella. Sprinkle with oregano, basil, olives, capers and green pepper; sprinkle with feta cheese. Bake in bottom third of 500°F (260°C) oven for 10 minutes or until feta is soft and crust is golden and slightly puffed.

 Use low fat cheese.

trivia clips

The islands of Greece are divided into the Aegean Islands, including the Northern Sporades, the Cyclades, and the Dodecanese; the large island of Crete (also Kriti); and the Ionian Islands off the west coast.
About 70 percent of the country of Greece consists of mountains, the highest being Mount Olympus at 9,570 feet (2,917 meters) in Thessaly.

mediterraneo

greek shrimp with feta cheese serves 4

This is served as a side to the pizza.

2 tbsp	olive oil
2	cloves garlic, minced
1 cup	green onions, sliced
1/2 cup	celery, thinly sliced
1/4 cup	parsley, chopped
1	28 oz can tomatoes, drained
1 tbsp	fresh oregano, chopped (or 1/2 tsp dried oregano)
1/4 tsp	each salt and granulated sugar
1 lb	uncooked shrimp, peeled and deveined
1 cup	feta cheese

- Heat olive oil in a large skillet over medium high heat. Sauté garlic, onions and celery in oil until tender. Stir in parsley, coarsely chopped tomatoes and seasonings. Simmer uncovered 10 minutes or until sauce has thickened and is no longer runny. Stir shrimp into mixture; simmer 3 - 5 minutes, stirring occasionally, until cooked through.

- Spoon into a 9-inch round baking dish; sprinkle with feta cheese. Bake at 400°F for 10 - 12 minutes or until cheese begins to melt.
Serve immediately with bread to scoop up sauce.

SETTING THE STAGE

Picture yourself arriving on a Greek island... the most predominant colours in your mind's eye will probably be the blue and white that are used to paint the charming homes on the Greek islands. Use these colours to create a Greek taverna like atmosphere. Tablecloths and dinnerware should be white or vibrant blue. Mix the two together by using one colour for side plates or chargers and the other as the plate for the main meal. You could even pick up a fish net at a sporting goods store and lay it over your tablecloth. Set a shell by each place setting to bring a bit of the Aegean to your table. Place votive candles in small claypots. Use a potted plant such as a geranium or hydrangea as a centrepiece. If you have a clay amphora, a traditional Greek vessel for wine, put some vines in and around it, and use that on your table too. Make sure you have some of the enchanting Greek folk music playing in the background. Perhaps you and your guests may be inspired to try your hand at some Greek circle dancing, there's probably someone in your group who has tried this, or at least seen it in a movie. Enjoy your Mediterranean evening outdoors, weather permitting. This would really enhance the atmosphere.

trivia clips

The Greek language comes directly from that of the ancient Greeks. The modern literary language has kept many features of ancient Greek, but the spoken language includes words and grammar borrowed from other languages. At present, the spoken form of the language is recognized as the official form for government and education.

pretty
woman (1990)

It was the movie that made young starlet Julia Roberts, a household name. Before her debut in the film Pretty Woman, Roberts was still a largely unknown actress. She delighted audiences and set her compass towards stardom with this blockbuster movie alongside veteran heartthrob, Richard Gere. What were the magic ingredients that turned out such a great concoction? Stars who really did shine in their roles, and a sharp witty script that made this fairy tale with an edge, just that bit more believable and made us care as deeply for the lead characters as they eventually did for each other. We fell in love with them and a decade later enjoyed seeing them share the screen again in Runaway Bride. The film Pretty Woman, is a surprisingly successful variation on an old formula: boy meets girl, but complications exist. Wealthy, emotionally cool business tycoon, Edward Lewis (Richard Gere), meets Hollywood Boulevard hooker, Vivian Ward (Julia Roberts). He hires her to be his companion for a week, spruces her up, and introduces her to his social scene. Edward is a rich, ruthless businessman who specializes in taking over companies and then selling them off piece by piece. Vivian has found a way of surviving by working as a prostitute on Hollywood Boulevard. When she runs into the prince of her dreams, who comes along on four wheels instead of a horse, she at first does not recognize him as her saviour. Edward does not at first realize that she could be more than just a girl from the streets, but he changes his opinion after the first night with the beautiful, candid stranger. Vivian is the first person in a long time that is able to surprise him. Edward, with all his emotional baggage, can now see the light at the end of the tunnel. He is on his way to becoming a better person, whereas Vivian has received a chance to start over again. This romantic comedy with its hilarious complications, makes this film a real treat, and of course the fairy tale ending makes the viewer feel good!

FEATURED ACTORS
Richard Gere (Edward Lewis)
Julia Roberts (Vivian Ward)
Jason Alexander (Philip Stuckey)
Laura San Giacomo (Kit De Luca)
Ralph Bellamy (James Morse)

DIRECTOR ~ Garry Marshall

menu
oysters rockefeller • roasted salmon with orange herb-sauce • herbed steamed rice • california gingered fruit salsa sundaes • southern night caps

oysters rockefeller
serves 6 to 8

The original recipe for oysters Rockefeller, created at the New Orleans restaurant Antoine's in 1899, remains a secret to this day. The appetizer, oysters topped with a mixture of finely chopped greens and copious amounts of butter and then baked in their shells, was considered so rich that it had to be named after the richest man of the day, John D. Rockefeller. A few years later, no self-respecting restaurateur would be without his own version on the menu. This lighter version features spinach, watercress, green onions and grated Parmesan.

1	garlic clove	2 tbsp	Pernod or other anise-flavored liqueur
2 cups	loosely packed fresh spinach	1 tsp	fennel seeds, ground
1 bunch	watercress, stems trimmed	1 tsp	hot pepper sauce
1/2 cup	chopped green onions	1 lb	rock salt
3/4 cup	unsalted butter, room temperature	24	fresh oysters, shucked, shells reserved
1/2 cup	dry breadcrumbs	1/4 cup	freshly grated Parmesan cheese

• Position rack in top third of oven and preheat to 450°F. Finely chop garlic in processor. Add spinach, watercress and green onions to garlic. Process, using on/off turns, until mixture is finely chopped. Transfer mixture to medium bowl. Set aside.

• Combine butter, breadcrumbs, Pernod, fennel and hot sauce in processor. Process until well blended. Return spinach mixture to processor. Process, using on/off turns, just until mixtures are blended. Season with salt and pepper. (Can be made 8 hours ahead. Cover; chill.)

• Sprinkle rock salt over large baking sheet to depth of 1/2 inch. Arrange oysters in half shells over the rock salt. Top each oyster with 1-tablespoon spinach mixture. Sprinkle with cheese.

• Bake until spinach mixture browns on top, about 8 minutes.

Count Agoston Haraszthy de Moksa started the California grape and wine industries. He planted Tokay, Zinfandel, and Shiras varieties from his native Hungary in Buena Vista, California, in 1857.

trivia clips
Richard is the second of five children born to Homer and Doris Gere. He attended the University of Massachusetts, but dropped out to pursue acting.
In 1999, Richard Gere was voted People Magazine's "Sexiest Man Alive".

pretty
woman (1990)

roasted salmon with orange-herb sauce *serves 6*

1	large orange, unpeeled, sliced
1	large onion, halved, thinly sliced
1-1/2 tbsp	olive oil
6	3-ounce skinless salmon fillets

3 tbsp	fresh dill, chopped
1/2 cup	orange juice
1/4 cup	green onions, thinly sliced
1-1/2 tbsp	fresh lemon juice
	additional unpeeled orange slices for garnish

- Preheat oven to 400°F. Place orange slices in single-layer in 13x 9x2-inch glass baking dish.

- Top with onion slices. Drizzle with oil. Sprinkle with salt and pepper. Roast until onion is brown and tender, about 25 minutes. Remove from oven. Increase oven temperature to 450°F.

- Push orange and onion slices to side of baking dish. Arrange salmon in center of dish. Sprinkle with salt, pepper and 1-1/2 tablespoons dill. Spoon orange and onion slices atop salmon. Roast until salmon is opaque in center, about 8 minutes.

- Meanwhile, mix orange juice, green onions, lemon juice and remaining 1 1/2 tablespoons dill in small bowl. Transfer salmon to platter. Spoon onion alongside; discard roasted orange slices.

- Pour orange sauce over fish. Garnish with additional orange slices.

herbed steamed rice *serves 6*

2 cups	long-grain rice
1/2 cup	chicken broth
2	garlic cloves, minced and mashed into a paste with 1/2 teaspoon salt
1 tbsp	fresh ginger root, peeled and minced

1/4 cup	scallions, finely chopped
2 tsp	fresh lemon juice
1 tsp	soy sauce
1/2 tsp	salt, or to taste
1 cup	packed cilantro sprigs, washed well, spun dry, and finely chopped

- In a large stock pot put 4 cups water. When it comes to a boil, add rice and return to a boil stirring. Boil rice 10 minutes. Drain rice in a large sieve and rinse. Set sieve over another pot of boiling water (rice should not touch water) and steam rice, covered with a kitchen towel and lid, 20 minutes, or until tender (check water level in pot occasionally, adding water if necessary).

- In a large bowl stir together remaining ingredients except cilantro, and add rice. Toss mixture until combined well. Cool rice to room temperature and stir in cilantro.

AWARDS

Best Actress (Julia Roberts)	1991 People's Choice Award
Best Actress— in Musical or Comedy (Julia Roberts)	1991 Golden Globe Award
Best Film	1991 PEO

trivia clips

A Buddhist for over a decade, Gere was banned from the Oscars once after making anti-China comments on the air at the 1993 ceremony. Gere is an accomplished pianist and music writer. He actually wrote and played the song in one of his scenes in the film.
Richard Gere's salary for the Runaway Bride, $12,000,000.

pretty
woman (1990)

BEVERAGES

Before dinner, have champagne of course, with fresh strawberries in each glass! Or you may want to serve a Kir Royale, which is made by topping champagne with Crème de Cassis, a liqueur made from blackberries.

With dinner serve some California white wine like: Ernest and Julio Gallo North Coast Chardonnay, Glen Ellen Chardonnay, Mondavi Woodbridge Sauvignon Blanc or Wente Chardonnay.

MUSIC

The soundtrack entitled "Pretty Woman" (EMI) is available and features hit singles by Roy Orbison and Roxette.

SETTING THE STAGE

Make the evening elegant, yet informal. Use your best china and silverware. First set the table with a crisp white tablecloth, and add fancy plates with chargers (a large, usually ornate metal or glass decorative base for dinner plates). Don't forget to use real linen napkins. Place white floating candles in a crystal bowl or set out some candles on a pretty plate or tray, and intersperse some greenery between the candles and sprinkle a few silver sparkles on the table.

Weather permitting set up your dinner outdoors on your patio or deck. String up some lights to create some Hollywood sparkle, and maybe even reminisce about fairytale moments in your own life!

california style gingered fruit salsa sundaes serves 6

1 cup	raspberries	10	large strawberries, finely diced
2 tbsp	sugar	1/2 cup	fresh pineapple, finely diced
3 to 4 tbsp	minced crystallized ginger, or to taste	1/2 tsp	balsamic vinegar
1	small firm-ripe mango, finely diced (about 2/3 cup)	1	container super-premium vanilla ice cream

- In a bowl, crush raspberries coarse with sugar and let stand 5 minutes. Stir in ginger, mango, strawberries, pineapple, and vinegar. Scoop ice cream into 6 sundae dishes and spoon fruit salsa over it.

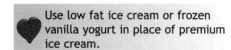 Use low fat ice cream or frozen vanilla yogurt in place of premium ice cream.

southern night-caps serves 4 to 6

Make this drink with decaffeinated coffee if it is a late evening, this soothing drink is ideal for sipping while watching the video.

2 cups	hot espresso or strong filter brewed coffee		sugar to taste
1/4 cup	coffee liqueur	1/2 cup	whipping cream
2 tbsp	Southern Comfort		grated semisweet chocolate

- Combine espresso, coffee liqueur and Southern Comfort in medium bowl. Flavor mixture with sugar to taste. Divide among 4 cups. Whisk whipping cream in heavy small saucepan over medium heat until hot and frothy, about 2 minutes. Spoon hot cream over coffees, dividing evenly. Sprinkle grated chocolate over and serve.

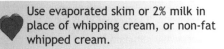 Use evaporated skim or 2% milk in place of whipping cream, or non-fat whipped cream.

trivia clips

A early version of the script had Vivian addicted to drugs.
Julia Robert's head was superimposed on Shelley Michelle's body for the poster.
Richard Gere's hair is brown on the poster, but graying in the movie.

the lover (1992)

menu vietnamese spring rolls • vietnamese dipping sauce • pho (vietnamese beef and noodle soup) • vietnamese style coffee • saigon style sweet bananas

This romantic tale of forbidden passionate love is an adaptation of a novel by Marguerite Duras. The setting is exotic French Indochina (Vietnam) in 1929. The main character is a young girl from France, who has been sent to boarding school in Saigon. While there, she meets a wealthy, handsome Chinese aristocrat. Sparks fly as soon as the two lay eyes on each other. Differences are set aside, and the two are soon arranging erotic trysts in his "bachelor room". From the onset, their relationship is written in the stars as doomed, —in order to inherit his father's wealth, he must go through an arranged marriage to a Chinese girl. The girl also has complications in her family life. Her brother is a drug addict and her mother is mentally unstable. Neither family would approve of an inter-racial marriage. Though their feelings run deep, the couple can not break free of their circumstances. This tastefully filmed sensual story is a pleasure to watch.

vietnamese spring rolls

Yield: 30 rolls

8 oz	chicken breast, boneless and skinless
2 tbsp	soy sauce
1 tbsp	hoisin sauce
1 tbsp	water
2 tsp	frozen orange juice concentrate
1 tsp	peanut butter
1/2 tsp	Oriental chili paste
1 tsp	sesame oil
2 tsp	cornstarch
8	Shiitake mushrooms, dried

2 oz	cellophane noodles
2 tbsp	peanut or safflower oil
1 tbsp	fresh ginger, minced
2	garlic cloves, minced
2	green onions, minced
1	red pepper, julienned
4 tbsp	fresh cilantro, chopped
30	rice paper triangles (or 16 rounds)
6 cups	vegetable oil (for deep frying)

- Cut chicken into 1-1/2 x 1/2-inch strips. In bowl, blend soy sauce and hoisin sauces, water, orange juice concentrate, peanut butter, chili paste and sesame oil until smooth. Stir in cornstarch. Add chicken and stir to coat; marinate for 15 minutes.

- Cover mushrooms with warm water; soak for 15 to 50 minutes or until softened. Drain and rinse; discard stems and slice caps into thin strips.

- Meanwhile, break noodles into 1-1/2 inch long pieces. Place in bowl and cover with water; soak for 5 minutes, then drain. In saucepan of boiling water, cook noodles for 2 minutes.

- Drain and rinse with cold water; drain well.

- In wok or skillet, heat peanut oil over med-high heat; cook ginger, garlic and onions for 30 seconds. Add red pepper and mushrooms; cook for 3 minutes. Add chicken with marinade; cook for 3 to 4 minutes or just until chicken is

no longer pink inside. Stir in noodles and cilantro; let cool.

- Dip rice papers, one at a time, into warm water to soften; lay out on damp tea towels in a single layer. Place about 2 tablespoons filling in centre of each triangular sheet (or 1/4 cup in each round sheet). Fold up bottom over filling; fold sides over and roll up tightly. (Rolls can be covered with damp tea towel in separate layers and refrigerated for up to 8 hours)

- In wok or a deep pot, heat oil over medium-high heat to 375°F. Fry rolls, in batches, for about 5 minutes or until crisp and golden on all sides. Drain on rack. Makes 16 large or 30 small rolls.

♥ Instead of deep-frying, steam spring rolls in greased steamer for 5 minutes, or bake for 20 minutes in 400°F oven.

🕐 Buy ready-made spring rolls in the frozen food section of Asian supermarkets.

FEATURED ACTORS
Jane March (the young girl)
Tony Leung Kar-Fei (Chinese aristocrat)
Frederique Meininger (mother)
Arnaud Giovaninetti (older brother)
Melvil Poupaud (younger brother)

DIRECTOR ~ Jean-Jacques Annaud

AWARDS WON
Best Music (Gabriel Yared)	1992 French Academy of Cinema Award

trivia clips

The country has a coastline of nearly 1,440 miles (2,317 kilometers), much of which fronts on the South China Sea. Border countries are China, Cambodia, and Laos. The latter two countries, along with Vietnam, constituted the former French Indochina.

the lover (1992)

BEVERAGES

Vietnamese beer would be ideal. Try: Hue Beer, or Saigon Export Beer.

Otherwise, stick with Asian brews like: Sapporo (Japan), San Miguel Pale Pils (Philippines), Tiger Beer (Singapore) and Tsingtao (China).

MUSIC

"The Lover" soundtrack (Varese Sarabande) is available. If you wish to listen to some authentic music from Vietnam, try: "Vietnamese Traditional Music" (Oliver Suddei) by Pham Duc Thanh; he is originally from Vietnam, but now lives in Canada.

vietnamese dipping sauce (for spring rolls)

Yield: 1 cup

1	carrot	1/4 cup	fish sauce
2	garlic clove, minced	1/4 cup	lime juice
1	shallot, minced	1/4 cup	water
1	hot chili pepper, minced	3 tbsp	rice wine vinegar
2 tbsp	sugar		

- Shave the carrot into thin strips with a vegetable peeler. Stack the strips up 3-4 layers high and cut lengthwise into hair-thin slivers. Combine the garlic, shallot, chili, and sugar and pound to a smooth paste with a mortar and pestle or use a food processor. Work in the fish sauce, lime juice, water and vinegar.

- Transfer the sauce to a bowl and stir in the carrot.

Buy ready-made dipping sauce at Asian supermarkets.

pho (vietnamese beef and noodle soup)

serves 4

This soup is a substantial meal! Serve in deep oriental soup bowls that can be purchased for a reasonable price at Asian stores or markets.

1 lb	boneless sirloin, fat removed and cut into fine julienne strips	6	leaves Romaine lettuce, shredded
2	cloves garlic	1/4 lb	vermicelli (rice noodles) broken into 2-inch lengths
1-inch	piece ginger, peeled		salt, to taste
1	stick cinnamon	2 tbsp	fresh lime juice
2 quarts	water	2 cups	fresh bean sprouts
1	large bunch cilantro	1/2 tsp	dried red pepper flakes
6	fresh basil leaves, shredded		

- Combine beef, garlic, ginger, cinnamon and 2 quarts water. Bring to a boil, skim off scum.

- Reduce heat to low and simmer gently until meat is tender, about 45 minutes. Continue skimming and keeping level of liquid constant by replenishing with fresh water. Meanwhile, rinse and chop the cilantro. When meat is tender, remove garlic, cinnamon and ginger. Add noodles and simmer until tender, about 5 minutes.

- Remove soup from heat, stir in salt, lime juice, bean sprouts, pepper, cilantro, basil and Romaine. Adjust seasoning and serve piping hot.

trivia clips

The Vietnamese are descended from both Chinese and Thai peoples. Originating in southern China, the Vietnamese people pushed southward over the course of several hundred years to occupy much of the current area of Vietnam. A strong sense of national identity was produced as a result of the struggle for political independence from China.

continued

vietnamese style coffee Yield: 1 serving

Special pots to brew this type of coffee are available at Asian supermarkets as is a special coffee blend; however you can replicate this style of coffee using any strong, rich tasting brew.

2 tbsp	sweetened condensed milk		1 cup	strong black coffee

- Place the milk in the bottom of an 8 ounce glass. Carefully pour in coffee, trying not to disturb the layer of milk. Stir milk up from bottom (serve coffee with long-handled spoons such as those for ice cream sundaes) and sip coffee. There may be some milk left at the bottom of the glass when you are finished.

- This coffee may also be served iced. Add ice cubes on top of the sweetened condensed milk and proceed as above.

 Use non-fat sweetened condensed milk.

saigon style sweet bananas serves 6

Many Vietnamese desserts are based on bananas. Banana desserts are usually simple to prepare, but quite tasty!

3 tbsp	shredded fresh coconut		4 tbsp	fresh lime juice
1/4 cup	unsalted butter		6 tbsp	orange liqueur
1 tbsp	grated ginger root		3 tsp	toasted sesame seeds
	grated zest of 1 orange			lime slices, for garnish
6	bananas			ice-cream (vanilla is best) to serve along side
1/4 cup	granulated sugar			

- Heat a large non-stick frying pan until hot. Add the coconut and cook, stirring constantly, for about 1 minute until lightly coloured. Remove coconut from the pan and allow to cool.

- Heat the butter in the frying pan until it melts. Add the ginger and orange zest and mix well.

- Peel and slice the bananas lengthwise. Place the bananas, cut-side down in the butter mixture and cook for 1 to 2 minutes or until the sauce mixture starts to become sticky. Turn to coat bananas in the sauce.

- Remove the bananas from the pan and place on heated serving plates. Keep warm.

- Return the pan to the heat and add the orange liqueur, stirring well to blend. Ignite with a long match, allow the flames to die down, then pour over the bananas.

- Sprinkle with the coconut and sesame seeds. Serve at once, decorated with slices of lime and a scoop of ice cream on the side.

 Use non-hydrogenated margarine instead of butter. Use low fat ice cream or frozen yogurt.

SETTING THE STAGE

An oriental or Asian theme is required. Prior to your event, shop in Asian stores to purchase the deep bowls required for the Pho. Ordinary soup bowls won't do—they're too small! Buy some that have an oriental motif. Don't forget to pick up some chopsticks, oriental spoons and some small bowls for the dipping sauce. You may also wish to purchase a square platter for the spring rolls. Set your table with a red tablecloth and place a lace tablecloth over it for an interesting effect. Use oriental paper lanterns for subdued lighting around the dining area. Paper fans may be placed on walls for decoration. Bamboo place mats would suit the theme or use some made of silk or a rich looking brocade in shades of red. Light small red and gold votive candles and place around the room in clusters. Enjoy the meal and linger over the delicious Vietnamese coffee!

trivia clips

Vietnamese culture, however, still reflects the strong influence of Chinese civilization. Nearly 100 years of French rule instilled many European cultural traits as well. The Vietnamese continue to maintain their own culture through such customs as attaching great importance to the family and observing rites honouring their ancestors.

the red
violin (1998)

This Canadian-Italian production features an interesting story about the journey of a famous and perhaps cursed violin through a series of different owners. The story is told in episodes. The film begins with an authority on violins, Charles Morritz, as he investigates the violin's authenticity. His quest links the four stories in the film. The violin was created in 1681, by an Italian master craftsman named Nicolo Bussotti. In this story line, we meet the master craftsmen and become engrossed in the perils that affect his family. The second episode features young orphans at an orphanage, under the tutelage of monks in 18th century Austria, playing the red violin. One young boy in particular, creates magic on the stringed instrument, but alas the violin does not stay long in his hands. The next owner is British composer Frederick Pope, a talented man with his share of idiosyncrasies. Many woman find him attractive, but he is having an erotic affair with novelist Victoria Byrd. This owner's life also ends in tragedy. After his death, his servant carries the red violin with him as he returns to his homeland, China. The final tale follows the fate of the red violin during the Cultural Revolution in China, a time when anything connected with Western culture was deemed dangerous and ordered destroyed. Somehow the red violin escapes this date with destiny and survives to end up at an auction in Montréal.

FEATURED ACTORS
Samuel L. Jackson (Charles Morritz)
Don McKellar (Evan Williams)
Carlo Cecchi (Nicolo Bussotti)
Irene Grazioli (Anna Bussotti)
Jean-Luc Bideau (Georges Poussin)

DIRECTOR ~ François Girard

menu

antipasto platter or artichoke bruschetta (see index) • continental style veal cutlets (see index) • "smashed" potatoes with caramelized onions (see index) • trio or four seasons salad (see index) • green tea ice cream (see index)

This eclectic menu follows the path of the violin. The starter is Italian, the main dish is Austrian and the side is English. The dessert is an ice cream flavoured with one of China's favourite beverages—green tea.

trivia clips

Members of the violin family have four strings tuned in intervals of fifths (except the double bass, which is tuned in fourths), an arched bridge and unfretted fingerboard, and a body that acts as a resonator of the instrument's sound.

trivia clips

The violin family appeared in Europe in the early 16th century and by the mid-16th century was found in paintings of the period. Since then, these instruments; the violin, viola, violoncello (or cello), and double bass have been the major component of symphony orchestras and chamber music ensembles all around the world.
A famous painting "The Death of Marat," is recreated in the film. This image recreated on film, occurs when British composer Frederick Pope leans back in the tub with the letter from his lover in his hand.

continued

BEVERAGES

A white wine such as Weingut Undhof Riesling-Sp‰tlese Kremser Kˆgl (Austria) is a good choice if you wish to serve wine. Polz Chardonnay (Austria) and Daruvarski Rizling (Croatia) would also be suitable choices.

English or Chinese tea after dinner.

MUSIC

Apart from the obvious choice of the wonderful soundtrack "The Red Violin" (Sony), there is an astonishing array of violin and fiddle musical selections. For something with a Celtic influence try anything by the following trio of Canadian performers: Natalie MacMaster, a Cape Breton fiddler who has two excellent CD's, the appropriately titled "Fit as a Fiddle" (Rounder) and "My Roots are Showing" (Rounder). Another Canadian solo artist is Ashley MacIssac from Nova Scotia. He has won acclaim for his "Hi How Are You Today" (A&M). The Chieftains "Fire in the Kitchen" (RCA), is also a delight for fiddler lovers!

If you prefer a Latin sound try: "Violincito" (Sony International) by Reyes Del Corrido or "Violin Romantico" (Mediterraneo) featuring various artists. "Violins of Europe" (Ocora) and "Violoini E Seranate a Canosa" (Columbia), feature various artists and tunes from a number of European countries. Finally, for classical violin music we suggest: "Violin Concertos" (Sony) by the English Chamber Orchestra, or "Violin Concertosî (EMI) featuring the music of Beethoven. Perhaps the best thing to do is listen to this marvelous and versatile instrument in a number of various genres to truly appreciate how amazing it really is!

SETTING THE STAGE

To continue with the theme of following the path of the red violin we suggest the following: serve the appetizer on ceramic or rustic looking dishes that look somewhat Mediterranean. The main meal should be served on a table set with red accents as red is considered lucky in Chinese culture. Perhaps red napkins or a centrepiece of lovely red flowers such as carnations in a crystal vase would be suitable. You could even use a red table runner. The table setting and dinnerware should be formal. If you have something in a floral motif that could reflect the English aspect of the violin's journey. The Austrian aspect is in the choice of wine and perhaps the playing of Beethoven during dinner. If you have a tea service whether traditional or Oriental you could use that to formally serve tea after dinner, just as is done in both England and China!

AWARDS WON

Best Original Score (John Corigliano)	1999 Academy Award
Best Motion Picture (François Girard/Niv Fichman)	1999 Genie Award
Best Screenplay (François Girard /Don McKellar)	1998 Genie Award
Best Music Score (John Corigliano)	1998 Genie Award
Best Overall Sound (Jo Caron /Bernard Gariépy-Strobl/ Claude La Haye/Hans Peter Strobl	1998 Genie Award
Best Achievement in Art Direction /Production Design (François Séguin)	1999 Genie Award
Best Achievement in Cinematography (Alan Dostie)	1999 Genie Award
Best Achievement in Costume Design (Renée April)	1999 Genie Award
Best Achievement in Direction (François Girard)	1999 Genie Award

trivia clips

The look of instruments in the violin family became standardized in the late 16th century. By that time they shared a sound hole in their bodies shaped like the letter f, square shoulders, and a belly and back that protruded and projected past the ribs. The "Messiah" violin by Stradivari is considered one of the finest examples of the Italian masters.

trivia clips

The greatest violins were from Italy, and no city was more renowned for its instruments than Cremona. The Amati family of Cremona, produced instruments that set the international standard for beauty of sound. Cremona has another famous son, Antonio Stradivari, whose name is still synonymous with the finest violins.

titanic

(1997)

It was the year's most popular movie hands down! A worldwide phenomenon occurred; fans lined up for hours to buy tickets and some theatre showings sold out. Due to the popularity of the film and in recognition of this historical sea disaster which occurred on April 15, 1912, numerous television documentaries and books were released that retold the story of the ill-fated maiden voyage of the R.M.S. Titanic. The film was ranked (at the time) the most expensive film in Hollywood history. It had the backing of two major film studios behind the production, 20th Century-Fox and Paramount studios were both involved. Canadian writer-director James Cameron, used state of the art digital special effects to make this historical story come to life.

The story begins with an American treasure seeker combing the waters of the North Atlantic. Inspired by the discovery of the Titanic in 1985, Brock Lovett (played by Bill Paxton) searches for priceless artifacts said to be still on board the ill-fated ship. His team searches through the remains of the ship and actually does find numerous artifacts still intact. Lovett was searching for gold and diamonds said to be still on board the ship, but instead he finds a nude drawing of a young woman wearing an exquisite necklace. The media gets wind of Lovett's search and the discovery. Not soon after, a 102 year old woman reveals that she is the person in the portrait. Rose (played by Gloria Stuart), is invited to the wreckage site and she re-tells the story of how she survived the horrific tragedy, the true love she met on the voyage and the fate of the many who did not survive. With her testimony, we are taken back in time and given a glimpse of how things might have been on the ill-fated super liner. This fictional, bittersweet story made us realize the immensity of the awful human tragedy that occurred on that fateful day in history when so many lost their lives not far from the shores of Canada.

menu — oysters rockefeller (see index) • cream of pea soup with a dash of mint · filet mignon lili • baby potatoes with rosemary (see index) • puff pastry parcels with salmon and rice • vanilla cream in puff pastry

The first 3 items on this menu were featured on board the Titanic.

cream of pea soup with a dash of mint serves 4 - 6

1	small onion, finely chopped		5 cups	chicken broth
2 tbsp	unsalted butter		1 cup	packed fresh mint leaves (reserve a few for garnish)
2 lb	frozen peas		1 cup	heavy cream

• In a large, heavy saucepan sauté onion in butter with salt to taste, over moderately low heat, stirring occasionally, until softened. Add peas and 3 cups stock and simmer, uncovered, until peas are tender, 5 to 7 minutes. Stir in mint and remaining 2 cups stock and remove pan from heat. In a blender purée soup in batches until very smooth(use caution when blending hot liquids), forcing each batch through a sieve into a

large bowl. (Discard solids in sieve between batches.) Whisk in cream (or cream-yogurt mixture) and salt and pepper to taste. If serving soup cold, chill, covered. If serving soup hot, reheat but do not let boil. Garnish with additional mint leaves.

 Use evaporated skim milk in place of heavy cream.

trivia clips

The Titanic sank during the last years of the Edwardian era before World War I. It was a decadent era where the privileged ate and drank with abandon. Food was rich and fatty, and courses were accompanied with selections of wine and liquor.

trivia clips

The movie cost about $200 million to make. Blueprints of the real Titanic were followed during construction of the replica of the ship for the film at Fox's custom-built Rosarito, Mexico studio. A hydraulics system moved the model in a 17-million-gallon water tank.

titanic

continued

filet mignon lili

serves 4

This dish was featured on board the Titanic in first class as a dinner entrée.

3 tbsp	butter	salt to taste	
2 tbsp	olive oil	freshly ground pepper to taste	
3/4 lb	Cremini mushrooms, thinly sliced		
		4	5-oz filet mignon steaks (each about 3/4-inch thick)
1/2 cup	shallots, minced		
4	garlic cloves, minced	1/2 cup	Madeira wine
1 tbsp	fresh thyme, chopped	1-1/2 cups	canned or homemade beef broth
1/2 tbsp	fresh parsley, chopped	1/2 cup	whipping cream

- Melt 2 tablespoons butter with 1 tablespoon oil in heavy large skillet over medium heat.

- Add mushrooms and sauté until tender, about 10 minutes. Add 1/4 cup shallots and half of garlic and sauté until shallots are soft, about 3 minutes. Stir in thyme and parsley; season with salt and pepper. Transfer mushroom mixture to medium bowl.

- Melt remaining 1 tablespoon butter with 1 tablespoon oil in same skillet over medium-high heat.

- Sprinkle steaks with salt and pepper. Add to skillet and cook to desired doneness, about 3 minutes per side

for medium-rare. Transfer steaks to plate. Add remaining 1/4 cup shallots and garlic to same skillet. Sauté 2 minutes. Add Madeira and boil until reduced by half, about 3 minutes.

- Add broth and boil until mixture is reduced to 2/3 cup, about 6 minutes. Add cream and boil until sauce thickens slightly, about 2 minutes. Stir in mushroom mixture. Season sauce to taste with salt and pepper. Return steaks to skillet and cook until heated through, about 1 minute.

- Transfer to plates. Spoon sauce over and serve.

FEATURED ACTORS
Leonardo Di Caprio (Jack Dawson)
Kate Winslet (Rose DeWitt Bukater)
Billy Zane (Cal Hockley)
Kathy Bates (Molly Brown)
Frances Fisher (Ruth DeWitt Bukater)
Gloria Stuart (Old Rose)

DIRECTOR ~
James Cameron Producer / Screenwriter / Editor / Director

AWARDS WON

Best Art Direction-Set Decoration Michael Ford	1997 Academy Award
Best Art Direction-Set Decoration Peter Lamont	1997 Academy Award
Best Cinematography Russell Carpenter	1997 Academy Award
Best Costume Design Deborah Scott	1997 Academy Award
Best Director James Cameron	1997 Academy Award
Best Film Editing James Cameron	1997 Academy Award
Best Film Editing Conrad Buff	1997 Academy Award
Best Film Editing Richard A. Harris	1997 Academy Award
Best Original Dramatic Score James Horner	1997 Academy Award
Best Picture	1997 Academy Award
Best Song Will Jennings	1997 Academy Award
Best Song James Horner	1997 Academy Award
Best Sound Gary Summers	1997 Academy Award
Best Sound Tom Johnson	1997 Academy Award
Best Sound Mark Ulano	1997 Academy Award
Best Sound Gary Rydstrom	1997 Academy Award
Best Sound Effects Editing Christopher Boyes	1997 Academy Award
Best Sound Effects Editing Tom Bellfort	1997 Academy Award

trivia clips

The British steamer Carpathia picked up the Titanic's SOS and radioed back, "Coming hard." Several hours later she rescued 712 passengers and crewmen from the Titanic's lifeboats. The film, Titanic, stayed at the top of the U.S. box office for 3 months. It was the most expensive film ever made up until that time. It grossed over $1.6 billion dollars internationally.

trivia clips

When the accident occurred, there was little excitement among the passengers. They were told only that there might be a slight delay. The ship's orchestra continued to play popular tunes. But the Titanic's bow was settling deeper by the minute. When the command was finally given to enter the lifeboats, many passengers still refused to believe that the ship was in real danger.

titanic

(1997)

BEVERAGES

Prior to dinner serve your favourite apertifs. With dinner wine is a must. Serve the following with the filet mignon: Casa Dos Vinhos Fine Old Madeira (Portugal) or Tedeschi Amarone Della Valpoilcella (Italy) or for a more full-bodied red try Banrock Station Shiraz Cabernet Sauvignon (Australia) or even Bersano Barbera D'Asti. With the salmon try: Fazi-Battaglia Sangiovese (Italy) or Banrock Station Unwooded Chardonnay (Australia)

MUSIC

"Titanic" the original soundtrack is available, it features the hit song by "My Heart Will Go On" by Canadian superstar Celine Dion.

puff pastry parcels with salmon and rice
serves 4

1/2 cup	long-grain white rice
2 tbsp	butter
1/2 cup	minced leek
6 oz	fresh shittake mushrooms, stemmed, chopped
2 sheets	frozen puff pastry (approx. one 17-1/4-ounce package), thawed
4	6-ounce (4 x 2-1/2-inch) skinless salmon fillet
1	egg beaten with 1 tablespoon water

Dill Sauce:

2/3 cup	bottled clam juice
1/2 cup	dry white wine
1 1/4 cups	crème fraîche or whipping cream
3 tbsp	minced fresh dill

- Bring medium saucepan of salted water to boil. Add rice; boil and uncovered until just tender, about 18 minutes. Drain.

- Melt butter in heavy, medium sized skillet over medium-low heat. Add leek; sauté until beginning to soften, about 4 minutes. Add mushrooms. Cover skillet; cook until mushrooms release their juices, stirring occasionally, about 5 minutes. Uncover skillet. Increase heat to medium-high; sauté until liquid evaporates, about 3 minutes. Transfer to bowl. Add rice.

- Season with salt and pepper. Cool completely.

- Preheat oven to 400˚F. Next, butter a large baking sheet. Roll out 1 pastry sheet on floured surface to 12-inch square. Cut into 4 equal squares. Divide rice mixture among centers of squares, mounding in oval shape with ends toward 2 corners of pastry. Set salmon atop rice.

- Sprinkle with salt and pepper. Bring pastry corners up around salmon (pastry will not enclose salmon completely.

- Roll out remaining pastry sheet on floured surface to 13-inch square. Cut into 4 equal squares.

- Lay 1 square atop each salmon fillet, tucking corners under bottom pastry to enclose salmon completely. Pinch edges together to seal, brushing with egg mixture if necessary to adhere. Arrange salmon packages, seam side down, on prepared baking sheet. Cover and chill 30 minutes. (Can be made 8 hours ahead. Keep chilled.)

- Brush top of pastry with egg mixture. Bake until golden about 30 minutes.

- Make dill sauce while salmon is baking: Combine clam juice and wine in heavy small stainless steel saucepan. Boil until reduced to 1/3 cup, about 5 minutes. Reduce heat to medium. Whisk in crème fraîche. Boil until reduced to 1 cup, about 5 minutes. Remove from heat. Stir in dill. Season with salt and pepper.

- Transfer salmon to plates. Spoon Dill Sauce around and serve.

trivia clips

Since there were not enough lifeboats, many of the men gallantly insisted that women and children be allowed into them first. Husbands, separated from their wives and children, were forced to remain aboard as the ship sank deeper into the icy waters. There were acts of cowardice and some lifeboats pulled away half empty.
Some of the first class passengers paid the equivalent of $124,000 in today's dollars for the ocean voyage.

titanic

continued

vanilla cream
in puff pastry
serves 12 to 16

Don't worry about the fact that this decadent dessert serves so many! Leftovers won't last long and we're sure that your guests will want seconds!

2 cups	evaporated 2% milk	2 tbsp	clear gelatin (Knox)
2 cups	milk	1/2 cup	cold water
8	egg yolks	1/2 cup	boiled water
1 cup	granulated sugar	2 cups	whipping cream
4 tsp	vanilla sugar (or substitute equal parts vanilla and sugar)	1 package	(16 ounces) puff pastry
1 cup	flour		powdered sugar for garnish
			strawberries for garnish (optional)

- Bring the evaporated milk and regular milk to a very gentle boil in a double boiler. While waiting for the milk to boil, in a separate bowl mix together the yolks, granulated sugar and vanilla sugar at medium speed with a mixer. Add flour to the yolk mixture until blended.

- Remove 2 cups of milk from the double boiler. Add this milk to the flour mixture while continuously beating at low speed. When blended, return this mixture to the milk still in the double boiler and continue to cook until thick while stirring v ery frequently.

- Mix together gelatin with the cold water, let stand for 1 minute and then add boiling water, mixing well with a fork or small whisk.

- Add the gelatin to your custard mixture in the double boiler and continue to cook for about 5 minutes, continually stirring as it thickens. Cool custard in ice water when removed from heat.

- In a separate bowl, beat the whipping cream until peaks form. Fold the whipped cream into the cooled custard (make sure the custard has cooled to room temperature before adding the whipped cream). Refrigerate this mixture for about 20 minutes so that it stiffens a bit and is easier to spread.

- Trim the edges of the puff pastry sheets to fit a deep tray or baking dish. Place one layer of puff pastry on bottom.

- Spread evenly with custard and then place second layer of puff pastry on top, pressing down slightly. Refrigerate for at least 4 hours. Sprinkle with powdered sugar on top prior to serving and cut into oblong pieces. Garnish with strawberry fans or chocolate dipped strawberries if so desired.

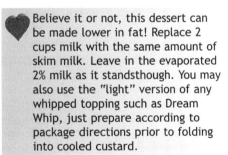 Believe it or not, this dessert can be made lower in fat! Replace 2 cups milk with the same amount of skim milk. Leave in the evaporated 2% milk as it standsthough. You may also use the "light" version of any whipped topping such as Dream Whip, just prepare according to package directions prior to folding into cooled custard.

SETTING THE STAGE

Prior to the event, send out invitations to your guests on fine writing paper in calligraphy styled writing. Put invitations in small, miniature bottles or roll into scrolls, and hand deliver them.

During the ship's maiden voyage all stops were pulled out! Only the finest china, silverware, serving pieces and crystal were used on the Titanic for her first class passengers. This menu should be served course by course with short pauses between courses to encourage conversation between guests. Use elegant china, place cards and crisp white linens to create a formal atmosphere. Add fancy plates with chargers (a large, usually ornate metal or glass decorative base for dinner plates). If you have any antique plates or serving pieces, use them to create an old world elegance. Prior to the event, scout for antique serving pieces at local garage sales or thrift stores. If you don't have any formal serving pieces, you can rent these items along with matching cutlery and other tableware. Pick up a few nautical items to decorate the house with, or search for small model replicas of the Titanic and use at place settings. Place white floating candles in a crystal bowl and sprinkle a few silver sparkles on the table. Buy a small floral arrangement to use as a centrepiece. For added elegance at the end of the meal, make available a platter of fresh fruits and cheeses, along with a variety of liqueurs for guests to sip with their coffee. Serve coffee and cigars (if desired) in another room to recreate the atmosphere of a drawing room or library.

trivia clips

Some experts say that had the lookout not sighted the iceberg and the helmsman not turned the wheel, the Titanic would probably have hit the iceberg head on. It is then likely that only the bow sections of the ship would have been flooded and, though seriously crippled, she would have remained afloat and been able to reach her destination.
Titanic received a record-tying 14 Oscar nominations.

train de vie (1998)

The setting is a small Jewish village or shtetl, in Eastern Europe during the summer of 1941. The village is in an uproar as the local village fool, Shlomo, has brought terrible news. The Nazi's are destroying entire Jewish villages and they are headed in their direction! A meeting of the village men takes place and Shlomo proves to be a visionary. He proposes a plan that is so crazy—that it must succeed! Rather than be deported, he suggests that they should buy a train and deport themselves. The villagers are elated, there is a way after all to avoid the fate of their brethren! Soon big plans are under way and almost everyone in the village is involved. The tailor is busy sewing Nazi uniforms for those Jews who will be impersonating officers of the Third Reich on the train carrying the deportees. Other villagers are fixing and painting the old rickety train they have managed to put together, while others are learning how to be conductors and engineers by reading old manuals on how to operate a train. Each of the villagers has unique comical traits, from the resident Marxist to the man who was selected to be the German commander, Mordechai, the village woodcarver. All those in command have to iron out their Yiddish accents and improve their German vocabularies. Through the film it becomes obvious that those in command are living up to the authority required by their uniforms. Once the train starts its roundabout journey to Palestine via the Soviet Union, the story gets complicated as they encounter actual Nazis and even a group of Gypsies who are also trying to pull off a stunt similar to the Jews. The musical jam session between the two groups of deportees is terrific and quite spirited, as they try to outdo each other! The passion of both groups is evident. Other complications occur as a group of partisans decides to dynamite the railroad tracks in hopes of doing damage to the Nazis, but they soon find out that all on the train is not as it appears at first!

This is a film that deals with a tragic time period in a comical way. The film is not about the destruction of a people. Rather it focuses on a small village that was under threat from the Nazis, and how the people there came together to deal with the threat. Other films, such as Life is Beautiful and Jakob the Liar, also used humour in their treatment of the same historical time period. Train de Vie is definitely worth watching, especially for those who appreciate European film.

menu

cabbage rolls with sauerkraut • "smashed" potatoes with caramelized onions (see index) • green salad with vinaigrette (see index) • pickled vegetables (store-bought) • crusty bread (store-bought) • poppy seed slices

This Eastern European menu reflects the film's setting. The food is simple and hearty.

cabbage rolls with sauerkraut   serves 10

These make a great winter meal. They taste even better when re-heated the next day!

3	medium-size heads soured or pickled cabbage (about 20 leaves)	1 cup	rice
1/2 cup	cooking oil	5 slices	smoked bacon and/or 1/2 pound smoked sausage or smoked pork ribs
6	onions, finely diced		bay leaves
1-3/4 lbs	ground meat (a mix of beef, veal and pork is ideal)	3	dried small chili peppers
	salt and pepper	1 tbsp	all-purpose flour
	salt-free herbal seasoning, such as Mrs. Dash or Spice Island Original Mix (optional)	4 tsp	paprika

- Remove the leaves from the heads of cabbage, and taste a small piece. If the taste is too strong or sour, soak the leaves in water for 30 minutes.

- While the leaves are soaking in water, prepare the filling. Heat 1/4 cup of the oil in a frying pan and sauté the onions until soft. Add the meat, salt, pepper and seasoning to taste.

- Add the rice and mix well, then remove from heat. Preheat the oven to 400˚F.

- Prepare each cabbage leaf for stuffing by peeling off any tough parts of the leaf with a small paring knife while being careful to leave the leaf intact.

- Lay the leaf down and add several tablespoons of the filling mixture. First fold over the side closest to you, folding towards the center of the leaf, then fold in one end. Then fold over the other side (towards you) and then finally the other end.

- Place the cabbage rolls in a large roaster with a lid. In between the rolls, place some of the bacon and/or other meat. Tuck in the bay leaves and crush the dried chilies over the cabbage rolls.

- Add enough water to cover the cabbage rolls by about 1 inch and place in the oven with the lid on the roaster.

- Roast until the water boils and then reduce heat to 350˚F. Heat the remaining 1/4 cup oil in a skillet and when it is hot add the flour and the paprika and stir to make a roux. Remove from heat.

- Take the roaster out of the oven and remove the lid. Pour the roux mixture over the cabbage rolls, shake the roaster so that it drizzles to the cabbage rolls on bottom too (you may also ensure that it drizzles down by gently moving aside cabbage rolls with a wooden spoon thus allowing the roux to pass through.

- Return the roaster to the oven and continue to bake for about 2 more hours, partially covered. Check the level of liquid every so often. If it is not covering the cabbage rolls, add more hot water (enough to cover). If the top cabbage rolls are browning then cover the roaster loosely with foil so that further browning doesn't occur but steam can still escape.

train de vie (1998)

poppy seed slices

Makes 3 dozen

Poppy seeds are synonymous with Eastern European desserts. If you have never tried desserts with poppy seeds you are in for a special treat!

Pastry:

1-1/4 cups	all-purpose flour
1 tsp	baking powder
1/3 cup	granulated sugar
1 tsp	vanilla sugar (or substitute equal parts vanilla and sugar)
1	egg
1/2 cup	(1 stick) unsalted butter, cold
	melted butter (optional)
	powdered sugar (optional)

Filling:

1 cup	milk
1 cup	granulated sugar
2 tsp	vanilla sugar
2 tbsp	honey
2-1/3 cups	ground poppy seed
2 tsp	rum extract
1/4 cup	raisins
1/8 tsp	cinnamon

- <u>Pastry:</u> grease a large cake or baking pan, about 9 x 13". Sift the flour and baking powder together on a pastry board. Make a well in the center. Put the granulated sugar, vanilla sugar and egg in well. Work a small amount of flour into the center to make a thick paste. Cut the cold butter into small pieces and work into the flour mixture, making a smooth dough. If the dough seems too sticky, chill it for about 20 minutes

- Preheat oven to 350°F. Divide in 2 balls, and roll out one of them to fit the baking pan. Place in bottom of pan. Reserve second ball for top layer of dessert.

- <u>Filling:</u> put the milk, granulated sugar, vanilla sugar, and honey and poppy seed into a saucepan. Stir to combine, bring to a boil over medium heat, stirring continuously. Blend in the rum extract, raisins and cinnamon.

Remove from heat and let cool. When cool spread over pastry in the baking pan.

- Roll out the second ball of dough to fit the baking pan. Cover the filling with the second layer of pastry. Prick a few holes with a fork over the top. Place in oven and bake for 30 to 45 minutes or until golden. Brush melted butter over the top a few minutes before removing it from the oven if desired. Or let cool, slice, and sprinkle with powdered sugar.

 Make the filling the day before and store in a tightly covered container.

 Use skim or evaporated skim milk for the filling.

MUSIC - CONTINUED

Eastern Europe has a long tradition of appreciating gypsy music, so there are many albums to choose from. We suggest: "Imre Magyari and his Gypsy Band" (Hungaroton) from Hungary, and "Gypsy Music from Eastern Europe" (Isba) which features erformers and songs from several countries. A few great albums from the former Yugoslavia are: Jovica Nikolic's "Gypsy Holiday" (Pro Arte), "Djelem" (Orange Music) and "Gypsy Esma" (Monitor)

SETTING THE STAGE

Create a village or peasant atmosphere. Use a traditional looking tablecloth for your table, perhaps a crocheted lace or embroidered one. Decorate with baskets of fresh fruit and nuts interspersed with greenery. Serve the food in ceramic, wood or rustic looking bowls and platters. Set the table with simple, traditional dinnerware. Serve wine out of a pitcher. If it is warm and you have a patio, take the meal outdoors and enjoy your nature-filled backyard. And of course don't forget the music in the background.

FEATURED ACTORS

Lionel Abelanski (Schlmo)
Rufus (Mordechai)
Clement Harari (Rabbi)
Michel Muller (Yossi)
Bruno Abraham-Kremer (Yankele)

DIRECTOR ~ Radu Mihaileanu

AWARDS WON

Best Foreign Film	1998 David di Donatello Award (Italy)
FIPRESCI Award	1998 Venice Film Festival
Audience Award	1999 Sundance Film Festival

BEVERAGES

Beer would best suit this menu. Try some beer from Eastern Europe like: Karlovacko Pivo (Croatia), Pilsner Urquell (Czech Republic), Okocim or Zywiec (both from Poland).

MUSIC

If you have never listened to klezmer music, we strongly suggest you give it a go! Klezmer is a Yiddish term for musician, and refers to a tradition of Jewish folk music with German and Eastern European roots. The violin and the clarinet are two of the most important instruments in this tradition. Klezmer music is being revived in North America by bands such as The Flying Bulgar Klezmer Band from Canada, whose album of the same name is found on the Agada label. You could also listen to "Yiddish American Klezmer Music" (Yazoo) by Dave Tarras. Another good choice for Jewish music is "Maramaros: The Lost Jewish Music of Transylvania" (Hannibal)

Other Eastern European suggestions include: anything by Marta Sebestyen, a leading Hungarian singer. She is often backed by Muzsikas, a young group that is comfortable with a number of ethnic Hungarian styles. We suggest the following CD's: "Muzsikas (Hannibal)", "The World of Eastern Europe" (Trace). This last CD features a variety of compositions from this area of Europe. The "Rough Guide to the Music of Eastern Europe" (World Music Network) is also a great compilation CD.

eat drink
man woman (1994)

This film centres around a Chinese widower who happens to be a retired chef, and his daughters. The widower prepares traditional Sunday dinners for his three daughters. The girls are an interesting lot; all very different from each other. The eldest is unmarried, and rather bitter about men and relationships. The middle daughter works as an executive in the airline industry and secretly dreams of being a chef, but that line of work isn,t open to women. The youngest is more free spirited and is attending college, she has numerous sexual liaisons which lead to her becoming pregnant. As the story progresses the oldest daughter finds herself attracted to a volleyball coach and pursues him relentlessly. The daughters find their relationships changing as they themselves change. This comedy drama is a snapshot into a somewhat conflicted relationship between the members of an ethnic family.

FEATURED ACTORS
Sihung Lung (Chu)
Yang Kuei-Mei (Jen)
Wu Chien Lien (Kien)
Ah-Leh Gua (Madame Liang)

DIRECTOR ~ Ang Lee

AWARDS WON
Best Foreign Language Film 1994 National Board of Review of Motion Pictures Award

menu
hot and sour soup • chinese chicken with cashews • sesame fried rice orange or tangerine sorbet (store-bought) • walnut and banana spring rolls with rum sauce

hot and sour soup
serves 4

1/2 cup	dried mushrooms
1 cup	water
3 cups	vegetable stock
1 tbsp	dry sherry
1/2 cup	bamboo shoots, sliced, cut in matchstick pieces or water chestnuts, sliced
4 oz	firm tofu, diced
1/2 cup	frozen peas, thawed
2 tbsp	white wine vinegar
1 tbsp	soy sauce
2 tbsp	cornstarch
1/4 cup	water
1/2 tsp	white pepper
1 tsp	sesame oil
1	egg, lightly beaten
2	green onions, cut into 1-inch diagonal slices
	salt

- Cover mushrooms with warm water and let stand for 30 minutes. Remove mushrooms; cut off and discard stems.
- Thinly slice mushrooms and set aside. Strain and reserve soaking water. Measure and add enough stock to make a total of 4 cups liquid.
- Place in a 2-quart saucepan and add sherry, bamboo shoots, and sliced mushrooms. Bring to a boil, then reduce heat; cover and simmer for 15 minutes.

- Add tofu, peas, white vinegar, and soy; heat for 3 minutes. In a small bowl, stir together cornstarch and the 1/4 cup water.
- Add to soup and cook, stirring, until slightly thickened. Turn off heat.
- Add pepper and seasame oil. Stirring continuously, slowly pour egg into soup. Sprinkle with onion; add salt to taste.

trivia clips

"Born to the earth are three kinds of creatures. Some are winged and fly. Some are furred and run. Still others stretch their mouths and talk. All must eat and drink to survive." Lu Yu, Ancient Chinese Philosopher.

trivia clips

Tradition is very important in Chinese culture as is family. Maintaining close relationships with every family member and most importantly the elderly, is customary for most Chinese. The birth of a baby is a joyous time and it is said in China that when a woman becomes pregnant that she has found true joy. The Chinese think a name may somehow determine the future of a child. Therefore, all possible factors must be taken into account when naming children.

eat drink
man woman (1994)

chinese chicken with cashews
serves 6

1	egg white
1 tbsp	soy sauce
1 tbsp	cornstarch
1-1/2 lb	chicken breasts, skinned, boned & cut into 1" cubes
1/4 cup	soy sauce
1 tsp	cornstarch
1 tbsp	dry sherry
2 tbsp	cider vinegar
1 tsp	sugar

1/4 cup	peanut oil
2/3 cup	unsalted cashews
1 inch piece	of ginger, peeled and quartered
2	scallions, peeled and sliced
1	8 ounce can water chestnuts, drained and sliced
1	medium green bell pepper, diced
	white rice, cooked

- Lightly beat the egg white in a small bowl. Add the tablespoon of soy sauce and tablespoon of cornstarch. Mix well. Add the chicken. Toss thoroughly.

- Let stand for 15 minutes.

- Combine the 1/4 cup of soy sauce, and the 1 teaspoon of cornstarch, the sherry, cider vinegar and sugar in a second small bowl.

- Mix very well. Set the sauce aside.

- Heat the oil in a large wok or skillet over medium heat. Add thecashews. Stir fry for about 1 minute. Use a slotted spoon to remove the cashews. Set aside.

- Discard 1/3 of the oil. Add the ginger, sliced scallions and water chestnuts to the wok. Stir fry for 1 minute. Add the chicken cubes, green pepper and sauce. Cook, stirring constantly, until thickened.

- Discard the ginger pieces. Return the cashews to the wok. Serve alongside rice.

BEVERAGES

Serve Chinese beer like Tsingtao (China). Otherwise, stick with Asian brews like: Sapporo (Japan), San Miguel Pale Pils (Philippines), Tiger Beer (Singapore).

MUSIC

The soundtrack "Eat Man Drink Woman" (Varese) is available. Other good choices are: "Chinese Bamboo Flute Music" (Legacy), "Chinese Classical Music" (CMS), and "Chinese Drums and Gongs" (Lyrichord). All of these are mainly instrumental. For music with accompanying vocals try "Chinese Folk Music" (Arc) or "Chinese Pop Solos" (China). For a fusion that's really different try "Chinese Turkestan/Xinjian Uighur Music" (Ocora), this CD features Chinese music with an Arabic influence. In Turkestan many of the ethnic Chinese are followers of Islam.

trivia clips

Never stick your chopsticks upright in the rice bowl. Instead, lay them on your dish. The reason for this is that when somebody dies, the shrine to them contains a bowl of sand or rice with two sticks of incense stuck upright in it.
So if you stick your chopsticks in the rice bowl, it looks like this shrine or it could be interpreted as a death wish!

trivia clips

What do foreign dignitaries drink when visiting China? Mao Tai: a potent 150 proof alcoholic concoction.
The difference between Chinese and Western eating habits is that unlike the West, where everyone has their own plate of food, in China the dishes are placed on the table and everybody shares. If you are being treated to a meal by a Chinese host, be prepared for a lot of food! The Chinese are very proud of their culture and world renowned cuisine, and will do their best to showcase it, hospitality is a matter of pride.

eat drink
man woman (1994)

SETTING THE STAGE

An oriental or Asian theme is required. Prior to your event, shop in Asian stores to purchase some Chinese or Asian motif dinnerware. Don,t forget to pick up some chopsticks, oriental spoons and some small bowls for the dipping sauce. You may also wish to purchase a square platter for the dessert spring rolls. Set your table with a red tablecloth and place a lace tablecloth over it for an interesting effect. Use oriental paper lanterns for subdued lighting around the dining area. Paper fans may be placed on walls for decoration. Bamboo place mats would suit the theme or use some made of silk or a rich looking brocade in shades of red. Light small red and gold votive candles and place around the room in clusters. Have some of the soothing Chinese music playing in the background and enjoy the delicious meal!

walnut and banana spring
rolls with rum sauce serves 6

This recipe is a North American creation with an Asian twist!

For sauce:

1 cup	sugar
1/2 cup	water
1/2 cup	whipping cream
1-1/2 tbsp	dark rum

For Rolls:

12	spring roll wrappers
3	small bananas, peeled, quartered lengthwise, trimmed to 4 inches
1/2 cup	toffee bits
1/4 cup	finely chopped toasted walnuts
	vegetable oil (for deep-frying)
	powdered sugar for garnish
	pinch of Chinese five-spice powder (very little or at your own discretion)

- Make sauce: Stir sugar and 1/2 cup water in heavy medium saucepan over medium-low heat until sugar dissolves. Increase heat and boil until syrup turns deep amber, brushing down sides of pan with wet pastry brush and swirling pan occasionally, about 12 minutes. Reduce heat to low. Add cream (mixture will bubble vigorously) and stir until caramel bits dissolve. Remove from heat. Mix in rum.

- Make rolls: Arrange 4 spring roll wrappers on work surface (keep remainder covered). Place 1 banana piece diagonally across 1 corner of each wrapper. Brush opposite corner with water.

- Drizzle each banana with 1 teaspoon caramel sauce, 1 teaspoon toffee bits and 1 teaspoon walnuts. Fold in wrapper corner closest to banana. Roll wrapper over banana once, then fold in sides and roll up as for egg roll, pressing ends to seal. Repeat filling and rolling remaining wrappers. (Can be made 2 hours ahead. Cover and chill.)

- Pour enough oil into heavy large saucepan to reach depth of 3 inches. Heat oil to 375°F. Working in batches, fry rolls in oil until deep golden brown, turning frequently, about 3 minutes per batch. Using slotted spoon, transfer rolls to paper towels and drain. Arrange 2 rolls on each plate. Sift powdered sugar over. Sprinkle with five-spice powder (optional).

- Drizzle caramel sauce around rolls and serve.

trivia clips

"Born to the earth are three kinds of creatures. Some are winged and fly. Some are furred and run. Still others stretch their mouths and talk. All must eat and drink to survive." Lu Yu, Ancient Chinese Philosopher.

drink recipes

Alcoholic

ACAPULCO

1-1/2 ounces Tequila

1/2 ounce Triple Sec

1/2 ounce Light Rum

1 ounce Sour Mix

Splash Of Lime Juice

Shake - Garnish with lime wedge.

ACAPULCO GOLD

1-1/4 ounces Tequila

5/8 ounce Grand Marnier

1 ounce Sweet and Sour Mix

Blend with ice, and serve in a cocktail glass.

AMARETTO COFFEE

1/2 cup amaretto

1/4 cup brandy

4 teaspoons sugar, or to taste

3 cups freshly brewed strong coffee

Lightly sweetened whipped cream to taste

Garnish: Lightly toasted sliced almonds

In each of the four 8-ounce mugs combine 2 tablespoons of the amaretto, 1 tablespoon of the brandy, and 1 teaspoon of the sugar, divide the coffee, heated if necessary, among the mugs, and stir the drinks until the sugar is dissolved. Top each drink with a dollop of the whipped cream and sprinkle the whipped cream with the almonds.

BANANA COLADA

3 ripe bananas, peeled and quartered

18 ounces unsweetened pineapple juice

4 ounces coconut milk

3 ounces dark rum

2 cups ice

1/4 cup toasted coconut

Place bananas and pineapple juice in a blender and blend until smooth. Add coconut milk, rum and ice and mix until frothy. Garnish with toasted coconut.

BANANA SANDWICH

1/2 ounce Kahlua

1/3 ounce Crème de Banane

1/6 ounce rum cream liqueur

Shake well and serve in a cocktail glass.

BETWEEN THE SHEETS

3/4 ounce rum

3/4 ounce brandy

3/4 ounce Cointreau

Splash of lemon juice or sour mix

Blend with ice, strain and serve up in a chilled cocktail glass.

BLACK RUSSIAN

4 ounce vodka

1 ounce Kahlua

Pour over ice in a glass.

drink recipes
continued

alcoholic

BLOODY MARY
1 ounce vodka
5 ounces tomato juice
3 drops Tabascoô sauce
2 drops of Worcestershire sauce
salt and pepper
lemon slice for garnish.

Mix together and serve over ice.

BOBBY BURNS
3/4 ounce Scotch
3/4 ounce sweet vermouth
1/2 ounce Benedictine

Stir over ice. Strain into a cocktail glass.

BRONX
1 ounce gin
1/2 ounce sweet vermouth
1/2 ounce dry vermouth
1 ounce fresh orange juice

Shake with ice and drain into a cocktail glass. Garnish with an orange slice.

CHAMPAGNE COCKTAIL
Chilled Champagne
Dash of Bitters and Simple Syrup

Put dashes in Champagne glass. Fill with Champagne and garnish with a twist of citrus.

COCO COLADA
1/3 cup pineapple, diced
2 tablespoons cream of coconut
1 1/2 ounces rum
1 tablespoon lime juice
1 1/2 cups crushed ice
1/3 cup pineapple-coconut ice cream

Put all ingredients in blender. Blend till slushy. Pour into large glass. Garnish with pineapple.

FLYING SCOTSMAN
1-1/2 ounce Scotch
3/4 ounce sweet vermouth
4 dashes of Angostura bitters
1 tsp sugar
Strain over ice. Strain into cocktail glasses.

FREEDOM FIGHTER
1-1/2 ounce sloe gin
1/2 ounce Crème Yvette
1/2 of 1 egg white
Shake over ice. Strain into small wineglasses.

GODFATHER
3/4 ounce white rum
1/4 ounce Galliano
5 ounces orange juice

Pour all ingredients over ice in a glass. Garnish with a slice of orange.

GODMOTHER
3/4 ounce vodka
1/4 ounce Amaretto

Pour all ingredients over ice in a glass. Garnish with a cherry.

HONOLULU COCKTAIL

1-1/2 ounces gin

1 ounce pineapple juice

1 teaspoon lemon juice

1 teaspoon lime juice

1 teaspoon orange juice

1/4 teaspoons sugar

1 dash bitters

Pour over ice, stir and serve with a citrus twist.

HONOLULU COOLER

Juice from 1/2 Lime

1 1/2 ounces Southern Comfort

Pineapple Juice

Pack a tall glass with crushed ice, add lime juice and southern comfort. Fill with pineapple juice and stir.

HOT WHITE RUSSIAN

2 1/2 cups freshly brewed coffee

1/2 cup heavy cream

1/2 cup Kahlúa or other coffee-flavored liqueur, or to taste

1/4 cup vodka, or to taste

whipped heavy cream for garnish if desired.

In a saucepan stir together the coffee, the 1/2 cup cream, the Kahlúa, and the vodka and heat the mixture over moderate heat until it is hot. Divide the mixture among heated mugs and garnish each drink with some of the whipped cream.

IRISH COFFEE

3/4 cup (4 jiggers) Irish whiskey

2 tablespoons sugar, or to taste

3 cups freshly brewed strong coffee

Lightly sweetened whipped cream to taste

In each of the four 8-ounce mugs, combine 3 tablespoons (1 jigger) of the whiskey and 1-1/2 teaspoons of the sugar, divide the coffee, heated if necessary, among the mugs, and stir the drinks until the sugar is dissolved. Top each drink with a dollop of the whipped cream.

KIR ROYALE

3/4 oz. Creme de Cassis

Champagne

Pour Creme de Cassis in bottom of wineglass or flute. Fill with champagne and garnish with a twist.

LEAVING LAS VEGAS

1 ounce Triple Sec

1 ounce vodka

1 ounce light rum

lemonade

2 tablespoons sugar

splash of Sprite

Mix all in highball glass and serve.

LEMON BLUE DOLPHIN

1-1/2 ounces lemon vodka

2 tablespoons blue curaÁao

1 1/2 cup crushed ice

1/3 cup lemon sorbet

Put all ingredients in blender. Blend until slushy. Serve in a tall glass. Garnish with lemon slice.

drink
recipes

LONG ISLAND ICED TEA

3/4 ounce rum

3/4 ounce gin

3/4 ounce vodka

3/4 ounce tequila

3/4 ounce Triple Sec

3/4 ounce sour mix

splash of cola

Shake liquors with sour mix and pour into a Hurricane glass or other large glass. Add a splash of cola. Garnish with a lemon wedge.

MANGO DAIQUIRI

1-1/2 ounces white rum.

1/2 ounce lime juice,

1/2 cup chopped mango.

Blend until smooth, pour into glass and enjoy!

MANGORITA

1/3 cup fresh mango, diced

1-1/2 ounces tequila

1 tablespoon triple sec

1-1/2 cups crushed ice

1/3 cup mango sorbet

Put all ingredients into a blender. Blend until slushy. Pour into a tall glass. Garnish with mango if so desired.

MANHATTAN

1-1/2 ounces whiskey or bourbon

3/4 ounce Sweet Vermouth

Dash of Bitters (if desired)

Build in a Rocks glass or stir over ice and strain into a chilled cocktail glass to serve up. Garnish with a Cherry.

MELON-BERRY SLUSH

1/3 cup diced watermelon, seeded

1-1/2 ounces raspberry vodka

1 tablespoon grenadine syrup

1-1/2 cups crushed ice

1/4 cup raspberry sorbet

Put in blender. Blend until slushy. Serve in a tall glass.

MEXICAN SPICED COFFEE

2 cups strong coffee

1 cinnamon stick

3-4 whole cloves

1/4 cup dark brown sugar

1/2 cup Kahula or coffee flavour liqueur

whip cream

In a small saucepan containing coffee, stir in cinnamon, cloves, sugar and Kahlua. Heat this over a medium setting, stirring occasionally until the sugar dissolves. Pour into individual serving glasses or mugs. Top with fresh whipped cream prior to serving.

MEXICOLA

1 fl ounce tequila

1/2 ounce fresh lime juice

chilled cola

Pour tequila and lime into a tall, ice-filled glass. Top with cola and stir mix.

MINT JULEP

1 ounce bourbon

1 tsp sugar

5 ounces soda water.

Garnish with crushed fresh mint leaves. Serve over ice.

MINT-MELON JULEP

1/3 cup honeydew melon, diced

3 tablespoons melon liqueur

2 tablespoons green mint liqueur

1 1/2 cups crushed ice

1/4 cup lime sorbet

Put all ingredients in a blender. Blend until slushy. Serve in a tall glass. Garnish with mint.

NEW ORLEANS HURRICANE

8 ounces lemon lime oda

1 ounce lime Juice

2 ounces passion fruit juice

2 ounces light rum

1 ounce 151 proof rum

Shake all except 151 proof rum with ice and pour into a Hurricane glass or other large specialty glass. Float 151 proof rum on top. Drink through a straw from the bottom first. Starts out calm, but gets stormy towards the end. Ginger Ale or Tonic Water can be used in place of lemon lime soda.

PINK LADY

1-1/2 ounces gin,

cream

dash of Grenadine

Shake with ice. Strain into a champagne flute or other long, narrow glass.

PEACHSICLE

3 tablespoons peach schnapps

1-1/2 tablespoons vanilla syrup

4 to 5 frozen peach slices (cut in thirds)

1-1/2 cups crushed ice

1/4 cup peach sorbet

Place in blender. Blend until slushy and serve in a tall glass. Garnish with peach wedge.

PUERTO RICAN PUNCH

3/4 ounce sloe gin

3/4 ounce peach schnapps

3/4 ounce vodka

3/4 ounce gin

3 ounces orange juice

3 ounces pineapple juice

grenadine

Mix into a large glass, with or without ice.

ROMAN HOLIDAY PUNCH

1/2 cup lemon juice

1 cup Marsala wine

1 cup rose wine

1 cup brandy

1 pint raspberry sorbet

Mix all ingredients together (except sorbet) in a large punch bowl. Add sorbet just before serving.

ROMAN SNOWBALL

2 ounces Sambuca

5 chocolate covered espresso beans (Starbucks sells these)

ice

Fill a wine glass with ice. Pour Sambuca over the ice and top with espresso beans. Serve with a straw. Remember the beans are edible!

SAN FRANCISCO

3/4 ounce sloe gin

3/4 ounce sweet vermouth

3/4 ounce dry vermouth

Dash Angostura bitters

Dash orange bitters

3 or 4 ice cubes

Maraschino cherry

Combine ingredients, except the cherry, in a cocktail shaker and shake vigorously.

Strain into a cocktail glass; add cherry.

drink recipes

SEX MACHINE

1-1/2 ounces Irish Cream

1-1/2 ounces coffee liqueur

8 ounces milk

Put liqueurs into glass top with milk.

STRAWBERRY BLONDE

30 mL vodka

60 mL cherry brandy

cola

splash of cream

Mix ingredients together in a cocktail glass.

TROPICAL DREAM

1 ounce Malibu rum

1 ounce Blue Curacao

1 ounce pineapple juice

Mix in a shaker with ice. Pour into glass and garnish with a red cherry on the rim of the glass.

TEQUILA SUNRISE

Serves 6

2/3 cup tequila

3 cups fresh orange juice

1 tbsp grenadine, or to taste

6 orange slices for garnish

In a large pitcher stir together well the tequila, the orange juice, and the grenadine.

Divide the drink among 6 glasses filled with ice cubes. Garnish the drinks with the orange slices.

VIENNESE COFFEE

1/2 cup whipping cream

6 ounces semisweet chocolate, chopped

6 cups freshly brewed coffee

Whipped cream

Ground cinnamon

Bring 1/2 cup cream to simmer in large saucepan. Reduce heat to low. Add chocolate and stir until melted and smooth. Gradually whisk in coffee. Ladle coffee mixture into cups. Top with dollops of whipped cream. Sprinkle cream with cinnamon and serve.

WHISKY TODDY

Hot water

Heather honey or sugar.

Lemon juice.

Dissolve a teaspoon of honey/sugar in a glass of boiling water. Add a glass of whisky and a little lemon juice, stir. Serve while still hot.

WHITE RUSSIAN

1-1/4 ounces vodka

1 ounce Kahlua

splash of cream or milk

Shake and serve over ice in a highball glass.

alcoholic

CAPPUCCINO PUNCH

4 cups freshly brewed double strength coffee

2 cans evaporated 2% milk

1 cup sugar

1 teaspoon vanilla extract

1 pint chocolate ice cream

chocolate curls for garnish

Pour coffee into a punch bowl. In a blender, whip the evaporated milk with the sugar until frothy.

Add milk mixture to coffee along with the vanilla. Next add scoops of ice cream to punch bowl.

Serve.

CITRUS MINT PUNCH

1 cup packed fresh mint leaves

grated peel of 1 lemon

grated peel of 1 orange

3 cups boiling water

1 can frozen lemonade concentrate, thawed

1 can frozen orange juice concentrate, thawed

6 cups cold water

Heat 3 cups of water in a large saucepan to boiling and remove from heat. Add mint leaves and grated citrus peel to saucepan. Steep 1 hour and strain into pitcher or punch bowl. Add the concentrates and water. Stir well to mix. Serve over ice. Garnish with fresh mint.

EGG NOG

12 eggs, separated

1/2 cup plus 4 tablespoons sugar, divided

3/4 cup whiskey

1 pint heavy whipping cream

In a large bowl, beat egg yolks and 1/2 cup sugar until thick and lemon colored. Add liquor slowly, beating constantly. Beat egg whites until foamy. Add remaining sugar and beat until stiff, but not too dry. Fold egg white mixture into yolk mixture. Whip cream and fold into mixture.

Refrigerate at least 1 hour before serving and keep thoroughly chilled, set in a bowl of ice, when serving. Serve in punch bowl with ladle.

HOMEMADE HOT CHOCOLATE

1/4 cup good quality cocoa

1/2 cup granulated sugar

1 1/3 cups powdered milk

dash of salt

Mix everything well, and store in an airtight container. To use, put three to four teaspoons of mix in a cup (adjust to taste) and add hot water and a drop of vanilla. Marshmallows may be added if so desired. Stir well.

ICE CASTLE FANTASY MOCKTAIL

1/2 cup apricot juice

1/2 cup pineapple juice

1/4 cup lemon juice

orange slices for garnish

Shake all ingredients (except orange slice) with ice and strain into a tall glass over ice cubes. Garnish with the slice of orange and a cherry (if desired) and serve.

drink recipes

MINT ICED TEA

Makes 12 to 14 servings

2 tablespoons English Breakfast or Darjeeling Tea

3 cups sugar

1 cup fresh mint leaves

1 cup lemon juice

crushed ice

lemon slices

mint sprigs

powdered sugar

Pour a quart of boiling water over the tea and steep for 3 hours. Make a syrup of the sugar and 1 cup of cold water by boiling for 10 minutes. Add the mint leaves and infuse for 2 hours or until the tea is ready. Strain tea and syrup and combine with the lemon juice. Serve in 12- or 14-ounce glasses filled with crushed ice.

Garnish with lemon slices and mint sprigs and dust the top with powdered sugar.

Without the garnish, this brew will keep for several days in the refrigerator.

MOROCCAN MINT TEA

Serves 4

10 fresh mint sprigs, plus 4 for garnish

3 teaspoons green tea

3 tablespoons sugar

4 cups water

Boil water. Pour a small amount in teapot and swish around to warm the pot. Combine the mint and green tea and sugar in the teapot, then fill it with the rest of the hot water. Let tea brew, stirring the leaves once or twice, for 3 minutes. Pour tea through a tea strainer into glass teacups to serve. Garnish with remaining 4 sprigs of mint

REFRESHING YOGURT DRINK

Serves 4

2 cups thick plain yogurt (preferably Balkan style)

2 cups cold water

a dash of salt

fresh mint leaves for garnish (optional)

Place all of the ingredients in a blender and whisk until frothy. Divide the froth among 4 glasses,

top with remaining liquid. Garnish with mint leaves.

ROSEMARY FRUIT PUNCH

1 large can pineapple juice

1 tablespoon fresh rosemary, chopped

1/2 cup sugar

1-1/2 cups lemon juice

2 cups water

1 bottle ginger ale

lemon slices and mint for garnish

Heat the pineapple juice in a saucepan. When warm, add rosemary and steep for 10 minutes.

Dissolve sugar in hot juice. Strain into pitcher or punch bowl. Add remaining ingredients (except ginger ale). Chill. Before serving add ginger ale and garnishes.

SHIRLEY TEMPLE MOCKTAIL

8 ounces ginger ale

1 dash grenadine syrup

Build in a highball glass. Add ginger ale over ice and sprinkle grenadine syrup over it. Garnish with a lemon slice and a cherry.

index

index

FISH AND SEAFOOD

MAIN DISHES

index

continued

SALADS AND SIDE DISHES

continued

SOUPS AND STEWS

MISCELLANEOUS

MAIN BEVERAGES

If you are unable to find More than Just Dinner and a Movie where you shop, please ask your retailer to contact us.. For your convenience, we offer a mail order service. Just fill out the coupon below and send it, along with payment to Spice of Life Books Inc. at : P.O. Box 84012 Burlington, Ont. L7L 6S2 or fax us at (905) 643-4410.

www.morethanjustdinnerandamovie.com

We offer discount for orders of more than 10 books. Please contact us for more details.

Mail Order Coupon

Please send me _____copies of MoreThan Just Dinner and a Movie @ $24.95each_____

Postage and handling: $2.00 for 1 book, $1.00 for each additional book_____

(Not applicable for orders of 5 to 10 books)

Canadian Residents add 7% GST_____

Total Amount Enclosed _____

Enclosed is my ☐ cheque ☐ money order

Name _____

Address_____

City_____Province_____

Postal Code _____Phone_____

E-mail_____

Please Make all cheques or money orders payable to Spice of Life Books Inc.

More Than Just Dinner and a Movie makes a great gift for birthdays, bridal showers, weddings, Mother's Day, Father's Day, Christmas, house warming gifts etc. We will ship the books directly to the recipients of your choice. Just provide us with their names and addresses, along with any personal note or card with your order form.

Acknowledgments

Vlado Pavicic- Who actually came up with this initial idea and let us run with it and turn it into something of our own.

John Roberts- Who believed in our project from the very early stages. Thank you for believing in us and for the support... couldn't have done it without you!

Corinne Nyffenegger- Graphic Artist and Art Director extraordinaire, who helped us put our ideas into a visually appealing format and who went the extra mile to complete our book on time.

Jean Saiphoo- Editor par excellence, who was able to decipher our late night writing and make suggestions for improving our manuscript with very short turnaround times! A thank you to her husband Reza for acting as courier.

Roy Timm- A talented photographer who can meet tight deadlines and overall nice guy. Glad you were on board!
Roy and Carole Timm are well known for their photography and photo-styling and appear in numerous publications.

Carole Timm- Thank you for supplying all of our props and tableware!

Gene and Murline Mallatte- Liaison College (Hamilton Campus) for continued support and use of their facilities for food preparation and photography.

Chef Randal Myers- for preparation of our recipes for photography. Chef Randal Myers is a graduate of the University of Toronto, George Brown College and the Italian Culinary Institute in Costigliole Piedmont, Italy. He has earned the designation of Chef de Cuisine.

Chef William Wallace C.C.C.- for preparation of our recipes for photography. Chef William Wallace graduated with "Honours" from George Brown College and with "Honours" in Post Graduate Italian Culinary Arts. He has earned the designation of Chef de Cuisine.

Chef Randal Myers and
Chef William Wallace C.C.C.

Bibliography

Berlin,Joey. Toxic Fame Celebrities Speak on Stardom. Visible Ink Press.1996.

Crawley, Tony. The Wordsworth Dictionary of Film Quotations. Wordsworth Editions Ltd 1991.

Harkness, John, The Academy Awards® Handbook, Winners and Losers from 1927 to Today. Kensington Publishing Corp. 1994.

Hunter, Allan. The Wordsworth Book of Movie Classics. Wordsworth Editions Ltd 1996.

Kozel, William and Maguire, Barrie. What Were Their Names Before? Real Names of More Than 300 Celebrites and the Stories They Tell. Contemporary Books Inc. 1993.

Martin, Mick and Porter, Marsha. Video and Movie Guide 2000. The Ballantine Publishing Group, 2000.

Eve Zibart, Stevens, Muriel and Vermont, Terrell.The Unofficial Guide® to Ethnic Cuisine & Dining In America. Prentice Hall Macmillan Company,1995.